C000268714

Praise for *Making I*

David Didau's latest edu-blockbuster is a compelling and endlessly fascinating read. Weaving together a wealth of evidence and ideas, from the practical to the philosophical, *Making Kids Cleverer* confronts the taboo topic of intelligence head-on. Didau shows us that by teaching children powerful, biologically secondary knowledge we not only increase their intelligence but also prepare them for the prospect of happiness, wealth and anything that adult life can throw at them.

I have not read another education book that brims with as much insight and stimulating thought as this one: every page serves up a new surprise or gentle provocation. Thoroughly recommended.

Andy Tharby, teacher, co-author of *Making Every Lesson Count* and
author of *How to Explain Absolutely Anything to Absolutely Anyone*

Written with great precision and clarity, and with a good dash of humility and humour too, *Making Kids Cleverer* is a truly magnificent manifesto. Everything David Didau says chimes deeply with what I know to be true and what I am trying to accomplish in our schools, and I am of course cleverer now than I was before reading it. It is an absolute joy to read, and an incredibly timely tour de force that can, and should, have a national impact.

A must-read for everyone in education, from trainee teachers to inspectors and policy makers.

Lady Caroline Nash, Director, Future Academies

Schools and parents alike invest so much energy in teaching children and yet often understand relatively little about what exactly it is they are trying to achieve. In *Making Kids Cleverer* David Didau reviews everything we know from cognitive science on how to enhance children's learning, and delivers a powerful argument that we can – and must – help all children succeed at school.

Rebecca Allen, Professor of Education,
University College London Institute of Education

In *Making Kids Cleverer* David Didau provides us with a brilliant and accessible account of why knowledge is opportunity, and of how we can increase children's knowledge through a thoughtful and scientific approach to schooling.

More than ever, children need a core set of ideas, facts, procedures and other forms of knowledge in order to help them navigate the ever-changing work environment they will encounter and to fully participate in the many opportunities afforded by the modern world. In this book, Didau offers an incisive argument for the importance of knowledge and a solid framework for how to improve the knowledge base of all children.

Making Kids Cleverer will be an invaluable resource for parents, teachers and policy makers.

David C. Geary, Curators' Distinguished Professor, Department of Psychological Sciences, University of Missouri

David Didau has done it again! *Making Kids Cleverer* is an engaging, highly readable analysis of the latest research on how we learn and what we can do to improve the achievement of our pupils.

Like his previous books, David's latest offering contains many strong claims. Your initial reaction, like mine, may be that he has made these claims for effect, but he sticks so closely to the research evidence that you have to take his arguments seriously.

Anyone involved in the care and education of children and young people would gain a huge amount from reading this book. Highly recommended.

Dylan Wiliam, Emeritus Professor of Educational Assessment, University College London

David Didau

Making Kids' Cleverer

A manifesto for closing the advantage gap

Foreword by Paul A. Kirschner

Crown House Publishing Limited
www.crownhouse.co.uk

First published by

Crown House Publishing Limited
Crown Buildings, Bancyfelin, Carmarthen, Wales, SA33 5ND, UK
www.crownhouse.co.uk

and

Crown House Publishing Company LLC
PO Box 2223, Williston, VT 05495, USA
www.crownhousepublishing.com

First published 2019.

Table 4.3, pages 101–103 – republished and adapted with permission of Thomas J. Bouchard, Jr, from Genetic Influence on Human Psychological Traits: A Survey, *Current Directions in Psychological Science* 13(4) (2004): 148–151 at 150; permission conveyed through Copyright Clearance Center, Inc.

Quotes from Ofsted documents used in this publication have been approved under an Open Government Licence. Please visit http://www.nationalarchives.gov.uk/doc/open-government-licence/version/3/.

Man image © aeroking – Fotolia.com

Images page 122 © vilisov – Fotolia.com, page 197 © Les Evans 2019, page 262 © vladgrin and monicaodo – fotolia.com.

British Library Cataloguing-in-Publication Data

A catalogue entry for this book is available from the British Library.

Print ISBN 978-178583366-3
Mobi ISBN 978-178583384-7
ePub ISBN 978-178583385-4
ePDF ISBN 978-178583386-1

LCCN 2018957742

Edited by Peter Young

Printed in the UK by
TJ International, Padstow, Cornwall

To my bold, brilliant and beautiful
daughters, Olivia and Madeleine.

Foreword by
Paul A. Kirschner

How do we make kids cleverer? How do we close the advantage gap? These are not easy questions to answer as the science of education and learning is far from exact. Our problem is made even more complicated by the fact that how a person learns is influenced by so many things – both internal and external – which are hard to grasp and even harder to control. This being said, there is one factor that can optimise learning, make kids cleverer and, potentially, play an enormous role in closing the advantage gap. That factor is the teacher.

As an educator and researcher in the field of educational psychology I've spent my whole academic career – which now spans four decades – studying how people learn and how the process can be facilitated through carefully designed interventions. What I've learnt in all those years, from all the studies I've conducted and from all of my attempts to help learners learn better (and maybe even to become cleverer), is that everything hinges on teachers.

For me, a teacher is an educational designer: a professional who designs, develops, implements and (hopefully) evaluates learning situations that are effective, efficient and enjoyable for the learner. That a learning situation is *effective* means that in the time allotted within a curriculum, either more is learned than was planned for or what is learned is done to a deeper level than expected or required. For a learning situation to be *efficient* the curriculum is mastered either in less time or is learned with less effort. Finally, *enjoyable* doesn't necessarily mean that lessons are fun (real learning is often difficult), but rather that the learner experiences success and, with that success, has a feeling of accomplishment and what is known as self-efficacy (i.e. I can do it!).

Ideally, a teacher should not be just a run-of-the-mill educational designer; they should strive to be the very best they can be: a top-quality teacher. In order to explain what I mean I will resort to an analogy with what it takes to become a top chef, both because I love to eat and because I myself – before I entered academia – worked as a chef in a restaurant. Top chefs perform their magic in restaurants that have attained the Nobel Prize of the gastronomic world, namely three Michelin stars. Such chefs are capable of planning and preparing tasty, healthy and beautiful dishes for anyone, be they children, finicky eaters, diners with allergies, or gourmets. And they can do this because they have deep conceptual knowledge and finely honed skills with respect to the tools (knives, ovens, pots, pans, stoves, mixers, blenders …), techniques (steam baking, hot-air baking, wood-fire baking, sautéing, deep frying, blanching, freezing, cryogenic cooking …), and ingredients (vegetables, meats, grains, spices, herbs …) of the trade. A top chef knows when, how and why to use each of the tools, techniques and ingredients and also has the skills to properly implement them to get the best results in any culinary situation.

Similarly, top teachers are capable of designing and preparing effective, efficient and enjoyable learning experiences for all students, be they average or advantaged, possessing special needs or blessed with particular talents. And they can do this because they have deep conceptual knowledge and finely honed skills with respect to *their* tools (whiteboard, textbook, e-reader, tablet, computer, laboratory …), instructional techniques that optimise different types of learning (lectures, discussions, debate, collaboration, formative and summative assessment, feedback techniques …), and ingredients of the teaching trade (different types of questions, prompts, tasks, examples, illustrations and animations, homework, simulations …). A top teacher knows when, how and why to use each of their tools, techniques and ingredients and also has the skills to properly implement them in different situations and with different students.

This being the case, I must confess that reading this book has made me really jealous! David Didau has essentially written what I would have loved to write myself. This is a book that can and will provide teachers – and anyone else interested in the project of education – with most if not all of the background knowledge they need to understand how kids learn and how to make them cleverer. As such, it can and will play an important role in closing the advantage gap. In my opinion, the book you have in your hands will help teachers to graduate from knocking out reheated meals in a second-rate diner to competent chefs turning out delicious, nutritious meals. Reading this book could help teachers become the equivalent of top quality chefs in Michelin starred restaurants.

Bon appétit!

Paul A. Kirschner

Professor of Educational Psychology and Distinguished University Professor at the Open University of the Netherlands

Fellow of the American Educational Research Association, the International Society of the Learning Sciences and the Netherlands Institute for Advanced Study in the Humanities and Social Sciences

Acknowledgements

I owe a number of people a great debt for this book being what it is. Many of them I've never met, but on whose research and thinking the arguments in it depend. I am grateful to be able to jump up and down excitedly behind their shoulders, if not to actually stand on them.

There are also a number of people who are due personal thanks. First of these is Andrew Sabisky for interesting me in the study of intelligence and for recommending Stuart Ritchie's excellent little book, *Intelligence: All That Matters*, which forms the backbone of much of the information in Chapters 3 and 5.

I must also thank Nick Rose, my esteemed co-author of *What Every Teacher Needs to Know About Psychology*, for refusing to pull his punches. As well as being grateful for his many insightful comments and criticisms, I have also leant heavily on a number of Nick's contributions to our book, and these crop up in Chapters 2, 6 and 10.

Thanks also to Adam Boxer for allowing me to reproduce the diagrams and some of the content from his article, 'Novices, Experts and Everything In-between: Epistemology and Pedagogy', which can be found on his blog, *A Chemical Orthodoxy*.

I'm also terrifically grateful to Dylan Wiliam for making so many helpful suggestions and observations; the book is much improved as a consequence.

And, of course, to my indefatigable editor, Peter Young, who read through some pretty ropey early drafts, pulled me up on countless errors and wrestled the whole thing into whatever shape it has.

Finally, and always, Rosie.

Contents

Foreword . . . . *iii*

Acknowledgements . . . . *vii*

Figures and tables xi

Preface xiii

Introduction 1

Chapter 1   The purpose of education 17

Chapter 2   Built by culture 37

Chapter 3   Is intelligence the answer? 55

Chapter 4   Nature via nurture 85

Chapter 5   Can we get cleverer? 113

Chapter 6   How memory works 149

Chapter 7   You are what you know 171

Chapter 8   What knowledge? 201

Chapter 9   Practice makes permanent 227

Chapter 10 Struggle and success 249

Conclusion: Shifting the bell curve 271

Notes *281*

Bibliography *299*

Index *321*

Figures and tables

Figure 2.1. Folk knowledge domains 42

Figure 3.1. Degrees of correlation 62

Figure 3.2. Piracy and global warming over the years 63

Figure 3.3. The correlation between autism and organic food sales   64

Figure 3.4. The normal distribution of intelligence 71

Figure 4.1. Normal IQ distribution curves for males and females . . 94

Figure 5.1. Example of a matrix reasoning question 119

Figure 5.2. Chess position based on the Caro–Kann advance . . . 122

Figure 5.3. The Flynn effect: rising IQ scores, 1947–2002 125

Figure 6.1. A simple model of memory 153

Figure 6.2. Baddeley and Hitch's working memory model 154

Figure 6.3. Representation of a schema – the individual nodes link to form one interconnected chunk 159

Figure 6.4. Ebbinghaus' forgetting curve 164

Figure 6.5. The new theory of disuse 166

Figure 7.1. Example of a maths question which can be solved using Pythagoras' theorem 180

Figure 7.2. The offside trap 196

Figure 7.3. The Coffey still 197

Figure 8.1. The domain, the specification and the test 219

Figure 8.2. The domain; a schema within a domain; a schema begins to be acquired 223

Figure 10.1. The task-switching penalty 258

Figure 10.2. The feedback continuum 262

Figure 10.3. The spacing effect 264

. . . .

Table 4.1.   Estimated influences of genes and environment on
reading ability at age 5 92

Table 4.2.   Estimated influences of genes and environment on
reading ability after one year of reading instruction 92

Table 4.3.   Estimates of broad heritability, shared environmental
effects and indications of non-additive genetic effects
for representative psychological traits 101

Table 5.1.   Accuracy of setting with a test of validity of 0.7 145

Table 9.1.   The difference between novice and expert 240

Table 10.1. Optimal intervals for retaining information 265

Preface

I've spent a good bit of the past five years thinking about and researching the contents of this book, and have learned a lot along the way. Not having a background in any field of science, at times I've struggled to appreciate some of the complexities, particularly those around behaviour genetics, heredity and gene expression. Consequently, when I started writing, I still had a confused belief that our personalities are more or less determined by our genetic inheritance. Even though I had repeatedly read about what heritability actually implies, I still found myself reverting to a folk biology explanation: we are who we are because we share the genes of our parents.

Although this hereditarian position has been passed confidently along in a more or less unbroken progression from the earliest origins of intelligence research to various current experts, it's a narrative that has given – and continues to give – comfort to eugenicists and racists and encourages the spread of the soft bigotry of low expectations. This is not the story I tell in this book.

Initially, I planned to include a chapter on the history of intelligence research – detailing the contributions of Galton, Spearman, Burt, Terman, Jensen and the like. Although Alfred Binet provides a rare example of an intelligence researcher who was neither a hereditarian nor a eugenicist (his motivations in measuring children's mental abilities are very much in the spirit of making kids cleverer), many of the others – despite being responsible for such useful inventions and discoveries as factor analysis, the positive manifold, and reliable and valid IQ tests – are found wanting on moral or intellectual grounds. I found myself in the position of having to condemn much of their research and conclusions while extracting precious little that added to my argument. Eventually, I decided it was a lengthy distraction from what I really wanted to write about and so ditched it.

What really matters is the environment in which our genes express themselves. This book is about what we *can* do. The measurement of individual differences is only really of interest to individuals; but the notion that intelligence is both malleable and correlated with a vast range of positive outcomes should be of interest to us all. This is the story of how we might go about improving society by improving the lives of every individual within it.

I'm painfully aware that my knowledge of the subjects I discuss is far from complete. Please assume that where there are mistakes or flaws of reasoning, these errors are my own and not those of the various sources I cite.

What is so thrilling about our time is that the privilege of information is now an instant and globally accessible privilege. It is our duty and our responsibility to see that gift bestowed on all the world's people, so that all may live lives of knowledge and understanding.

Kofi Annan

Wrong does not cease to be wrong because the majority share in it.

Leo Tolstoy, *A Confession*

Introduction

Who's afraid of Charlie Gordon?

What did you expect? Did you think I'd remain a docile pup, wagging my tail and licking the foot that kicks me? I no longer have to take the kind of crap that people have been handing me all my life.

Daniel Keyes, *Flowers for Algernon*

Given the choice, who wouldn't want to be cleverer? Who wouldn't wish for greater insight and understanding? Who wouldn't strive to see further and know more? What teacher wouldn't wish these things for their students, and what parent wouldn't wish them for their children?

When I started researching this book, I thought the answers to these questions were obvious. But it turns out that the very idea of intelligence makes many people extremely uncomfortable. When I started asking these questions of friends and family, instead of the resounding positivity I'd expected, I got equivocation. "Maybe" was the most popular answer. When asked if they would want their children to be cleverer, parents would say things like, "I just want them to be happy." When I asked my youngest daughter, she was concerned that if she was cleverer then perhaps she wouldn't be the same person anymore – maybe the way she thought would become fundamentally different and, if this was the trade-off, she'd rather stay as she was. Others, particularly those who work in education, are often concerned that if some people were more intelligent, where would that leave those of us who weren't?

In Daniel Keyes' novel, *Flowers for Algernon*, Charlie Gordon, a man with an IQ of just 68, undergoes a surgical procedure to artificially raise his intelligence. The story concentrates on Charlie's changing perspective and how he is treated by those around him. At the outset, Charlie is frustrated by his inability to make sense of the world, but finds that the consequences of getting cleverer are not all positive. He is rejected by his workmates and plagued with resentment at the way he had been treated when everyone believed him to be retarded. Perhaps intelligence is not such a blessing.

Leaving aside the fact that no one has yet come up with a technique to raise intelligence as described in the novel, Charlie's story taps into some popular misgivings about the consequences of making kids cleverer. Maybe ignorance is bliss? Maybe children would be more content if they knew less and therefore could think less about the world?

This squeamishness about intelligence seems to be the norm. We're assailed by popular images of the geek, the nerd, the dysfunctional scientist and the mad professor. Brainiacs have fewer friends, lack empathy and don't know how to have fun. You may have heard that IQ doesn't really mean anything in the real world and that being more intelligent leads to more problems than it solves. These pervasive, but false, ideas infect society to the point that, very often, especially during the school years, it's just not cool to be clever and being brainy is social suicide.

Fascinatingly – and much to the contrary of these enduring myths and misconceptions – intelligence appears to govern many other traits, and having more of it is connected to increases in almost every other desirable human characteristic. If you are cleverer, not only will you do better in school, but you'll also be more creative, demonstrate better leadership skills, earn more, be happier and live longer. In fact, the only downside to intelligence is a slightly greater tendency to wear glasses!*

---

*   Before the bespectacled among you get too smug about your eyewear, the correlation between IQ and wearing glasses is about 0.4 (see page 62 for details on degrees of correlation), which means that although on average those with glasses are a bit cleverer than the rest of us, there are still plenty of less smart glasses wearers out there. See Rosner and Belkin (1987).

You're not gifted *or* talented

As a child I never thought of myself as being particularly clever. Let me rephrase that: I never considered myself to be particularly academic. I did, however, pride myself on my quick wit and tended to gravitate towards the position of class clown. Too much of my time in school was spent cracking inopportune jokes and generally making a nuisance of myself. To my parents, I was something of a disappointment. My father loved Jesus and mathematics. He was disgusted with both my irreligious soul and my inability to manage more than the most slippery of grasp on anything to do with numbers. I also struggled to learn to read and, as you'll hear more about later, I was briefly home-schooled by my mother. To really rub salt into my intellectual wounds, I'm the eldest of three boys and my middle brother, 18 months younger than me, was always the clever one. He took the entrance exam for a local selective school; no one ever suggested that I might.

My first inkling that I might not be a complete duffer came as the result of a primary school quiz. I was selected as a last minute replacement for the school team when another boy – I can no longer remember his name – was taken ill. *Why me?* I wondered. No one told me, but whoever made the decision's instincts were pretty good as our team ended up winning and, if I didn't cover myself in glory, I certainly didn't disgrace myself. Looking back, this was probably the first time I made the link between being clever and knowing a lot.

Whatever my own opinion of my intellect, my teachers never seemed impressed. When I began secondary school, I was considered distinctly average. I worked reasonably hard in history and English and clawed my way into higher sets, but this was balanced against my performance in maths and science, where I seemed to sink ever lower. By the time I reached my last year of school, I'd given up trying at most subjects and only passed three of my GCSEs – further confirmation of my lack of scholarly prowess. I left school, got a job in a record shop and turned my back on education.

I drifted from job to job until, a few years later, working on a building site, I decided that there must be more to life and signed up to do an A level in classical studies at night school. As a child I'd had a much-treasured copy of *Heroes of Greece and Troy* but, apart from the *Asterix* comics, I really didn't know all that much about ancient civilisations. Suddenly I was reading Homer, Thucydides, Herodotus, Aeschylus, Virgil, Tacitus, Suetonius and Ovid (all in translation, of course), and I loved it. My mind felt enlarged like never before. Suddenly I had so much more to think about. As the end of the course loomed I asked my foreman if I could have a day off to sit my exams. Apparently, no one had ever asked him that before and he was impressed. When I came back on site the following day, I'd been promoted from general labourer to engineer's mate. Instead of having to haul bricks around all day I got to hold a theodolite and everyone took to calling me 'professor'. Such are the rewards of education.

Rather than bore you with further indulgent anecdotes, suffice it to say that from there I took another A level, this time in English literature, was persuaded to go to university, graduated and, after some further perambulations, became a teacher. I taught English in a series of state secondary schools for 15 years. Like most young teachers, I wanted to change the world. I wanted to set young minds on fire and instil in them a love of learning. And, like most young teachers, I rapidly realised it wasn't going to be easy. I was stunned that so many of the children I taught seemed to take such defensive pride in their ignorance and were so dismissive of the world beyond their narrow experience.

A few years into my career, the job of gifted and talented coordinator came up at my school and I decided to apply. (Back in those days, English schools were required to identify their gifted cohorts and put together a programme to enrich them beyond what was on offer to other students.) I happened to mention to my mother that I was interested in the role. She responded with some surprise and said, "That's funny because you're not gifted or talented." How we laughed.

You'll be pleased to hear that I got the job. I now see the idea of identifying a minority of children as gifted and talented as a terrible one. I've got no problem with giving children enriching experiences, but I object strongly to the notion that enrichment should only be accessible to those already considered more able. But back then I threw myself into the role. I organised all sorts of activities, visits, speakers and intellectually stretching experiences for my students, many of whom came from fairly deprived backgrounds, knew little of the world and felt their ignorance sharply.

One of my schemes was to put together a public speaking team. We entered a competition held in a local independent school. When we arrived, it turned out that our team was one of only two from state schools. My little group felt hugely intimidated by the other students. They kept asking me things like, "Why do they sound like that?" and "Why is their hair like that?" When these other children spoke they were confident, controlled and articulate, but what really set them apart was what they knew. They all seemed ferociously intelligent. When it was my students' turn to speak they were nervous wrecks. Needless to say, we came last.

I've no idea whether these other children really *were* more intelligent than my students, but it didn't matter. The power of knowing things struck home. Being clever and being knowledgeable may not be the same thing, but, as was clear to me and my students, knowledge trumped all else. The way I thought about what I did shifted profoundly. At about the same time my eldest daughter was born and I began asking of the education I was providing, "Is this good enough for my own child?" Increasingly, the answer seemed to be no.

What do we really want?

Education isn't cheap. On top of the Herculean efforts of teachers, we spend millions every year on keeping the system going and so it's important that education provides some sort of value for money. But, important as this might be, it also has to satisfy us on a more human level. To that end, it's worth thinking about what we most want for the next generation.

When I asked my wife what she wanted for our children she said she'd settle for about £100 each. After we'd stopped chuckling she explained that, although she's ambitious for them, mostly she wants them to be content. This is in line with what most people say: we'd like our children to be successful, but only as long as that doesn't make them unhappy. We also want our children to be healthy, safe and secure. All parents tend to put financial security near the top of their lists; there's a recognition that contentment is more likely if you've got a decent job. Nothing extravagant, but enough to pay the bills without being soul destroying. And, of course, we want them kept out of harm's way and to live a long, illness- and accident-free life. The question is, how best to arrive at these ends?

Contentment, happiness, call it what you will, can seem a meagre ambition, but without it, little else is likely to be worth savouring. But what *is* it? How do you acquire happiness? The most useful definition I've encountered suggests that happiness is best thought of as being derived from both pleasure and purpose.[1] Pleasure involves doing what makes us feel good, and purposefulness requires that we head towards some sort of goal. None of us want a life of pure hedonism for our children, and few would see happiness as being achieved by a life spent relentlessly pursuing an ambition. So, pleasure and purpose must be taken in moderation and in harmony. They temper and complement each other.

For life to be purposeful, we have to be able to choose a goal that seems meaningful. Being able to choose is, at least in part, a function of how well educated we are; the better we do in school, the more choices there are before us. Of course, there are always stories of successful people whose success has come despite flunking their exams, but this is survivorship bias; such folk are the exception rather than the rule.

For most of us, our chances of being happy are greatly increased by having been successful at school, but we also recognise that education is more than examinations and qualifications. We tend to agree that children, no matter their backgrounds or starting points, need the best chance of becoming rounded young people who are ready to face an uncertain future. Like everyone else does, I want young people to be creative, skilled at collaborating with others to solve problems, able to clearly and critically communicate their thoughts, take on new challenges and persist in the face of setbacks. I want them to be prepared for whatever the unknowable future places in their paths. And, of course, I want my children – and yours – to be tolerant, compassionate, open-minded, curious, cooperative and to help leave the world in a better condition than the shambles it currently seems to be in.

In 2012, I left the classroom and turned to the dark side to become a full-time writer and consultant. When I'm not working in schools and training teachers, I tend to read academic papers and books. In doing so, I have become aware of a huge body of research indicating that intelligence appears to be connected with all sorts of other good stuff. I began to wonder whether it might be possible to get what I wanted by making kids cleverer. What if, by raising children's intelligence, not only would they do better at school, but their lives beyond school might also be improved?

This, then, is my contention: whatever it is we might want for our children, making them cleverer appears to be the best way to go about making it happen. Over the course of this book, I will explain that, unlike many other qualities we might value, intelligence has the advantages of being malleable, measurable and meaningful.

Intelligence is a social good. The greater the number of individuals with higher intelligence, the safer, happier and more productive the society in which we live. It's also an individual good, and, contrary to popular belief, intelligence correlates strongly with creativity, leadership, happiness, longevity and most other factors we tend to view as worth striving for. It therefore seems reasonable to suggest that if we want to make children more creative and better critical thinkers, we need first to make them cleverer.

By 'making cleverer' what I really mean, of course, is raising intelligence – increasing children's intellectual capacity. Intelligence means different things to different people. It has been described as a faculty for logic, understanding, self-awareness, creativity, problem solving and the ability to learn new information more quickly. According to some, it's the ability to acquire and apply knowledge, while others see it as plain old 'good sense'. Whatever it is, it seems safe to agree that it's not simply a single thing. One widely accepted definition is offered by Linda Gottfredson. She defines intelligence as:

> ... a very general mental capability that, among other things, involves the ability to reason, plan, solve problems, think abstractly, comprehend complex ideas, learn quickly and learn from experience. It is not merely book learning, a narrow academic skill, or test-taking smarts. Rather, it reflects a broader and deeper capability for comprehending our surroundings – 'catching on,' 'making sense' of things, or 'figuring out' what to do.[2]

We'll add some flesh to these bare bones as we go, but for now, this is the definition I'm happiest with and what you should assume I mean whenever you see the word.

The gap

The arguments in this book are aimed at both parents and those involved in education. As parents, we are most interested in what is likely to make our children more successful. It's not that we don't care about other people's children, but ours, rightly, come first. I hope you will find much in these pages to guide you in your endeavours and to be more knowledgeable about what goes on in schools.

I'm also writing for teachers, policy makers and all those who, directly or indirectly, influence what happens in schools and classrooms. Your priority is the well-being and success of all children in the system. You will be concerned that some children fare far less well than others and you will be interested in whether there is anything we can do to arrest and narrow the advantage gap. According to a report by the Education Policy Institute, while the situation may be improving, the gap between rich and poor children is still very wide:

> The gap between disadvantaged 16 year old pupils and their peers has only narrowed by three months of learning between 2007 and 2016. In 2016, the gap nationally, at the end of secondary school, was still 19.3 months. In fact, disadvantaged pupils fall behind their more affluent peers by around 2 months each year over the course of secondary school.[3]

The Sutton Trust report *Global Gaps* found that while children in England do better at school than those in most other countries, "bright but poor" children – those in the top 10% for achievement but in the bottom 25% for socio-economic status – are almost three years behind the Organisation for Economic Co-operation and Development (OECD) average. For girls, the situation is even worse.[4] These facts are stark but they are not the complete picture. All children, in every country in the world, are better off today than at any other point in human history. Yes, of course, some children are unfairly disadvantaged, but this is not fate. Children from less advantaged backgrounds are only failing when viewed through a particularly distorted lens. Not only can we change the future, but the present is not what we think it is.

In his book, *Factfulness*, the Swedish statistician Hans Rosling warns us against the gap instinct: the tendency to divide the world into two distinct and conflicting groups – poor and rich – with, in his words, "a chasm of injustice in between". This instinct distorts our ability to see the world as it actually is. Rosling asks, "How do you like your bathwater? Ice cold or steaming hot?" Of course, we choose our bathwater to be any temperature between these extremes. He points out that when asked whether the majority of people live in low, medium or high income countries, most people tend to guess the first option. This is wrong. In fact, 75% of the world's population live in middle income countries – right where the gap is supposed to be. In Rosling's view, "there is no gap".[5]

We have the same tendency to divide children up into two discrete categories: rich and poor; more and less advantaged; those from secure backgrounds and those from chaotic backgrounds. This is just as absurd. The overwhelming majority of children are somewhere in the middle. Trying to create education policy based on the experiences of the few per cent at the top and bottom of the distribution is unlikely to work because it ignores most children. Instead, we need to think in terms of what is likely to work for *all* children.

That said, we ought not to be complacent about the least advantaged. The message of this book is that all children can become cleverer and, in so doing, increase the chance that they will lead a happy, healthy and prosperous life. Currently this is not the case. Children from more deprived backgrounds are disproportionately more likely to struggle at school. This often leads to a cycle of failure with children learning that school is for other people and growing into adults who pass this suspicion of education on to their own children. It wasn't always like this. Arthur Scargill, tub-thumping leader of the National Union of Mineworkers, who led the opposition to Margaret Thatcher's struggle to break the power of the trade unions, wrote, "My father still reads the dictionary every day. He says your life depends on your power to master words."[6] This view of education – that it confers power and choice – is one that must be reclaimed. Mastering words, along with all other forms of knowledge, is the mechanism for becoming cleverer.

A gap – a difference between those at the top and bottom of a distribution curve – is inevitable. We can't all be equally intelligent. But that gap does not have to be based on something as arbitrary and unfair as your parents' income. The information and arguments in this book will, I hope, provide you with both practical strategies to apply to the classroom and an intellectual and moral underpinning for creating the schools our children need, altering your thinking about those who succeed and those who fail. This is my manifesto for making education benefit all children, regardless of their beginnings.

A chain of reasoning

Before we plunge further into the book, here is a brief summary of the arguments I will go on to make in support of the idea that education should be about making children cleverer.

The first chapter considers the various competing claims about what the purpose of education ought to be. The three proposed purposes we shall review in detail are: preparing children for employment, moulding children's characters, and transmitting culture. The conclusion I offer is that, while each of these purposes has individual merit, all are best achieved by making children cleverer. This, then, should be the purpose to which we bend our collective will.

All well and good, but if we're serious about making children cleverer then we need to consider the means to make it so. Chapter 2 is a discussion of the ways our brains have been shaped to learn and think. The fact that we find some things easy to learn doesn't mean we find all things equally so. Evolutionary psychology provides us with some sensible ideas about why this might be and suggests an explanation as to why human beings came to invent schools. There is good reason to think that skills like creativity and problem solving are actually evolutionary adaptions so important to the survival of the species that we've evolved to find them easy to learn.

Next we need to think more seriously about what intelligence is and isn't. This is the subject to which we turn in Chapter 3. Although myths and misconceptions about intelligence and IQ abound, there's compelling evidence that higher intelligence is positively associated with pretty much everything we tend to regard as important and worth valuing. By unpicking the more persistent and pernicious of these beliefs, we should get a better, less biased understanding of what we mean by intelligence. Along the way, we will also examine the data suggesting that intelligence might be the root cause of all other good things, whether we can trust this data and what the implications are.

From here we move onto a discussion about where intelligence comes from. Chapter 4 takes on the nature vs. nurture debate and explores the implications of a hereditarian view of intelligence, as well as the notion that we are entirely the product of our experiences. Intelligence (and pretty much everything else) is influenced by our genes. Some children are just born with a greater potential for cleverness than others. However, there's good reason to believe that we are already getting cleverer in some respects as we become more knowledgeable, and, by concentrating on those environmental factors that can be changed, we might be able to make all children cleverer, and in the process benefit not just society as a whole but every individual within it.

Just as everyone isn't equally tall, equally healthy, equally talented at playing the piano or equally good at maths, we can't make everyone equally intelligent. However, it may be possible to address the difference between the most and least advantaged in society. Trying to develop children's ability by teaching generic skills directly is fundamentally unfair. Children with higher fluid intelligence and those from more advantaged backgrounds will be further privileged. If we make a concerted attempt to increase children's intelligence by expanding what they know about the world, we may also be able to shift the whole curve upwards. I will argue that while both matter, currently there's nothing anyone can do about their genes, so our power to shape children's environments is all we have. And perhaps all we need.

Chapter 5 returns us to intelligence research, but this time the focus is on what actually increases our store of intelligence. The concept of intelligence can be broken into two subcomponents: fluid intelligence and crystallised intelligence. Fluid intelligence is our raw reasoning power, and is, as far as we can tell, fixed. Nothing we've tried as yet is able to increase it. Crystallised intelligence is the ability to apply what we know to new problems and can certainly be increased by adding to our store of knowledge. This is the central thesis of the book: more knowledge equals more intelligence. But it may not be the only way to get what we want, and there are plenty of other competing theories. Before we move on we need to assess these alternatives and so we will evaluate the merits of growth mindset, brain training and cognitive acceleration, to name but a few.

If I'm right that knowing more leads to us becoming cleverer, then we need to think more about how children are going to remember all this additional knowledge. To that end, Chapter 6 examines what our memories are composed of, what limits our thinking and how much space we've got to fill with precious cargo. We possess a working memory – the ability to hold things in mind when trying to solve a problem or perform a task – and a long-term memory – the ability to store huge quantities of stuff that can be dredged up as needed. It turns out that our working memory capacity is strictly limited and cannot be easily increased, but its limits can be 'hacked' by storing information more robustly in long-term memory. When we store knowledge in long-term memory, it organises itself into schemas which, when we use them to think about complex problems, take up less of our limited reasoning capacity. While those with less fluid intelligence may find it more difficult to create long-term memories, the capacity of their long-term memory, like that of anyone else, is essentially infinite. All children can remember stuff, regardless of how able we perceive them to be, but some better than others. While the difference might be explained by higher fluid intelligence, we should also look at ways we might train our memories to be more efficient and work out what to do about our natural tendency towards forgetfulness.

But understanding memory is not much use without considering the stuff of which our memories are composed. The somewhat contentious view I present in Chapter 7 is that knowledge is all there is. We take in some of the early philosophical explorations of knowledge before settling on the notion that everything is knowledge. No one can think about something they don't know. Equally, the more you know about a subject, the richer and more sophisticated your thinking on that subject becomes. It's my view that '21st century skills' depend on knowing things rather than on simply being able to look stuff up on the internet. What we know is composed both of what we are able to bring to mind and consciously think about and those things we're not always aware of but which we think with. Some of what we normally refer to as skills can, with practice, be made effortless and invisible so that they take up practically no space in working memory, giving us a far greater capacity with which to think. If children automatise powerful procedural knowledge in long-term memory and encounter culturally rich knowledge, they will become cleverer and therefore more creative, better problem solvers and able to think more critically.

Certain types of knowledge are particularly worth automatising because they recur so often, both in education and in subsequent life. This leads us, in Chapter 8, to think about what knowledge (whose knowledge) children ought to learn. Not all knowledge is equal. Some kinds of knowledge are much more likely to enhance children's intellectual capacity than others. We will consider several mechanisms for selecting knowledge and organising it within a curriculum, packaged and ready for children to embark on an exciting voyage of discovery. We will think about whether the curriculum ought to be divided up into subjects and how we can organise and sequence the things we want children to learn.

Chapter 9 takes on the concept of practice. We all know that expertise only develops as a result of hard work and effort, but how much? You may have come across the neat sounding, but ultimately unhelpful, idea that we should practise for 10,000 hours if we want to achieve mastery. Sadly, as with knowledge, not all practice is equally effective. We will look at the type of practice most likely to result in expertise and then consider what makes experts expert. Fascinatingly, when experts operate within their area of expertise, they develop entirely different cognitive architecture to the uninitiated.

Novices and experts are very different beasts and, for the purposes of education, must be treated as such. The vast majority of school students are currently novices. Explicit instruction will very likely be the most effective way for them to be taught. Context has very little to say on this matter; not nothing but very little. If, for example, you want to pay for your child to attend a private school then that's fine. You're exercising a choice. The fact that you can afford the fees means that your children will almost certainly be fine, no matter how they're educated.

It may be true that "everything works somewhere but nothing works everywhere",[7] but, if so, it's trivially true. I would accept that pretty much any approach to teaching *can* be made to work – sort of – but it's not whether an intervention works but *how well* it works in comparison to other interventions. Better to say, some things work in most contexts and other things rarely work anywhere. Some approaches to the curriculum and instruction have stood the test of time and are better suited to achieving the ends most people value.

In Chapter 10, we turn our attention to what is most likely to lead to children learning the knowledge they need to become cleverer. When it comes to the best way to teach there are no certainties, but there are some pretty clear probabilities. For instance, explicit instruction appears to be much more effective than discovery learning for novice learners. Ends never justify means. There's little point in judging someone by their intentions – the road to hell is paved with high hopes and grand plans. Instead, we should all be judged by our actions. If your actions fail to achieve your aims, what then? This is a social justice argument.

The book concludes by returning us to the gap in attainment between the most and least advantaged. For those children endowed with high fluid intelligence and a privileged background, it probably doesn't matter much what schools choose to do. But for those without these advantages, a school provides choice. With greater access to knowledge, taught explicitly, disadvantaged children are more likely to live happy, healthy, prosperous lives. We all agree that children should be happy, virtuous and successful; where I diverge from the received wisdom is on how we can best achieve these aims. Although making kids cleverer doesn't rely on causing any other outcome to be worthwhile, the fact that intelligence appears to correlate with so much of what we want is a possibility we should not ignore.

All this applies most to those children who are often overlooked, assumed to be plodders and consigned to bottom sets. I'm not claiming that what I suggest in this book will work magically to make all children cleverer, but that we can, and should, seek to increase the intellectual capacity of all children. To this end, resources should be targeted at those who struggle to master the basic academic tools of reading, writing and arithmetic, to help them overcome these difficulties by whatever means are effective. Leaving school without an acceptable level of competence in each of these areas is entirely unacceptable; those who do so have been failed by their school and by the system.

....

Once the arguments I will present have been absorbed, making children cleverer becomes a very useful framing device. It provides a mechanism for interrogating many educational issues:

Q. What is the purpose of education?

A. Making children cleverer.

Q. How do we make children cleverer?

A. By getting them to know more.

Q. How do we get children to know more?

A. By teaching them a knowledge-rich curriculum and focusing on strengthening their access to knowledge stored in long-term memory.

Q. What is a knowledge-rich curriculum?

A. One built around the most powerful and culturally useful information.

Q. How do we focus on strengthening children's access to knowledge stored in long-term memory?

A. By teaching in a way that prioritises opportunities to recall what has been learned and minimises distractions and irrelevances.

Q. Why should we be interested in making children cleverer?

A. Because this seems to be the best bet for improving children's welfare and because getting children to know more is something that's relatively straightforward for schools to do.

And so on.

Whenever I'm confronted with some new initiative or policy proposal, my first question is, will this help make children cleverer? I hope that once you've read the book and chewed over the arguments, you'll find this simple formulation as useful as I do.

Chapter 1

The purpose of education

Our top priority was, is and always will be education, education, education.

Tony Blair

The greatest university of all is the collection of books.

Thomas Carlyle

- Why do we need schools when we have libraries (and the internet)?
- How can we shape children's characters?
- How do we prepare children for an unknown and unknowable future?
- How do we open children's minds? And how do we keep them open?

Despite the esteem in which it's held, education is as hotly contested and ideologically riven as any other field of human endeavour, probably more so than most. Much of the disagreement stems from the troublesome fact that there's little consensus on what education is actually for.

Most people readily accept that the purpose of medicine is to make people healthier. There's no such consensus about the purpose of education. One of the things that makes education different from other areas of enquiry is that everyone has spent a lot of time in schools and we all feel we know what makes them successful. We might also have spent time in hospitals or law courts, but we tend not to assume we could do what doctors or lawyers do. But teachers? They just, well, teach, don't they?

Schools vs. libraries

If you're anything like me, at times you probably wondered why you were at school. In most developed societies, school is taken utterly for granted and, like death, taxes and other things that are unavoidable, we often view it with a mixture of resentment and disdain. I look back at my time in school and remember it as being three parts mind-numbing tedium to two parts social battleground. I wasn't a good student. I didn't know how to study and, as I said, wasn't at all sure why I was there. By the age of 13, I had started voting with my feet.

Although I'm not a Catholic, I went to a Catholic school. It was about 15 miles away from my home and I had to catch two buses in order to get there. This could have been prohibitively expensive, but for some reason the local education authority took pity on children in my position and gave us free bus passes. This was somewhat ironic, as my free bus pass became my ticket out of school. For months at a time, I would leave home in the morning in my school uniform and catch the bus into central Birmingham. Where do you go if you're a 13-year-old with no money in the middle of England's second biggest city? The library, obviously.

Birmingham Central Library was my refuge, my sanctuary and, in some ways, my alma mater. Not only was it warm, but it was big enough that a teenager in school uniform went unnoticed. In memory it was vast. There were escalators to several floors, and one of my favourite ways to pass the time was to ride up to the top floor and use the microfiches to hunt through old newspapers for diverting nuggets and tidbits. In retrospect, this must be akin to the kind of aimless surfing through YouTube and BuzzFeed that my teenage daughters engage in today. I say akin, but there was one acute difference: as far as I could tell, I was the only child who seemed to spend his time in this way.

When I wasn't flicking through decades-old headlines, I'd scour the shelves for interesting sounding books and take a handful into the reading room to peruse. I read all sorts. As well as indulging my penchant for science fiction and flicking through encyclopaedias, I wrestled with aging classics like *The Decline and Fall of the Roman Empire*, *On the Origin of Species* and *The Prince*, as well as more popular titles like *I'm OK – You're OK*, *The Selfish Gene* and *Surely You're Joking, Mr Feynman?* And for some now unknowable reason I became a devotee of Russian literature:

I read *Crime and Punishment*, *The Gulag Archipelago*, *The Master and Margarita* and *Anna Karenina*. I didn't understand them all that well – and I certainly didn't like them all – but I stubbornly ploughed through them, day after day. And no one in the library ever questioned my right to do so.

But it couldn't last. Eventually I was found out. My school – after many blissful months – finally worked out I wasn't turning up and got around to calling home to ask my parents whether I was attending another school. I won't detail the exquisite agonies of my punishments here, but the one accusation that still rings in my ears is that I was throwing away my education. At the time I went along with it, but now this seems rather bizarre. After all, what is education? My memory of school is that I spent a lot of time being bored, staring out of windows and playing squares.[*] For years, I thought of myself as something of an autodidact and that I learned practically nothing at school. I now know that this is incorrect, but more on that later.

What, we should ask ourselves, is the point of going to school? Why do we make children wear uniforms, sit at desks and do homework? What's it all for if children can learn as much – or more – from libraries (and, of course, the internet)? The point, as I've slowly come to realise, is that most children are not like I was. If I'm honest, even I wasn't much like the way I remember myself. At the library I only read what interested me. At school I had to learn about blast furnaces, quadratic equations, osmosis and *The Mayor of Casterbridge*, whether I wanted to or not. Much as I might try to deny it, something of each of these things is lodged somewhere in my brain. I am my own example of survivorship bias!

In a society where we no longer believe it ethical to put children to work in factories, school gets young people out of bed and gives them something productive to do instead of just snapchatting each other all day. As an adult, with children of my own, I have sympathy with this. I instinctively dislike the idea of children purposelessly meandering through their days, as seems to be the case at weekends, and going to school is, on the face of it, better than sending them up chimneys.

....

[*]   In case you don't know, squares is a two-player game in which the players construct a grid made up of dots and then take turns connecting the dots with lines in the hope of making a square. The player who captures the most squares is the winner.

There are no end of cynical takes on what education is, as opposed to what it ought to be. Matt Ridley complains, "Rarely, if ever, has the purpose of state education been to add to scholarship and generate knowledge." He quotes the American journalist H. L. Mencken as saying, "The aim of public education is not to spread enlightenment at all. It is simply to reduce as many individuals as possible to the same level, to breed a standard citizenry, to put down dissent and originality."[1] A depressing thought.

But, less selfishly and cynically, when we think about why we send children to school, the answers tend to fit into three broad areas: socialisation, enculturation and personal development.

- *Socialisation* – in this view, education is primarily a tool of the state, employed to make its citizens more productive. In this way of thinking, children should be prepared both for work and to become loyal and enthusiastic participants in the activities of the state.

- *Enculturation* – the notion that the towering achievements of our culture should be passed along, like the Olympic torch, from one generation to the next to allow young people to fully participate in the intellectual and cultural life of their society.

- *Personal development* – many take the view that education ought to address 'the whole child' and aim to make children flourish in as broad a sense as possible. This includes the belief that education should be both therapeutic and concerned with developing character.

Underlying each of these is the notion that education is our best chance for eradicating inequality. This includes the belief not only that all children, no matter their start in life, should be afforded the advantages enjoyed by the most privileged, but also that all children have the capacity to rise to the top if their disadvantages are specifically addressed and playing fields are systematically levelled.

But it's worth enquiring whether school – or schooling – does an adequate job in these regards. To that end, we will address some of the details of these three broad visions for the purpose of education.

The content of our characters

The idea that schools should be educating children's characters has been gathering momentum in recent years, but if we're going to educate children in a way that moulds their characters, we need to be very clear about what kind of character we want them to have.

We all agree that a good character is, well, good. But what should this include? Is grit, tenacity, resilience (or whatever you want to call it) part of a good character? Or is character more about being polite, well-mannered and able to smoothly navigate through the world? Or might it be to do with morality, ethics and conscience? Is it about doing the 'right thing'? And if it is, who decides what's right? Should we be guided by the so-called 'British values' of fair play, tolerance and self-deprecation? On some level all of these things are desirable, but are they teachable?

Obviously, schools can't do everything. Like it or not, some schooling has to be about acquiring the knowledge in order to be able to do stuff. In *Education is Upside-Down*, American educator Eric Kalenze offers the intriguing idea that if we get children to struggle with troublesome concepts, work hard and delay gratification as they work towards examinations, we will be simultaneously and implicitly developing their ability to acquire these traits without having to teach anything explicit.[2] And these traits may well be the very ones which best prepare young people for higher education, satisfying careers and a fulfilling life. The either/or nature of character development vs. academic learning is problematic. But maybe by giving children the very best academic education, character may just follow along.

But what of the other aspects of character? How far should we seek to mould children's personalities? The Sutton Trust report on character education, *A Winning Personality*, concluded that extroversion correlates strongly with career success. It recommends that schools focus their efforts on improving less advantaged children's knowledge and awareness of professional careers, using "good feedback to improve pupils' social skills", providing "suitable training in employability skills and interview techniques" and on ensuring that attempts to improve outcomes for less advantaged children are "broad-based – focusing on wider skills as well as academic attainment".[3] These are relatively uncontroversial, but the much trumpeted headline was that people from more advantaged backgrounds are significantly more extroverted than those from less advantaged backgrounds. The implication is that these children ought to be taught to be more extrovert.

I feel uncomfortable at the idea of extroversion being preached as a gospel of success. To the extent that career success might correlate with such personality traits, this is more an indictment of the shallowness of our society than a reason to force quieter, more introspective children to be as loud and brash as their more extrovert peers. Also, a careful reading of the report reveals a negative skew in the relationship between agreeableness (things like modesty and humility) and earnings potential. If we were to follow that line of reasoning, one might argue that as well as encouraging children to be extroverts, we should also teach them to be less agreeable! Maybe, instead, we should do more to consider why we value such super-ficialities rather than rushing to lionise those who shout the loudest.

I'm not the only one who's troubled. The Jubilee Centre, an organisation which exists to further the aims of character education, is at pains to distance itself from the Sutton Trust report. The thrust of their objection is that the authors of *A Winning Personality* failed to understand that personality and character are not the same thing:

> An elementary distinction is circumvented by both the report and its discontents between *personality* and *character*. ... Personality traits, such as extroversion and conscientiousness and others posited and measured via the proverbial Five-Factor Model, are mostly non-malleable after an early age. They are genetic up to at least 50% and otherwise shaped in early childhood. In academic parlance, those traits would be described as *content-thin, non-morally evaluable, non-reason-responsive and mostly non-educable*. No amount of rational dissuasion or character education is ever going to turn an introvert into an extrovert. ... Character traits, in contrast, are *content-thick, morally evaluable, reason-responsive and highly educable*.[4]

It's almost certainly true that personality traits, along with every other trait, are heritable to some degree, although I'm less sure of the claim that the remaining factors are "shaped in early childhood". As we'll see in Chapter 4, there's compelling evidence to suggest that peer effects in early to late adolescence are much more powerful than early childhood factors. What's really interesting is the idea that the 'Big Five' personality traits – openness to experience, conscientiousness, extroversion, agreeableness and neuroticism* – might be distinct from character traits. This is important because in her book, *The Cult of Personality*, Annie Murphy Paul casts doubt on the idea that personality traits are stable – that is to say, they seem to change depending on the context in which they're measured.[5] If our personality is dependent to some degree on context, would it perhaps be better to think of personality as just a collection of learned habits? Openness to experience depends on mood; how conscientious we are depends greatly on how we feel about what we're doing. We are agreeable in some situations and not others; we change to adapt to the circumstances we find ourselves in.

So, what about the idea that character traits, or virtues, might be "content-thick, morally evaluable, reason-responsive and highly educable"? Can we really educate children to be virtuous? And what virtues should we educate them in? The Jubilee Centre claims that "Character is a set of personal traits or dispositions that produce specific moral emotions, inform motivation and guide conduct."[6] The virtues they reckon we should value are courage, justice, honesty, compassion for others, self-discipline, gratitude and humility. These seem like pretty good things to be, but are they really "highly educable"?

Another question to consider is, where do these virtues come from? Are they innate or acquired? Might there be genes for good character or is it soaked up along with mother's milk? In short, is our character the result of nature or nurture? Well, you'll probably be unsurprised to find that it's a bit of both.

Apparently one in every 100 men is a psychopath. (Interestingly, the figure is much lower for women.) Evidence appears to suggest that being a psychopath isn't a choice or the result of some early childhood trauma, but a genetically heritable condition. While most psychopaths don't end up as serial killers, they do all lack moral emotions like guilt, shame and compassion. They just don't seem to care what others think about them.** Now, if psychopathy can be passed on through genes, it follows that the ability to experience these emotions must also, at least to some degree,

---

*   The 'Big Five' are often referred to by the acronym, OCEAN.

**   That's not quite true. They probably *do* care what others think, but only in so far as they want to manipulate or exploit other people. See Millon et al. (1998) for details.

be inherited. Further, it suggests that these feelings have evolved through natural selection because they have some evolutionary advantage.

The moral psychologist Jonathan Haidt suggests that morality is the product of maintaining our reputations within social interactions.[7] Very often we can be guilty of trying to *look* good, rather than putting our effort into *being* good. One benefit of being a psychopath is that you will care far more about what you think of yourself than the good opinion of others. But for the rest of us, we need to consider how social pressures could encourage us to prefer being good over looking good.

The political scientist Philip Tetlock came up with three conditions under which this might occur. They are:

1. The knowledge that we will be accountable to an audience.

2. The audience's views must be unknown.

3. The belief that the audience is well-informed and interested in accuracy.[8]

If these conditions are met, people tend to do the right thing.

Research into self-consciousness has shown that the idea of self-esteem is dodgy at best. People who identify as having high self-esteem actually believe they stand high in the esteem of others; they think well of themselves because others think well of them. In an experiment, participants who identified themselves as possessing high self-esteem saw that sense of self deteriorate as they spoke about themselves to camera and received unflattering rankings of their performance from a hidden audience. As Haidt puts it, "They might indeed have steered by their own compass, but they didn't realise that their compass tracked public opinion, not true north."[9]

Depressingly, this suggests that you can't really instil good character; we're only likely to display the right kind of character traits when we're held accountable for our behaviour by, as Adam Smith put it, an "impartial spectator". In *The Theory of Moral Sentiments*, Smith argued that morality emerges through a human desire to get on with others. When they're born, children know nothing of morality but discover, through trial and error, which behaviours are considered acceptable and which aren't, resulting in "a mutual sympathy of sentiments".[10] Most people will conform to social norms, and what is accepted quickly becomes acceptable. Morality emerges. So, if we want children to develop positive character traits, we should make sure that the culture of schools is pretty intolerant of indolence, rudeness and general arsing about.

Developing children's character depends not on attempting to explicitly teach some ephemeral set of 'non-cognitive'* skills but on a combination of high expectations, accountability and modelling. As Kalenze suggests, probably the best way to teach resilience is to give children challenging work to do; the best way to teach respect and politeness is to model it; the best way to teach children how to be functional, happy citizens is to set up systems which hold them to account for their behaviour.

Does the future change everything?

Employers tend to be vocal about what they think schools should be teaching. They usually agree that literacy and numeracy are valuable skills, but they also want children to be taught a whole host of other work-friendly competencies such as creativity, critical thinking, problem solving, collaboration and the like. An increasingly common argument that is often advanced is that the internet has changed everything. The 21st century has been variously referred to as the second machine age, the fourth industrial revolution and the information economy – but has technology *really* changed everything?

The reality is that technology has been transforming education for as long as either has been in existence. Language, arguably the most crucial technological advancement in human history, moved education from mere mimicry and emulation into the realms of cultural transmission; as we became able to express abstractions so we could teach our offspring about the interior world of thought beyond the concrete reality we experienced directly. This process accelerated and intensified with the invention of writing, which Socrates railed against, believing it would eat away at the marrow of society and kill off young people's ability to memorise facts. He was right. The transformative power of writing utterly reshaped the way we think and how we use knowledge. As soon as we were able to

---

* The term non-cognitive is an irritating misnomer. Anything that takes place in the brain is the result of cognition.

record our thoughts in writing, we no longer had to memorise everything we needed to know. But education was very much a minority sport until the advent of the printing press, when suddenly books started to become affordable for the masses. Before Gutenberg, there was no need for any but a privileged elite to be literate, but as the number of printed works exploded exponentially, the pressure on societies to prioritise universal education slowly grew until, by the 20th century, education became increasingly to be viewed not only as a requirement but as a right.

The rate at which we now produce knowledge is staggering. In his 1981 book, *Critical Path*, the architect and inventor Richard Buckminster Fuller identified what he called the 'knowledge doubling curve'. He noticed that until 1900 human knowledge doubled approximately every century. By the mid-20th century knowledge was doubling every 25 years.[11] Today, on average, human knowledge doubles in just over a year. Some estimates suggest that soon what we collectively know is set to double every 12 hours.[12]

It's no wonder so many have been persuaded that there is no longer a need to learn facts because what we know will quickly be superseded, and, after all, we can always look up whatever we need to know on the internet. This sort of rhetoric has certainly had a transformative, if largely negative, effect on education in the last decade or so. I say negative because there's a fundamental confusion about the difference between information and knowledge. Information is inert, passively awaiting somebody to stumble over it and make use of it; knowledge is a product of living tissue. Knowledge is only knowledge if it lives and breathes inside of us. Much more on this later.

The pace of change is now so great that the future is less certain and less predictable than it has ever been before. Our children will be doing jobs which haven't been invented yet, so the claim goes, so teaching them the knowledge of the past will be useless in this unknown, unknowable future.* To be successful, young people will require skills. What skills? Why, 21st century skills, of course.

....

* This claim is dubious. The top ten 'in-demand' jobs in 2017 included truck driver, home health aide, emergency medical therapist, physician assistant, occupational therapist, nurse, business manager and financial advisor. It would appear that a career in health care seems a pretty safe bet for some years to come. See https://www.careercast.com/jobs-rated/in-demand-jobs-2017 and https://www.cnbc.com/2017/03/27/the-9-most-in-demand-jobs-of-2017.html.

The past few years have seen an endless round of experts telling us that in the 21st century children need to be creative, collaborative, problem solvers, critical thinkers and communicators. In response, schools started reinventing themselves as places where children learn these transferable skills, thereby allowing them to navigate the shifting, uncertain world we now inhabit. Maybe the traditional curriculum of school subjects has had its day. Maybe all we have to do is show kids how to use Google and they will magically teach themselves all they need to know. After all, most of what schools taught in the past will be a waste of time in the future, right?

There is nothing more philistine, more impoverished than reducing the curriculum to the little that is visible through the narrow lens of children's current interests and passing fancies. How do *they* know what they might need to know? And, in any case, do we really want to educate the next generation merely in what futurologists and business leaders guess they might need? It's not that there's anything wrong with wanting children to be more creative and better at solving problems, it's that these things don't work the way some people suppose. If we engage in a spot of critical thinking for a moment, we'll see there are at least three problems with this argument.

Firstly, these things have always been important. It was just as important for Socrates to think critically, for Julius Caesar to solve problems, for Shakespeare to communicate, for Leonardo da Vinci to be creative and for the builders of the Great Wall of China to collaborate as it is for young people to do so today. In an important way, we're born with the ability to acquire these skills without instruction. We'll discuss how this works in the next chapter, but there's good reason to believe that we have evolved the capacity to be creative, solve problems and think critically.

This is not to say that every child is equally creative or that we all share the same capacity for successful collaboration; as with every human characteristic there will be a normal distribution of ability. But it does mean that *everyone* has a natural ability to solve problems. Were this otherwise, some people would never work out how to get out of bed and put their pants on! Of course, we can encourage children to be *more* creative, critical and collaborative, but the question is, can children be taught these things? While it's an obvious waste of time to teach children things they have already mastered, we could argue that because there's a difference in natural ability, some children will benefit from additional practice in creativity or critical thinking. This sounds like a reasonable argument. After all, we all get better at things we practise, don't we? This leads us to the second problem.

How, exactly, would we go about teaching someone to communicate or to solve problems in more sophisticated ways? The mistake that's often made is to neglect thinking about the *what*. *What* is it we want children to communicate? *What* sorts of things do we want them to create? *What* do we want them to collaborate on? The problem with attempting to teach a generic skill like critical thinking is that you must have something to think critically *about*. If you know nothing about molecular biology, no amount of training in critical thinking is going to help you come up with much on the subject that is very profound. Likewise, to be truly creative we need to know a lot about the form or discipline we're trying to be creative in. Such skills, divorced from a body of knowledge, are bland to the point of meaninglessness. We are innately disposed to be creative, we solve problems as a matter of course and collaboration comes to us naturally. What makes people appear to struggle with these attributes is that they cannot use them to manipulate abstract concepts and culturally specific knowledge. Anyone can collaborate on a playground game, but to collaborate on finding a cure for cancer you would need a lot of highly specialised expertise. The only thing that makes these skills especially desirable in the 21st century is the background knowledge on which they depend.

If anything, those children who are most lacking in the skills seen as essential for the future have the most to lose from having their time wasted receiving lessons in things that can't be taught. The product of knowledge is ever more knowledge. Because of the accumulation of human cultural understanding, an ever-expanding number of people are freed from things like food production and are able to specialise in different disciplines, allowing us to make discoveries and produce new information at an exponential rate. Apparently, when Newton formulated the laws of force and invented calculus he knew everything that was then known about science. This is no longer possible; as our collective knowledge grows our individual ignorance expands with it. We're long past the point where any individual could ever hope to learn anything but the tiniest fraction of what is known, but that doesn't imply that children don't need to acquire *any* facts.

While it might be the case, then, that the amount of new information is doubling every year, is it really true that half of what students studying a four-year technical degree learn in their first year will be outdated by the third year?[13] Possibly those studying highly specialised areas of computer science will find the programming languages they learn are quickly superseded, but that doesn't make the practice and discipline of learning them in the first place totally useless. And in most other fields of human endeavour – medicine, engineering, law, teaching – new discoveries and practices build upon a settled body of knowledge and change is iterative. No doubt it's true that the complexity of the modern world means that we benefit from being able to think in new and creative ways – what Leonard Mlodinow calls "elastic thinking"[14] – but all this means is that a firm foundation in the thinking of the past is even more essential today than ever before. The historian Daniel Boorstin said, "Education is learning what you didn't even know you didn't know."[15] No one knows which disciplines a child might want to specialise in, so all children need a broad and rich curriculum within which to find the areas to which they might – one day – contribute. Depriving children of this foundation is in no one's interest and will do nothing to prepare young people for an uncertain future.

The underlying assumption of the socialisation argument is that education promotes economic growth. If that's true, then clearly it is a very good reason for sending children to school, but is it? Well, it's certainly true that better educated countries are more prosperous, but this might be to mistake cause for effect. It could be truer to say that more prosperous countries have better educated citizens. Maybe education is an effect of prosperity rather than a cause. This is the view that Alison Wolf comes to in *Does Education Matter?* Case by case, and in exhaustive detail, she shows that countries which have spent more on education have grown more slowly than those which have spent less. The idea that education causes economic growth is, in Wolf's view, "a chimera".[16]

None of this implies that education is not a social good. Clearly, education benefits individuals and education is unlikely to happen without schools. Contrary to my experience, most children are no keener on libraries than schools. But beyond the need to make sure that children become numerate and literate, the purpose of education cannot be economic.

The soul of a society

In *The Closing of the American Mind*, the philosopher Allan Bloom says, "We are like ignorant shepherds living on a site where great civilizations once flourished. The shepherds play with the fragments that pop up to the surface, having no notion of the beautiful structures of which they were once a part."[17] If that's true of us, might it not be even more true of our children? They're more than capable of downloading apps, subscribing to Netflix and popping ready meals in the microwave, but do they have a sense of where all these things came from, and does it matter?

Well, it matters to some. Michael Gove, then the UK education secretary, in a letter on the design of the new national curriculum, paraphrased Matthew Arnold's totemic phrase that children deserve access to "the best which has been thought and said in the world".[18] Gove urged that in order "to set ambitious goals for our progress as a nation we need clear expectations for each subject. I expect those aims to embody our sense of ambition [and] to democratize knowledge by ensuring that as many children as possible can lay claim to a rich intellectual inheritance."[19] Although it may have come as a shock to many in education, this is not a new idea.

In *Culture and Anarchy*, Arnold, the eldest son of the celebrated headmaster of Rugby School Thomas Arnold, argued for the civilising effect of great literature. He was scathing of the idea that culture is little more than a badge signifying membership of an elite. In his view, true culture is "the study of perfection".[20] Arnold believed that a full apprehension of the virtues of culture is attained by induction into the best that human culture has to offer by the free play of the mind over these facts and by a sympathetic attitude towards all that is beautiful.

Arnold posed questions that continue to bedevil us. In a mass society, what kind of life should individuals be encouraged to lead? How can such societies best ensure that our quality of life is not impoverished? Is it possible to preserve an elevated and exclusive freedom of thought in an age of democratic fervour? This isn't all that far from the clergyman and social reformer Henry Ward Beecher's proposition: "That is true culture which helps us to work for the social betterment of all." Certainly, that's the basket in which I'd like to place my eggs.

Martin Luther King, Jr is often quoted as saying, "Intelligence plus character – that is the goal of true education." While this is usually co-opted to support the arguments of those who think education should primarily be focused on developing children's character, it may have more to say in support of cultural transmission. In his 1947 essay on the purpose of education, King goes on to suggest:

> The complete education gives one not only power of concentration, but worthy objectives upon which to concentrate. The broad education will, therefore, transmit to one not only the accumulated knowledge of the race but also the accumulated experience of social living.[21]

Even if developing the content of our character is the aim, culture is the vehicle. This view of education sees knowledge of the past as a liberation and that genuine intellectual development depends on the creation of a strong and deep foundation of knowledge. To have a firm footing in an uncertain future, children require solid foundations – and how long a thing has lasted is a good indication of its dependability.

This is the Lindy effect, named after a delicatessen in New York where actors and comedians used to get together for post-show gossip, which led to the observation that the longer a show had lasted, the longer it was likely to continue to last. This, it turns out, can be applied to some but not all domains. Nassim Nicholas Taleb reckons that if a book has been in print for 40 years, we can expect it to still be in print in 40 years' time.

> This, simply, as a rule, tells you why things that have been around for a long time are not 'aging' like persons, but 'aging' in reverse. Every year that passes without extinction doubles the additional life expectancy. This is an indicator of some robustness. The robustness of an item is proportional to its life![22]

This may, on first glance, look like a post hoc fallacy (seeking to explain events after the fact) but it actually allows us to make interesting and accurate predictions. Obviously, many things – like people – are the victims of senescence. The rule only applies to the realm of ideas, not to the realm of things. The survival of an object tells you nothing about its likely continued survival. Things break, technological inventions are superseded. But if an idea spreads and takes on a life beyond its original context, it has the capacity to last for generations. Some ideas die early, but we can bet that those ideas that have persisted for hundreds or thousands of years will still be around long after we're gone. And the longer ideas and traditions have existed, the more they will have been enhanced and refined by exposure to time.

Of course, this is not to suggest that children merely need to uncritically imbibe the thoughts and works of 'dead white men'. In *A History of the World*, Andrew Marr suggests there needs to be a balance between new ideas and what he calls "the wisdom of the tribe":

> What is the right balance between state authority and individual liberty? No successful state is a steady state. All successful states experience a relentless tug-of-war between conservatism, the wisdom of the tribe, and radicalism, or new thinking. The wisdom of the tribe really matters: it is the accumulated lessons of history, the mistakes as well as the answers, that a polity has gathered up so far. But if this wisdom is not challenged, it ossifies. The political revolutions of the British and then the Americans encouraged individuals to alter the balance of powers, without destroying their states. In France, where a conservative monarchy collapsed, revolutionaries tried to wipe out the past entirely and create a new present based only on radical questioning, or 'reason'; it was a bold but bloody failure, copied again and again.[23]

The tug-of-war between tradition and radicalism is as alive, and as necessary, in education as it is in politics.

The wisdom of the tribe tells us that throughout history experienced adults have passed on their accumulated knowledge to their inexperienced children. At one time this knowledge represented the skills needed to survive in a hunter-gatherer society and would have been a necessarily informal process. As we settled down into agrarian communities, excess food supply allowed various members of the tribe to specialise in particular trades or crafts. Trade secrets were passed down from master to apprentice to ensure that essential knowledge was preserved, but also as a way of guarding interests and making sure that individuals were needed by the community at large.

With the inventions of writing and, many long years later, printing, mass literacy began to be seen as desirable, and educating the young in the knowledge needed to participate in an increasingly advanced economy meant that education needed to be formalised. Economic necessity dictated that schools be built where many students could be instructed by a small number of teachers. Schools began to take on the forms and structures we still recognise today: classrooms, boards on which the teacher writes, desks, chairs, pens and paper. Technology has made refinements and improvements but schools remain essentially the same. Why?

The wisdom of the tribe tells us that schools have remained the same because, by and large, they work. New thinking might suggest the reasons are more hidebound and display a fear of change. The early 2000s saw something of a French Revolution in English schools. Old, established practices were guillotined and there was a mass bonfire of textbooks and the trappings of tradition. Walls were, quite literally, torn down and shiny new schools built without libraries, staffrooms or much that a visitor from the past might recognise. Teachers were told that teaching was of the past and that digital technology had made knowledge obsolete. Punishment was barbarous and discipline doctrinaire. Christine Gilbert and her educational inquisition tried, quite deliberately, to wipe out the past.[*]

Like most teachers, I assumed this was done for sound reasons, because the old ways had been proved ineffective, and did my best to adapt. I facilitated group discussions, I planned engaging lessons in an attempt to control my students' increasingly unruly behaviour and I taught a curriculum that was relevant, authentic and exciting.

Then, with the growing imposition of iron-fisted accountability, I was forced to analyse data and saw, to my horror, that students' results had plummeted. Along with legions of other teachers, I desperately intervened with 16-year-olds who were struggling to read or write to ensure they could pass their exams. We 'improved' coursework, taught to the test and heaved a relieved sigh when the results began to bob up. Then came grade inflation, dumbing down and 'the blob'.[**] I surveyed the scorched

---

[*] Christine Gilbert was the head of Ofsted – also known as Her Majesty's Chief Inspector of Education, Children's Services and Skills – between October 2006 and June 2011.

[**] *The Blob* was a 1958 sci-fi film in which Steve McQueen had to defeat an ever-expanding, amorphous and ravening, er, blob. Michael Gove, education secretary between 2010 and 2014, referred to those who opposed his brand of counter-reformation – teaching unions, consultants, university education departments – as possessing similar qualities to McQueen's nemesis.

landscape and saw these well-intentioned innovations had been a "bold but bloody failure, copied again and again".[24]

Radicalism had become traditional and it wasn't working. Piece by broken piece, schools started to put together a new way of thinking from the fractured shards of the past. It became obvious that teachers should be allowed to talk, that 'independent learning' results only in dependence, that high standards can and should be demanded of children's behaviour, and that if the curriculum isn't good enough for our own children, it isn't good enough for anyone else's. Obviously, no one wants to go back to Victorian classrooms, corporal punishment and the other inequities of the past, but there's good sense in accepting that what has stood the test of time is likely to be more worthwhile than what is new and tawdry. In the words of G. K. Chesterton, "Education is simply the soul of a society as it passes from one generation to another."

....

You might believe that education should be about cultural transmission, making children nicer or better preparing them for the world of work. Or you might think it's a mix of all three. Each of these approaches fractures into myriad splinters and sub-groups. It's possible to hold aspects of each of these beliefs while simultaneously denigrating others. We can, for instance, claim that it is more important to enrich certain aspects of a child than others; that wisdom is more important than intelligence. We can earnestly applaud efforts to make children easier to govern while raising an outcry against the pragmatic ideal of fitting children to jobs.

Although this maelstrom of conflicting ideas and ideologies swirls beneath the level of consciousness in the minds of most, it nevertheless shapes how we think about what we do and why we do it. What we choose to teach, how we choose to teach it, how we organise our classrooms and how we treat children are all shaped by attitudes and opinions we might not consciously share or explicitly approve of, but have, nevertheless, been absorbed osmotically through the policies and practices that more obviously govern teachers' professional lives.

But, whatever you believe, all endeavours are strengthened when imbued with a sense of purpose. In the chapters to follow, I will build the case that if we focus education on making kids cleverer, all else is likely to follow.

Chapter 1: key points

- Although there's little agreement about what education is for, making children cleverer might be the best way of achieving many diverse aims.

- If the purpose of education is to make children cleverer, schools don't always do a good job.

- The aims of character education – instilling positive qualities in children – might best be achieved by teaching an academic curriculum and holding students to our high expectations.

- '21st century skills' can only be applied to 21st century problems if children have a broad base of academic knowledge.

- The aims of cultural transmission build the broad knowledge base that children require to navigate an uncertain future.

- The longer an idea has been around, the more likely it is to be useful and true.

Before we go on to address in detail the whys and wherefores of making children cleverer, we have a few questions to answer about how our brains have developed in the way they have. This is the subject we turn to in Chapter 2.

Chapter 2
Built by culture

Evolution is cleverer than you are.

Francis Crick

- Do we learn best by copying or by trying out new things?

- Why is it that we find some things so easy to learn while others require years of patient study to master?

- Why do so many people – especially teenagers – prefer fiddling with objects, chatting with friends and flirting with each other rather than focusing on the academic study of school subjects?

- If children can learn to walk and talk without being taught to do so, why do we need to bother with schools?

Why our brains are the way they are

All these questions – and many others – can be answered with a basic understanding of evolutionary theory. In order to comprehend ourselves we need to know that we have been forged in the crucible of natural selection. In our distant past, we naked apes had few advantages beyond our big brains and opposable thumbs. In order to survive we needed to band together with other members of our species and share any useful survival tricks we came up with. These good tricks were collected, refined and passed down the generations, forming the basis of human culture.

It's tempting to view culture – "the extensive accumulation of shared learned knowledge and its iterative improvements over time"[1] – as that which sets human beings apart from all other species. While a few other species make very limited use of tools, we have invented smartphones, 3D printers and the Large Hadron Collider. But our capacity for culture must also have evolutionary roots. And it does. The evolution of culture took place side by side with the evolution of our genes. In fact, who we are and how our brains work is the result of 2.5 million years of gene–culture coevolution. The evolution of genes is painfully slow, yet culture can evolve incredibly rapidly and have the effect of galvanising the selection process *on* genes, resulting in far faster biological innovation. (One of the most well-known examples is the evolutionary relationship between the genetics of lactose tolerance in humans and the cultural habit of dairy farming.[2]) This time period saw a quadrupling in the size of the human brain,[3] unprecedented changes in human gene expression,[4] and archaeological finds detail bewilderingly rapid progress in the complexity and diversity of our technology and knowledge base.[5] Our reliance on each other and the tools we have designed to assist us in our efforts to stay alive have shaped our brains. In the words of evolutionary biologist Kevin Laland, "Human minds are not just built for culture; they are built by culture."[6] But what we've ended up with is just good enough to survive and reproduce; in essential ways, our brains are the same as those of our Palaeolithic ancestors.

When we think about how and what to teach, we should consider the role of evolution in shaping the way humans have adapted to think and learn. In our distant past, learning was a costly strategy – time spent learning was time we couldn't spend surviving and reproducing – so it makes sense that we have evolved to learn as efficiently as possible. Evolutionary biologists think of learning as being either social or asocial. Social learning is essentially copying (what's everyone else doing?), whereas asocial learning is accrued by interacting with the environment through trial and error. Everything we know is either learned socially or asocially, through mimicry or experimentation, emulation or innovation.

Both types of learning have associated advantages and disadvantages. The advantage of asocial learning is that you get accurate, up-to-date, first-hand information about what works and what doesn't, but the cost is high. You might waste a lot of time on strategies that are minimally effective or, worse, you might try something that turns out to be fatal, like eating a funny looking mushroom or being bitten by an interesting looking beetle.

The advantage of social learning is that it's easier, safer and more likely to result in productive survival strategies. Human beings, like many other species, operate in groups, and so copying the behaviour that others – especially those in your kinship group – have adopted seems a sensible strategy. After all, if everyone around you is getting on well, why would you risk trying something different? Copying something that doesn't work means you are less likely to survive and reproduce than those who copy things that do, and so being good at copying is selected for. The downside to relying on other people's experiences of what's most likely to be effective means that we might not understand why we do what we do. When environmental conditions change rapidly or a new predator is introduced, old strategies may prove ineffective and those who can adapt the quickest are those who will survive.

It used to be believed that the number of social to asocial learners in a group would be fairly evenly balanced – that environmental change would favour asocial learning, whereas stability would favour social learning – but it turns out that social learning forms the basis for the remarkable growth and success of human culture.[7] This might seem counter-intuitive: surely, new innovations gleaned from asocial tinkering must be the most important driving force in human ingenuity? The thing is, although we need a minimal amount of asocial learning, most people get on most of the time purely using socially learned strategies, and that's because we copy strategically. Only the most successful ideas get passed on and spread throughout the group. Each new generation hones in on optimal solutions, so as long as there's a little bit of experimentation going on – either through asocial learning or through copying errors – culture accumulates and is continually refined. This is the Lindy effect in action (or what Richard Dawkins calls mimetic reproduction[8]).

In the modern world, we support a very small number of people – scientists, artists and the like – that they may spend a fraction of their time on asocial learning. The rest of us spend our lives directly copying those around us or accessing the vast accumulation of human culture through word of mouth, books and the internet. Pretty much every moment of every day is spent engaged in tasks which are directly or indirectly copied. As the Bible tells us, "The thing that hath been, it is that which shall be; and that which is done is that which shall be done: and there is no new thing under the sun."[9] If we choose to engage in a brief bout of asocial learning, we do it for fun and because we're safe enough not to worry about it going too far wrong.

Obviously, when the zombie apocalypse comes, asocial learners will be in much demand; those who work out how to survive in the new paradigm fastest will have an enormous advantage over the rest of us. But then, if humanity is to survive, it will be because we copy the new 'good tricks' they come up with and begin the fightback against the undead.

So, what does all of this have to do with education? Simply this: while we might all enjoy a small amount of asocial experimentation, almost everything we learn – and almost certainly everything useful – will be due to our ability to observe and emulate. A school curriculum that favours a trial and error approach to reacquiring what has previously been discovered as the result of several millennia of iterative copying is fighting against biology. We're just not fitted to learn that way. Even Jerome Bruner, a champion of the discovery learning cause, could see that existing knowledge and culture were not generally passed on by discovery. He wrote:

> You cannot consider education without taking into account how culture gets passed on. It seems to me highly unlikely that given the centrality of culture in man's adaptation to his environment – the fact that culture serves him in the same way as changes in morphology served earlier in the evolutionary scale – that, biologically speaking, one would expect each organism to rediscover the totality of its culture – this would seem most unlikely.[10]

By far the most effective way to pass on the fruits of human culture is to share what has already been discovered and invented as clearly and as explicitly as we can.

This gets to the heart of what we believe schools are for. Should they be safe spaces in which we allow children to tinker about at the margins of human culture, maybe discovering something useful for themselves? Or are they, as education professor Michael Young has said, places that "enable young people to acquire the knowledge that, for most of them, cannot be acquired at home or in the community"?[11] The first choice is a Darwinian jungle in which those fortunate enough to have wealthy, educated parents will thrive and the devil take the hindmost. If you believe in social justice and giving children a fair chance to escape the constraints of this lottery, using schools to promote effective social learning is the only option.

Some things are easy but others are hard

Our ancestors needed to find food, avoid danger, mate and ensure their children survived to adulthood. The need to find food selected for minds which could attend to and remember the characteristics and behaviour of plants and animals, the resourcefulness to provide shelter and defend against predators, and the ingenuity to consider how inanimate objects might be used as tools. The ability to compete and cooperate in groups, whether for food gathering or mating opportunities, selected for minds which were able to anticipate the motives and emotions of others, and better communicate needs and ideas. These are the folk disciplines: folk psychology, folk physics and folk biology.

Folk psychology is an interest in people and an awareness of ourselves; folk physics is an interest in movement, tools and time; and folk biology is an interest in plants and animals (see Figure 2.1).

Over the millennia, our minds have adapted to acquiring this folk knowledge quickly and easily. Instinct and learning are often seen as opposites: instinct is genetically determined whereas learning is the product of experience. But it might be better to say that we have an instinct for learning, and learning some things might be more instinctive than learning others. As far back as 1896, James Mark Baldwin struggled with the conundrum of why some things are preprogrammed while others have to be learned. Instincts are hugely time-saving; anything we have to learn for ourselves makes it more difficult for us to survive and reproduce. Baldwin saw that there was a clear limit to the returns of innate abilities and that being able to acquire new knowledge provided more flexible advantages. He concluded that the reason why humans developed intelligence was to enable children "to learn things which natural heredity fails to transmit".[12]

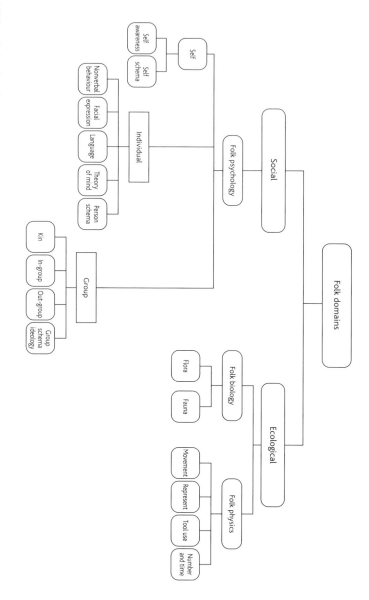

Figure 2.1. Folk knowledge domains

Source: David C. Geary and Daniel B. Berch, Evolution and Children's Cognitive and Academic Development. In David C. Geary and Daniel B. Berch (eds), Evolutionary Perspectives on Child Development and Education (Basel: Springer International Publishing, 2016), pp. 217–250 at p. 220.

In 'Educating the Evolved Mind', evolutionary psychologist David Geary calls these domains of folk knowledge "biologically primary adaptations".[13] Such adaptations are universal traits shared by people from all cultures since at least the Upper Palaeolithic period about 40,000 years ago. What is universal is clearly the result of evolutionary adaption; if it wasn't, it wouldn't be universal. These emergent modules of folk knowledge are so important that they have come to be essentially human characteristics. Every culture possesses language and has easily acquired systems for learning about the natural and social world. These are species-constant, universal inheritances that we can trace back to the first appearance of Homo sapiens. In Baldwin's terms, we have an evolved instinct for readily acquiring this kind of knowledge.

Geary refers to other branches of knowledge as "biologically secondary". Where human cultures diverge, so does culturally specific, biologically secondary knowledge. Laland points out that "Humanity's success is sometimes attributed to our cleverness, but culture is actually what makes us smart. Intelligence is not irrelevant of course, but what singles out our species is an ability to pool our insights and knowledge and build on each other's solutions."[14] As well as 'hard wiring' our brains to rapidly and effortlessly learn the folk disciplines, nature has also made use of the brain's natural plasticity to enable us to learn any cultural innovations which may prove useful to us. This ability to learn is the ultimate 'good trick'. The trouble is, although we can 'rewire' our brains to learn all sorts of new and useful culturally generated knowledge, it doesn't come nearly as easily as learning what is biologically primary. We tend not to pick up biologically secondary knowledge from the environment, instead requiring some sort of apprenticeship or instruction.

This is in part because we have a motivational bias towards learning such things as peer interaction, play hunting of other species and exploration of the physical environment within the biologically primary domains. So adaptive were these kinds of knowledge that over time we evolved the ability to create symbolic representations of experiences and techniques, like storytelling, to communicate our experiences. The human brain – shaped by evolutionary pressures – is adapted to run off rules of thumb or heuristics such as: 'Avoid weird-looking food', 'Don't mess about with potential predators', 'If someone shares with you, share with them in return', 'Smile at strangers to avoid conflict,' * and so on. We acquire this knowledge rapidly through social learning – Joe ate those red spotted mushrooms and now he's dead – and generalise it as widely as possible. Most of the time the heuristics we pick up can be very useful.

The problem is, we increasingly find ourselves in environments that require more abstract thinking and where knowledge from folk domains doesn't necessarily generalise well to the situations we encounter. For instance, all of our experience tells us that for an object to move with a constant speed we must apply a force to it, otherwise it will slow down. Newton's second law directly contradicts this – but this is so at odds with what we learn about the world through direct observation that we find it extraordinarily challenging. The probability that children would rediscover this through asocial experimentation is staggeringly small. Indeed, it took thousands of years and an awful lot of giant shoulders for Newton to discover it!

We're going to think about knowledge in a lot more detail later in the book, but for now consider how Geary's big idea might be one of the most useful and important ways of demarcating different categories of knowledge. In this view, everything we store in our brains is either the product of evolved instinctive responses to environmental stimuli or the result of learning, probably through copying. What we learn is then divided into those things we learn easily and rapidly without the need for instruction, and the hard-won discoveries that make up our culturally acquired information about the world and how to get on in it.

Seeing knowledge as either biologically primary or secondary provides us with a useful framework for deciding what should be covered in a school curriculum. I've already provided several reasons to be sceptical of the 21st century skills agenda, but Geary's theory allows us to add one more: these skills have always been vital for the survival of the species, so much so that we have evolved an enhanced capacity for developing them. They are biologically primary modules. Every child naturally learns to collaborate, solve problems and be creative without the need for explicit instruction. As the philosopher of science Karl Popper said, "All life is

---

*   For instance, it's been speculated that the reason babies are disproportionately likely to smile at strange men is to counter the threat of infanticide. In our more primitive past, unrelated males were one of the biggest threats to babies' survival, so it makes excellent evolutionary sense to make yourself as cute as possible.

problem solving."[15] Environmental pressures have shaped our minds to respond to scarcity and threat with solutions. If a food source has dried up, where else should we look? If a new predator arrives, how should we escape? This problem-solving instinct often operates below the level of conscious thought, but sometimes we have to get creative: if in the past you've escaped predators by climbing trees, but this one can climb better than you can, what then? This forced us to make tools – at first fire hardened spears, then stone axes, later machine guns – and collaborate. We banded together and fought off threats we couldn't defeat alone. '21st century skills' would be better thought of as 'Stone Age skills'.[16]

With this in mind, we should think very carefully about whether what we are seeking to teach is biologically primary or secondary. If it's culturally acquired it needs to be taught; if it's a primary adaption, then demonstration and coaching is all we need. A major problem with teaching 'domain-general skills' is that while they are obviously learnable, they may not be teachable. Time spent teaching children abilities they have already acquired through emulation is time wasted; time that could be better spent either teaching them things they don't already know or how to apply primary adaptions within secondary domains.[17] But using curriculum time to teach biologically primary knowledge is more pernicious than that. Some children may be born with a greater capacity for solving problems and thinking critically than others. These children are lucky. At the same time, some children will possess more (and more useful) knowledge of the world on which to apply these skills. These children will tend to be from more privileged backgrounds. What happens in school matters far less to both these groups of children than it does to the less fortunate and the less advantaged. The killer argument against a curriculum that focuses on 21st century skills – or any other kind of generic competencies – is that it is inherently iniquitous.

That said, we may need to make sure that children's environments are conducive to acquiring the folk knowledge we all take for granted. Just because we have an evolved predisposition to attend to and rapidly learn this stuff, it doesn't follow that we will automatically do so. If you spend your formative years locked in a darkened room or raised by wolves, you definitely won't. Luckily, we're highly motivated to learn these things and, just so long as we encounter them in our environment, we almost certainly will. This might provide an argument in favour of coaching and modelling approaches in the early years of education to ensure all children are immersed in the kind of environment in which they pick up speech, group cooperation and a sense of self. But if we're tempted to teach these kinds of things explicitly later on, then we will be wasting our time.

Where we can perhaps salvage the notion of domain-general competencies is in using them to assess the application of knowledge within different subjects. If we agree that it's useful to solve problems within mathematics, to be creative in science, to think critically in history and to collaborate in languages, then we can both teach children how to use their subject knowledge in these ways and use these competencies as a means to assess how well this is done. Dylan Wiliam suggests that 21st century skills are "best thought of as a way of ensuring that our standards are sufficiently broad".[18]

Evolutionary psychology not only provides convincing arguments against a curriculum based around developing general competencies, it also tells us something important about why schools exist.

The evolution of schools

Education is a technology that tries to make up for what the human mind is innately bad at.

Steven Pinker, *The Blank Slate*

Although schools are an important technological invention, it's not clear whether anyone ever sat down and dreamed up the idea of a school. It's more likely that schools, along with many other aspects of human culture, emerged as the most effective way to pass on biologically secondary knowledge. Children don't need to go to school to learn how to walk, talk, recognise objects or remember the personalities of their friends, even though these things are much harder than reading, adding or remembering dates in history. This is Moravec's paradox: contrary to the initial expectations of artificial intelligence researchers, robots and computers are excellent at learning how to do many of the things we're bad at, but – thus far – have struggled to learn those things we find easy.*

Geary tells us that "In contrast to universal folk knowledge, most of the knowledge taught in modern schools is culturally specific; that is, it does not emerge in the absence of formal instruction."[19] Schools emerged to teach those things children won't learn elsewhere. We send children to school to learn written language, arithmetic and science because these bodies of knowledge were invented far too recently for any species-wide knack for acquiring them to have evolved, even if such a mechanism *could* arise through natural selection.

Think about the example of language. In *The Language Instinct*, Steven Pinker argues that we have an instinct for learning our mother tongue.[20] Children's ability to intuit previously unheard structures and formulations from minimal grammatical knowledge is remarkable. For instance, when learning English, most children infer that the past tense of the verb to go is 'goed'. But how? No adult ever says this; children independently work out the rule that you add 'ed' to the end of the verb to indicate that it happened in the past. It's only later that children learn that 'to go' is an irregular verb and 'went' is the correct formulation. This is just one of many thousands of examples which makes it clear that we have an instinct for learning language but that specific vocabulary must be acquired the hard way. Compare this to the way we learn to read and write. While human beings have been using spoken language for tens of thousands of years, writing is a relatively recent invention. It's only been in the past few hundred years that it's been considered important for the majority of people to learn to read and write. As such, it should be clear that we can have no evolved instinct for written language in the way that we do for spoken language.

Schools – institutions for giving formal instruction – have only existed in literate cultures where biologically secondary knowledge has outstripped universal folk knowledge. If we look at ancient Sumer – where cuneiform, the earliest known writing system developed – we also find the first archaeological evidence of schools, which were set up to induct

---

* Machines are only now beginning to mimic these basic human abilities. For example, robots can now run and jump, as well as assemble IKEA furniture – after a fashion. See *The Guardian*, 2018a and 2018b.

budding clerks into the mystery of scribing. These *edubas* (scribe schools) were probably fairly informal, usually taking place in private homes, but some sites, where particularly large numbers of school tablets have been unearthed, are considered by archaeologists to be 'school houses'. We know a surprising amount about how *edubas* operated as various cuneiform tablets contain stories attesting to what life was like as a scribal student.

Sumerian students began their education as young children, and although most students were boys, there is also evidence of some female scribes. The *eduba* literature paints a vivid picture of daily life for these young students. Lessons included reciting texts learned previously and forming new tablets to inscribe. Punishments for misbehaviour – talking out of turn, leaving without permission, writing poorly and so on – could be harsh. In one account, a student describes being beaten no less than seven times in a single day:

> The door monitor said, 'Why did you go out without my say-so?' He beat me.
>
> The jug monitor said, 'Why did you take beer without my say-so?' He beat me.
>
> The Sumerian monitor said, 'You spoke in Akkadian!'* He beat me.
>
> My teacher said, 'Your handwriting is not at all good!' He beat me.[21]

And so on. Then, after a day at school, the students would return home to their parents, where they might have to recite homework assignments.[22] Charmingly, there is even evidence of Sumerian teachers complaining about their students and students about their teachers.[23]

It was ever thus. In the 11th century, Egbert of Liège noted that "Scholarly effort is in decline everywhere as never before. Indeed, cleverness is shunned at home and abroad. What does reading offer to pupils except tears? It is rare, worthless when it is offered for sale, and devoid of wit."[24] A 14th century student at the University of Bologna moaned that other students "attend classes but make no effort to learn anything ... The expense money which they have from their parents or churches they spend in taverns, conviviality, games and other superfluities, and so they return home empty, without knowledge, conscience, or money."[25] And, in

---

*   Akkadian was the language people spoke on a daily basis. Sumerian was probably regarded similarly to the way medieval monks would have thought of Latin.

a letter from a 10th century Byzantine scholar to the father of some of his students:

> I hesitated whether to write to you or not but decided that I ought. Children naturally prefer play to study: fathers naturally train them to follow good courses, using persuasion or force. Your children, like their companions, neglected their work and were in need of correction. I resolved to punish them, and to inform their father. They returned to work and studied for some time. But they are now occupied with birds once again, and neglecting their studies. Their father, passing through the city, commented acidly on their conduct. Instead of coming to me, or to their uncles, they have run away to you or to Olympus. If they are with you, treat them mercifully as suppliants. Even if they have gone elsewhere, help them return to the fold. You will have my gratitude.[26]

Why is it that education appears always to have had this effect on young people? Some commentators suppose the fault to be with the way schools operate and express despair that they have not moved with the times. It is, as psychologist Douglas Detterman says, "a sad commentary on education" that the only educational innovations of note have been printed books and the blackboard:

> If Plato or Aristotle walked into any classroom in any school, college, or university they would know exactly what was going on and could probably take over teaching the class (assuming they had a translator). They would certainly be amazed by the extent of what has been learned since their deaths but not at how it is taught.[27]

Should we be amazed that the way children are taught today hasn't changed much in the last few thousand years? Is it really a "sad commentary on education" that new technologies haven't transformed schools in the way that books and blackboards have? What if the way the *edubas* went about teaching ancient Sumerian was, broadly speaking, the best way to go about things?*

Great efforts have been made in the last century or so to 'revolutionise' schools. This has gathered pace in recent years because 'technology has changed everything'. As we saw in the previous chapter, this isn't really true, and yet everything we take for granted as being synonymous with schools is under threat. Various reformers have done away with (or would like to do away with) classrooms, desks, books and even teachers

----

*   Obviously, without the beatings!

talking to students. Understandably, these efforts have met with some resistance. Why, reformers wonder, are some teachers so resistant to change? This is entirely the wrong question. Teachers, like everyone else, tend to love change. What they (and everyone else) tend to hate is loss. Consider a scenario in which a school informs its staff that they are all required to work one day less a week for the same pay. Will anyone resist the change? Teachers complain about ill-conceived ideas about how to run schools and classrooms that add considerably to their workloads. This seems entirely rational.

Where schools are not imposed, they emerge. In the poorest slums and most remote villages of India, Nigeria, Ghana, Kenya and China, low cost private schools have sprouted up spontaneously. James Tooley first recorded this phenomenon in the Indian city of Hyderabad, which contains over 500 private schools catering to the children of day labourers and rickshaw pullers. These schools even offer free tuition to the children of the poorest and most illiterate members of the communities they serve.[28] People everywhere seem to recognise that where these sorts of institutions don't exist, or where they are so corrupt they may as well not, adults can gather children in rooms and teach them culturally accumulated wisdom. Obviously, these schools are unlikely to conform to our expectations of what schools in developed nations should look like, but the way in which they operate is essentially the same as the Sumerian *edubas*. Schools – spaces where children are taught biologically secondary knowledge by adults – have evolved as the simplest, most effective way to handle the business of education.

For what it's worth, I suspect Messrs Plato and Aristotle would be quite startled by modern schools. The fact that what we do today is recognisably similar to what we did in yesteryear is a testament both to the fact that our brains haven't changed in the intervening time, and that teaching is far simpler than some would like us to believe. So simple, in fact, that some have argued that the ability to teach may well be another biologically primary adaption.

Is teaching natural?

Psychologists call the ability to infer how other people think and feel 'theory of mind'. Theory of mind enables us to make sense of what others do and predict what they're likely to do next by inferring the mental states which cause that behaviour. If someone smiles at us we infer that they have friendly intentions. If they clear their throat we infer that they want to speak. If they glare murderously at us we run away. The philosopher Daniel Dennett calls this the "intentional stance" – understanding that other people's actions are goal-directed and arise from their beliefs or desires.[29] From his studies of imitation in infants, Andrew Meltzoff has argued that theory of mind is an innate understanding that others are 'like me' – allowing us to recognise the physical and mental states apparent in others by relating them to our own actions, thoughts and feelings.[30]

Sidney Strauss and colleagues have proposed that theory of mind is an important prerequisite for teaching. Although a few other animals (e.g. meerkats) appear to engage in limited teaching activities, as far as we know only humans teach using the ability to anticipate the mental states of the individual being taught. As evidence that teaching is an innate ability, they point to the fact that the ability to teach arises spontaneously at an early age without any apparent instruction and that it is common to all human cultures. Teaching, despite its complexity, evolved alongside our ability to learn.

In one study, preschool children were shown how to play a board game. Strauss and his team then observed the children's behaviour when teaching others and witnessed a range of teaching strategies being deployed, including demonstration (actively showing the learner what to do), specific directions, verbal explanations, questions aimed at checking learners' understanding, explicit reference to the act of teaching ("I will now explain to you how to play") and instances of teachers responding to the utterances and actions of learners.[31]

Teaching ability doesn't appear to improve all that much with maturation; thus, compared to 3-year-olds, 5-year-olds relied more on verbal explanations, were more responsive to the learners' difficulties and asked questions aimed at checking the learners' understanding. Still, this is somewhat alarming as it suggests that much of what teacher training and professional development consists of are competencies possessed by the average 5-year-old! Maybe the only real difference between qualified teachers and most 5-year-olds is our subject knowledge.

In *The Orator's Education*, the Roman writer Quintilian set out pedagogic practices that we would still recognise and approve of today. Not only did he prefer classrooms to private tuition, he also argued that students required persistence, practice and an expert teacher to guide them. While he believed that students possessed natural inclinations to reason and remember, he saw knowledge – particularly the knowledge required to be an orator – as something students must make an effort to learn. He even used guides to help students learn to write by tracing letters.[32] If teaching is a biologically primary skill, it goes a long way to explaining why classroom practices have been so remarkably persistent over the generations: the way we teach is an evolutionary adaption that has developed as being an efficient, effective way to transmit culturally specific knowledge. Why would we want to reinvent this particular wheel?

This is the lure of the new – the idea that the future should be shiny, different and, preferably, sciency. We have developed a tendency to believe that what is old is outdated and needs to be replaced. This wasn't always the case. Previous generations had more of a 'make do and mend' mentality, but today we're used to built-in obsolescence and crave new laptops and phones every year. Gimmicks come and go, fads pass, but the Lindy effect predicts that what has worked for the entirety of human history will, in all probability, still work in the 21st (and 22nd) century.

That said, it takes biologically secondary knowledge to teach biologically secondary knowledge. While the act of teaching may well be an evolutionary adaption, *what* we teach is not (or at least not directly). Rather neatly, it would seem that nature has equipped us to find it easy to teach things to others that they would otherwise find hard to learn. The fact that schools were invented to transmit this hard to learn stuff provides some clear clues about *how* to teach. If biologically secondary knowledge is difficult to master, the aim of teaching should be to make this process as straightforward and clear as possible.

As well as suggesting the degree to which we should be explicit in our instruction, Geary's theory also tells us something important about motivation. As previously noted, we are inherently motivated to learn knowledge that has an obvious evolutionary advantage. Few children have to be persuaded to socialise or to mess about with objects – the tendency is part of being human. Similarly, few children are motivated to put in the effort required to learn algebra without direction. Our brains – so well adapted for learning biologically primary knowledge – have been unceremoniously co-opted for the purposes of learning culturally acquired knowledge. As information diverges from its folk knowledge base, it becomes increasingly harder for us to wrap our heads around it. We easily fall prey to naive misconceptions and get frustrated at the tedious practice needed to master secondary knowledge. This is why schools need rules and well-administered behaviour systems; without these things, children – especially teenagers – are likely to drift off into those activities which come more naturally and induce more pleasure, such as chatting, twanging rulers, looking at cat memes on the internet and trying to get off with each other.

Learning to read or learning mathematics are not natural human activities, in the sense that these technologies have been around for such a short time that evolution through natural selection hasn't had much of a chance to shape our brains to learn them easily. As a result, such things typically require much more effort to master. The purpose of schools, as much as anything else, is to provide an environment where children are made to attend to what they would otherwise prefer to avoid.

....

One of the central planks in assembling the arguments in this book is the importance of acquiring biologically secondary knowledge. This will be explained in more detail in later chapters, but for now, it is important to stress that learning new information requires a secure foundation of prior knowledge. The good news is that, with effort, our brains are more than capable of automatising secondary knowledge to the point where it can become effortless to use. The bad news is that this doesn't just happen.

Chapter 2: key points

- Evolutionary pressures have shaped every aspect of our brains.

- Our genes have co-evolved with the development of culture to accelerate this process.

- We find some things easy to learn because they offer an evolutionary advantage; the capacity to rapidly learn these things is a biologically primary evolutionary adaption.

- Although our brains are remarkably plastic, we do not find it nearly so easy to acquire abstract, culturally specific information.

- We have a motivational bias to prefer the biologically primary over the secondary.

- Schools were invented specifically to teach biologically secondary, culturally specific knowledge that students are not motivated to learn independently.

- Teaching seems to be a good example of a biologically primary adaption, which suggests that maybe we shouldn't try to reinvent how we teach according to new fads and ideas.

Now that we've surveyed the evolutionary basis for learning and why children find some things so much easier to learn than others, we're ready to begin thinking about why making kids cleverer might be both desirable and possible.

Chapter 3
Is intelligence the answer?

I once spoke to a human geneticist who declared that the notion of intelligence was quite meaningless, so I tried calling him *un*intelligent. He was annoyed, and it did not appease him when I went on to ask how he came to attach such a clear meaning to the notion of lack of intelligence. We never spoke again.

Peter Medawar, *Advice to a Young Scientist*

- What is the point of being clever?

- Should we screen children for intelligence in school?

- Are IQ tests biased or meaningless?

- Are there different types of intelligence?

It may be that we'll never fully understand the complexity of the human mind. If our brains were simple enough for us to understand, we'd be too simple to understand them. But we know a lot more now than we used to. Brain research progresses at a rapid pace and everything we currently know is contingent and subject to addition, but that doesn't mean we can ignore the findings of cognitive science or pretend we don't know enough to draw some fairly sound conclusions. Despite the many myths surrounding it, intelligence is a good candidate for being the best researched and best understood characteristic of the human brain. It's also probably the most stable construct in all psychology. By stable what I mean is that an IQ test is likely to result in pretty much the same score if taken on multiple occasions (i.e. it doesn't tend to change much). This is quite unlike many widely used personality constructs like MBTI (Myers–Briggs Type Indicator) or MMPI (Minnesota Multiphasic Personality Indicator) which both produce widely varying results.

The fact that intelligence has been so thoroughly researched means we have a hell of a lot of data to dig through to understand what it is and isn't. We also need to consider a few other topics. Everyone's heard of the intelligence quotient (IQ) – more on that shortly – and may also have heard of a number of other qualities that have acquired the label of intelligence. These include the cuddly sounding emotional intelligence and the doggedly enduring notion of multiple intelligences. We therefore need to investigate whether these distinctions are valid and supported by research, so that we can decide what to focus on if we want to make kids cleverer.

What is intelligence?

Although the word intelligence (from the Latin *intelligere*, meaning to comprehend) has been in use since the medieval era, it's only become part of our regular lexicon relatively recently. This was probably in part because rationality used to be seen as something God-given – something to be thankful for rather than to boast about; but also because education – the sphere in which intelligence most comes into its own – was, for centuries, a rare and solitary pursuit. Very few people received much in the way of formal education, and it was easy to look at differences between the educated elite and the unwashed masses and think of each as belonging to an entirely different species. It was only with the dual development of increasingly affordable printed books and aspirations for universal literacy that it came to matter how intelligent a person might be. At roughly the same point, laws mandating education for all began to be passed across Western Europe, as well as in the United States and Japan. Suddenly, being clever mattered.

Justice Potter Stewart famously described his threshold for identifying what is obscene as "I know it when I see it."[1] Intelligence is similarly obvious but hard to pin down. In 1921, a symposium on intelligence asked 14 of the then leading experts what they thought intelligence was; they provided 14 different definitions including "the power of good responses from the point of view of truth or facts"; "the ability to carry on abstract thinking"; "having learned or ability to learn to adjust oneself to the environment"; "the capacity for knowledge, and knowledge possessed";

and "the capacity to acquire capacity".[2] A few years later, Edwin Boring rather snarkily came up with, "Intelligence is what the tests test."[3] Fast forward to the 1980s, and Robert Sternberg and Douglas Detterman decided to have another go at a symposium, and again failed to produce anything like a consensus.[4] In 2007, Shane Legg and Marcus Hutter finally managed to winnow down competing definitions to arrive at this: "Intelligence measures an agent's ability to achieve goals in a wide range of environments."[5] The journalist David Adam pithily truncated this to "Using what you've got to get what you want."[6]

None of these is entirely satisfactory, and it should be clear that a single, all-encompassing definition is probably impossible. Let's think again about the one offered by Linda Gottfredson on page 7. Her definition included reasoning, planning, abstract thought, comprehension of complex ideas and quickness of learning. While these things are important, it's still not the full story. Most definitions seem to assume that intelligence is a natural, innate capacity for reasoning and learning, but the position I will advance in this book is that intelligence is as much a product of what we know as it is a mechanism for acquiring knowledge.

What does it mean to be clever? Is it being able to generate revolutionary new thinking? Is it seeing links and connections between different concepts and ideas? Or is it simply the quality and quantity of what we know? Rather than attempting a neat but incomplete definition, the political philosopher and intelligence researcher James Flynn suggests that a number of factors make up an individual's intelligence:

- *Mental acuity* – the ability to come up with solutions to problems about which we have no prior knowledge.

- *Speed of information processing* – how quickly we assimilate new data.

- *Habits of mind* – the ways in which we are accustomed to using our minds; if we practise thinking in certain ways we are likely to improve at thinking in those ways.

- *Attitudes* – how the society in which we live tends to view and think about the world. As we'll see in Chapter 5, Flynn argues that seeing the world through 'scientific spectacles' has changed the way we think from being essentially concrete to being much more abstract.

- *Memory* – our ability to retrieve information when it will be useful.

- *Knowledge and information* – the more you know, the more you can think about; no one can think about things they have no knowledge of.[7]

Of these, mental acuity and speed of information processing are probably not amenable to being improved through social or educational interventions. That is to say, what you've got is all you'll ever have. The other factors are all, to a greater or lesser extent, subject to various environmental factors and are therefore more or less malleable. In order to see how best we might go about making children cleverer, let's consider the relative profitability of concentrating on these remaining four aspects.

Habits of mind are inherently subject to practice. If you've never done a cryptic crossword before, you'll probably struggle no matter how good you are at dreaming up novel solutions or how rapidly you accumulate new ideas. As you get used to doing crosswords you learn to spot patterns. You have to learn to think about how the same word can be used as a noun or a verb, or how to recognise and solve an anagram to find an answer. Children can be profitably directed to think in particular ways about the subjects they study. Although possessing mathematical knowledge will be a prerequisite for solving mathematical problems, it's also true that solving these problems will be a great help in learning to recognise the structure of different problems. That said, too much effort at simply developing students' habits of mind without an equal or greater focus on knowledge and information could be costly.

Although social attitudes may sometimes shift fairly rapidly, more commonly change is slow and incremental. We are often unaware of the power of these attitudes to shape our thoughts. Today most people think with 'meta-beliefs', such as those we can trace back to Romanticism or the Enlightenment. Whenever we cite research we are drawing on the meta-belief that evidence is sufficient justification for action. When we uncritically accept the word of academics or authority figures over our own experience, we acquiesce to a meta-belief that those who are best qualified are most qualified to offer an opinion. We see Enlightenment meta-beliefs in action in the pseudoscientific jargon used to advertise shampoo, and some of the worst examples of mumbo-jumbo in education come dressed in neuroscientific jargon. There have been theories suggesting that listening to Mozart can boost intelligence, foot massages can improve children's impulse control, fish oil boosts brain power and, I kid you not, that breathing through your left nostril will enhance creativity.

Romantic meta-beliefs tell us that anything 'natural' is good and anything processed is bad. This suspicion of 'unnatural' intervention leads to such tropes as the 'factory model of education' and convinces us that education should be as natural as possible. Anyone who talks about unleashing or unlocking children's hidden potential is acting on Romantic meta-beliefs.

As a result, it's hard for us now to understand the religious attitudes which permeated our forebears' patterns of thought, and it would be even more difficult to think our way back to the pre-agrarian ways of thinking that our hunter-gatherer ancestors might have possessed. Although the mental attitudes of an individual don't necessarily have to reflect those of the social group in which they live, deviations from the norm are relatively rare and subtle. As such, this aspect of intelligence is probably one which is resistant to the efforts of teachers.

There's no doubt we can improve aspects of our memory – or, more specifically, our ability to retrieve information. In Chapter 10, we'll discuss the promise of techniques like spacing, interleaving and retrieval practice in improving our ability to recall what we know. These sorts of approaches are very well supported by evidence, and so there's every reason to believe that they should be effective in supporting children's ability to recall what they have been taught. But, and this is something that is probably not considered often enough, what is it that children are able to recall? I've taught many students who appear to have a fabulous memory for football statistics or rap lyrics, but few teachers would see this as appreciably improving children's intelligence.

This leads us to the final category of intelligence: knowledge and information. It's the *quantity* and *quality* of what we know that, to a large extent, determines how clever we are. Although it's no doubt true that those children with greater mental acuity and faster information processing are likely to be given opportunities which mean they also learn more (e.g. the quicker you learn things, the more likely you are to be labelled as bright and put into top sets). It's also true that *what* you know is entirely dependent on your environment. If a child is raised in an environment where they are read to and where the adults in their lives include them in discussions about current affairs, then they're infinitely more likely to be able to think about these things than those children who haven't had these advantages.

The quantity and quality of what children know is, I believe, the most important individual difference between them. Those who know more are, on average, cleverer than those who know less. Although we might perceive some children to be more 'able' than others, this is unimportant because there's not really anything we can do about it. We can, however, do an awful lot about developing the quantity and quality of what children know. This perspective, which puts knowledge at the heart of what it means to be clever, offers both hope and a clear way forward. We can, deliberately and systematically, introduce them to the concepts and information that are most prized by society and, with care and patience, we can ensure that they know them with real fluency.

So, why is raising intelligence such a big deal? As everyone knows, intelligence is measured by IQ tests, and these tests provide surprising evidence of the importance of being clever. An IQ test is not a single test but a whole battery of tests designed to assess a range of different mental capabilities and provides a fairly accurate proxy for what we think of as intelligence. The capabilities tested include reasoning ability, memory, knowledge (including vocabulary and general knowledge), spatial ability and processing speed. Intuitively, we tend to believe that being good at one of these things is evened out by being bad at others. You might have a great memory but struggle to add up columns of numbers, you might possess an extensive vocabulary but struggle to see patterns, or you could score well on tests of processing while being a bit rubbish at, say, rotating 3D objects. However, it turns out that people who do well at one aspect of an intelligence test tend to do well at all aspects. In other words, intelligence seems to be general.

Added to that, IQ scores turn out to be unexpectedly accurate at predicting behaviour in all sorts of other areas. That is to say that, on average, IQ scores correlate startlingly well with how people perform on tests of creativity and leadership, as well as many real-world situations like how well you're likely to perform in your job,[8] how physically and mentally healthy you're likely to remain,[9] and how long you're likely to live.[10]

Correlation ≠ causation

To make sense of this finding we must resist the temptation to think in anecdotes and instead attempt to think statistically. Claims which may not be true for individuals may well be the case when we make them about a representative sample of a population. The points I will make about intelligence in this and subsequent chapters are true *on average*. They are probabilistic. Of course, there will always be some people who fall outside the norms, but that doesn't mean we're unable to identify patterns which describe the majority. Bear in mind that these patterns are correlations – that is, imperfect links between two variables which, on their own, say nothing about causality. So, if I were to claim that intelligence is correlated to creativity – and I will – this would mean that both factors appear to be connected but not that one necessarily causes the other.

Correlation should never be confused with causation. We can only ever see effects, never the causes of those effects. But this doesn't stop us believing that we understand the reasons for complex events. Human beings are natural pattern seekers. We automatically seek to find meaning in the chaos that surrounds us, and so we have an in-built tendency to create stories that 'explain' how things happen. I can be pretty certain that if I kick a ball, the ball's trajectory is caused by my kick, but the same would not necessarily be true if I were to kick a dog. We see faces in wallpaper and fantastical creatures in clouds. We look at the world around us and assume that we understand the reasons why things occur. In our primitive past we assumed a thunderstorm was caused by an angry god, but now we know – for science has revealed it to be so – that thunder and lightning are caused by the collision of ice particles within cumulonimbus clouds.

We might believe that our child's immaculate public behaviour is caused by our wonderful parenting, but anyone who has had more than one child knows that no two children respond in exactly the same way to the same stimulus. I shouldn't be so certain that if I reprimand my impossibly difficult teenage daughter that her tears are caused by my stern words. Me yelling my head off may well have *something* to do with her sudden onset of uncontrollable weeping, and I should perhaps feel rightly ashamed of myself, but her emotional life is far more complex than that. Sometimes

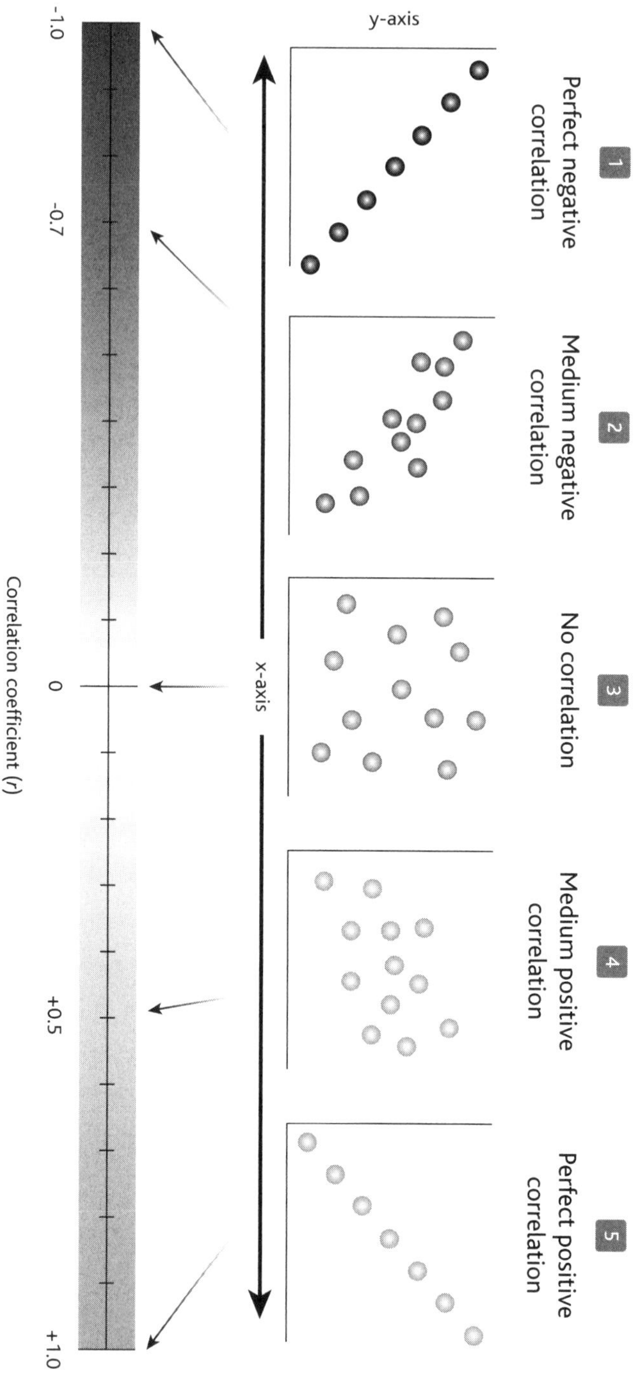

Figure 3.1. Degrees of correlation

when I tell her off she laughs, other times she rolls her eyes and occasionally she's contrite. I know from experience that gentle teasing will, on one occasion, be met with hearty, good-humoured banter and on another with utter and unexpected devastation.

Correlation is a tricky business. Perfect correlations tend not to exist so the relationships we find are always, to a greater or lesser extent, imperfect (see Figure 3.1). No matter how clear a signal we think we've identified, there is always noise.

In order to understand some of the figures in this chapter, it's worth briefly explaining a bit about what correlations mean. A perfect positive correlation is +1.0 and a perfect negative correlation is -1.0. If we see $r = 0.5$, it means there is a medium strength correlation between two identified sets of variables, which is a lot more than you'd expect to see by chance. Even though a medium strength correlation suggests a plausible link between these variables, it doesn't mean that one is causing the other.

Some correlations are amusingly spurious, such as the finding that the rise in global temperature has mirrored a decline in international piracy (see Figure 3.2).

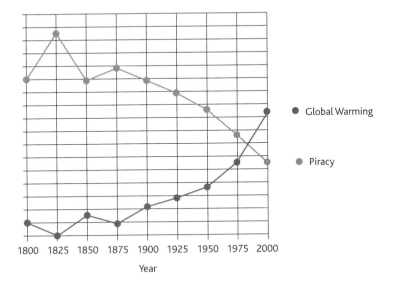

Figure 3.2. Piracy and global warming over the years

© Idolum Australian Laboratories for Purile Research (2011)

But other correlations can seem more plausible. Take the hyperbolic reports claiming that the rise in autism diagnoses were caused by vaccinations. Yes, autism has increased over a similar time period that has seen vaccinations rise, but for this to represent a causal connection we would need to have a testable hypothesis to link the two phenomena. The increase in autism also happens to correlate with "the rise in chemtrail sightings,* terrorist attacks on U.S. soil, the New England Patriot's cumulative win total – and organic food sales".[11] It just so happens that symptoms of autism arise around the age that children are usually vaccinated. This is true regardless of whether or not vaccines are given, and any reports that a link has been established are junk science. Rises in autism correlate with pretty much everything that's risen over past the 20 years.

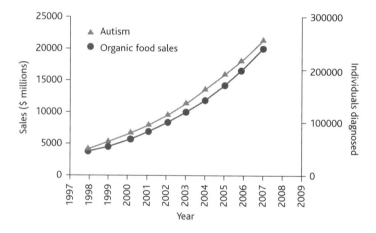

Figure 3.3. The correlation between autism and organic food sales

Source: Arvind Suresh, Autism Increase Mystery Solved? No, It's Not Vaccines, GMOs, Glyphosate – Or Organic Foods, *Genetic Literacy Project* (22 September 2016). Available at: https://geneticliteracyproject.org/2016/09/22/autism-increase-mystery-solved-no-its-not-vaccines-gmos-glyphosate-or-organic-foods/.

Even where epidemiologists find plausible correlations between, say, eating spinach and living longer, we still can't be clear of the causal

----

*   The chemtrail conspiracy theory is the false claim that long lasting condensation trails, called 'chemtrails' by proponents, consist of chemical or biological agents left in the sky by high flying aircraft and are deliberately sprayed for purposes undisclosed to the general public. In fact, chemtrails are caused by air turbulence at a plane's wing tips.

connection. It may be that spinach increases our lifespan but it could also be that spinach is purely a confounding factor. For instance, it's well established that men live longer if they're married. It could be that married men eat more spinach to please their wives. Maybe the spinach has nothing to do with it. Equally, maybe marriage has nothing to do with men's life expectancy; if they'd just eat spinach as bachelors perhaps they'd be fine.*

Anyway, you can see the tangled skein produced when correlations are all we have to rely on. The correlational claims made by other sciences, such as behaviour genetics, are more robust because they are able to analyse whether there are two-way mechanisms and to establish if the cart is being placed before the horse. We'll go into this in more detail later, but, as an example, adoption studies are really useful for isolating the effects of environment and heritability: if there's no correlation between the traits of adopted siblings, we can be pretty sure the differences will be due to heritable causes. Likewise, twin studies do a decent job of showing the reverse: if identical twins share 100% of their genes then any differences *must* be down to environmental factors.

What IQ predicts

While we cannot state with certainty that a high IQ score *causes* people to be more creative or to live longer, there is a correlation connecting these factors which is down to more than chance. This could mean that creativity causes intelligence, or that some other factor — maybe social background — causes both intelligence and creativity. Or it could be some combination. The point is, the connection is not random. When we say that people who are good at reasoning also have better vocabularies, we're saying that this isn't a matter of luck. While correlation is not proof that one thing causes another, causation is implied. The same is true of the finding that when we look at IQ test results for a reasonably large sample of people, their scores in different areas correlate positively. This is what has become known as the positive manifold — the idea that all variables

---

* I know I've reduced a complex science almost to absurdity. Epidemiology is a lot more sophisticated than I'm painting it, but *reductio ad absurdum* can be a useful tool in testing an idea to destruction.

are positively correlated – and led Charles Spearman to conclude that intelligence is general.* This is referred to as the general factor of intelligence, or the g-factor, or just g. Nobody knows for sure exactly why this should be the case but, nevertheless, intelligence researchers tend to agree that it is.

Far from being merely a measure of how good people are at taking tests, IQ is more strongly related than any other single measurable human trait to a whole host of important educational, occupational, economic and social outcomes. Whatever it is that IQ tests measure, it's of great practical and social importance. Maybe the most surprising finding to come out of this field of research is that intelligence is a good predictor of longevity; the higher your IQ, the longer you're likely to live. It's difficult to understand how the kinds of things measured by IQ tests could correlate with lifespan, but correlate they do.

It seems much more reasonable for longevity to correlate with physical health, and indeed it does, but better health is also positively correlated with higher IQ. This might have something to do with the connection between intelligence and education; the better educated you are, the more likely you are to know how to take care of yourself and be able to afford to do so because, you guessed it, intelligence also correlates with success in the workplace and higher job status, which is, in turn, associated with better medical benefits.

It's probably not too much of a shock to find out that higher IQ scores are related to higher income, but more surprising is research that demonstrates the correlation between cognitive ability and workplace performance. The more intelligent an employee, the more conscientious they're likely to be. In fact, the correlations just keep coming:

- Job performance (high complexity) – 0.58

- Job performance (medium complexity) – 0.51

- Job performance (low complexity) – 0.4

- Training success (civilian) – 0.55

- Training success (military) – 0.62

---

* As explored in his 1904 article '"General Intelligence," Objectively Determined and Measured.'

- Objective leader effectiveness – 0.34

- Creativity – 0.37[12]

There are pretty strong correlations with performance in jobs designated as 'high complexity' and 'medium complexity', and intelligence even makes a difference when the job is relatively straightforward. IQ even shows correlations with leadership and creativity indicating that, on average, cleverer people will have more ideas and be better at getting others to implement them.[13]

It's often argued that IQ tests don't measure important cognitive qualities like creativity, but studies into the links between g and creativity have consistently shown a moderately positive correlation. One problem is that creativity is tough to pin down – it ranges across fields as diverse as writing a new software app, designing a garden, reducing the effects of climate change and so on. Therefore, researchers rely on proxies which can be measured more easily, like 'divergent thinking'. Divergent thinking is assessed by the alternative use test (e.g. How many uses for a paper clip can you come up with?), and we find that people who do well on this test also have high IQ scores.[14] Even more interestingly, those who score well on IQ tests also do better on tests of musical discrimination[15] and have even been shown to register more patents for new inventions and receive more awards for artistic endeavours.[16]

If you're not already convinced of the importance of intelligence, then what about the fact that higher IQ is positively correlated with not only better physical health but also better mental health. The more intelligent you are, the lower the likelihood you will be hospitalised for a psychological condition.[17] Contrary to many popular myths, there's an especially strong negative correlation between higher IQ and schizophrenia.

While it seems to be the case that a higher IQ makes for a happier, healthier, longer life, clearly it can't be the only causal factor. Before we get too excited, we also need to consider the connection between social class and intelligence, and whether we're pointing the causal arrow the wrong way round. Maybe higher social class, with its many attendant advantages, causes higher intelligence. This is certainly plausible. The correlation between social class and IQ scores is certainly there, but it's not as strong as you might expect ($r = 0.3–0.5$).[18] There's no doubt that your background has an effect on your life chances, but there's also evidence of a connection between higher IQ and social mobility; the cleverer you are, the more likely you are to improve your socio-economic standing. Where you start off will be an important determining factor in where you end up, but so will your intelligence.

And if all that wasn't enough, there's also a pretty strong connection to happiness. People who score more highly on IQ tests tend to report being happier.[19]

Possibly the strongest correlations are those with educational outcomes. The higher your IQ, the more likely you are to do well in school and the longer you're likely to stay in school. It might seem self-evident that people who score better on IQ tests go on to do better at school, because educational success is predicated on measuring the same kind of ability. But it's worth knowing that the correlation between IQ tests taken five years previously and GCSE results at age 16 is one of the strongest yet found in psychology ($r = 0.81$).[20] The predictive power of the IQ test seems astonishingly accurate.

Accurate, but far from perfect. Before you start wondering whether we could do away with examinations in school altogether and just give a single, one-hour IQ test, you need to know that some people with high intelligence did not perform well in other tests and that some people who did well in their GCSEs did poorly on an IQ test. There are, it would appear, other factors involved in educational success, such as conscientiousness, motivation and self-control. We will discuss the evidence that education may cause increases in intelligence in Chapter 5.

Importantly, intelligence is not just an individual good, it's also a social good. The cleverer we are, the better society will be for everyone. The more intelligent you are, the less likely you are to commit a violent crime and, even more interesting, the less likely you are to have a violent crime committed against you or be murdered.[21] This might just be because you can afford to live in a low crime area. However, in his magisterial study of violence and its decline in the modern era, *The Better Angels of Our Nature*, Steven Pinker argues that the cleverer you are, the more likely you are to cooperate with other people, weigh the consequences of your actions and think in such a way that allows you to escape the confines of your own limited experiences.[22] Amazingly, the more intelligent you are, the lower the probability that you'll be racist or sexist and the greater the likelihood that you'll be socially liberal.[23] Social liberalism is a near cousin to liberal democratic values and there's good evidence to suggest that democracy – the form of government which is least likely to commit violent actions against its own people or go to war against another state – is most likely to take root and flourish in a literate, knowledgeable population. (More on this in Chapter 5.)

Whatever the question, it seems that intelligence is always at least part of the answer. If we want our children to be happier, healthier and more successful, to live long and to earn more, then it will pay to try to make them cleverer.

If you're already convinced by this argument then you may want to skip ahead to the next chapter. But if you need some further persuasion, the rest of this chapter will discuss the various myths and misunderstandings that surround the concepts of intelligence and IQ.

Everything you've been told about intelligence is wrong

Naturally, lots of people will possess lots of correct information, and many people will know a whole lot more than I do. However, if my experiences are anything to go by, a lot of what many people believe about intelligence is just plain wrong.

My experience falls into two categories. Firstly, what I used to believe about intelligence was confused and erroneous. I unquestioningly accepted a lot of myths and half-truths because I'd heard them trotted out so often. Repetition does a wonderful job of persuading us of anything; if we're sufficiently familiar with an idea, we're many times more likely to believe it than if it's new or unfamiliar.* And then, once we've become convinced of a thing's veracity, there are all kinds of biases that help to protect us from alternative perspectives. Most of the time we're far happier being wrong but certain than troubled by inconvenient truths that shake our status quo.

....
* This is the 'mere-exposure effect', a cognitive bias which leads to people developing a preference for things merely because they are familiar with them.

The other source of my experience is the result of talking to people about intelligence from a position of having done some reading on it. My finding is that many people, even highly knowledgeable, otherwise insightful folk whom I respect and admire, don't really have a proper grasp of what the research into intelligence actually says and tend to dismiss it all as unpalatable bunk.

I want you to try to set aside everything you might have assumed or been told about intelligence. While some of what you've heard may be true, much of it will be a seething mix of misinformation, ignorance and lies.

Charlie Gordon, the hero of *Flowers for Algernon*, who we met in the introduction, knows what it would mean to get smarter but has very little idea of what IQ might be. He's not alone:

> Prof. Nemur said it was something that measured how intelligent you were – like a scale in the drugstore weighs pounds. But Dr. Strauss had a big argument with him and said an I.Q. didn't *weigh* intelligence at all. He said an I.Q. showed how much intelligence you could get, like the numbers on the outside of a measuring cup. You still had to fill the cup up with stuff.
>
> Then when I asked Burt ... he said that some people would say both of them were wrong and according to the things he's been reading up on, the I.Q. measures a lot of different things including some of the things you learned already and it really isn't a good measure of intelligence at all.[24]

These kinds of differences and disputes are more the norm than the exception. IQ is controversial and it causes regular bun fights between the various tribes of intelligence researchers. To help thread a path through some of this confusion, here are some of the most potent and enduring myths about intelligence and IQ:

Myth 1: IQ measures intelligence

Although the terms are often used interchangeably, they're not the same thing. Being intelligent is the ability to adapt quickly to new surroundings and to use the information at hand to solve problems. This is too vague and imprecise to be readily measured. IQ is a proxy for intelligence. That is, it measures how well individuals perform on a standardised test that attempts to simulate some of these real-world applications. IQ scores are based on population statistics, and an individual's score on a test is defined in relation to the standard deviation of scores. IQ is the ratio of attainment age to chronological age. Your score is placed somewhere on the bell curve relative to everyone else's. These scores happen to follow a normal distribution (see Figure 3.4), but that is a consequence of the definition, not the definition itself.

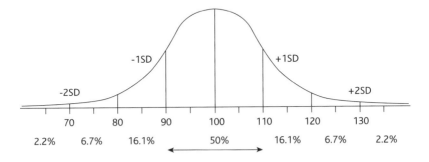

Figure 3.4. The normal distribution of intelligence

Note: SD = standard deviation

As we'll see, doing well on an IQ test requires abstract and hypothetical thinking. It's no doubt true to say that there are very many people who cope excellently with the diverse challenges presented by the world around them who might not do well in a test. It's probably also true that there are some people who score well in test situations who would fall to pieces when presented with the challenges of surviving in a harsh and previously unfamiliar environment. It might be better to call IQ a measure of relative intelligence. IQ is actually a mathematical construct – a number derived from performance on the various sub-tests that make up an IQ test. Numbers seem to have a peculiarly magical effect on our brains; if we can give something a number we can start adding and averaging these numbers. We start seeing these numbers as inherently real, as the thing itself. But a number is just a number – it means nothing in and of itself. And in the case of IQ, the number is a way of approximating a person's intelligence as compared to other people's.

Some critics of IQ tests contend that the scores are meaningless – or less important than others would like to claim – because they only measure a single, narrow form of intelligence and that, in the real world, many more things come into play. IQ tests, the claim goes, only measure how good individuals are at taking IQ tests. The popular cliché of the bumbling mathematician who can solve complex equations at lightning speed but struggles to butter his toast has an enduring appeal, but it's largely a myth. In fact, IQ tests attempt to measure *general* intelligence – an all-round ability to perform a wide range of mental activities. Those who do well at one aspect of an IQ test will tend to do well at all other aspects.

Myth 2: There are different kinds of intelligence

In 1983, Howard Gardner came up with his theory of multiple intelligences.[25] Basically, he said that instead of there being one general intelligence there were lots of different types of intelligence: logical-mathematical, linguistic, musical, intra and extra personal and so on. He claimed that while someone might have a low linguistic intelligence, they might do very well in, say, naturalistic intelligence. This is a seductive idea, but one which is conceptually confused and for which there is absolutely no empirical evidence. Gardner never tested his theory nor conducted any studies. It was just a hunch. A popular and enduring hunch to be sure, but even Gardner himself has said, "I readily admit that the theory is no longer current."[26]

Of course, he's not quite ready to entirely abandon his theory. While he admits that he never carried out any experiments designed to test the theory, he is not willing to accept that it lacks empirical support. He says, "The theory is not experimental in the traditional sense ... but it is strictly empirical, drawing on hundreds of findings from half-a-dozen fields of science."[27] I'm not at all sure this is good enough. Just because you've got a lot of data, it doesn't mean that you know how to interpret it, nor that you understand what it's telling you. Gardner's argument is a classic closed circle: I'm right because I have a lot of data which says I'm right. How does he know the data is correct? Because he's got a lot of it.

But maybe there's a ray of hope. Recent research claims to provide much needed empirical support for multiple intelligences. After reviewing 318 neuroscience reports, one study concluded that "there is robust evidence that each intelligence possesses neural coherence".[28] That sounds pretty convincing, but what does it actually mean? Basically this: researchers trawled though neuroscience studies to find indications in cortical areas for each of Gardner's eight intelligences. And guess what? Brain imaging reveals that people really do have brain regions dedicated to each area. Does this provide support for multiple intelligences? No. All it tells us is what we could have guessed: there are brain regions associated with musical ability, physical movement, communication, handling figures and so on. It really shouldn't come as much of surprise to find out that mental abilities are located in the brain. This has never been in doubt. And this is the whole problem with Gardner's theory. He himself admits that if he'd steered clear of the word 'intelligence' no one would have given his idea a second glance. It's completely uncontroversial to say different people have different talents, but by calling these talents intelligences he poisoned the well of intelligence research and strayed into pseudoscience.

If you make an empirical claim, then it should be falsifiable. There comes a point when twisting your ideas to fit the facts becomes pseudoscience, otherwise we can all believe whatever the hell we like and damn the evidence. We can argue that what we like 'works' because we like it. And if it's unsuccessful on verifiable metrics then the metrics are worthless. This is how closed circle arguments work: you can explain away any amount of disconfirming evidence as not fitting your paradigm. You've given yourself permission to ignore reality, and anyone who suggests you might not be wearing any clothes can be safely dismissed as having a fixed mindset. The redoubtable Richard Feynman put the problem like this: "It doesn't make a difference how beautiful your guess is. It doesn't make a difference how smart you are, who made the guess, or what his name is. If it disagrees with experiment, it's wrong."[29] If you can't accept that there could be conditions in which your guess is wrong, there's a good chance you're fooling yourself.

Let's be charitable for a moment and ask ourselves, *what if Gardner were right?* What difference could it possibly make to discover that some children are musical and others like nature? How would this change how we educate children? Just because someone has 'naturalistic intelligence', does this mean they need to be taught maths in a garden? Would possessing high 'linguistic intelligence' mean you wouldn't appreciate art? As we know from research into learning styles, matching instruction to children's perceived preferences only serves to narrow their experiences. The bottom line is this: the theory of multiple intelligences is conceptually confused, lacks experimental support, flies in the face of more generally accepted, mainstream scientific research on intelligence, predicts nothing in the real world and, most importantly, provides absolutely nothing of any practical value.

But what about emotional intelligence, or EQ (emotional quotient) as it's sometimes called? On the face of it, emotional intelligence – the ability to perceive, identify and manage emotions – sounds like a wonderful thing. Far nicer than the cold brutality of IQ. Although it made its first appearance in a 1964 paper by Michael Beldoch,[30] emotional intelligence was popularised by Daniel Goleman in his 1995 book, *Emotional Intelligence: Why It Can Matter More Than IQ*.[31] While Goleman has claimed that emotional intelligence accounts for up to 67% of the qualities deemed to be essential for leadership, this has been flatly contradicted by Flavia Cavazotte and her colleagues who found it to have no significance in tests of leadership qualities.[32] Although there are some studies showing a positive correlation between EQ and performance at work, these are much less strong than the correlations between IQ and performance we looked at earlier.

It seems that EQ doesn't actually seem to tell us anything we don't already know from looking at IQ and existing personality tests. It may not even be a thing. Much criticism has focused on the way emotional intelligence is measured. Basically, you answer a series of multiple-choice questions and respond to statements with 'never', 'rarely', 'sometimes', 'often' or 'consistently'. The obvious problem with this sort of assessment is that it's very easy to predict the 'right' or socially acceptable answer. This methodology is hard to take seriously when compared to the rigour with which intelligence is measured. Despite the claims, there is very little correlation between emotional intelligence and job performance.[33] So perhaps, at least for now, we'd be better off consigning this to the pile of good guesses that disagree with experiment.

But what of other attempts to invent different intelligences? As far back as 1920, Edward Thorndike proposed that intelligence should be divided into three types: abstract (ideas), practical (objects) and social (people). Social intelligence is the ability "to act wisely in human relations".[34] This seems fair enough. We readily understand what is meant by the idea of social intelligence and will have a store of acquaintances who we might recognise as possessing the qualities encapsulated by it. But is "social intelligence just general intelligence applied to social situations"?[35] In order for it to be accepted as a separate concept it would need to be measurable in a way that is both reliable and valid – that is to say, test scores would need to make meaningful predictions in the real world.

The first attempt to measure social intelligence was the George Washington Social Intelligence Test. Like IQ tests, it consisted of a variety of sub-tests including judgement in social situations, memory for names and faces, observation of human behaviour, recognition of the mental states behind words and from facial expressions, social information and sense of humour. The problem was that test scores were so highly correlated with IQ scores that it became increasingly hard to argue that they are actually different things.

Later attempts to distinguish social intelligence from abstract intelligence relied on self and peer ratings of social competence and the judgement of interviewers. The finding that self and peer ratings correlated more with the interview judgements than IQ did is interesting, but hardly impressive.[36] Essentially, all this tells us is that likeability and intelligence are not synonymous, which will surprise no one. The best we can say is that on the basis of intuitive evaluations of folk psychology, social intelligence 'feels right'. It also probably corresponds with various personality traits such as openness to experience and extroversion.

Unlike social intelligence, Thorndike's notion of practical intelligence has proved much harder to pin down and at least 27 different attributes have been bundled under the label.[37] The difficulty with accepting practical intelligence as something separate is that it already seems to be included in Linda Gottfredson's definition (see page 7). As she says, general intelligence is "not merely book learning, a narrow academic skill, or test-taking smarts. Rather, it reflects a broader and deeper capability for comprehending our surroundings: 'catching on,' 'making sense' of things, or 'figuring out' what to do." These things all seem nothing if not practical.

On the other hand, some have argued that while IQ tests are useful for identifying individuals at the extremes of the distribution of ability, they're not much help in differentiating between the vast majority whose scores fall between 85 and 115. As I've argued, what truly distinguishes these people is the quality and quantity of what they know. Exponents of practical intelligence argue that what we know, as well as our personality and interests, should be taken into account when trying to establish how intelligent we might be in everyday circumstances, and that attempts to measure such a construct should focus on what's typical rather than what's possible.[38] In other words, it's more useful to know what someone is normally like rather than what they could achieve with a downhill slope and fair trailing wind.

As this idea fits so well with the arguments in this book, I'm tempted to allow it. However, my real problem with slapping the label 'intelligence' on things that aren't intelligence is that as well as devaluing the currency, you just end up with conceptual confusion. Howard Gardner acknowledged that he very deliberately labelled his different categories of accomplishment as intelligence rather than talents to challenge "those psychologists who believed that they owned the word 'intelligence' and had a monopoly on its definition and measurement".[39] Perhaps it's also true to say that if he hadn't, no one would have been interested.

Myth 3: Intelligence cannot be increased

There are some who believe that everyone has an allotted and immutable measure of intelligence. The argument goes that our intelligence is inherited from our parents and that our genes account for the entirety of our IQ score. Of course, others believe the opposite – that everything depends on the environment and that with the right kind of practice anyone could achieve anything. The reality is that pretty much all human characteristics appear to be the products of both our genetic inheritance and the environmental pressures we encounter throughout our lives. Estimates vary, but research suggests that our genes account for at least half of our intelligence, with the remaining fraction being the product of the unique circumstances of our lives.

Much of what we call intelligence depends on experience. If you were locked in a box from childhood and deprived of all stimuli you'd perform poorly on an IQ test, whereas if you've been fortunate enough to be exposed to a wide range of ideas and information, you'll do much better. For genes to be the only influence on intelligence, everyone's environment would need to be equal. It might be true to say that our intelligence is limited by our genes, but that doesn't detract from the central tenet of this book: that we can all get cleverer.

As we'll see in Chapter 5, intelligence is partly fluid and partly crystallised. The fluid aspects of intelligence may not be particularly malleable, but crystallised intelligence – what we know – is relatively straightforward to increase. While fluid intelligence increases during childhood development, peaks in our mid-twenties and then gently declines, our crystallised intelligence can go on accruing across our entire lives. Using the environment to increase crystallised intelligence is central to making kids cleverer; fluid intelligence, and its associated individual differences, is largely a distraction.

IQ tests measure attainment broadly enough to make a general prediction of how test-takers are likely to fare compared to others. As we explored, tracking how IQ scores correlate with other outcomes allows us to see the possible effects of higher intelligence on health, wealth and a range of other factors. Obviously, measuring mental ability in this way is totally different from being able to pinpoint an individual's capacity. Predicting how most kids will get on is not at all the same as stating what any individual kid can do. In an article for *The Psychologist*, Michael Howe explains that while IQ scores are highly stable there is, as we've seen, plenty of evidence that they can be raised. He points out that "stability does not imply unchangeability" and gives the rather amusing example that although your telephone number tends to remain stable from one year to the next, no one would argue that it couldn't be changed. Telephone numbers and IQ scores are unlikely to change unless there is some pressing reason for them to do so; in the absence of such a reason they will both be stable.[40]

It might be more useful to think of our cognitive abilities as being similar in some ways to our physical abilities. Although some people will always have the capacity to be stronger, fitter and healthier than others, whether or not they are depends on what they do. If you want to get healthier you can change your diet and exercise regime. By eating well and taking regular exercise you will become fitter and healthier. You might never be as fit or as healthy as someone else but, relative to your starting position, you're definitely better off. However, if you quit going to the gym and revert to eating junk food, these benefits are unlikely to last.

The same seems to be true of intelligence. If you work in a cognitively demanding environment, read interesting books, chose smart friends who engage you in challenging debate and generally work at being cleverer, you will be. But, as with your health, this depends on continued effort. If you decide to quit your current job and do something less demanding, choose a peer group who all nod and smile at whatever inanity spills from your lips and spend your leisure time watching docu-soaps, your intelligence will probably ebb away. IQ scores vary as we reach maturity, peak in our mid- to late twenties and begin to decline thereafter. Of course, this isn't fate. Sometimes IQ scores go up, sometimes they go down.

Myth 4: IQ tests are unfair

A common criticism of IQ tests is that they are culturally biased. This argument usually rests on the finding that the average IQ scores of different identified groups is not the same. If we find that the average score of group X is higher than group Y, we might be tempted to say that those in group X are naturally more intelligent than those in group Y, or we might conclude that the life experiences of those in group X are substantially different to those in group Y, ensuring an unfair advantage in the test.

As we've already seen, IQ cannot be wholly dependent on a person's genetic material and must, in some part, depend on a person's experiences. It's not unreasonable to suppose that if some groups of people are disadvantaged economically or socially, then the environments in which they've grown up also disadvantage them when it comes to sitting an IQ test or any other measure of academic ability. Dismissing such data as unfair allows us to ignore the problem. Instead, it should make us realise that the unfairness and inequality experienced by some groups must be tackled if we want to give all children the same opportunities for getting cleverer.

In 1979, Robert Serpell found that the media in which a task is presented makes a great deal of difference to how children from different cultural backgrounds perform. His study compared the performance of British and Zambian children and found that when they were asked to reproduce a figure using wire, the Zambian children outperformed their

British counterparts, but when the children were given pen and paper, the British children did best. Serpell concluded that we develop highly specific perceptual skills depending on our experiences and what we have practised. Almost all British children have extensive experience of using pen and paper to make drawings, whereas Zambian children have less access to expensive writing materials but much more practice at manipulating found objects, such as wire, to represent the shapes of animals and people.

Serpell recommended that tests should be designed to reflect the contexts with which the subjects are most familiar. He suggested that Western-educated subjects possess the cultural knowledge which forms the infrastructure on which test performance depends, whereas those from non-Western backgrounds don't. His conclusion was that using non-verbal pictorial tests to measure the intelligence of children who have had little or no cultural experience of pictures would be as pointless as testing children in a language with which they were unfamiliar.[41]

Fair point. In his masterwork, *Guns, Germs and Steel*, the anthropologist and biologist Jared Diamond goes further. For many years, Diamond lived and worked in Papua New Guinea and his book is an attempt to explain why people of Eurasian origin, and not the native New Guineans, were the first to export the building blocks of colonialism. The question he set out to answer was why wealth and power became distributed as they now are rather than in some other way.

A typically racist answer to this question might be that because white immigrants managed to create a modern, industrialised society in less than a hundred years, then the Australian Aborigines must be either lazy or stupid. Diamond goes on to demolish such a fatuous explanation and points out that there are two problems with the data showing differences in IQ between peoples of different geographic origins now living in the same country. Firstly, as adult cognitive abilities are influenced by the social environments experienced by children, how can we untangle genetic differences from social ones? Secondly, what IQ tests measure is culturally specific and so tell us little about innate intelligence.

Diamond then makes a fascinating, if anecdotal, observation that New Guineans are "on the average more intelligent, more alert, more expressive, and more interested in things and people around them than the average European or American is". He argues that living in a 'civilised' urbanised environment makes it relatively easy for anyone to pass on their genetic material, as opposed to in a more 'primitive' hunter-gatherer society. He says, "natural selection promoting genes for intelligence has probably been far more ruthless in New Guinea than in more densely populated, politically complex societies".[42]

Could it be that people from non-Western societies are actually cleverer, and that all IQ tests are doing is providing flimsy evidence that those people with access to Western education are better at those things most valued by the Western educated elite?

For IQ tests to be unfair, getting the right answer to a question would have to depend on factors other than intelligence, such as education and social class. In order to interrogate this idea we must distinguish between the terms 'fair', 'valid' and 'biased'. Of course, we mustn't get mixed up between the properties of tests and those of our inferences; a test is just a tool and it is our interpretation that gives it meaning or validity. That said, most people would be happy to say that a question is fair if they get the right answer, but is a question biased against you if you can't answer it?

Or, to put it another way, does getting a low score on an IQ test mean you're not intelligent? Well, probably. Being intelligent is essentially a combination of how quickly you learn and how much you've learned. There are several possible reasons why you might not know the answer to a question. It might be that you were never taught the answer, you never learned it on your own, you might have forgotten it, you might not know how to reason it out or, knowing how, you're still not able to reason it out. It might be that, for some reason, you've never been taught to read. You might conceivably do well at spotting visual patterns but would be unable to answer questions measuring verbal ability. Whatever the case, most of these reasons relate, in some way, to general intelligence.

Getting a high score, on the other hand, means you know the answers. But does it matter *how* you know the answers? Have you had the advantage of a good education? Have you got a better than average memory? Are you perhaps just one of those people who are good at taking tests? Once again, general intelligence covers each of these things.

Regardless of how well they do on IQ tests, no group of people is in any way superior to any other group. There's no doubt that IQ has been (and still is) used by racists to justify their beliefs in the superiority and inferiority of different races, but IQ itself is just a mathematical construct. We can condemn the uses IQ scores are put to without rejecting their validity. IQ scores can never predict the worth of an individual. Everyone deserves to be treated fairly and with respect. The idea that we can or should select for some people's idea of desirable traits or engage in any other form of social engineering is reprehensible.

The fact that various studies show differences in the IQ scores of men and women, different ethnic groups and people of different socio-economic status has no bearing whatsoever on whether we should pursue a progressive political agenda. Differences in the average IQ scores of different groups are caused by the unfair distribution of wealth and access to education and by systematic discrimination. These are things that social policy should seek to address. It doesn't matter at all whether some children are more intelligent than others; all children can be made cleverer.

Myth 5: IQ doesn't matter in the real world

IQ tests are very far from perfect. If the same person takes an IQ test on consecutive days they're likely to get a slightly different score. And that score is a very dark lens through which to sum up the intelligence of a human being. This has led to probably the most pernicious of all these myths – the belief that IQ tests don't measure anything meaningful. It's become widely accepted that success in life is due to a combination of personality, motivation and socio-economic advantage, and that IQ scores predict nothing of value. The truth is that whatever IQ measures, it provides surprisingly accurate predictions about a huge range of things, from academic success to conscientiousness at work.

Of course, an IQ score can never reveal what a person is actually like, but it's a remarkably accurate predictor of almost everything our society values. In fact, despite the limitations of the test, it's all the more remarkable how accurate the predictions of IQ scores can be. We always need to remember that what's true of population statistics isn't necessarily true of an individual within that population. IQ may correlate with better health, wealth and happiness, but any individual could get lucky or unlucky. What's important is that at a population level 'good things' tend to be correlated with higher IQ. It could be possible that it is the presence of these good things that leads to higher IQ, but a more compelling possibility is that creating an environment in which intelligence can thrive will allow children to enjoy more of the benefits with which intelligence correlates.

As we saw earlier, IQ is particularly good (although not perfect) at predicting academic success, even when we control for socio-economic status, age, sex, ethnic origins and other variables. It also predicts various brain characteristics such as cortical thickness and cerebral glucose metabolic rate.[43] If intelligence tests were meaningless, they wouldn't be able to predict anything. The fact that they can and do predict such a wide range of things – including quantifiable brain characteristics – proves they have meaning.

What IQ tests don't do is tell us what the scores mean. That is a matter of interpretation. All we know is that something real and meaningful is being measured which we have decided to call intelligence. We know IQ has implications for areas as diverse as functional literacy, job performance and being involved in road traffic accidents, but it doesn't tell us whether these things are good or bad. For instance, the US military won't accept recruits with scores below 90 because, on average, such people tend to find it harder to learn what's required and run a greater risk of being killed in training. Is this fair? At the level of an individual, probably not. But at the level of thousands of potential recruits, that is what the military has decided is in everyone's best interests.

This is a numbers game, and making such decisions in an education context would be entirely wrong, not least because IQ is highly influenced by background when young. Trying to use IQ tests to academically select kids fails because they are likely to measure more about children's socio-economic status than act as a reasonable proxy for intelligence.

....

To summarise, everyone agrees on the sorts of things we want for children. It's absolutely uncontroversial to say that children ought to feel fulfilled and possess the capacity to thrive in an uncertain future.

Intelligence, as measured by IQ tests, seems to be the best predictor we have of whether people possess these capacities. Therefore, the purpose of education ought to be to make children cleverer.

Chapter 3: key points

- Intelligence is a combination of how easy we find it to learn and the product of what we have learned.

- Intelligence is not fixed at birth. While some aspects probably can't be changed, other aspects – what we know – are easy to change.

- There's good evidence that intelligence is general and that someone who is good at one area of cognition is likely to be good at all areas of cognition.

- IQ tests, although they imperfectly measure it, provide a reliable and valid proxy for what we mean by intelligence.

- IQ scores correlate with a wide range of real-world outcomes – such as income, health and happiness.

- Comparing people from widely varying cultures using an IQ test is probably pointless and unfair.

- Selection by IQ is both abhorrent and unnecessary. The most useful and fair form of testing in schools is to test children on what they have been taught, what they know and what they can do.

- There's good reason to believe that we can increase children's intelligence, so perhaps we should.

Now that we've had a chance to think about what is and is not covered by the term intelligence, it's time to consider where our intellectual capabilities come from. This age-old debate is normally characterised as being between, on the one hand, nature and, on the other, nurture. This will be the subject of the next chapter.

Chapter 4
Nature via nurture

We are not born equal, we are simply born different.

Adam Rutherford

The difference of natural talents in different men is, in reality, much less than we are aware of ... The difference between the most dissimilar characters, between a philosopher and a common street porter, for example, seems to arise not so much from nature as from habit, custom, and education.

Adam Smith, *The Wealth of Nations*

- Does our understanding of genes provide a road map for education?

- What might it mean to have genes for low or high intelligence?

- What role does parenting and schooling have on determining intelligence?

Whose fault is it anyway?

As a teenager, I wanted to blame my parents for everything. I felt scarred by their belief in the efficacy of corporal punishment, blighted by their fervent Christianity and hampered by their small-minded, provincial take on just about everything. How could I ever make a success of my life with such a parental albatross to drag around?

So embittered, frustrated and impatient did I feel that I left home at the tender age of 16, convinced I knew more than they did about everything.

I don't intend this to be any sort of memoir so I think it best to gloss over most of what I now think of as my wilderness years. Suffice it to say that I got in with a bad crowd and experienced a wider variety of human degradation than you probably care to imagine.

Eventually, after many perambulations, I finished a degree, began a career as a teacher, married a wonderful woman and became the proud father of two breathtakingly beautiful, alertly intelligent and utterly unique girls.

As you might expect, I feared for their fates. What if they took after their wayward father instead of their sensible, civic-minded mother? Happily, I'm pleased to report that, at the time of writing, they're both conscientious, happy and utterly square. Both have vowed never to drink alcohol or smoke cigarettes, and I'm happy to accept that (for now at least) they mean it. Maybe there's hope for them. They've never seen, and hopefully never will see, the old me, and only know me as a somewhat irascible, unpredictable old curmudgeon. I do my best.

Genes and the environment

Common sense tells us that how kids turn out is down to a combination of who they are and what happens to them; their genes and the environment they grow up in; nature and nurture. The extreme hereditarian position is that all differences are due to our genes and that the environment counts for nothing. As Stephen Jay Gould puts it, "The hereditarian fallacy is not the simple claim that IQ is to some degree 'heritable' [it is] the equation of heritable with inevitable."[1] While this may have had some currency in the past, I've not been able to find anyone who holds this view today. The extreme environmental position is that genes are irrelevant and our environment and our efforts are all that matters. This is very much a minority position, but there are a few who hold firm to it. For instance, in an interview, Anders Ericsson (about whom we'll hear more in Chapter 9) said, "I have no problem conceptually with this idea of genetic differences ... but nothing I've seen has convinced me this is actually the case. There's compelling evidence that if [performance is down to] length of bones, that cannot be explained by training. We know you can't influence diameter of bones.* But that's really it."[2] However, the majority of researchers agree that both genes and environment play a part in how we turn out.

There have been several occasions so far in this book where I've referred to the finding that when we consider differences in people's intelligence, our genes account for roughly half of those differences, with our environment being responsible for the other half. This is often misinterpreted as meaning that at least half of our intelligence is due to our genes. That would be an understandable mistake to make, but it's not right. Here's how it actually works: if we take a roughly representative sample of 100 people and give them an IQ test, we can be fairly sure that we'll get a range of IQ scores from about 70 to 130. Roughly 68% will have a score between 85 and 115, with an average score being somewhere between 90 and 110. When trying to account for these different scores we can be reasonably sure that at least half of the variation will be due to genes and the remaining portion due to environment.[3]

Although it coincides with the common-sense view, this is a troublesome finding because we tend to be pretty squeamish about saying that some people are just born cleverer than others. In a very obvious sense no one is 'born clever'. Babies would universally perform poorly on IQ tests, but some may have a greater potential for intelligence than others. The mistake is to believe that our genes represent our fate. The science of behavioural genetics is probabilistic *not* deterministic. That said, common sense and the evidence of experience tells us that some people really *are* cleverer than others. Even though there is no end of academic quarrelling about exactly what intelligence might be and what IQ tests measure, we naturally find ourselves thinking of some people as brighter than others. And, despite our difficulties in pinning down a definition of intelligence, we know what we mean when we call someone clever.

Let's see how the interplay between genes and the environment unfolds with a less controversial trait like height. It's widely accepted that height, within a given population, is about 90% heritable. Or, to state the same thing more accurately, 90% of the variation in height differences is due to genetic factors. We also know that in the 30-year period between 1979 and 2009 the average height of male South Korean high school seniors

---

*   Ericsson is actually wrong about this, as David Epstein explains in *The Sports Gene*.

increased by 3.5 inches, to 5 foot 8 inches, and girls grew by an average of 2 inches, to 5 foot 3 inches.[4] Now, height was just as heritable in 1979 as it was in 2009. Confusing as this may seem, the variation in differences between how tall one South Korean is compared to another is *still* explained by genes. We'll explore why in a moment.

This can be hard to get your head around. The problem is caused because we assume that *heritability* is synonymous with *inherited* and reflects the portion of a trait which is genetically determined. It's not. Heritability is "the proportion of variation in the characteristics in a given population that is accounted for by genes".[5] The concept of heritability comes from animal breeding experiments where the variation of genes and the environment are tightly controlled by researchers. In the real world genes and the environment run free. We have no way of controlling their variation, and so talking about percentages of a trait as if they are genetically determined is a nonsense. All we know for certain is that if genes vary in a population then the heritability of a trait cannot be zero, and if the environment varies at all it cannot be 100%.

Simple observation tells us that just as children look similar to their parents, their personality traits are also similar. We know that children share 50% of the genes of each of their parents, and we have identified the genes responsible for a range of genetic medical conditions. If we can pass on the genes responsible for causing cystic fibrosis, it's not too much of a stretch to suggest that we also pass on genes responsible for intelligence. A word of caution here. Although there are a handful of medical conditions (like cystic fibrosis) which have been identified as having a single genetic cause, this is the exception rather than the rule. Most traits, certainly ones as complex as intelligence, are caused by the interaction of multiple genes. So, while we think we've discovered some of the genes that contribute towards intelligence, we are very far away from having anything like a complete genetic picture.

Anyway, back to the extraordinary growth of South Korean high school students. The difference across time from 1979 to 2009 is explained by changes in the environment. Standards of living in South Korea went through the roof during this period and, as you would expect, improvements in healthcare and nutrition rose in tandem. The fact that differences in height are due to genes is true but trivial; with improvements to the environment, *everyone* gets taller. Why would the same not be true for intelligence? Think of it as a Grand Prix with genes as the drivers and cars as the environment. Both are required to compete. Without the very best Formula 1 car, a driver's skill and experience will count for little. Likewise, without the most talented and experienced driver, even the best engineered car is unlikely to win.

Not everyone is born equal and nor are children blank slates. We don't all have the same potential and not everyone can do anything, no matter how hard they might try. But what should we do with this information? How might this change our aim to make all children cleverer? Well, just as everyone gets taller with improvements to the environment, maybe everyone can get cleverer by changing children's experiences. One thing that all children experience – at least in developed countries – is school. So, if we change the school environment, couldn't this lead to children becoming more intelligent?

Our genes don't just sit there making us tall or clever; they interact with our environment. Your genes partly explain how healthy you are, but, unsurprisingly, so does the environment you select for yourself. No matter how healthy you are predisposed to be, if you eat junk food all day every day, you won't be healthy. Likewise, it's hard to see how you would gain weight on a starvation diet.

At best our genes indicate a statistical probability, but these probabilities change markedly depending on the environment. When we compare the IQ of children of similar socio-economic status, most of the variance is explained by genes; but when the IQ scores of children of lower socio-economic status are compared, most of the variation is explained by environmental differences. Heritability can be as high as 70% for middle-class children and as low as 20% for less advantaged children.[6] Why might this be?

It's probably down to the *Anna Karenina* principle. Tolstoy's novel starts with the sentence: "Happy families are all alike; every unhappy family is unhappy in its own way." For a family to be happy several key factors must apply: the good health of all family members, acceptable financial security, mutual affection and so on.[7] The family will be unhappy if there is a deficiency in any one or more of these factors. Maybe families with higher socio-economic status are all alike in important ways, but the financial pressures experienced by families of lower socio-economic status mean that any one of a range of important indicators could be adversely affected.

If you're from a nice middle-class home all your basic needs will be met. You're more likely to be exposed to a broad range of cultural experiences, more likely to be read to by doting parents and more likely to discuss current affairs around the dinner table. All this expands your vocabulary, increases your general knowledge and helps to prepare you for school. Because the home environments of middle-class children don't vary all that much, genetic variation explains more of the differences between children. That is to say, if most middle-class children come from a background favourable to developing intelligence, differences in their intelligence are more likely to be rooted in their biology. But environments vary more greatly for children from less advantaged backgrounds. Some children will come from poorer families whose parents will be every bit as nurturing as their middle-class peers', while others may come from backgrounds that are chaotic or deprived. Your genes might indicate something about your potential, but you're far less likely to develop a high IQ if you're abused and neglected.

Other factors have been shown to have some effect on IQ. For instance, alcohol consumption during pregnancy is likely to have a negative impact on children,[8] whereas breastfeeding could cause an IQ gain of between 6 to 8 points.[9] There's also evidence that talking to children matters. According to one study in the United States, the children of professional parents have heard, on average, about 30 million words by the age of 3, whereas children of working-class parents will have heard 20 million, and the children of unemployed lone mothers hear only 10 million words. In addition, the vocabulary used in professional homes is substantially more sophisticated than that in working-class homes.[10] These figures have been disputed and more recent research suggests the gap is more likely to be in the region of 4 million words, but this may still represent an important environmental disadvantage.[11] Now, of course, there's no way to be sure how many of the gains associated with the quantity and quality of the vocabulary children encounter are actually caused by parents passing on their genes. It may be that parents who read to their children are more intelligent parents, and perhaps the fact that they're in a higher income bracket is also partly explained by their intelligence. Nevertheless, it seems safe to say that these environmental effects are unlikely to be trivial: no one, no matter how intelligent they are, can learn a word they have never read or heard. School programmes that attempt to teach children vocabulary are likely to have an effect not only on the academic outcomes of those children but also on their intelligence.[*]

Let's leave intelligence for a moment and consider the effects of nature and nurture on reading ability. In *G is for Genes*, Kathryn Asbury and Robert Plomin estimate that genetic heritability accounts for 60–80% of reading ability. This leaves as little as 20% down to the nurturing effects of our environments. Admittedly, this is horribly oversimplified:

> Genetic variation exists from the moment we are born, but is multiplied and magnified as our genes interact with each other and with our environment. It is likely that some environmental effects are hidden within our heritability estimates because they are effective indirectly, via their interplay with genes.[12]

In one study, researchers investigated this interplay by comparing children's reading ability in three quite different environments: Colorado, New South Wales and Scandinavia.[13] Each of these territories exerts different environmental pressures: in both the United States and Australia children are required to attend school from the age of 5, but in New South Wales children attend school from 9 a.m. to 3 p.m. and the state decrees that 35% of this time is devoted to mandated literacy instruction, whereas in Colorado children only attend kindergarten for three to four hours a day and the curriculum is left entirely in the hands of individual schools. In Scandinavia children do not begin reading instruction until the age of 7. Unsurprisingly, the researchers found enormous differences in the relationships between genetic and environmental factors on children's reading ability (Table 4.1). But after each of the different population groups had each received one year of reading instruction, environmental differences largely disappeared (Table 4.2).

---

[*]   Alex Quigley's book *Closing the Vocabulary Gap* is a useful addition to any teacher's bookshelf.

Table 4.1. Estimated influences of genes and environment on reading ability at age 5

	Genetic influences	Shared (parenting) and non-shared environmental influences (school, peers, etc.)
New South Wales	80%	20%
Colorado	66%	33%
Scandinavia	33%	66%*

Table 4.2. Estimated influences of genes and environment on reading ability after one year of reading instruction

	Genetic influences	Shared environmental influences (parenting)	Non-shared environmental influences (school, peers, etc.)
New South Wales	80–90%	0%	10–20%
Colorado	80–90%	0%	10–20%
Scandinavia	80–90%	0%	10–20%

When non-shared environmental factors are broadly similar, genes account for the vast majority of the difference in reading ability. The fact that there is some variance is down to differences between schools – some are better run and provide better reading instruction than others. As we'll see shortly, shared environment (growing up in the same household with the same parental influences) vanishes as a source of influence by adulthood.

This is all deeply counter-intuitive. As Asbury and Plomin put it, "More school – that is, more environmental input – leads to greater genetic influence rather than greater environmental influence."[14] As children's

---

* These figures have been rounded, so don't add up to 100%.

environments become more similar, genetic differences become more noticeable. At first glance, this might sound a bit fatalistic and dispiriting, but actually there is a much more positive message that should be taken from these findings.

Reading is a very useful indicator of heritability because it's so unnatural; genetically speaking, it's a very recent development in human communication. As explained in Chapter 2, we readily pick up speech without formal instruction, but relatively few people spontaneously learn to read, no matter how genetically predisposed they might be to having a high reading ability. If we look at samples of children before they receive formal reading instruction at school, it seems reasonable to infer that the greater part of their reading ability is a product of their environment. Parents who value reading and read to their children are more likely to have children who can read.

The ad hoc reading instruction in Colorado results in some non-shared environmental reading influence. Some schools teach children to read, others don't. Compare this with the lack of any formal instruction in Scandinavia before the age of 7 and we can see that reading ability is almost entirely attributable to parents' efforts to teach their children to read.* But education is the great leveller. When all children receive similar reading instruction, the differences between them are mainly explained by genetic influences, resulting in a bell curve with a normal distribution of reading ability. This corresponds to an uncomfortable degree with the normal distribution of intelligence. What we should conclude is that some children end up doing better in school than others not because they're more intelligent, but simply because they get better (and unfair) access to the environments that are most likely to improve intelligence. The more egalitarian the society, the more genetic influences will matter.

Science writer Matt Ridley puts it like this:

> If intelligence was not significantly genetic, there would be no point in widening access to universities and trying to seek out those from modest backgrounds who have much to offer. If nurture were everything, those children who had experienced poor schools could be written off

....

*   It's important to note that due to very sensible spelling reforms, Swedish has a much shallower orthography than English. You can make 35 different sounds in Swedish and there are 40 ways to represent these sounds in writing. In comparison, English has 44 phonemes and over 170 graphemes.

as having poor minds. Nobody thinks that. The whole idea of social mobility is to find talent in the disadvantaged, to fund people who have the nature but not the nurture.[15]

Group differences

Socio-economic background is not the only factor that affects IQ. The differences between males and females and between different racial groups have been exhaustively explored and have become the source of huge controversy.

There's no doubt that boys and girls are biologically different. But, as the novelist and poet Gertrude Stein put it, "A difference to be a difference must make a difference."[16] Do the very obvious biological differences between the sexes actually make a difference to their academic performance? Apparently for most human characteristics, while the mean scores are identical for men and women, there are more men at the extremes (see Figure 4.1).

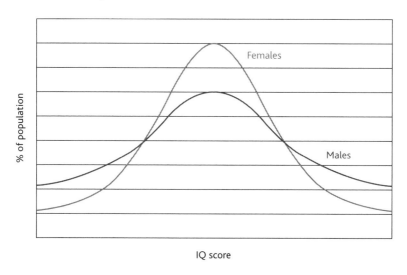

Figure 4.1. Normal IQ distribution curves for males and females

While the average IQ for men and women is the same, there is more variability in the data set of all men than in the data set of all women. To put it another way, if there are more male geniuses, there are also more male dunces. It tends to be the case that women are more likely to do well on the sub-test for verbal abilities, whereas men seem to do better at mental rotation – the ability to imagine what an object would look like if it were rotated. Despite the fact that average brain size varies greatly between the sexes (on average, the male brain is 8–14% larger than the female brain), male intelligence really doesn't differ all that much from female intelligence. We are far more similar than we are different, and group differences tell us nothing about an individual's potential.

Much more disturbing is the finding that people who identify as belonging to particular racial groups seem to have different average IQs to the wider population. Broadly, people who identify as Jewish or East Asian have higher IQs than those who identify as white, while people identifying as black or Hispanic fall somewhat lower.[17] While the 15-point difference between the average IQ of white and black Americans is a matter of fact, what has caused that difference is not. Racists have taken comfort from studies that claim the difference is largely explained by genetic differences, but then racists are idiots. The fact that 50% of the difference in intelligence is due to genes *only* applies to individuals, not to groups. It is both logically false and empirically wrong to claim that the differences in intelligence between different racial groups is due to genes; there is no evidence that the difference between racial groups is in any way heritable.

The scientific consensus is that race, as applied to human beings, is a biologically meaningless term. Although people who identify as belonging to specific racial groups may share certain identifying physical attributes, such as skin colour, their genetic code does not differ substantially from those who identify as belonging to other racial groups with quite different skin pigmentation. What differences there are will be individual rather than group differences. Biologists define race as a group or population differing in gene frequency from that of others in the same species. These differences usually occur when geographic barriers limit interbreeding, so that the two otherwise similar genetic populations begin to drift apart. This does not apply to humans.[18] The fact that so many people struggle with this idea is a good example of the clash between folk knowledge and a biologically secondary understanding of scientific knowledge (see

Chapter 2). To be clear, if race is biologically meaningless, it *must* follow that race has no causal effect on genetic differences in IQ.

But just because race is biologically meaningless, it doesn't follow that the term has no cultural, political or economic meaning. As such, the fact that people identify as belonging to different racial groups tells us much more about their cultural, political and economic circumstances than it does about their biology. A far more compelling and plausible explanation is that the environments of white and black Americans are substantially different, and that the lower average IQ score of black Americans is attributable to inequitable environmental conditions.

Of course, the objection to discussing racial differences in IQ stems from the now thoroughly discredited belief in eugenics. Eugenics (from the Greek *eugenes*, meaning well-born) argues that only people with the 'right' genes should be allowed to have offspring. It's astonishing to us now that such an unpleasant and inherently racist ideology was once so fashionable. Winston Churchill was keen on the idea and various countries even went as far as implementing eugenic polices on a national scale, notably the United States and Sweden, both of which enforced the sterilisation of those deemed to be of undesirable stock. Even though many thousands of people – particularly those of Native American and African-American descent – underwent forced sterilisation in the United States, this is hardly the worst of it. The efficiency with which the Third Reich went about exterminating millions of Jews, Gypsies, Slavs, homosexuals and mentally ill individuals makes it hard to focus on anything else.

The belief that human beings can be selectively bred in the hunt for good genes is now rightly and roundly condemned, and the eugenics label utterly abhorred as both monstrous and intellectually incoherent. Gregor Mendel's research into pea plants led to the discovery of particulate inheritance and recessive genes, which makes a nonsense of the idea that undesirable characteristics could be weeded out through selective breeding. There is simply no way to spot people who carry but don't express a gene. Attempting to do so would lead inexorably to inbreeding, resulting in more, not fewer, heterozygous conditions. Just in case anything here seems ambiguous, let me be absolutely clear: eugenic attempts to raise intelligence are not only morally repugnant, they are also deeply stupid.

Simply denying that there are differences in the IQ scores of different groups won't help anyone or solve anything. This is the moralistic fallacy.* It makes no logical sense to leap from 'what ought to be' to 'what is' and claim that the way we would like things to be is the way they actually are – or, in this case, because everyone ought to be treated equally that there are no meaningful genetic differences between different people. Acknowledging that the difference exists and seeking to alter 'what is' to be more in line with 'what ought to be' seems to be the fairest possible approach. Ignoring or explaining away these differences is only in the interest of privileged groups and acts to discriminate against the most disadvantaged.

The good news is that in recent years, with a rise in the affluence of black communities, some of the disparities are beginning to fade and the difference in average IQ scores narrowed by over 5 points between 1972 and 2002.[19] While this should not make us complacent, it is further evidence of the powerful effect of the environment and an encouragement to those who believe that we can make children cleverer.

The Larkin hypothesis

Being a parent is a terrifying responsibility. The poet Philip Larkin warns, "They fuck you up, your mum and dad." The message of his poem, 'This Be the Verse', is that parents cannot help but pass on their failings to their children, and that the reason we are as we are is an inevitable consequence of how we were brought up. The thought that I probably can't help filling my daughters with my faults can seem an alarming inevitability, but one of the most troubling truths I've had to grapple with as a parent is that parenting doesn't really matter. OK, that's not quite right: parenting matters a great deal in how happy we make our children's childhoods and in how our relationships with them evolve into adulthood. But the simultaneously terrifying and liberating finding from behaviour genetics and developmental psychology is that the effects of parenting wear off almost completely by adulthood. As we'll see, the reason we're like our parents is

---

*   The assumption that an aspect of nature which has socially unpleasant consequences cannot exist. Its converse is the naturalistic fallacy: that which is natural is automatically good.

that we share half of their DNA. Estimates vary but it's generally agreed that the portion of IQ variance which is accounted for by our genes rises from about 50% in childhood to around 80% in adulthood. And the proportion that is due to our shared environment (parenting) starts at about 30% and washes out almost entirely by adulthood. At the same time, other environmental effects (usually referred to as 'non-shared environment') become increasingly important, with education and peer groups taking over the role of parents.

Just in case you weren't concentrating, I'll say it again: roughly half the differences between how we turn out are attributable to our genes, half to the peer groups we choose for ourselves and approximately none to the way we were raised.

Before I get into explaining the evidence for such a preposterous sounding claim, I want you to think about accents. Both my parents spoke with a typically neutral, middle-class, standard English accent. My father grew up in Cheshire and his parents had the lovely flat vowels of northern England. He passed the 11-plus and went to a grammar school where he made friends with bright boys from mainly middle-class families, and the accent he developed as an adult reflects this influence. My mother was born in Ireland to fairly well-off Irish Protestant parents. My Irish grandparents' accents weren't like those of most people I've since met in Ireland – I can only describe their accents as 'posh Irish' – but they sounded nothing like my mum. Her family relocated to England when she was 9 and, as she tells it, she was victimised mercilessly by both her teachers and the other children in class for sounding like a 'bog trotter' and a 'duck egg'. She was sent to a succession of private girls' schools and, unsurprisingly, she learned that if she was going to fit in, she'd better speak the way they did. The accent she has now can best be described as a bit cut glass.

I grew up in Birmingham, went to a comprehensive school and developed a Brummie accent. At home I spoke more like my parents, but at school and with friends I sounded – and still sound – like a native West Midlander. I honestly wasn't aware of how I switched codes between home and everywhere else until, one night, I phoned home from a nightclub in central Birmingham – I must have been all of 15 – to leave an answerphone message explaining that I would, yet again, be late home. Next morning, or probably more accurately afternoon, when I finally surfaced, my mother thanked me for leaving the message, but said, "Oh, David, you do sound common." While I could see she meant it despairingly, something inside me thrilled. My main aim in life was to be as little like my parents as possible and this new piece of evidence was proof that I was succeeding.

My own children sound, more or less, like their mum. My wife married beneath her and speaks like a lady. We live in Bristol and for a while we worried that the girls would grow up speaking 'Brizzle', as the local dialect is fondly referred to.* Apart from one memorable lapse, when my youngest daughter, on being told she had to walk home by herself and noting the cloudy sky, asked, "What be I do if it rains?" they speak perfectly normally. This surprised me at first, but being aspirational, middle-class parents, we moved house so we would be within the catchment area of the school we wanted them to attend. Judging by the house prices, lots of other similar parents seem to have made the same calculation and, as a result, my daughters' friends all sound like their parents, who (how weird is this?) sound a bit like us. Not the same, but enough alike that the girls' peer groups, very deliberately, don't want to speak like West Country bumpkins.

Now, this is all entirely anecdotal, but I'm sure you've spotted the pattern: we end up sounding more like our peer groups than we do our parents. If this is true of accent, might it not be true of other things? To consider that question, we need to understand a bit about group socialisation theory and the research of Judith Rich Harris.

Harris was an academic outsider. After being told by Harvard University that she didn't have what it takes to study for a doctorate in psychology, she contented herself with writing textbooks on developmental psychology. From her outsider vantage point, she began to notice inconsistencies between what the research said and what she observed in the world. Textbooks on developmental psychology were very clear: children's characters were shaped partly through the pressures of heritability (nature) and partly by the environment provided by their parents (nurture). But why was it, she wondered, that the children of her Russian immigrant neighbours spoke perfectly inflected American English? Why didn't they at least have their parents' Russian accents? And why was it that, in 19th

---

* If you've never heard it before, imagine a cross between a farmer and a pirate.

century Britain, scions of the aristocracy were brought up by nannies, sent off to prep school at the age of 7 and thence on to Eton, Harrow or Rugby, before ending up at Oxbridge, and still managed to sound exactly like their fathers when, if they were lucky, they only saw their parents for brief intervals at infrequent points dotted throughout the year?

If two adopted children are brought up in the same home they will be no more similar in personality than two adopted children raised in completely different homes. Similarly, a pair of identical twins reared in the same home are not much more alike than twins reared in separate homes. As everyone knows, identical twins share 100% of their genetic material,* but despite this there are often observable differences in their behaviour and personalities. What accounts for these differences is referred to as 'the environment'. Behaviour geneticists have identified two broad categories of environmental effects: *shared* and *non-shared*. Shared environmental effects are those that siblings have in common and, by definition, these cannot account for the differences between identical twins because, if they are raised in the same family, they share them. Therefore, all differences must be non-shared in origin. Essentially these are environmental factors that are unique to each twin. Possibly they have different friends, maybe they're in different classes at school and so have different teachers and so on.

This is not to say that parenting has no impact – clearly it has a huge impact on the environment a child experiences – but this doesn't account for the differences between people brought up in that environment. This runs counter to every parent's lived experience. We see our children ape our mannerisms and take on our beliefs and values – how could this not be the result of parenting? As with accent, so with religious belief: we only retain the beliefs of our parents to the degree that they are not in conflict with those of our peers.

Since 1979, the Minnesota Twin Family Study has been tracking down and reuniting pairs of separated twins from all around the world and collecting data on their personalities and IQs. Other studies have focused on comparing the IQs of adopted children to their adoptive parents. Taken together, these studies present an intriguing picture. The IQ score of the same person taking a test on different days would produce a correlation

---

*   Except for a few minute mutations.

of about 0.87. The scores of identical twins raised together produce a correlation of 0.86. This suggests that the IQs of identical twins brought up in the same family are pretty much indistinguishable. So far, so predictable. But the scores of identical twins raised apart produce a correlation of 0.76. When compared to fraternal twins raised together (0.55) and biological siblings (0.47), this is impressive. The scores of parents and children living together is 0.4, whereas parents and children living apart is 0.31. Not much different. The real shock is that there is no more correlation between adoptive siblings than there is between any two unrelated people living apart.[20]

While shared environmental effects are often strong during childhood, they wear off by adulthood. This makes some sense. After all, children have little control over their environments when they're at home. But as soon as they start school, alien mannerisms and foreign values begin to enter a child's repertoire. It's only by the time we reach adulthood that we are free to behave exactly as we please (except perhaps when we return to visit our parents).

Thomas J. Bouchard, Jr summarises much of the research into the role of genes on human behaviour and finds that, "Shared environmental influences are often, but not always, of less importance than genetic factors, and often decrease to near zero after adolescence."[21]

Table 4.3. Estimates of broad heritability, shared environmental effects and indications of non-additive genetic effects for representative psychological traits

Note: NR – not relevant

Trait	Heritability	Non-additive genetic effect	Shared environmental effect
Personality			
Openness	0.57	Yes	No
Conscientious-ness	0.49	Yes	No

Extroversion	0.54	Yes	No
Agreeableness (aggression)	0.42	Yes	No
Neuroticism	0.48	Yes	No
Intelligence (by age)			
Age 5	0.22	No	0.54
Age 7	0.40	No	0.29
Age 10	0.54	No	0.26
Age 12	0.85	No	No
Age 16	0.62	No	No
Age 18	0.82	No	No
Age 26	0.88	No	No
Age 50	0.85	No	No
> 75	0.54–0.62	Not tested	No
Psychiatric illnesses (liability estimates)			
Schizophrenia	0.80	No	No
Major depression	0.37	No	No
Panic disorder	0.30–0.40	No	No
Generalised anxiety disorder	0.30	No	Small (female only)
Phobias	0.20–0.40	No	No
Alcoholism	0.50–0.60	No	Yes

Antisocial behaviour (children)	0.46	No	0.20
Antisocial behaviour (adolescents)	0.43	No	0.16
Antisocial behaviour (adults)	0.41	No	0.09
Social attitudes			
Conservatism (under age 20)	0.00	NR	Yes
Conservatism (over age 20)	0.45–0.65	Yes	Yes (in females)
Right-wing authoritarian-ism (adults)	0.50–0.64	No	0.00–0.16
Religiousness (age 16)	0.11–0.22	No	0.45–0.60
Adults	0.30–0.45	No	0.20–0.40

Source: Adapted from Thomas J. Bouchard, Jr, Genetic Influence on Human Psychological Traits: A Survey, *Current Directions in Psychological Science* 13(4) (2004): 148–151 at 150.

As you can see in Table 4.3, shared environmental effects are very low or non-existent for most traits in adults. Aha! you might be thinking – it looks like parenting can affect 'religiousness' to a moderate degree, and look, various other traits show some small effects. Clearly the claim that parenting has no effect is bunkum.

Well, that *could* be the case, but these small estimates are often equally attributed to measurement errors and unaddressed confounding factors. It's also true that if children experience extreme neglect or abuse (especially before the age of 5), parenting can cause lasting damage and often results in permanent cognitive impairment. While parents should not expect their values or beliefs to be adopted wholesale by their children, we naturally have a duty of care. Making sure they eat their vegetables, brush their teeth and go to school may not result in habits that persist into adulthood, but they make for a healthier, happier childhood. The effects of parenting on IQ seem particularly conclusive. Shared environmental effects decrease steadily from 0.54 at age 5 to 0.26 at age 10, before disappearing entirely. The good news is, Larkin was wrong!

Interestingly, heritability estimates for many traits, including intelligence, increase as we age. Typically, the portion of differences in IQ scores explained by genes increases from 20% to 80%. In very young children genes only explain 20–30% of the differences in intelligence.[22] At this age the environment matters far more. Among the elderly, less of the difference in IQ scores can be explained by the environment. Much will be due to the choices made in adulthood. If you choose to work hard at school, you're more likely to go to university. If you graduate from university, you're more likely to get a professional job. If you have a well-paid, cognitively demanding job, your colleagues are more likely to be intelligent and so you're more likely to engage in stimulating discussions and other highfalutin stuff. And vice versa.

The power of the group

If children's shared environment has little lasting effect on their intelligence, what accounts for non-shared environmental effects? We don't know for sure. The non-shared bucket contains everything that isn't genes and parenting. One theory is that children are shaped to a significant extent by other children.

Harris states that "Children are socialized, and their personalities shaped, by the experiences they have outside the home, in the environment they share with peers."[23] Group socialisation theory predicts that the most important variable for determining children's educational success is the peer culture at their school. In a selective school, parents go to some trouble to make sure their children pass a demanding entrance exam and, although some people don't want to admit it, grammar schools serve largely homogenous populations of parents with similar socio-economic status. Parents' values are handed down to children while they're at home and continue to hold sway as long as these are values shared by a critical mass of the child's peer group. If a small minority of students from different socio-economic backgrounds attend the school, they will take on the values shared by their peers and abandon those of their parents. They will start to speak differently – at least while at school – and because the school is academically selective, they're likely to take on beliefs about the value of hard work and be increasingly motivated by academic achievement.

But if the minority group is large enough – how large Harris admits she doesn't know but speculates it could be as few as three or four – then the children will identify with those most like themselves and be socialised in opposition to the dominant group. Small initial differences tend to balloon over time as groups become increasingly distinct. This has a particularly pernicious effect on intelligence. As we've seen, the heritability of intelligence actually increases over time, so the cleverer you are, the better the choices you are likely to make, and the more likely you are to get cleverer still. Group contrast effects can have an indirect but profound effect on the heritability of IQ. If your peer group values hard work and good behaviour, individuals within the group will learn more; if the group thinks school is for geeks and trying hard is for losers, individuals within the group will learn less. "What starts as a different attitude to schoolwork might well end up as a difference in average IQ."[24]

The stereotypes espoused by a group can have a lasting influence on group members. If the group values hard work then it becomes important to identify as a hard worker. If our group values mucking about and being defiant then that's how we're likely to identify. When we find ourselves in situations where we're torn between two sets of values, we experience what Claude Steele dubbed 'stereotype threat'. Steele found that African-American students performed worse on a test if they were given a pre-test questionnaire which included a question about race.[25] Other researchers have found similar priming effects on women when reminded about their sex.[26] Simply being reminded of our group affiliations may be enough to trigger the associated stereotypes about who we are supposed to be.*

Academically selective schools work for most of their students because gaining status within their peer groups is about being academically successful. This might also explain why children from lower socio-economic status homes tend to do worse in academically selective schools. If there are sufficient students from a background different to the majority, but similar to each other, they're likely to band together around their own shared values and see themselves as distinct to the majority.

Selection is fairer the older you get, and by the time students are deciding whether to apply to university, academic selection is probably a good idea. But before then the effects of selection are more likely to repress the cognitive potential of children from the most disadvantaged backgrounds. Although academic selection might appear to work for the majority of students who attend selective schools, such students form like-minded groups with shared values within non-selective schools and are successful regardless of the school they attend.

This isn't really the problem though. The real issue is that the environments of non-selective schools where those who have failed the selection test end up will exaggerate heritable differences in IQ downwards. Whenever there is academic selection, children categorise themselves as clever or not-so-clever. Groupness makes us like those in our groups best, and instead of feeling low self-esteem at being in the not-so-clever group, children gain self-esteem through gaining status within their group. If the group thinks school is for losers, then they'll feel better about themselves if they muck about and don't try. This is an example of what the psychologist and child development expert Keith Stanovich called the Matthew effect: "For unto every one that hath shall be given, and he shall have abundance: but from him that hath not shall be taken away even that which he hath."[27]

We'll talk more about selection and ability grouping in the next chapter, but for now it should suffice to say that if we want all children to get

....

*   As with many other examples of social priming, this finding has failed to replicate. The debate is summarised on the Replicability-Index blog: https://replicationindex. wordpress.com/2017/04/07/hidden-figures-replication-failures-in-the-stereotype-threat-literature/.

cleverer then we need to address the peer culture in schools. Fortunately, teachers have some real power in this regard. Group leaders can do much to change the characteristics of a group and leaders do not have to be group members to affect peer culture.

Harris points out three ways in which teachers can shape peer culture:

1. *By defining group norms.* You don't have to influence every member of a group, you just need to nudge enough of the most influential members. This then generates a kind of 'herd immunity' against poor choices and bad behaviour.

2. *By defining the boundaries of the group.* We can, to a greater or lesser extent, control who is in and who is out, who is us and who is them. Of course, it's possible for subcultures to form within classes and schools, but by engendering strong social norms we can make belonging to the in-group both inclusive and desirable.

3. *By defining the image or the stereotype children have of themselves.* If we encourage children to value hard work and disciplined behaviour in each other, then we will have done our job; they will police the social norms themselves.[28]

This is, I think, how successful schools in disadvantaged areas operate. They create an in-group where 'we' are different to everyone out there. 'We' feel privileged to be in the in-group and appalled at the idea of what it must be like to be a member of the out-group. 'We' notice everything that makes us different from 'them' and revel in the differences.

You may be wondering what the point of parenting is if genes and peer groups between them explain how children turn out. Does there need to be a point for us to do the best for our children? The point, if there needs to be one, is that being nice to your kids improves the quality of their childhoods. And, if you need further incentive, the one enduring effect of parenting is the quality of the relationship you will have with your adult children: the more effort you make to be kind, fair and supportive, the more likely your children are to like you and the less likely they will be to dump you in a retirement home. If they do go off the rails though, it's probably not because of your parenting.

Why health and intelligence might be similar

It should be clear by now that understanding the interplay between children's in-built genetic predispositions and the environments they find themselves in are crucial to the endeavour of making kids cleverer.

For the sake of argument, let's agree that we're all born with a different predisposition for healthiness and possess a measurable health quotient (HQ). We know genes cannot account for the entirety of our HQ as it's an observable fact that eating burgers and doing press-ups both have an impact on our health. We can see that, as children, how healthy we are depends in large part on the environment our parents create for us. If they force us to eat our greens, get plenty of sleep and refuse to let us sit around playing computer games all day every day then we will be healthier as a result of their interventions. When we grow up and leave home, our parents are no longer the boss of us and we can do whatever we want. We decide whether we want to go to the gym or stuff our face with cream cakes. How we decide will be partly due to our genetically influenced predisposition for healthiness and partly due to factors such as trying to impress friends or potential mates. We mostly stop caring about what our parents might think if we don't eat up our broccoli.

If you decide you want to run a marathon, you could commit to eating more healthily and sticking to a training regimen. For the duration of your training, the environmental impact on your HQ dramatically increases. After you've successfully completed your marathon you might decide to stop training and eat what you like. Then the environment you experience starts to make you less healthy. However, you might instead decide that you love training and pick up a lifelong habit for healthy living. Of course, training will never entirely overcome your genetic propensity for health; no matter how hard you train not everyone can be Paula Radcliffe or Mo Farah.

Our intelligence follows a similar path. As children, our parents can positively affect our environment by reading to us, giving us a positive attitude towards school and helping with our homework. All of this equates to a shared environmental contribution to intelligence. But as children become teenagers, parents have less and less effect, until their adult children finally fly the nest entirely. The environmental role of parents is overtaken by that of peers, choice of leisure time activities, jobs and so on. If we decide to become the cognitive equivalent of a couch potato, we will lose some of our intelligence. If we decide to 'exercise' by reading improving books, being part of a peer group who are interested in the world and prepared to challenge us, and choose a cognitively demanding career, then we should see a boost to our intelligence.

How long will this boost affect our intelligence? Well, how long does physical exercise and good nutrition affect our health? Eventually, our environment will catch up with us. Just as some people develop an intrinsic love of healthiness, so others settle on an approach to life that has a self-sustaining effect on their intelligence. Few environmental effects will be anything like permanent (a serious head injury is an obvious exception) so we have to keep working at being clever if that's what we want to be. This helps to explain why IQ gains seen in early childhood interventions like Head Start in the United States and Sure Start in the UK seem to wash out over time.

Because the environment is so important in our formative years, early interventions will lead to substantial increases in IQ. If this then leads to being placed in an academically challenging school where you continue to experience a cognitively enhancing environment, then the IQ gains will persist. But if, as is the case with these programmes, the idea is that underprivileged children will be given an early IQ boost which will hold them in good stead for the rest of their lives, no matter what kind of school they end up in, it shouldn't be that much of a surprise that the IQ gains don't last.

We should also be aware of how our genes co-opt our environment. As Kathryn Asbury and Robert Plomin put it, "genes are generalists and environments are specialists".[29] Our genes may give us general advantages, but it is up to the environment to provide the opportunities that will shape us into particular forms and send us in specific directions. If you're very tall and quick and live in a society that values basketball, then your environment is likely to change in order to give you more practice at playing basketball, which will in turn have a direct impact on your HQ. Eventually, most young basketball players, no matter how talented, will stop playing basketball. Unless they've internalised a habit of healthiness, they will likely see their HQ decrease.

Likewise, children with a genetic endowment that helps them to perform well academically will tend to seek out and be given opportunities where they can shine ever more brightly. They're likely to value academic success more and thus work harder. They're more likely to experience a cognitive boost by staying in education for longer. Eventually, most people will leave academia and their environment will shift. One way in which the effects of the environment may have a more or less permanent effect on intelligence is in the choices that open up for us. Better academic qualifications correlate well with a more cognitively demanding job, which also increases the likelihood that we will have brighter colleagues. Hence, what might have begun as a fairly small genetic advantage is multiplied by positive environmental factors and becomes a significant advantage.

All of this is to say that it seems plausible that our intelligence is, in some important ways, similar to our physical health. Just as we have to keep working to maintain our health, the same appears to be true for our intelligence. There's no doubt that attending school for longer results in clear IQ gains in adulthood, but unless children acquire a habit for intellectual curiosity and challenging themselves, these gains may eventually dissipate. Just as we're not really sure how to create a society in which everyone develops an intrinsic desire to be healthy, there's no certainty about how to support young people to acquire an internalised love of learning.[*]

By this way of thinking, much of what we do in school would be unlikely to have a permanent effect. But the following suggestions offer the possibility of inducing longer lasting effects:

- Open children's intellectual vistas by exposing them to the most powerful and culturally rich knowledge available, and then encouraging them to critique this information to arrive at new ways of thinking. Never devalue knowing things and always encourage thoughtful questions.

....

[*]   When I say 'love of learning', it's important to distinguish between biologically primary and secondary modules. A love of biologically primary learning is probably a species-wide adaption and does little to improve abstract reasoning. A love of secondary learning is dependent on cultural innovation and does not come to us naturally.

- Encourage children to stay in academic education for as long as possible by exciting their curiosity and providing an environment where intellectual pursuits are supported and rewarded. The longer children stay in education, the wider the choice of possible careers to which they will have access.

- Make what efforts we can to shape the peer culture in schools so that children come to believe it's cool to be clever and that hard work is its own reward. Although most of these relationships might not survive into adulthood, anyone can acquire a taste for thinking more about the world and therefore be more positively disposed towards others who think similarly.

Whether or not this results in a measurable increase in IQ is largely irrelevant. I think we can all agree that intellectual curiosity and a lifelong love of learning are things we want for all children, and these suggestions seem like a reasonable bet for getting what we want.

Chapter: 4 key points

- Our intelligence is partly a product of our genes and partly due to the environment in which we live.

- Although our genes play an important part in making us who we are, heritability is widely misunderstood. Genetics is not deterministic.

- Potential is irrelevant if we don't experience the right environmental triggers.

- Our genes effect our environment (as well as vice versa) – we tend to seek out opportunities in which we are more likely to excel, enhancing our natural abilities through experience and practice.

- Genes do not determine the difference between racial groups – if some groups do worse than others on IQ tests this is due to unequal environmental factors.

- Parenting has little or no effect on how we turn out as adults – our peer groups have a much more substantial impact.

- Teachers can do much to harness the power of peer effects on intelligence (and a range of other factors).

- The choices we make in school are only likely to have short-term effects – we need to develop habits that help us choose environments that make us cleverer.

In the next chapter we'll discuss what else we can do to make kids cleverer, as well as consider some of the things we should probably avoid.

Chapter 5
Can we get cleverer?

Oh how fine it is to know a thing or two.

Molière, *The Middle Class Gentleman*

- Does going to school make us cleverer?

- Are we cleverer today than people were in the past?

- Is growth mindset or brain training a good bet for making children cleverer?

The question of whether or not we can get cleverer is a crucial one for this book, but there is also some evidence that people are becoming more intelligent as a matter of course. In *Are We Getting Smarter?* James Flynn answers his own question thus:

> If you mean 'Do our brains have more potential at conception than those of our ancestors?' then we are not. If you mean 'Are we developing mental abilities that allow us to better deal with the complexity of the modern world, including problems of economic development?' then we are.[1]

If you believe intelligence has a biological basis and that environmental effects are trivial, then you may be sceptical. But as we saw in the last chapter, environment matters. And it matters most for those from the most socially disadvantaged backgrounds. If we were only worrying about the middle classes, then maybe there would be little scope for further improvements, but we're not. The arguments laid out here are rooted in a belief in social justice. The most vulnerable children not only have the most to gain, but they are also the ones *most likely* to gain from our efforts to make them all cleverer.

School makes you smarter

One thing we can be fairly sure will raise children's intelligence is sending them to school. For as long as education has been compulsory, average IQs have been rising. We've seen in previous chapters that education and intelligence have a two-way interaction: the more intelligent you are, the longer you stay in school and the longer you stay in school, the more intelligent you become. To understand how we know this, we have to head back to Norway in the 1960s. The government of the day decided to mandate an additional two years of schooling for all children, but, as luck would have it, they made the decision to roll out the new policy over a number of years with some regions of the country lagging behind others. As a further piece of luck, young Norwegian men were required to serve a period of military service and – more luck – all conscripts had to sit an IQ test. This means that researchers can see the effects of the additional two years of schooling by comparing the average IQs of men from those parts of the country in which the new policy had been implemented with men from those parts in which it hadn't. Each extra year of schooling accounted for 3.7 IQ points.[2] Something similar happened over the border in Sweden where men entering military service at age 18 were also given routine IQ tests. Those with less schooling had lower IQ scores than those with matched IQ scores at the age of 13 and similar socio-economic status but who stayed in school for longer.[3] These sorts of effects have been demonstrated again and again.[4]

There are two main arguments against the effects of schooling on intelligence. One is that gains to intelligence are temporary and tend to disappear over time. This is exactly what happens to Charlie Gordon in *Flowers for Algernon*: although his IQ is raised to genius levels, it rapidly retreats back to where it was and the story ends as it began. Does life imitate art? As noted in the previous chapter, attempts to raise IQ through preschool interventions seem to quickly fade. But why would we expect a transitory change in our environment to have a permanent effect on our intellect? This is just wishful thinking. However, we can perhaps change children's habits of mind and instil in them a desire to keep cognitively fit as well as expanding what they know.

The second objection is that gains to intelligence are hollow. It's well known that anyone can improve at anything through practice. This applies to taking IQ tests as much as anything else. If you practise taking IQ tests, your score will go up, but will you be any more intelligent? Measured intelligence may not be the same as genuine intelligence.[5]

Perhaps schools teach the kind of knowledge IQ tests are looking for; Stephen Ceci has argued that "it makes intuitive sense that much of the knowledge that aptitude tests, including IQ tests, tap is accumulated through directed encounters with the education system".[6] This does indeed make intuitive sense. But why would anyone think that would be a bad thing? Ceci goes on to suggest that the effects of education on IQ are due to the kinds of knowledge schools teach. If a test asks what an apple and an orange have in common, full marks are awarded for classifying them both as fruit, but only half marks for pointing out their shape, taste or that they contain seeds. As we'll see later on in this chapter, the cultural shift towards abstract and hypothetical thinking not only leads to higher IQ scores, but also to real-world advantages. If this is the case, then calling such gains hollow is to miss the point entirely. Indeed, a recent meta-analysis has shown that increases in IQ brought about by changes to educational policy are very durable, lasting at least until people reach 70 years of age.[7]

So, could there be an argument for staying in school indefinitely? If we extrapolate from the Norwegian study, we could assume that staying in education for 11 years will raise IQ scores by over 40 points! Too good to be true? Perhaps. Given that the average IQ is set at 100, this would be a phenomenal difference. Unfortunately, this isn't something that has ever been directly tested because it would require a large scale randomised controlled trial in which some children are prevented from attending school. While many of the children I've taught over the years might have been willing to take part in such an experiment, I think most parents would baulk at the idea.

Happily, developmental psychologists Sorel Cahan and Nora Cohen came up with a nifty experimental design that circumvented this problem.[8] They used the fact that in a given school year children's ages can vary by up to a year. My youngest daughter was born in August, right before the cut-off date for the next academic year starting in September. As a result, she's very close in age to children who are a whole academic year behind her. In this way, Cahan and Cohen were able to measure the effects of a year's schooling on the IQ scores of children with roughly the same ages. They found the effects of education were twice as great as the effects of aging. This has since been confirmed by a number of subsequent studies.[9]

In a report challenging the hereditarian view that intelligence is mainly a product of our genes, Ulric Neisser and his colleagues point out that "schooling itself changes mental abilities, including those abilities measured on psychometric tests". They go on to say: "There is no doubt that schools promote and permit the development of significant intellectual skills, which develop to different extents in different children. It is because tests of intelligence draw on many of those same skills that they predict school achievement as well as they do."[10]

Although we know that education has lasting effects on specific aspects of cognitive ability, no one knows for sure what it is about education that causes the increases. This is important because if we did know which bits resulted in the greatest increases, we could make sure we did more of what was most effective. Douglas Detterman is emphatic that schools account for very little of the variance between students' outcomes, estimating that 90% of the differences will be due to variations in children's cognitive abilities, with just 10% accounted for by schools.[11] While this may be true, few children will acquire biologically secondary knowledge without going to school, and while 10% could be true on average, schooling will probably account for far more of the variance for less advantaged children. Indeed, there is some evidence that the children who benefit most from going to school are those who are most disadvantaged.[12] Keeping children in school for as long as possible is likely to help close the advantage gap regardless of us understanding exactly why, but how much better it would be if we knew.

Various commentators have speculated that the effect of education on IQ might be caused by changes in children's thinking styles, increases in self-control brought about through having to comply with standards of behaviour imposed by schools or the effects of both learning to read and reading to learn.[13] All are interesting potential candidates, but the question of what precisely education affects has now been fairly comprehensively addressed by Stuart Ritchie, Timothy Bates and Ian Deary.[14] They considered whether education directly affects general cognitive ability (*g*) or has a more specific effect on particular cognitive skills. They took a sample of over 1,000 people and tracked their cognitive development over a 60-year period from the age of 11 to 70. The 70-year-old subjects were given a battery of 10 different cognitive tests, and from these Ritchie and colleagues were able to conclude that the effects of education only persist in specific IQ sub-tests, but do not bestow a long lasting increase for *g*. So, what was education affecting?

The sub-tests that showed no persistent improvement were in fluid areas of intelligence like processing speed, working memory and reasoning, whereas tests for crystallised aspects – vocabulary, verbal reasoning and arithmetic – showed persistent gains. It seems that those aspects of intelligence that flatten off are biologically primary modules, whereas those that continue to improve are the product of secondary knowledge. As we saw in Chapter 2, that which is biologically primary is learnable but not teachable, while that which is biologically secondary is the result of learning culturally accumulated knowledge. To explore this idea further, we now need to turn our attention to the idea that intelligence is both fluid and crystallised.

Fluid and crystallised intelligence

In the 1940s, the psychologist Raymond Cattell first proposed that intelligence should be separated into fluid and crystallised intelligence, and he continued working on the idea for decades.[15] Fluid intelligence is our raw reasoning power. It's usually defined as the ability to handle data and use logic to solve novel problems without relying on prior knowledge. It includes the capacity to store new information in long-term memory and is correlated with working memory capacity as well as our ability to focus our attention and impulse control. Crystallised intelligence is the ability to access and utilise information stored in long-term memory. This includes our vocabulary, knowledge of arithmetic and understanding of how the world works, as measured by questions like, 'Why do streets have consecutively numbered houses?'* While both these aspects of intelligence are correlated with each other, their separate existence has important implications for making kids cleverer. As we'll see, increasing

---

* To make it easier to find individual houses. House numbering first occurred for the convenience of the Royal Mail.

crystallised intelligence is relatively straightforward, whereas fluid intelligence appears to be much less malleable.

Consider the example of a Swedish study showing an IQ gain associated with additional days of school. Like Ritchie and his colleagues, the researchers noted that extra schooling had a marked effect on synonym recognition and technical comprehension, while scores on logic and spatial reasoning tests showed no improvement.[16] It should be clear that recognising a synonym is a product of what we know, as is the ability to comprehend a passage of text. Logic and spatial reasoning sub-tests tap into the fluid aspects of intelligence and so we should not be surprised to see that they don't improve. The rule seems to be that education raises crystallised intelligence but not fluid intelligence.

While we might be getting smarter, we're not getting any faster. In 1981, researchers tested the vocabulary and processing speed of children aged between 6 and 13 and then returned to the same school 20 years later to assess a different group of children with the same tests. The later generation had better vocabularies but their ability to process information was no better.[17] Processing speed is clearly linked to working memory and, as we will see, working memory is closely correlated with fluid intelligence. The crystallised nature of vocabulary seems to confirm that we can raise one but not the other.

What IQ test questions are like

As we've been considering IQ sub-tests, it's past time to have a look in more detail at the sorts of questions used to measure each of these components. Matrix reasoning tests are widely considered to be the best test of fluid intelligence because you are meant to be able to work out the answer without prior knowledge.* Figure 5.1 is a fairly straightforward example.

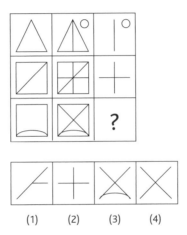

Select a suitable figure from the four alternatives that would complete the figure matrix:

(1)   (2)   (3)   (4)

Figure 5.1. Example of a matrix reasoning question

They can get a lot harder.

An example of something that would test crystallised intelligence is a vocabulary test. Clearly, you can only answer the following question with

---

*   It is probably naive to claim *no* previous knowledge. While a test-taker may not know about particular patterns, most people have had years of experience of finding similarities and making analogies – something the brain is hard-wired to do. For example, we are well able to sit on previously unknown chairs, open doors never encountered before, press buttons in lifts or keys on a phone all based on unconscious analogy-making. Maybe a better question would be to identify the extent of our unconscious natural ability, and where it merges into similarity, and find out what is more challenging and requires conscious effort. See Hofstadter and Sander, *Surfaces and Essences*.

any confidence if you have previously encountered the answer in some other context:

What is the best synonym for dismay?

1. Display
2. Jealousy
3. Provocation
4. Disappointment

A test of verbal reasoning may assess both fluid and crystallised intelligence. A question will require you to engage in some reasoning for which you won't be expected to have any specialised prior knowledge, but the better your vocabulary and general knowledge, the easier you're likely to find it.*

As children mature they get better at reasoning, as well as becoming more knowledgeable as they learn more about the world. But whereas crystallised intelligence continues to rise into our sixties, we start to haemorrhage fluid intelligence from our late twenties.[18]

These components of intelligence interact differently with memory. It turns out that while they're not the same thing, fluid intelligence correlates surprisingly well with working memory capacity. One of the most important things to understand about working memory is that no matter how clever you are – and contrary to the myth of multitasking – your capacity to pay attention to different ideas and facts at the same time is strictly limited. Although everyone's working memory is fragile, there's no doubt that some people have greater capacities than others. This confers a real advantage, and if we're interested in making children cleverer, it seems sensible to investigate how we can improve their working memories. Sadly, as we'll go on to explore, despite the claims of various brain training gurus, it doesn't actually appear to be possible to increase working memory capacity or fluid intelligence – what you've got is what you get.

However, although there is a link between fluid intelligence and learning – making changes in long-term memory – it's obviously true that everyone who falls within the normal range of human intelligence is capable

---

* For an example of this see www.verbalreasoningtext.org.

of storing memories. Due to their greater working memory capacity, someone with higher fluid intelligence will process more information in a given time and is more likely to retain more of it than someone with lower fluid intelligence. But given sufficient time everyone can remember stuff. The more knowledge we possess, the higher our crystallised intelligence will be. We'll explore the link between intelligence and memory further in Chapter 6.

We've seen that the general cognitive factor (g) suggests that being good at one aspect of an IQ test means you're likely to be good at all aspects. This in turn suggests that those people with higher fluid intelligence will also have higher crystallised intelligence. This is probably because a better ability to reason and process new information means you're likely to learn new information more quickly. But this is not fate. As we've seen, there's not much we can do to increase our fluid intelligence, but crystallised intelligence increases as our knowledge of the world expands – and what is this knowledge except distilled environmental influence?

The fact that at least some of what makes up intelligence is environmental is very important – it means we can do something about it. If we make a concerted and deliberate effort to help children to encounter and remember more information, they will be at a distinct advantage. If part of the measure of general intelligence is the ability to access items stored in long-term memory, then the good news is that there's no limit to the amount of stuff we can cram into the brain. Of course, what we know is subject to forgetting, but, as we'll see, we can improve access to our long-term stores of knowledge quite considerably.

The other good news is that no matter how poor you are at reasoning or solving abstract problems, you can still commit facts to long-term memory. Fluid intelligence governs how much information we can process at a given time, and because we can only remember what we think about, it stands to reason that those who think more quickly will end up remembering more. This does not imply that children with lower fluid intelligence cannot remember, just that they may need more repetition and patience. Happily, knowledge is cumulative: the more you learn about a subject, the easier it becomes to remember additional related items of knowledge.

The real benefits become clear when we understand that by improving crystallised intelligence we can 'hack' the limits of our fluid intelligence. For instance, if I know nothing about chess and try to memorise the positions of pieces on the board in Figure 5.2, the task is a formidable feat and I'll most probably give up.

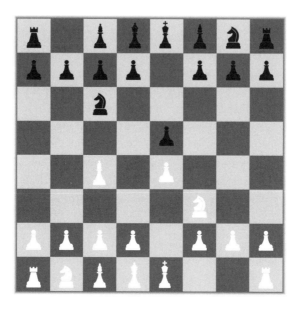

Figure 5.2. Chess position based on the Caro–Kann advance

However, if I already know the starting set-up of a chessboard then the task becomes much easier. Now, I only have to track which pieces have moved or are missing. And if I were a very experienced chess player, I might recognise this configuration as a variation of the Caro–Kann advance. In that case, the entire board becomes just a single item and the task becomes trivially easy. This is how crystallised intelligence acts upon the world.

We'll go on to explore the idea that knowing more makes us cleverer in greater depth. But, for now, let's draw together what we've learned so far in this chapter: that schools definitely seem to make us cleverer and that the way they achieve this is probably by increasing our crystallised intelligence. With this in mind, let's think about the startling discovery that IQ scores have been increasing massively over the past century.

Scientific spectacles

Back in the 1980s, intelligence researcher and political scientist James Flynn noticed something peculiar about the measurement of IQ. As we've already seen, IQ distributes normally across a population. What this means is that we can represent the intelligence of a large enough group of people with a bell curve (Figure 3.4 on page 71).

Average IQ is set at 100, with approximately 68% of people scoring within 15 points of the average mark and 96% within 30 points. If you're in the top 2% (with an IQ of 130 or above) you're in genius territory, and if you're in the bottom 2% you'll have trouble functioning in society. Because scores appear to be increasing over time, every now and then IQ tests have had to be recalibrated so that 100 continues to represent the average.

What Flynn noticed was that the average seemed to be steadily increasing. In fact, it's been going up by about 3 points per decade ever since the earliest years of testing.[19] We don't just get a few more questions right on IQ tests, we get far more questions right with each succeeding generation. On the face of it, this seems to suggest that we're all getting considerably cleverer. In fact, if you scored 100 on an IQ test and were somehow able to go back in time 50 years, you'd have an IQ of about 119. If you went back 100 years, you'd have a score of over 130 – better than nearly 98% of people alive at that time! And if that same time machine allowed an average person from 100 years ago to travel forward to us, their IQ score would now indicate mental retardation. Clearly, it's daft to suppose that the majority of people in previous centuries were retarded, and it's equally silly to think that most people alive today are geniuses. There must be another explanation for what's become known as the Flynn effect.

Various people have proposed various solutions to this enigma, including the idea that test questions have become common knowledge or that we've just got better at taking tests through practice. Weirdly, though, the biggest gains do not come from those questions that would seem to directly assess crystallised intelligence, like vocabulary and general knowledge. Rather, the questions we seem to score better on are mainly tests of abstract reasoning: similarities (What do caterpillars and tadpoles have in common?), analogies (ALL is to MANY as _____ is to FEW) and visual matrices (like Figure 5.1).

But it shouldn't take too much critical thinking to see that similarity and analogy sub-tests do test crystallised intelligence – we have to know what each of the items are before we can do much in the way of reasoning. And as Figure 5.3 shows, tests of general knowledge, vocabulary and mathematic ability have risen, but not nearly by as much. But if matrix reasoning tests are one of the best tests of fluid intelligence, how can we account for that increase? Answering this question will take some detective work.

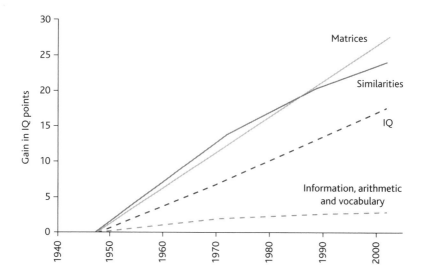

Figure 5.3. The Flynn effect: rising IQ scores, 1947–2002

Source: James R. Flynn, *What is Intelligence? Beyond the Flynn Effect* (Cambridge: Cambridge University Press, 2007), p. 6.

To say that the Flynn effect came as a surprise to the scientific community is something of an understatement. The one thing we can be clear about from the Flynn effect is that it's not caused by a change in our genes – evolution just doesn't work that quickly. As Sherlock Holmes tells us, "Eliminate all other factors, and the one which remains must be the truth."[20] So, if the rise in IQ isn't down to changes in the human genome, it must be something to do with the modern environment. It might seem reasonable to suggest that improved education and nutrition have played a part. Both are certainly correlated with rises in IQ, but no one is willing to accept they could account for a rise of 30 points over a century. As Neisser notes, "Whatever *g* may be, scores on tests that measure it best are going up at twice the rate of broad-spectrum tests ... while the tests most closely linked to school content show the smallest gains of all."[21] On the face it, this is a bit of a puzzler. If general intelligence was rising, all sub-tests should have increased in proportion. If schools were causing the increase, vocabulary, arithmetic and general knowledge scores should have gone up by as much as other components.

However, *g* may be only one factor affecting intelligence. If we are to make sense of the Flynn effect we should also think about our cognitive environment. Flynn himself reckons that social pressures reward acquiring skill in certain areas disproportionately more than in others, and that the biggest social change over the period of these IQ increases has been the increasing tendency to view the world through 'scientific spectacles' and think in more abstract terms. He suggests that this social pressure has caused some cognitive attributes to "swim freely of *g*".[22] Although this is conjecture, I find Flynn's thesis compelling and it's currently the only one which adequately fits the facts.

Imagine, thousands of years in the future, archaeologists picking over the remains of our civilisation and finding evidence that people's ability to shoot had dramatically improved. In the 1860s people were getting one bullet on target, by the turn of the century this had gone up to five bullets in the bullseye and by 1918 people were averaging 100 bullets on target. What would they conclude? That our hand–eye coordination had undergone an unprecedented evolutionary surge? Or that gun technology had undergone rapid advances?

Over the past century, our minds have altered dramatically in the way they perceive the world, but this has nothing to do with evolution and everything to do with the remarkable technological advances we've seen in human culture. Flynn cites the research of the late, great Russian psychologist Alexander Romanovich Luria, who tested Russian peasants with the sort of questions commonly asked in IQ tests. When they were asked what a horse and a dog had in common they answered that both were used in hunting rather than classifying them both as mammals. When given the following scenario: "There are no camels in Germany. Hamburg is a city in Germany. Are there camels in Hamburg?" the reply was, "If Hamburg is a large city, there should be camels there." When challenged, one interviewee allowed that maybe Hamburg was a small village and so there would be no room for camels. Because he was used to seeing camels in villages he couldn't imagine a town of any size that did not contain the odd camel or two. He was unable to ask the hypothetical question, *What if there were no camels in Germany?*[23]

Flynn takes this as evidence that our experience shapes the way we think. If we spend our lives thinking about practical concerns, such as where our next meal is coming from, then we're much more likely to think in concrete terms about what immediately concerns us. Without direction, most educated people might struggle to see the connections made by Luria's subjects. But being familiar with scientific taxonomy and the kind of abstract thinking required to operate a computer is how we have trained ourselves to think. Human beings have, Flynn argues, shifted from being people who thought in predominantly concrete terms about what might benefit them in the immediate environment, to people who think primarily in abstractions.[24] In addition, many more people get a lot more schooling now than was the case in the past, and that schooling tends to focus on abstract thinking rather than concrete facts.

Consider these examples of exam questions for 14-year-olds from 1912:

- How long a rope is required to reach from the top of a building 40 ft. high, to the ground 30 ft. from the base of the building?
- What properties have verbs?
- Diagram*: The Lord loveth a cheerful giver.
- Tell what you know of the Gulf Stream.
- Locate the following mountains: Blue Ridge, Himalaya, Andes, Alps, Wasatch.
- Name and give boundaries of the five zones.
- How does the liver compare in size with other glands in the human body? Where is it located? What does it secrate?
- Name the organs of circulation.
- Name and define the three branches of the government of the United States.

---

* Sentence diagramming is a way of dividing a sentence up into parts of speech.

- Describe the manner in which the president and the vice-president of the United States are elected.
- During what wars were the following battles fought: Brandywine, Great Meadows, Lundy's Lane, Antietam, Buena Vista.
- Who invented the following: Magnetic Telegraph, Cotton Gin, Sewing Machine, Telephone, Phonograph.[25]

With the exception of the maths questions, children today tend not to learn this kind of information. Research systematically documenting the content of school exams between 1902 and 1913, comparing them to similar exams in the 1990s, found that when it comes to factual knowledge, far less is expected of modern students. Instead, they are more likely to be taught transferable skills which, it is hoped, they will be able to apply in a range of contexts.[26] As we've seen, there is reason to doubt that such skills actually transfer in any meaningful way. The consequence may be that we are better at hypothetical and abstract thought, but know much less.

So, have we actually become cleverer, or have we just improved at the kinds of thinking measured by IQ tests? It should be obvious that any rise in IQ scores does not mean that people living today are cleverer in any functional sense than our ancestors. People in the past thought in ways that were suited to the world in which they lived, and so do we. You might think this is a bit of a trick and evidence that IQ tests don't actually measure anything important, but it turns out that the kind of thinking that allows us to do better in IQ tests has important real-world applications. The ability to divide the world into scientifically useful classifications, think hypothetically and frame our thoughts in abstract, universal terms seems to lead to us making better moral decisions.

Flynn notes that our ability to take universal and hypothetical statements seriously has changed the way we think. He argues that changes in the way we reason have improved the quality of moral debate. He recounts trying to confront his own father's racial bias by asking, "But what if your skin turned black?" In response, his father, a man born in 1885, would reply by saying, "That is the dumbest thing you've ever said – whom do you know whose skin has ever turned black?"[27]

If you can't take seriously the idea that you could be black, then you are less able to empathise. If you can universalise your moral principles and see how they would apply to other people in other situations, then you are more likely to make better decisions. Stephen Pinker speculates that this may have led to a moral Flynn effect, "in which an accelerating escalator of reason carried us away from impulses that lead to violence".[28] He reviews the fact that consensus attitudes towards ethnic minorities and women 100 years ago are considered disgustingly immoral by today's standards. We find it hard to imagine that Thomas Jefferson was a slave owner, that Theodore Roosevelt described Native Americans as "squalid savages",[29] that Woodrow Wilson was an admirer of the Ku Klux Klan[30] or that Winston Churchill could describe Indians as "a beastly people with a beastly religion".[31] Such sentiments are now so beyond the political pale that to most people they are unthinkable, let alone unsayable. It wasn't just politicians who thought this way, many writers including T. S. Eliot, D. H. Lawrence, Virginia Woolf, George Bernard Shaw and Gustave Flaubert expressed similarly contemptible racist ideas.[32]

Has our growing fluency with abstract reasoning and hypothetical thinking helped us to overcome such prejudice? Well, as recent elections in Europe and the United States have demonstrated, racism is alive and well, although it is perhaps more muted and far less mainstream. More tellingly, we know that the higher your IQ, the less likely you are to commit violent crime,[33] the more inclined you are to cooperate with others[34] and more likely you are to be politically liberal.[35] This is just the beginning of a long list of correlations between higher intelligence and more moral behaviour that Pinker elucidates in *The Better Angels of Our Nature*.[36] Of course, none of this should be taken as proof that making kids cleverer will result in a safer, fairer society, but it seems a good bet.

There is, however, a potential downside to all this. Even if the ability to think hypothetically generally allows us to be more empathetic, the fact that children are often ignorant about the facts of the world in which they live severely curtails their ability to think rationally. If today we are unable to answer questions like those on pages 126–127, then we are unable to think about those things. The implications for this will become clearer in later chapters.

Some scientists have argued that the Flynn effect may be coming to an end. They point to the fact that the rise in IQ in undeveloped countries is far steeper than that in the developed world.[37] Other reviews suggest that the Flynn effect shows no immediate signs of petering out, even in the most developed countries.[38] Whatever the cause – and Flynn's idea of 'scientific spectacles' seems as good an explanation as any – it may be slowing down but, despite some evidence to the contrary, it doesn't seem to be going away.[*]

Four legs growth, two legs fixed

Perhaps the most popular of the current approaches to raising children's intelligence is Carol Dweck's growth mindset – the idea that we can become cleverer by *believing* we can become cleverer. This is a beguiling idea, but is it more than just wishful thinking? After all, if wishes were fishes we'd all have salmon for supper. Obviously, no one becomes an astronaut just because they believe they can. This is mindset-lite: the undifferentiated and naive belief that the right kind of thinking leads to wonderful things. Like most well-intentioned educational fads, there's a kernel of truth in these sorts of claims. Hard work *does* make a difference; beliefs *do* matter. As always, though, reality is a little more complicated.

Dweck argues that how children attribute their successes and failures affects how they respond to the challenges and obstacles they face in life. Some people possess an 'incremental theory' of intelligence – what has become known as a growth mindset. This means they tend to see ability as something that can be increased with effort and time. Others possess an 'entity theory' of intelligence – a fixed mindset – and see ability as something that is static and inflexible. Children with a growth mindset generally focus on learning goals and are more willing to take on challenging tasks in an effort to test and expand rather than defensively prove their intelligence or ability. Hence, they rebound more easily from negative feedback and failure. Accordingly, if you believe that your intelligence and ability can be enhanced, you will tend to perform better on a variety of cognitive tasks and in problem-solving situations. Whenever we fail at something we look for reasons. If those reasons are seen as within our power to change ("I didn't try hard enough") then we can do something

....

[*]   A recent study of 730,000 Norwegian men born between 1962 and 1991 has shown that IQ scores peaked in 1975 and then declined at a rate of about 7 points a generation. The researchers have speculated that this decline could be due to falling educational standards and screen-based entertainment. See Bratsberg and Rogeberg (2018).

about it, but if we find reasons that are outside of our sphere of control ("I'm not clever enough") then we're stuffed. It should go without saying that we will be better able to cope when our failure is attributed to lack of effort rather than to lack of ability.

This is not entirely uncontroversial. As we shall see, other studies have been unable to replicate Dweck's original results, finding instead that if students with a growth mindset were overly concerned with academic performance they tended to behave similarly to those students with a fixed mindset.[39]

To find out what kind of mindset you have, Dweck has devised a series of statements like, "You can always substantially change how intelligent you are", to which you respond by saying whether you agree or disagree.[40] Not only are these sorts of self-report surveys notoriously unreliable,[41] there is also a question as to whether we have the same mindset across all subjects and challenges, or whether we adopt a fixed mindset for some things and a growth mindset for others. Most of us cut our losses and give up on some things in order to improve on others. It may be that a fixed mindset about, say, our ability to perform quadratic equations, saves us from a good deal of frustration and wasted time. In essence, the fixed mindset may be an adaptive response – an evolved strategy preventing us from wasting effort where we have experienced frequent failure and where the opportunity for future success is low.

But what if we could change our mindset? Dweck makes some pretty bold claims:

> We found that if we changed students' mindsets, we could boost their achievement. More precisely, students who believed their intelligence could be developed (a growth mindset) outperformed those who believed their intelligence was fixed (a fixed mindset). And when students learned through a structured program that they could 'grow their brains' and increase their intellectual abilities, they did better. Finally, we found that having children focus on the process that leads to learning (like hard work or trying new strategies) could foster a growth mindset and its benefits.[42]

No one would deny that hard work and learning new strategies make a huge difference to how well children perform academically, but hard work and a growth mindset are not enough. In fact, it seems likely that practising more without getting results will probably erode beliefs about self-efficacy. No wonder children learn that they 'can't do maths' or that 'French is impossible' if they're practising in the wrong way. If we believe that the difference between successful and unsuccessful students is their mindset then we could be adding to a potentially toxic cocktail. It's much more likely that a growth mindset follows from experiencing success. If we get good early results then our self-confidence can become invincible, but if we don't … Well, only a fool continues to believe anything is possible in the face of increasingly contradictory evidence. Dweck acknowledges this problem: "Students need to know that if they're stuck, they don't need just effort. You don't want them redoubling their efforts with the same ineffective strategies. You want them to know when to ask for help and when to use resources that are available."[43]

But what about the idea that we can grow our brains? Can such an approach really increase our intellectual ability? One of the central claims made by growth mindset proponents is that "the brain is like a muscle".[44] It's not. For this to be true the brain would have to behave like a leg: if you exercise your leg muscles, you get better at everything you use your legs for. The same muscle groups are used whether you're running, jumping, dancing or sitting in the full lotus position. The claim that the brain is like a muscle supposes that doing one kind of mental exercise would make you better at every other kind of mental exercise. The economist Bryan Caplan argues that this claim is improbable:

> You don't exercise your legs to improve your bench press. You don't even exercise your right leg to strengthen your left leg. Instead, you exercise the muscles you seek to build. Why would 'mental muscles' be any less specific? Furthermore, when you stop going to the gym, your physical muscles soon atrophy. Why would 'mental muscles' be any slower to wither?[45]

And, as we shall see, empirical evidence doesn't really support such a claim either.

Another common claim is that "mistakes make your brain grow".[46] In interviews, Jo Boaler – professor of mathematics education and Dweck devotee – cites research indicating that whenever we make a mistake a synapse fires. But if you didn't know you had made a mistake how would a synapse know to fire? Moreover, it's not at all clear that a synapse firing is the same as your brain growing.

The research Boaler refers to details an experiment conducted by Jason Mosel and his colleagues in which 25 participants were wired up with electrodes and asked to spot whether a string of five letters were all the same (congruent) or whether the central letters were different (incongruent). For instance, the string 'MMMMM' is congruent and 'NNMNN' is incongruent. In order to make it more challenging, participants saw each string for less than a second. Mosel established whether participants had a growth or a fixed mindset by asking them to respond to statements such as, "You have a certain amount of intelligence and you really cannot do much to change it." The survey results were then crossreferenced with the results of the electrical activity recorded when the subjects made a mistake on the test. They found that those participants who were identified as having a growth mindset showed more electrical activity of the type they were looking for than did those with a fixed mindset.[47] What should we conclude from this?

The first problem is that Mosel and colleagues only measured the types of electrical activity known to occur when mistakes are made, but nothing else. We have no idea what they might have found if they had looked for something else. Secondly, it's not clear that electrical activity is in any way synonymous with brain growth. Thirdly, the questionnaire used to establish the subjects' mindset seems like an absurdly blunt instrument (indeed, Dweck herself has said, "Everyone is a mixture of fixed and growth mindsets"[48]). Finally, the type of test used in the experiment – one where participants had no problem knowing if they were right or wrong – is a far cry from the sorts of situations in which people are likely to find themselves in real life. This seems like scant evidence to support the claim that our brains grow when we make mistakes.

Although Dweck's claims appear to rest on solid empirical foundations, there are some concerns that we should address. Mindset theory makes several falsifiable predictions:

1. Having a growth mindset towards academic study leads to better academic achievement.

2. Having a fixed mindset towards academic study leads to poorer academic achievement.

3. Giving students a growth mindset intervention (which focuses on explaining the neuroscience involved) improves students' academic performance.

Dweck's studies, and those of her colleagues, provide impressive data, but – and it's a big but – when schools try to implement a growth mindset intervention it often doesn't work. Maybe you've tried telling kids about growth mindset and how this can turn them into academic superheroes? Has it worked? If it has, great. If it hasn't, the problem might be that either you or your students have a 'false growth mindset'.

Dweck talks about the false growth mindset as a way of explaining away some of the difficulties I have with her theories. Basically, if you don't get the benefits of a growth mindset it's because you haven't really got a growth mindset. You're doing it wrong. In fact, you're probably just pretending to have a growth mindset because having a fixed mindset means you're a bad person.[49]

As we saw in our discussion of multiple intelligences, the problem with a theory that explains away all the objections is that it becomes unfalsifiable. There are no conditions in which the claim could not be true. For instance, when fossil evidence disproved the widely believed 'fact' that the world was created in 4004 BC, Philip Henry Gosse came up with the wonderful argument that God created fossils to make the world look older than it actually was in order to fox us and make Himself appear even more fabulous and omnipotent.[50] Adjusting the definitions of your theory in order to fit the facts is a hallmark of pseudoscience. If no amount of data or evidence can prove Dweck's claims false, isn't mindset theory unfalsifiable?

Perhaps this explains the trouble other researchers have had in replicating Dweck's findings. The Education Endowment Foundation's *Changing Mindsets* report found no statistically significant evidence of impact,[51] and in 2017, Yue Li and Timothy Bates forensically recreated Dweck's experiments and found no correlation between mindset interventions and improvements in students' performance. They say, "Mindsets and mindset-intervention effects on both grades and ability, however, were null, or even reversed from the theorised direction. ... This contradicts the idea that beliefs about ability being fixed are harmful."[52]

Dweck is dismissive of the idea that her research might be easy to replicate:

> We put so much thought into creating an environment; we spend hours and days on each question, on creating a context in which the phenomenon could plausibly emerge ... Replication is very important, but they have to be genuine replications and thoughtful replications done by skilled people. Very few studies will replicate done by an amateur in a willy-nilly way.[53]

This is the Bargh fallacy – the phenomenon of original authors calling researchers who try (and fail) to replicate their work 'amateurs'. This fallacy takes its name from psychologist John Bargh who launched a scathing personal attack on researchers who had failed to replicate a version of stereotype threat which found that older people performed worse in tests when primed to think about their age.[54] Not only is this bad science, it's also self-defeating. If it's true that replicating Dweck's studies takes "hours and days" to create the right context and cannot be done by amateurs "in a willy-nilly way", then what chance does your average teacher have? Despite the widespread appeal of mindset theory, the US study *Mindset in the Classroom* suggests that over 80% of teachers who have attempted to implement Dweck's suggestions have failed to make effective changes in their classrooms.[55]

Another study of the effects of growth mindset interventions on students' grade point averages in the United States had a huge sample of over 12,500 students in 65 different schools. It found that the "intervention reduced by 3% the rate at which adolescents in the U.S. were off-track for graduation at the end of the year".[56]

This sounds like good news but, as ever, we should proceed with caution. The study appears to show that giving students two 25-minute sessions on how the brain forms synaptic connections when we struggle has a small but real effect on students' outcomes for a very low cost. The authors also note that some students benefitted far more than others, and those who seemed to benefit most were lower achieving students and students in schools with "supportive behavioral norms". What this might suggest is that students who have previously underachieved improve when told that if they take more responsibility and work harder they might do better and that good behaviour makes a positive difference to any intervention, neither of which are all that surprising.

Were the results down to students believing that basic ability is malleable, or is it that working harder improves results? The first option – the growth mindset hypothesis – asks us to believe in magical thinking, whereas the second is about how conscientious we are. Beliefs about the malleability of basic ability appear to be largely irrelevant: achievement is all about work. Sadly, although the study reports that growth mindset interventions work, there's no way to determine what is actually affecting results.

More evidence comes from two meta-analyses into the circumstances in which growth mindset interventions are effective. Researchers examined the strength of the relationship between mindset and academic success and found that "Overall effects were weak for both meta-analyses. However, some results supported specific tenets of the theory, namely, that students with low socioeconomic status or who are academically at risk might benefit from mind-set interventions."[57]

Again, this sounds like it might be positive, but over 40 individual studies into the effects of mindset interventions reveal something of a mixed picture. We can summarise the main findings thus:

1. The correlation of growth mindset interventions with achievement is small (correlation = 0.1).

2. The effect of growth mindset interventions on achievement is also very small (an effect size of = 0.08).[*]

3. While 86% of interventions had an impact, this was almost as likely to be negative as positive.

Researchers concluded that it's worth giving students from lower socio-economic status backgrounds, or who those who are academically at risk, 50 minutes' worth of cartoons about synapses and brain cells. Maybe. But we should also reflect on the fact that, as things stand, there's no reason to believe that spending any more time on this sort of intervention is likely to be worthwhile. If nothing else, we should take away the well-worn truths that well-behaved students in orderly, supportive environments, and students who understand the relationship between effort and outcomes, do better than those who don't.

....

[*] In fairness, Dweck refutes this, saying, "These effects don't look so small when you use the right comparisons" (Dweck, 2018) .

What ought to be obvious to anyone who has spent any time reflecting on their own habits and behaviour is that we all try hard at things we believe we are good at, and we all quit things we think we suck at. This is human nature. If we're serious about changing children's beliefs about their ability, we ought to commit far more time to ensuring they can be successful at the subjects we teach.

To be clear, I'm not saying that growth mindset is wrong or useless, but it does contradict research in other fields. It also flies in the face of many people's lived experience: there really are people with fixed mindsets who are actually very successful and not helpless at all.

Can you train your brain?

Earlier in this chapter, we explored the differences between fluid and crystallised intelligence and established that while crystallised intelligence (the ability to retrieve and apply information stored in long-term memory) can be improved relatively straightforwardly by teaching children knowledge and then giving them practice in retrieving and applying this knowledge in a variety of contexts, fluid intelligence is well correlated with working memory capacity and appears to be fixed. This is a shame because, as cognitive scientist Daniel Willingham says:

> The lack of space in working memory is a fundamental bottleneck of human cognition ... if a genie comes out of a lamp and offers you one way to improve your mind, ask for more working memory capacity. People with more capacity are better thinkers, at least for the type of thinking done in school.[58]

Does such a genie exist? Is there evidence that we can, in fact, increase fluid intelligence through specialised 'brain training' programmes? Some people certainly think so. For instance, Robert Sternberg argues that "Fluid intelligence is trainable to a significant and meaningful degree."[59]

Sternberg was writing about a 2008 study conducted by Susanne Jaeggi and colleagues which claimed to show evidence that practice at brain training games transfers to increases in fluid intelligence:

> This transfer results even though the trained task is entirely different from the intelligence test itself. Furthermore, we demonstrate that the

extent of gain in intelligence critically depends on the amount of training: the more training, the more improvement in Gf [fluid intelligence].[60]

Sounds encouraging, doesn't it? Sternberg certainly thought so. He
suggested that Jaeggi's results had "important educational-policy implications, because they suggest that the results of conventional tests of
intellectual abilities and aptitudes provide indices that may be dynamic
rather than static and modifiable rather than fixed".[61]

Practising mental arithmetic improves your ability to do mental arithmetic. Similarly, if you practise memorising the order of a deck of shuffled
cards you will get better at that, and if you practise playing brain training
games you can become significantly better at playing brain training games.
But these improvements don't seem to transfer to everyday measures of
intelligence. The specific claim of Jaeggi's research is that, by engaging in
a specialised form of brain training programme, an increase in working
memory capacity can be *transferred across domains*. This flies in the face of
everything we know about our ability to transfer skills across unrelated
domains.[62] If Jaeggi were right, it would make sense for schools to focus
on brain training programmes.

David Moody throws cold water on these hopes: "A close examination
of the evidence reported by Jaeggi et al. shows that it is not in fact sufficient to support the authors' conclusion of any increase in their subjects'
fluid intelligence." Moody is critical of the way in which the tests were
designed and administered, and points out that far from the training
exercises being entirely different from the tests, some actually seem to
have been specifically designed to help subjects perform better on final
tests. He concludes by saying, "Whatever the meaning of the modest
gains in performance ... the evidence produced by Jaeggi et al. does not
support the conclusion of an increase in their subjects' intelligence."[63]

This is a debate that has rattled on and on. A 2013 report concluded: "It
is becoming very clear that training on working memory with the goal
of trying to increase fluid intelligence will likely not succeed."[64] Whereas
in 2014, a team (including Jaeggi) which conducted a meta-analysis into
improving fluid intelligence with training on working memory found that
"it is becoming very clear to us that training on [working memory] with
the goal of trying to increase fluid intelligence holds much promise".[65] All
this is anything but clear.

Most recently, a comprehensive review by Daniel Simons and colleagues attempted to put the matter beyond doubt. They found "little evidence that training enhances performance on distantly related tasks or that training improves everyday cognitive performance". They also pointed out that most of the studies showing the effectiveness of brain training games were poorly designed "and that none of the cited studies conformed to all of the best practices we identify as essential to drawing clear conclusions about the benefits of brain training for everyday activities".[66]

To the best of our current knowledge, brain training games make you better at brain training games, but they don't seem to result in a generalisable increase in working memory capacity and do not increase fluid intelligence.[67]

Let's think about thinking skills

It's very tempting to believe that if we teach children how to think, they will think better. After all, when we teach children to read, they read better and when we teach them to juggle, they get better at juggling. Why should thinking be any different?

Well, first we have to identify what we mean by thinking. There are two common usages of the term: one holds that thinking is everything the conscious mind does. This would include perception, mental arithmetic, remembering a phone number or conjuring up an image of an elephant-headed zebra. The second use of the word covers the many varieties of unconscious thought. These unconscious cognitive processes are doubtless tremendously important in shaping the way we make sense of the world but, fascinating as the unconscious mind is, this is beyond the scope of this book.

Simply equating thinking with any and all conscious cognitive processes is too broad to be useful. I discuss thinking as an essentially active process and therefore distinct from the more passive 'thought'. Thought is the product of thinking and thinking is the process of getting from A to B. So, for our purposes, thinking is both conscious and active. It is the kind of deliberative cognitive process that can make new connections and create meaning.

So, what might a 'thinking skill' be? Depending on who you ask, you get stuff like this:

- Organising gathered information.

- Forming concepts.

- Linking ideas together.

- Creating, deciding, analysing and evaluating.

- Planning, monitoring and evaluating.[68]

The thing is, these skills are worthless unless tied to a body of knowledge. In order to organise information, for example, you must have some information to organise, but organising information is something we do automatically. Likewise forming a concept. A concept is formed out of what we know, and again our minds appear to be wired in order to make forming concepts easy. As an intellectual exercise – practising thinking skills, if you will – why not work your way through the rest of the list and suggest how any of these items could possibly exist in the absence of propositional knowledge.

As we saw in Chapter 2, we all possess an evolved capacity to readily learn these things. We're born with the ability to organise environmental stimuli into schemas, which then form concepts and categories and so forth. We do this unconsciously without the need for thought. Other things like planning and evaluating also happen unconsciously, but we can also decide to pay additional attention when our experience is such that we're not sure as to outcomes. It might be useful to prompt children to do these things and briefly demonstrate how to do them, but investing much more time than that is likely to run into a considerable opportunity cost (see page 216).

The idea that thinking skills taught in one context will transfer to other unrelated contexts is one of the holy grails of education. But the evidence is not positive. Such transfer rarely, if ever, occurs. Bryan Caplan says that "Though some educational psychologists deny that education *must* yield minimal transfer, almost all admit that actually existing education does yield minimal transfer." He points out that teachers' claims of being good at teaching transferable thinking skills are "comically convenient" and that "When someone insists their product has big, hard-to-see benefits, you should be dubious by default – especially when the easy-to-see benefits are small."[69]

However, if you want to, you can take an A level course in thinking skills.[70] The skills assessed in this course are our old friends problem solving and critical thinking, as well as 'problem analysis and solution' and 'applied reasoning'. Now, of course, you can learn a body of knowledge which includes recognising and identifying biases, questioning assumptions and identifying logical fallacies. These are things everyone would probably benefit from learning about, and they will, no doubt, increase your crystallised intelligence. However, as we've seen, although we can measure raw reasoning power (fluid intelligence), to the best of our knowledge there is nothing we can do to increase it.

Here's the sort of question that might crop up on a thinking skills exam paper: "If P is true, then Q is true. Q is not true. What, if anything, follows?" The idea is that you need no prior knowledge to answer such a question, but, of course, that's absurd. If you've encountered this sort of logical problem before, your experience will be a great advantage. This is a product of crystallised intelligence. Some of the questions on the thinking skills paper are more insensitive to instruction than others,[71] but that just means there's little gain in teaching thinking skills beyond a certain point. Exposure to, and practise at, these kinds of questions improves our ability to answer them but, ultimately, some people are just better at reasoning than others.

But what about cognitive acceleration – specifically Cognitive Acceleration through Science Education (CASE)?[72] The basis of the CASE intervention requires a mediator to ask questions that allow 'guided self-discovery' with children working together in groups to solve a problem. The claim made by Philip Adey and Michael Shayer is that by teaching their science course to 12-year-olds, their English language GCSE results were improved at age 16.[73] Too good to be true? If it were true it would contradict decades of research in cognitive science and be the ultimate vindication for proponents of discovery learning and group work.

In 2016, a randomised controlled trial funded by the Education Endowment Foundation was unable to replicate the miraculous findings documented by Adey and Shayer. In fact, the conclusions drawn by the research team were that there was "no evidence that Let's Think

Secondary Science [LTSS] improved the science attainment of children by the end of Year 8". Furthermore, "Children who received LTSS did worse than the control group on the English and maths assessments", although they do allow that "this result could have occurred by chance and we are not able to conclude that it was caused by the programme".[74] Not only was there no effect of cognitive acceleration programmes on science, there was also no evidence of far transfer.

Despite a significant investment in tailored training, the Education Endowment Foundation noted that "Many schools did not implement the programme as intended by the developer", which can be a problem with educational interventions that teachers find difficult to deliver. It may be that CASE – or Let's Think Secondary Science as it's now branded – is actually wonderful and the poor results are just the fault of incompetent teachers messing up the researchers' hard work, but, equally, it may be that if the interventions are so hard to get right then they are not worth considering.

If we are to accept that something as implausible as minimally guided group work in science leads to far transfer years later in unrelated domains, then we need a spectacularly good reason to do so. This has become known as the Sagan Standard, named after the astronomer and science writer Carl Sagan, who said: "Extraordinary claims require extraordinary evidence."[75]

Psychology professor Douglas Detterman relates his personal journey to the depressing realisation that transfer doesn't just happen:

> When I began teaching I thought it was important to make things as hard as possible for students so they would discover the principles for themselves. I thought the discovery of principles was a fundamental skill that students needed to learn and transfer to new situations. Now I view education, even graduate education, as the learning of information. I try to make it as easy for students as possible. Where before I was ambiguous about what a good paper was, I now provide examples of the best papers from past classes. Before, I expected students to infer the general conclusion from specific examples. Now I provide the general conclusion and support it with specific examples. In general, I subscribe to the principle that you should teach people exactly what you want them to learn in a situation as close as possible to the one in which the learning will be applied. I don't count on transfer and I don't try to promote it except by explicitly pointing out where taught skills might be applied.[76]

Although I've take a couple of swipes at Detterman in previous chapters, in this respect his journey precisely mirrors my own. The irony is that both he and I had to discover the principle for ourselves. In my case this took 15 years of frustration. How much better would it have been for us, and our students, if someone had simply told us what we needed to know? But would we have believed them if they had?

David Ausubel, also a professor of psychology, is similarly sceptical:

> ... it hardly seems plausible that a strategy of inquiry that must necessarily be broad enough to be applicable to a wide range of disciplines and problems can ever have, at the same time, sufficient particular relevance to be helpful in the solution of the specific problem at hand.[77]

If 'thinking skills' are a body of knowledge that adds to crystallised intelligence, thereby making us better thinkers, then, yes, of course we can teach them. But let's not assume that such skills are likely to have any effect beyond this. We should only teach things because we value them in and of themselves. By all means teach children chess or the music of Mozart, but don't bother if you only hope it will make them better thinkers. If you're still convinced of the plausibility of transfer between unrelated domains then I have some magic beans you might be interested in ...

Is ability grouping a good idea?

Does putting bright children in elective environments work? In Chapter 4, we concluded that academic selection is unlikely to have more than a marginal benefit for the most fortunate and is likely to reduce the intelligence of the less fortunate. But is the same true of segregating children by ability within schools? The evidence on ability grouping is relatively well known. The Education Endowment Foundation Toolkit summarises the research findings thus:

> Overall, setting or streaming appears to benefit higher attaining pupils and be detrimental to the learning of mid-range and lower attaining learners. On average, it does not appear to be an effective strategy for raising the attainment of disadvantaged pupils, who are more likely to be assigned to lower groups.[78]

It appears that children who are deemed to be 'low ability' fall behind pupils with equivalent prior attainment at the rate of between one and two months per year when placed in ability groups. Conversely, high attainers make, on average, an additional one to two months' progress per year when they are set.

There's much speculation about why this is the case. It could be that low ability groups are assigned less capable teachers. Top sets are often seen as a reward, bottom sets as a punishment. If low attainers are viewed as unlikely to make good progress then it might not make strategic sense to assign them your best teachers. A second explanation is that behaviour in bottom sets prevents children from learning. If so, it's scandalous that some schools continue to allow classes for lower ability children to be sinks of low expectations and poor behaviour. This leads to another possibility: when children are corralled together by ability, they learn that they are either 'bright' or 'thick' and then rise or sink to meet these expectations.

It's no surprise that we usually experience what we expect to experience. Most likely, you're already aware of the placebo effect – the phenomenon in medicine that an inert tablet triggers a psychological response, which in turn impacts, usually positively, on a patient's health. Research into the placebo effect has focused on the relationship between mind and body. One of the most common theories is that physical responses may be due to our expectations: if we expect a pill to do something, then it's possible that our body's chemistry can trigger effects similar to those the actual medication might have caused. It seems reasonable to suggest that a child's belief about their learning could be influenced in a similar way.

We should also be aware of the Pygmalion effect. According to legend, Pygmalion invested so much love and care in sculpting a statue of the most beautiful and inspiring woman he could imagine that he fell in love with it. Too ashamed to admit he'd fallen for a statue, he prayed for a bride who would be a living likeness of his impossibly beautiful sculpture. The gods granted his wish and the statue became flesh.

Pygmalion's unreasonably high expectations for the woman of his desires resulted in him getting what he wanted. Likewise, teachers' expectations can be a self-fulfilling prophecy. Our beliefs about children have a tremendous impact on their progress and attainment. The self-defeating corollary of the Pygmalion effect is the Golem effect – the idea that negative expectations lead to decreases in performance. Robert Rosenthal and Lenore Jacobson's landmark 1968 experiment demonstrated that if teachers were led to expect enhanced performance from certain children, then the children's performance was indeed enhanced. In the study, children were given a disguised IQ test and teachers were told that some of their students (about 20% of the cohort, chosen at random) would be, in Rosenthal and Jacobson's rather unfortunate turn of phrase, 'spurters', and likely to make sudden and rapid progress over the following year. At the end of the study, all children were re-tested and the results showed statistically significant gains favouring the experimental group. The spurters had spurted. The conclusion is that teachers' expectations can have a strong influence on students' achievement.[79]

And so they can, but maybe not as much as is commonly believed. Lee Jussim and Kent Harber argue that teacher expectancy effects may be overstated: "Self-fulfilling prophecies in the classroom do occur, but these effects are typically small, they do not accumulate greatly across perceivers or over time, and they may be more likely to dissipate than accumulate."[80] They conclude that there appears to be a high degree of correlation between teacher expectations and reality; maybe the reason our expectations come true is because they're accurate.

Instead of teacher expectations, maybe it's actually children's experiences in school *causing* differences in ability. Graham Nuthall puts it like this: "Ability appears to be the consequence in differences of what children learn from their classroom experience."[81] It's a fascinating idea that our intelligence is the consequence, not the cause, of what happens to us. It may not be completely true, but as we've seen, genes interact with the environment and small initial differences get larger over time. Nuthall's hypothesis may be the one most likely to lead to equitable experiences for all children.

As we will go on to establish in later chapters, the biggest and most important individual difference between children is the quality and quantity of what they know. Let's imagine a scenario where two students – Katie and Liam – join school mid-year and need to be placed into sets. Katie has experienced successful phonics teaching and mastered decoding in her first year of school, moving quickly to more interesting and sophisticated reading material. Liam, on the other hand, suffered with undiagnosed glue ear and was unable to properly make out the fine distinctions between different vowel and consonant sounds.* Although he can decode, his ability is halting and laborious. Too much of his fragile working memory capacity is spent on sounding out letters, with little left to spare for much in the way of higher level comprehension. Both pupils are assessed using a reading comprehension test; Katie scores well, while Liam does poorly. As a result, Katie is placed in the 'top set' and Liam in the 'bottom set'. While on the face of it this appears entirely reasonable, it could be the case that Liam is actually more intelligent than Katie but just knows less.

This might sound far-fetched, but Dylan Wiliam estimates that when tests are used to select children for ability groups "only half the students are placed where they 'should' be" (see Table 5.1).[82]

Table 5.1. Accuracy of setting with a test of validity of 0.7

		Should actually be in			
		Set 1	Set 2	Set 3	Set 4
Students placed in	Set 1	23	9	3	
	Set 2	9	12	9	
	Set 3		9	7	4
	Set 4		4	4	7

Source: Dylan Wiliam, Reliability, Validity, and All That Jazz, *Education 3–13* 29(3) (2001): 17–21 at 19.

There's no doubt that some children are more intelligent than others, but that doesn't mean teachers are especially good at identifying which children are more or less able, and it could be that schools are creating

---

* According to various sources, including NHS Direct Wales, "It's estimated that one in five children around the age of two will be affected by glue ear at any given time, and about 8 in every 10 children will have had glue ear at least once by the time they're 10 years old."

self-fulfilling prophecies by ensuring that some children learn less than others.

Let's return to our fictitious students. In the top set, Katie is given more challenging material at a faster pace. Her early advantage is compounded. Liam is given simpler things to do at a slower pace, ensuring that, relatively speaking, he knows less and less. The more we know, the more we can think about and the cleverer we become. This is yet another example of the Matthew effect: the rich seem to get richer while the poor get poorer. Of course, this poverty is comparative not absolute. No one is actively stripping away what children know, but through low expectations and faulty understandings those who most need to progress are stymied and cast adrift on a sea of chance. Children's experiences in school determine, to a large extent, their ability. After all, no one rises to a low expectation.

Of course, as I keep accentuating, none of this is fate; the research reports what has been, not what could be. Conceivably, a school could design an approach to setting in which middle and low attainers are not held back, but we can be reasonably sure of what is likely to happen to children if a school's approach to setting is broadly similar to those that have gone before.

If we're interested in making all children cleverer, we should delay grouping pupils by ability for as long as possible. If some children are holding back the progress of others because they have not mastered basic, foundational knowledge – such as how to decode text at a minimum of 200 words per minute – they can and should be taught what they need to know as an intervention and then returned to normal lessons.[*]

....

To summarise this chapter, the scientific-sounding claims of brains growing when mistakes are made, and the efficacy of brain training, thinking skills and cognitive acceleration are seductive. No doubt there will be many more pitfalls and false starts, and no small amount of snake oil to add to other failed theories of increasing intelligence – such as playing chess, listening to Mozart and taking fish oil supplements. The truth is

....

[*]   See James and Dianne Murphy's book *Thinking Reading* for clear and practical guidance on how to achieve this.

more mundane and less sciency, but there are excellent reasons to believe that we can all get cleverer than we are currently by enlarging our store of knowledge, thereby increasing our crystallised intelligence.

Chapter 5: key points

- The longer children stay in school, the cleverer they get.

- Intelligence is made up of fluid and crystallised intelligence. While we probably can't increase our fluid intelligence, crystallised intelligence is highly malleable.

- Crystallised intelligence is the ability to apply stored knowledge. If children know more then they will be cleverer as a result.

- The past century has seen massive average IQ gains. This is probably attributable to the modern need to think more hypothetically and abstractly.

- Raising intelligence is a social as well as an individual good: the cleverer we are, the more likely we are to make better moral decisions.

- Too many approaches in education disproportionately benefit children with higher fluid intelligence and those from advantaged socio-economic backgrounds, whereas a focus on increasing crystallised intelligence would disproportionately benefit the least advantaged.

- Having a growth mindset may not have much impact on our intelligence or academic outcomes.

- Playing brain training games only makes us better at brain training games.

- Thinking is not generic and so attempts to develop thinking skills are unlikely to make much difference.

- Ability grouping can become a self-fulfilling prophecy. What we experience in school is the cause, not the consequence, of our academic ability.

The more knowledge we have at our disposal, the easier we will find it to make new connections and solve problems we recognise. This thinking is inextricably bound up with what we know, therefore the next step is to consider how we come to know things. What we know is broadly synonymous with what we remember and so, in the next chapter, we turn our attention to memory.

Chapter 6

How memory works

Lulled in the countless chambers of the brain,

Our thoughts are linked by many a hidden chain.

Awake but one, and lo, what myriads rise!

Samuel Rogers, 'The Pleasures of Memory'

- Is memory anything more than a handy metaphor to help us understand where we put information we're not currently thinking about?

- Is there more than one kind of memory?

- What can we do to improve our memories?

- Is forgetting as bad as we think it is?

Your memory isn't just a list of facts, it's a repository of everything you've ever experienced. "Everything we see, hear, and think about is critically dependent on and influenced by our long-term memory."[1] When we think about deliberately acquiring facts we conjure up words like 'memorisation' and 'rote learning', which give us the idea that the process of getting stuff into our heads is a brute force activity that requires sweat and effort. In reality, remembering stuff is easy. Think of all the things you just seem to know: what you look like; your mother's birthday; whether you prefer your eggs poached or scrambled; what an aubergine is; which side of your car the fuel cap is and so on. No one sits down and deliberately commits these things to memory, but nevertheless, there they are. This chapter is an attempt to explain how we acquire knowledge and how it shapes our ability to think once we've learned it.

Memory metaphors

One of the problems we face is how we think about memory. What happens and what we think happens are two dramatically different things. Memory is not a single static edifice; it's both a *selective* and an *interpretive* process. One of the most common misconceptions about memory is that we record events in the same way a video camera does — that we store our memories accurately and intact, as on a computer drive, and then replay faithful copies of these events whenever we desire. This is appealing but just plain wrong.

Memories are constructed based on our feelings about what we are experiencing. We then filter these events through our own unique set of values, knowledge and previous experience. We remember the peak of these occurrences, good or bad, and tend to forget how long they lasted. It is because memories are reconstructed from the most intense of our experiences that two people can witness the same event but end up remembering something quite different.

As we've seen, increasing children's intelligence requires expanding the store of knowledge on which crystallised intelligence depends. When we think about the academic content children have to learn in school, we sometimes take the view that learning dates in history or the names of chemical elements is hard. The idea of learning a poem by heart might seem daunting, but then anything will seem hard if you try to accomplish it through sheer will power. It's not true to say that some children can't remember. Memory, as we'll see, is the great leveller.

The other common complaint with getting children to remember things is that it's trivially easy. Remembering doesn't require thinking; surely, understanding is far more important than *merely* remembering. Can you spot the inconsistency? We're worried that remembering things is simultaneously too hard and too easy. Maybe you agree that it's more important for children to understand rather than merely remember. My contention is that the two are inseparable. Our ability to reason is our memory, and vice versa. Making a distinction between memory and, say, reasoning suggests there is some sort of central system which governs all our mental processes. Daniel Dennett says this belief in a mythical 'centre' which houses our consciousness causes us to underestimate how much processing must be accomplished by the relatively peripheral systems of the brain.[2]

Obviously, it's impossible to understand something you cannot remember – you may once have understood it, but what use is that? Can we remember something we don't understand? The obvious answer is, yes, of course we can. Plenty of people remember Einstein's formula $E = mc^2$ or the mnemonic Richard Of York Gave Battle In Vain. That doesn't mean they comprehend how light is dispersed through a prism or have any kind of understanding of how nuclear power works. Isn't this evidence of remembering without understanding? Well, no. If I remember an item of knowledge, like a formula or mnemonic, then I *understand* what this item is. I *know* it's different from understanding a complex scientific theory. My problem is that I *neither understand nor remember* the theories – I merely know what I don't know. But if I laboured mightily to understand these concepts then I would also remember them, at least for as long as I was able to use my understanding to act appropriately. When the memory fades, so does the understanding.

Plato expressed the same idea much more eloquently:

> Now see if it is possible in the same manner to possess knowledge without having it. Suppose a person had caught wild birds, doves or any other sort, and built a dove-cage in his dwelling and fed them. In a certain way we should say he always had them, because he possesses them. ...
>
> In another sense we should say he has none of them, but he has got a power over them, since he has made them subject to him in a domestic enclosure of his own. He can take and hold them when he likes, catching any one he wishes, and he can let it go again. And it is up to him to do this as often as he thinks proper.[3]

Simply having the birds isn't enough; you have to catch them when you need them. Through reasoning and understanding we can learn when and how to catch the birds we need. As Dennett puts it, "Learning to reason is, in effect, learning knowledge retrieval strategies."[4]

Human beings have been speculating about the vagaries of memory for thousands of years, and as far back as Plato it's been clear that there are at least three separate processes involved in remembering: encoding (acquiring memories), storage (putting them somewhere) and retrieval (finding them when we want them). Each of these processes might have implications for how we attempt to make kids cleverer.

We intuitively feel that remembering Pythagoras' theorem is different from remembering where we left our car keys, so it seems clear that memory is not a single monolithic edifice but a set of connected processes. These are generally divided into working memory and long-term memory.

Now and then, in my years as a classroom teacher, I taught what seemed to be a successful lesson. I'd explain challenging content, check for understanding, get some great responses to consolidation activities and, at the end of the lesson, the students would troop out happy, confident and certain they had grasped whatever it was I had taught, only for them to have seemingly forgotten it all by next lesson. Sound familiar? How is it that children can appear to have understood one day but forget the next? Well, as Paul Kirschner and colleagues put it, "If nothing has changed in long-term memory, nothing has been learned."[5]

A simple model of memory

In order to remember something, we first have to think about it. We can't think about everything in the environment because we have a limited capacity to pay attention (see Figure 6.1).

Working memory is synonymous with awareness. It is the site of conscious thought. The act of paying attention, of reading these words, of listening to your children complain about how much homework they've got to finish for Monday morning, fills up working memory. In practical terms, our working memories are always active, even when we're not focusing on something in particular. We're constantly absorbing and processing sensory data from the world around us.

Our working memory is used to process new information from the environment in which we currently find ourselves, as well as drawing on things already stored in long-term memory. Anything we think about is stored in long-term memory. Once something we've thought about is transferred to long-term memory it becomes knowledge.

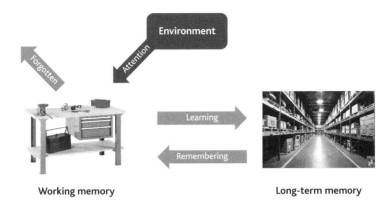

Figure 6.1. A simple model of memory

Alan Baddeley and Graham Hitch's widely accepted working memory model contains four distinct components. The *central executive* focuses our attention on the information we want to process. Where there are competing stimuli – listening to the teacher vs. making sculptures out of the contents of a pencil case – it will decide which should be attended to at any given moment. But even the most conscientious children are liable to switch focus if a bee flies into the classroom or someone farts. The central executive uses three dynamic sub-components to process information: the *phonological loop* which deals with verbal information; the *visuo-spatial sketchpad* which processes visual information and the spatial relationships between objects; and the *episodic buffer* which integrates new information from the phonological loop and visuo-spatial sketchpad with information already stored in long-term memory.

In Figure 6.2, the components of working memory are marked as 'fluid', whereas those of long-term memory are 'crystallised' (we met these terms in the previous chapter). The suggestion is that working memory, like fluid intelligence, is our in-built capacity to process information. As with fluid intelligence, there is very little reason to think that working memory can be improved. But, just as crystallised intelligence is relatively easy to increase, so is our knowledge of language and the semantic and episodic memories we acquire over our lives.

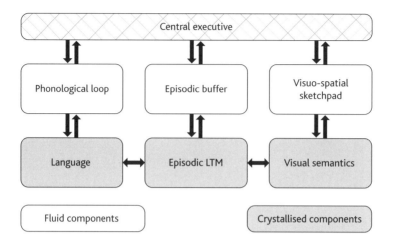

Figure 6.2. Baddeley and Hitch's working memory model

Source: Adapted from Alan Baddeley, Working Memory: Theories, Models, and Controversies, *Annual Review of Psychology* 63 (2012): 1–29.[6]

But what about the central executive? It appears to be neither fluid not crystallised, so what is it? According to John Sweller, Paul Ayres and Slava Kalyuga its theorised functions are performed in long-term memory. They argue that evolution has no need for an additional controlling component and that "an independent central executive disassociated from knowledge held in long-term memory results in an infinite regress of central executives".[6] What tells the central executive what to focus on? Another even more central mental component? And what tells that what to tell the central executive? Instead, our ability to focus on different inputs is more likely to be the product of what we know. As we'll see in the next chapter, knowledge stored in long-term memory prompts us to attend to those things we recognise as meaningful.

Regardless of what precisely directs our working memory, our ability to pay attention is both fragile and finite. We're only able to think about a few things at once before we start losing track and getting confused or frustrated, and if we get distracted, then everything disappears and we struggle to remember what we were thinking about just seconds before. In the 1950s, George Miller suggested that the capacity of our working memory was seven (plus or minus two) items.[7] While this may well be true for holding very simple things in mind, more recent research suggests that for more complex ideas this is something of an overestimate. In 1973, William Chase and Herbert Simon developed chunking theory – the idea that smaller units of information connect together to form chunks or schemas.[8] Even when working memory capacity is at its highest during early adulthood, we may be limited to handling an average of only about four chunks of information at any one time.[9]

Despite the bottleneck of working memory, we can hold information in different components of working memory at the same time without too much difficulty. For instance, images processed in the visuo-spatial sketchpad can be used to anchor verbal instructions and explanations held in the phonological loop. So, if I were to explain what a sepulchre was while also showing an image of what one looked like, working memory would not be in danger of becoming overloaded; in fact, the image would support the explanation. The general rule is that while we should avoid overtaxing any of the individual components, visual and verbal information can be processed simultaneously without overly taxing us.

Not only is the capacity of working memory limited, it's fixed. There's nothing much we can do to get more. This has been explored by all sorts of studies – for instance, when psychologists tested the capacity of air traffic controllers to keep track of aircraft in the sky they appeared to find something remarkable: working memory increases with experience. Air traffic control students could manipulate an average of 23 variables, but for experienced air traffic controllers the number was 30% higher.[10] Isn't this evidence that we can train working memory? Sadly not. Just as we saw with brain training programmes, while practice can lead to notable improvements within a specific field, this doesn't transfer to any other area. The improvement was really caused by the fact that the air traffic controllers had stored lots of information relevant to their job in their long-term memory.

Discussing his finding that most people are only able to hold a very small number of musical tones in mind, Miller wrote:

> Most people are surprised that the number is as small as six. Of course, there is evidence that a musically sophisticated person with absolute pitch can identify accurately any one of 50 or 60 different pitches. Fortunately, I do not have time to discuss these remarkable exceptions. I say it is fortunate because I do not know how to explain their superior performance. So I shall stick to the more pedestrian fact that most of

us can identify about one out of only five or six pitches before we begin to get confused.[11]

What confused Miller can be explained by the interaction between working memory and long-term memory. The limitations of working memory only apply to novel, and not to familiar, information. When dealing with subjects we know well, our working memory seems able to process huge amounts of data. To understand why, we need to consider how long-term memory works.

The human capacity to store information is unimaginably vast: there's more than enough space to store everything we'll experience in our long lives. This is at odds with popular belief. For instance, in *A Study in Scarlet*, Sherlock Holmes tells Dr Watson:

> Depend upon it, there comes a time when for every addition of knowledge, you forget something that you knew before. It is of the highest importance, therefore, not to have useless facts elbowing out the useful ones.[12]

This is categorically not the case. Although the capacity of long-term memory is unknown, there are some clues – for example, cases of hyperthymesia. Hyperthymesia is a condition where an individual possesses an extraordinarily detailed autobiographical memory and is able to recall precise details of everyday life events since childhood. A recent study attempted to estimate this capacity by looking at how much information might be stored at each synapse (the tiny gaps between neurons which control the flow of information in the brain). Scaling up from their sample, researchers judged that the total memory capacity of the brain was in the region of a petabyte (a million gigabytes) which – to give you some sense of scale – is roughly the total contents of the World Wide Web.[13] For all practical purposes, the limits of long-term memory are infinite.

This is very difficult for us to conceptualise because we have no ability to introspect about our long-term memories; the only knowledge we have direct access to, and are conscious of, must necessarily be held in working memory – the site of consciousness. This will only ever be the tiniest fraction of what we know. Because we're unaware of just how much we have stored in our long-term memories, it is easy to assume that domain-specific knowledge is relatively unimportant to thinking. This problem is neatly summed up by André Tricot and John Sweller: "It may be difficult to comprehend the unimaginable amounts of organised information that can be held in long-term memory precisely because such a large amount of information is unimaginable."[14]

Happily, anyone can memorise stuff. You might believe you have a terrible memory, but everyone reading this has memorised many thousands of vocabulary items, hundreds of letter/sound correspondences and a complex system of grammar and semantics. Although it might seem like an impossible task to sit down with a list of these things and attempt to deliberately memorise them, in practice it's something we do with relatively little effort. Children who are perceived as 'less able' will still have memorised vast quantities of stuff: football statistics, pop lyrics and any other information they deem important. The main reason children end up not learning what they're taught in school isn't that they're not capable of remembering it; it's that their teachers don't sufficiently value kids knowing stuff and don't use the sorts of consolidation strategies which would help them to remember. These strategies are discussed at length in Chapter 10. The main point, though, is that everything we've ever experienced is flying around in the birdcage of our mind, whether we're aware of it or not. There are, of course, things we're not aware of knowing or that we've forgotten.

One of the reasons we get confused about how our memory works is that the process of storing information as knowledge is invisible to us. We infer the presence of long-term memory because we must put our memories somewhere when we're not thinking about them. Our memories of events are influenced by the context in which we experienced something and are sensitive to the cues available when we retrieve them. A cue in the environment – Proust's smell of madeleines is a famous example – can prompt unbidden recollection. But the point remains: we have no direct ability to introspect about the contents of our long-term memory, how knowledge is stored or organised, or how some things are recalled to working memory. But without these cues it can be hard to bring to mind what we want to think about. Remember the scene at the end of *Raiders of the Lost Ark* where the Ark of the Covenant is nailed into a wooden crate labelled 'Top Secret' and stored in a vast warehouse full of identical crates? It's safe, but no one will ever find it.

This helps to explain why we can't always find what we're looking for. If we don't know very much about a subject, it can be very hard to remember the few things we do know; but the more we know, the easier it seems to become. When we travel abroad and try to learn a few words in a foreign language, it's tricky to recall them, whereas remembering the same words in our native tongue is much easier. The speculation is that when information is stored in long-term memory, it organises itself into an interconnected web of facts, ideas, examples, impressions and experiences which psychologists refer to as *schemas*.

Schema acquisition

Storing memories is about making links and connections between our experiences in a vast network of interrelated concepts and contexts. This is the aviary within which the captured birds of our knowledge roost. But the birds don't just sit in the aviary waiting to be called upon; what we have stored in long-term memory actively helps us to overcome the limits of our working memory capacity within a domain or type of activity. The more we know about a subject, the easier we find it to think about that subject. While we may be able to do very little to directly improve working memory in a generic way, we can help children to reason in complex and creative ways when they possess lots of background knowledge. The more you know, the more complex and interesting the connections you can make.

A schema can be thought of as an organised framework representing some aspect of the world, and a system of organising that information. A frequently used example is going to a restaurant. The schema for getting a table, ordering food and drink, and paying for the meal makes visiting a new restaurant for the first time, even in another country, a pretty straightforward process, as we deal with new situations by linking them to things we've encountered in the past. Most of the time we can rely on a pre-existing schema as a heuristic or rule of thumb; it requires little thought and acts as a cognitive shortcut when dealing with new information. Schemas help us to get around the working memory bottleneck because we don't need to think about them.

Here's an example of how a schema might form. If you learn a single word in a new language it won't be connected to much else other than the translated word in your own language. Take, for example, the phrase *ni hao*. Maybe you've encountered it before. If so, there's a good chance you'll remember what it means. At the very least you can probably remember what language it comes from. But if you've never seen or heard the phrase before, you're unlikely to remember it for very long. There are few potential cues to help you recall it.

However, when you learn that *ni hao* is the Mandarin for 'hello', all this information is stored together. You now know that *ni hao* is Mandarin and that it means hello.* The individual items become connected together and, when we recall one of the three pieces of knowledge, the rest of the *ni hao* schema is dragged along, making it easier for us to think about the new knowledge we've learned. If you committed to learning a bit more Mandarin, your schema would expand with each new vocabulary item and its meaning, connecting to an ever more complex web of data. Recalling your entire Mandarin schema is no more taxing than trying to remember the meaning of *ni hao*. If you practised enough, you would become fluent in Mandarin. At that point, the schema takes no space at all in working memory because it has been automatised. You never get fluent Mandarin speakers who suddenly forget how to say hello. They don't bump into acquaintances and think, now, what is the word you use for greeting someone? They 'just know it'.

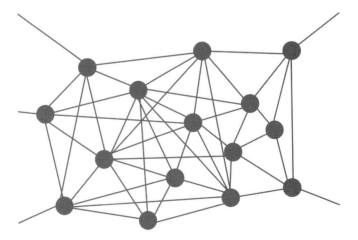

Figure 6.3. Representation of a schema – the individual nodes link to form one interconnected chunk

....

*   More literally it translates as 'you good'.

Thinking back to those seemingly successful lessons in which my students appeared to have grasped a tricky concept, in reality, all that had happened was that they had become familiar with the subject matter. Psychologists tend to divide long-term memory into two separate but interlinked systems: *declarative memory* (that which is consciously available) and *non-declarative memory* (that which can be retrieved without awareness).[15] To have a complete picture of how to make children cleverer we need to understand both these aspects.

Non-declarative memory

What we know we know and are able to put into words is a tiny portion of all we have stored in long-term memory. Non-declarative memory is a catch-all term for everything that might exist in our memory that we are unable to put into words. These are the things we have no memory of having learned, like the phoneme–grapheme correspondences needed to be able to read. Even though we can't list off this information, we wouldn't be able to read without it, so it's definitely in there somewhere. There are other procedural skills that defy our ability to explain – we 'just know' how to do them. This leads to the idea of 'muscle memory'. Clearly, there is no biological process whereby memory could be stored in muscles, but because we're not aware of storing memories in our brain, this can seem like a superficially satisfying explanation. The truth is more mundane. We will discuss this kind of tacit knowledge in the following chapter.

Another aspect of non-declarative memory is the associative memories produced by priming and by simple classical conditioning. Classical conditioning involves an unconscious association between a stimulus and a subsequent response. Everyone knows about Pavlov's dogs: the famous experiments of Ivan Pavlov, in which he trained dogs to salivate at the sound of a bell. By ringing a bell shortly before the presentation of food, the dogs learned an association between the two and began exhibiting the reflex behaviour normally provoked by food at the sound of the bell alone. Unlike conditioning, priming involves making unconscious associations between visual representations, words and concepts. So, if I say "egg", you're more likely to think of a chicken than a chestnut.

Declarative memory

Declarative memories are those memories we can declare: "She is 12 years old," "I used to like pink but now my favourite colour is orange," "I think I left my jacket on the back seat of Peter's car," "Not all Dundee cakes are made in Dundee," "The square of the hypotenuse is equal to the sum of the squares of the other two sides" and so on. Declarative memory can be either episodic or semantic. Episodic memories are those of experiences and specific events, and also how we felt at different moments, and allow us to reconstruct events from our past in vivid detail. Semantic memories are a more structured record of facts, concepts and meanings. While episodic memories tend to be context dependent, semantic memories are stored independently of the specific context in which they were first learned and so can be more generally applied across a range of contexts.[16]

Episodic memory differs to semantic memory in that we often remember an experience but forget the specific details of what actually occurred. This can be especially frustrating in a classroom context. If a teacher asks, "Do you remember when we studied the Vikings?" the children will feel a sense of familiarity and say, "Oh yes, I remember that." But if the teacher then asks what information they can specifically recall about the Vikings, they may struggle to remember anything relevant. This explains why I – and many others – come to believe that we didn't learn anything in school. I remember the episodic experience of being bored and that is the story I tell myself. Conversely, the episodic memories I have of reading in Birmingham Central Library are vividly intertwined with the idea that I was learning. In all honesty, if you were to ask me to recount the plot of *The Master and Margarita*, I'd struggle to remember much beyond the fact that the devil keeps cropping up and that I found it really confusing. In reality, I learned all sorts of stuff at school; I just can't remember learning it. Strong semantic memories are formed when we have to retrieve factual information. This is why retrieval practice is so effective at helping children to learn content.

If, instead of practising retrieval, we simply re-encounter information we've previously studied, we get a familiarity effect: *Oh yes, I remember that*. But this familiarity leads to an illusion of knowledge (see Chapter 6) rather than a fluent ability to be able to independently recall what we think we know. But if we've practised trying to retrieve information, we'll have a much more accurate picture of the extent of our ignorance. Knowing we don't know something is far more useful to us than falsely believing we do.

Eventually, semantic memories may detach from the context in which we learned them, and this can lead otherwise sensible people to believe that they learned nothing at school. What they can remember is episodic – messing about with friends, Mr Garlick's terrible halitosis, being given a detention for smoking behind the history classroom and so on. They may also know loads of stuff – how to read, long division, the causes of the First World War – but have no memory of where they acquired this information.

A number of studies reveal evidence of the links between semantic and episodic memory. For instance, divers were asked to memorise and recall lists of words in four different contexts. One group learned the words on land and had to recall them underwater; the second group learned underwater and recalled on land; the third learned underwater and recalled underwater; and you can probably work out what the fourth group got up to. When the context of learning and recall was the same, the participants found it easier to recall the information.[17] It seems reasonable to conclude that the episodic memory of how and where the information was learned made it easier to access the semantic information.

Conversely, semantic memory may sometimes influence episodic memory. For example, research into eye witness testimony has shown that giving witnesses misleading information after an event can alter their recall of that event. A famous study by Elizabeth Loftus and John Palmer, in which participants were shown a series of films involving car collisions, found that the estimation of how fast the cars were travelling could be manipulated by changing the verb used in the question. When participants were asked, "About how fast were the cars going when they hit each other?" they gave lower speed estimates compared to where the word "hit" was replaced with a more intense verb like "smashed".[18] The language used appeared to create a 'fact' about the collision which influenced the participant's memory of the event they had witnessed.

Similarly, if people are shown a list of words (e.g. *class, learn, chalk, pupil, teacher, whiteboard, bell, assembly, corridor, lesson, detention, book, hall*) and then later are asked to recall the words, about 40% of individuals 'remember' words that weren't on the list they memorised. In this case, *school* was suggested because all the other words were semantically linked.[19] This tells us that much of what we believe to be memories of real experiences and factual data is in fact illusory. We substitute what we actually saw or heard with what seems likely or what we'd prefer to be true. And, for the most part, we do it entirely unwittingly.

Another example comes from a classic experiment in which Frederic Bartlett examined the reconstructive character of memory using a culturally unfamiliar Native American folk story called 'The War of the Ghosts'. Participants read the story twice at their own pace and then attempted to reproduce the story a number of times. Bartlett found that the stories changed in the retelling. A new story would be created from fragments and snippets of the original. Participants would omit material they found unfamiliar, irrelevant or unpleasant, but would persistently recall otherwise trivial details. The reproductions tended to dramatise and rationalise the material to fit the more familiar format of a Western folk story. Overall, the reconstructions were moulded to the framework of prior knowledge – the schema – already possessed by the participants.[20]

We can link these ideas to the problems children face in learning new material when they possess misconceptions related to the topic of study. For example, in a science lesson where students are learning about forces, they will possess a great deal of folk physics about the behaviour of objects being pushed or pulled. One natural observation is that objects will slow down of their own accord, given things like friction and air resistance, after being given an initial push. So, it's reasonable to suppose that you need to apply constant force to make an object keep moving. Even after it has been explained that an object will travel at a constant speed until another force affects it, this misconception continues to assert itself. Unless the new schema is used repeatedly, it's likely that 'The War of the Forces' story will revert to the more familiar folk physics conception.

So, a schema is assembled of non-declarative and declarative memories. Some of what we can articulate is semantic, some episodic, but it's all stored as a biological process in the brain. We turn now to thinking about what happens when our neurons fail to fire. If the capacity of long-term memory is limitless, why do we seem to forget so much?

The power of forgetting

Some of the earliest experiments into semantic memory were carried out by the German psychologist Hermann Ebbinghaus in the 1880s. In many ways, Ebbinghaus was ahead of his time. He wanted to show that higher mental processes could actually be studied empirically using experimentation. His plan was to learn a list of words by listening and then repeating them back until he was able to recall them perfectly, but his problem was that using actual words would result in potentially confounding variables. He needed something simple to remember which had no prior associations and settled on lists of nonsense syllables.

In order to find the relationship between the time elapsed since material is learned and how much is retained in memory, he underwent an intense schedule – often up to three sessions per day over seven months – studying his list of nonsense syllables and practising until he could perfectly recall them twice in a row. He then examined his performance over repeated sessions.[21]

His experiments formed the basis of the well-known 'forgetting curve' (Figure 6.4) – the negatively exponential curve indicating the decay of information that occurs in the first minutes and hours after learning.

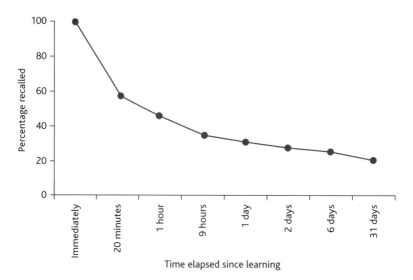

Figure 6.4. Ebbinghaus' forgetting curve

Likewise, the 'learning curve' – how quickly new information is learned – is also exponential, with the largest gains on the first try and increasingly smaller gains on subsequent attempts. Because the curve is based on his attempts to memorise nonsense, we should not expect the same rate of forgetting to apply to other material. The rate at which we forget depends on a range of factors including our prior knowledge, motivation to learn, the contextual cues present at the time of instruction, how long information needs to be retained and, most crucially, the type of material we want to learn. Some things are inherently stickier than others; we're excellent, for instance, at remembering stories.

Ebbinghaus also calculated the 'savings' – the amount of time saved on the second learning trial as a result of the first – and discovered that each subsequent learning attempt was quicker than the last. Most of us believe that as we learn we build up memories which then decay with lack of use. This is wrong. The presence of 'savings' tells us that information we think is lost – such as how to conjugate the French verb *avoir* or the process for working out the internal angles of a triangle – can be relearned much more rapidly than if we had not previously learned it. It turns out that memories are never really forgotten but lurk somewhere beneath conscious awareness. Even when we are unable to retrieve it, information is still stored in long-term memory.

Although it would be foolish to say exactly how much an individual might remember and forget, what is useful to know is that forgetting is both endemic and predictable – people forget at broadly similar rates over time. In an attempt to explain this, Robert and Elizabeth Bjork came up with the 'new theory of disuse'.[22] The old theory of disuse suggested that if memories were not accessed they would eventually decay away to nothing. In contrast, the Bjorks' theory states that everything we've stored in memory has both a retrieval strength (how easily we can recall it right now) and a storage strength (how durable it is) (see Figure 6.5).

Memory retrieval involves revisiting the neural pathways the brain formed when encoding the memory. The strength of those pathways probably determines the durability as well as the ease of subsequent recall. Although retrieval strength determines our ability to recall memories, it is storage strength that governs how quickly we forget and regain information. Some things – like the formula for finding the circumference of a circle or the first line of *Pride and Prejudice** – have extremely high storage and retrieval strength; we can recall these things whenever we need them because we've accessed the memory so many times over such a long period.

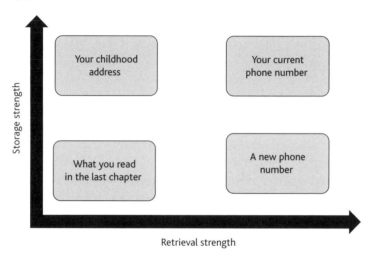

Figure 6.5. The new theory of disuse

Other items are well stored but we're not always able to recall them when needed. What about all the other mathematical formulas and lines of poetry you learned all those years ago? At one time you may have been able to remember them with ease, but now it's a struggle. Sometimes we *know* we know something we are unable to recall – it's on the tip of our tongue but we can't bring it to mind. Just because a memory is stored doesn't mean we will always be able to access it. If you can't find a thing when you need it, you might as well not know it. This is akin to being unable to catch the birds in Plato's birdcage.

Then there are items with poor storage strength but high retrieval strength. Imagine you've just been given a new phone number – what do you do? If you're like me, you'll repeat it over and over until you've stored it in your phone. We panic at the thought of forgetting the number, but once it's in the phone's memory we can relax. But, as we'll see,

---

*   C = 2π*r* or C = π*d* (*r* is the radius and *d* is the diameter) and "It is a truth universally acknowledged, that a single man in possession of a good fortune, must be in want of a wife."

by focusing our attention on something and attempting to increase its retrieval strength, we might prevent it from being stored.

Counter-intuitively, if we really want to make sure we don't forget something, the best approach is to put off trying to consolidate our memory until we're struggling to remember it. The higher the retrieval strength of an item of memory – that is, how easy it is for us to recall a piece of information *right now*, the smaller the gains in storage strength from additional study or practice. If something is highly accessible, virtually no learning can happen. No matter what you do, there will be no additional increases in storage. This makes evolutionary sense: if we never forgot anything we would end up overgeneralising horribly and be unable to act. For speed and efficiency, we have developed brains that ruthlessly prune away those memories that are unlikely to be useful in the here and now in favour of those that offer more obvious survival advantages. Intelligence could be defined as a judicious balance between remembering and forgetting. But – and this is the exciting part – as we forget and retrieval strength dips, when we study or practice there's a noticeably larger increase in storage strength. In Robert Bjork's words, "Forgetting, rather than undoing learning, creates the opportunity to reach additional levels of learning."[23] So, as time passes and we're unable to retrieve what we once could, any re-presentations of information will result in a boost to learning in the long term. Harnessing the power of forgetting might be the best way to increase the amount we learn.

Can we train our memories?

We have already noted that everyone – at least, everyone in the normal range of human ability – can remember. We all know children have no problem remembering what they find interesting, but how can we get them to remember academic content? In Chapter 2, we saw that children, especially teenagers, find anything biologically primary very motivating but tend not to be as interested in what is biologically secondary. Schools exist to teach culturally accrued knowledge, which, on the whole, is an uphill battle. Some school subjects – English and history – have an advantage in that they are constructed of stories, which we find much easier to remember and integrate into schemas. Other subjects don't come with this advantage, and getting students to remember more abstract information is tough. If we're committed to the idea of making kids cleverer, we need to help children build semantic memories that strengthen academic schemas. But this is not easy.

Wouldn't it be great if there was something we could do to make ourselves better learners and improve our ability to remember what we want to know? Remember the scene in the sci-fi film *The Matrix* where Keanu Reeves' character Neo plugs his brain into a computer database to study thousands of different martial arts? After a few seconds he jerks awake and says, "I know kung fu!" It's a wonderful idea, but sadly the emphasis here is on fiction rather than science. But are there real ways we can speed up the arduous process of learning?

The story of science journalist turned memory champion Joshua Foer offers some hope. In *Moonwalking with Einstein*, he recounts going, as a budding journalist, to cover the US memory championship in New York.[24] He was blown away to find people who could perform these incredible feats of memory. They could remember the order of a shuffled deck of cards in minutes or memorise pi to thousands of decimal places. We often talk about people with great memories as though it were some sort of innate gift they possess, but that's not the case. All of the memory athletes he interviewed insisted they were perfectly ordinary people with entirely ordinary memories. They had simply learned a set of tricks. One of these athletes offered to train him, and Foer promptly agreed. He spent the next year in training and then, one year later, he was back at the US memory championship. And, incredibly, he won.

So, what's the secret? Foer says, "We remember when we are able to take a piece of information and experience it. We remember when we pay attention. We remember when we are deeply engaged."[25] Most importantly, we remember when we transform new information so that it fits into the interconnected webs of our schemas and 'makes sense'. He suggests a process called elaborative encoding, which is really just a fancy way of saying that information should be made more meaningful. Consider the Baker/baker paradox. We are much more likely to be able to remember that someone has the job of a baker than we are to remember that their name is Baker. That's because we have all sorts of rich associations with bakers: the smell of fresh bread, flour dusted aprons, white paper hats. Whereas the name Baker is essentially meaningless; it doesn't connect to anything else we know.[26]

The ancient technique of the method of loci is one way to take advantage of our brain's excellent visuo-spatial memory.* Essentially, you create intense visual images of whatever you want to remember – the more ridiculous and, apparently, the more erotic, the better – and then place these images along a path in a building or location with which you're familiar. Then, when you mentally retrace your route, you simply scoop up the images and decode them into the information you were trying to store.

What if we could use these techniques to store things like the complete works of Shakespeare? While this might be something everybody could learn, it's not something that would be possible without a great deal of effort. It may be worth getting children to focus on acquiring these elaborative techniques in order to memorise some basic factual information for examinations, but I'm not sure it's worth the effort for longer term projects. Certainly, the time required would mean there wouldn't be much left to cover the breadth of abstract academic concepts children need to learn. In order to become a memory champion, Foer had to spend a frustrating year of his life in training. Most of the memory athletes he wrote about didn't seem to have many friends. Like any other form of training, it requires continued practice and doesn't transfer between different domains. There is, it would seem, no way to short cut the process of learning.

....

This chapter has attempted to build the case that memory, knowledge and thought are all inextricably intertwined, with each depending on the other to increase crystallised intelligence.

....

* Sometimes referred to as the memory palace, this technique is employed by those who enter memory competitions to remember vast amounts of information. Items to be remembered are mentally associated with specific physical locations. The method relies on remembering these spatial relationships to establish, order and recollect unrelated, context-less information.

Chapter 6: key points

- Memory doesn't work in the way we often assume – what we 'remember' is actually a process of reintegration and post hoc invention.

- In general, we find it easiest to recall those things we think most about.

- Learning involves making changes in long-term memory.

- Everyone's working memory is strictly limited – we are only able to think about approximately four 'chunks' of information at any one time.

- The capacity of long-term memory is apparently limitless, but just because we've stored something doesn't mean we can retrieve it.

- Information we know to be related connects together in long-term memory to form schemas which make it easier to retrieve and think about. Theses schemas can be retrieved as chunks, giving us more space in working memory.

- Some procedures can be made automatic so they no longer take up space in working memory.

- Retrieval strength is best enhanced indirectly by improving storage strength – the better an item is stored, the easier it will be to retrieve.

- We can train our memories to be capable of remarkable feats, but it may not be worth the effort in most instances.

These ideas will be enlarged upon in the next chapter as we get to grips with what knowledge actually is and how we use it to think.

Chapter 7
You are what you know

'Now, what I want is, Facts. Teach these boys and girls nothing but Facts. Facts alone are wanted in life. Plant nothing else, and root out everything else. You can only form the minds of reasoning animals upon Facts: nothing else will ever be of any service to them. This is the principle on which I bring up my own children, and this is the principle on which I bring up these children. Stick to Facts, Sir!'

Charles Dickens, *Hard Times*

- Is knowledge the same as facts?

- Are skills more important than knowledge?

- What's the point of teaching knowledge when children can look up whatever they need to know on the internet?

Gradgrind was a fictional character that Dickens invented as a caricature of what was doubtless some fairly awful teaching in Victorian England, into whose mouth he put the opening words of this chapter. But he isn't real. If they ever did, no one thinks like that today. Or if they do, I've yet to encounter them.

If you've never seen Hans Rosling speak about the power of facts, you've missed a treat. Rosling was one of the world's great scientific communicators (recordings of his talks are widely available on the internet). No one could watch him speak and come away unimpressed at the beauty and power of facts. Consider as well Charlie Gordon's view of knowledge when he's at the height of his powers – he describes himself as "living at a peak of clarity and beauty I never knew existed".[1] In this chapter we will attempt to unpick this much broader, more satisfying description of what knowledge actually is.

It's all Greek to me

Knowledge is not the same thing as facts. Facts are just one part of a much greater whole. Philosophers have been trying to work out what knowledge is for millennia. When Greece was still ancient, Aristotle broke it into three components which he called *episteme*, *techne* and *phronesis*. For Aristotle, *episteme* was timeless universal knowledge, such as the quality of the base angles of an isosceles triangle, while *techne* was knowledge that was dependent on time and place. *Phronesis*, sometimes translated as practical wisdom, is less concerned with what it true and more concerned with what is right.

We can think of *episteme*, or propositional knowledge, as what we know, whereas *techne* (procedural knowledge) is know-how and is basically synonymous with skill. *Phronesis* can perhaps best be thought of as tacit knowledge and is made up of those things we're unable to articulate and don't necessarily know we know. Pretty much all propositional and some procedural knowledge is equivalent to declarative memory, whereas tacit knowledge, as well as some procedural knowledge, equates roughly with what is stored as non-declarative memory.

From *episteme* we get epistemology – the study of knowledge. Philosophers tend to think about knowledge as justified true belief. Getting to grips with this would involve recapping some drawn out, tangled philosophical debates. We're not going to do that here.* Instead we're going to think about knowledge from the perspective of cognitive science – structured collections of information acquired through perception or reasoning. It doesn't have to be justified, or true, or even necessarily believed; it just has to be stored in the repository of our long-term memory. Our brains are as full of misconceptions, confusions and falsehoods as they are anything else.**

My contention is that you are what you know. Knowledge is all there is. All knowledge is biological – stored in the organic substance of our brains – and everything stored biologically is knowledge. This might

....

* Suffice it to say that, broadly speaking, I'm an empiricist with a dash of idealism.

** This view does not represent a consensus. I would agree that beliefs contain a position which can be assessed as being either true or false, and as being justified, unjustified or irrational, and that those beliefs which are both true and justified ought to be privileged over those which are not.

sound a little extreme and is sometimes dismissed as unduly 'cognitiv-ist', so I'll try to explain what I mean. Psychologists used to believe that people could be entirely understood by observing their behaviour and that behaviour could be explained in terms of conditioning. Importantly, behaviourists believed that the mind was a blank slate, or *tabula rasa*, on which any instructions could be written. One of the founders of behav-iourism, John B. Watson, even went so far as to claim:

> Give me a dozen healthy infants, well-formed, and my own specified world to bring them up in and I'll guarantee to take any one at random and train him to become any type of specialist I might select – doc-tor, lawyer, artist, merchant-chief and, yes, even beggar-man and thief, regardless of his talents, penchants, tendencies, abilities, vocations, and race of his ancestors. I am going beyond my facts and I admit it, but so have the advocates of the contrary and they have been doing it for many thousands of years.[2]

He *was* going beyond his facts and, as we've seen, it's now widely accepted that all human traits are in some part influenced by genes. As we dis-cussed in Chapter 2, there is good reason to believe that our genes have co-evolved with human culture to acquire adaptive capacities that make it easy for us to learn some forms of knowledge and ways of behaving, and that our genes, in part, select our environments.

Behaviourism fell from grace and was replaced by cognitivism. Argu-ably, the so-called 'cognitivist revolution' began with Noam Chomsky's observation that human language has universal features, and that, given the vast complexity of these features, if they really were blank slates, 3-year-olds should not be able to deduce the rules of language given the limited exposure they typically have by that age. He argued that we must therefore have an innate capacity for learning language. This was revolu-tionary thinking indeed, and from there psychologists began to focus on our inner mental activities.*

Cognitivism – and, in particular, the computational theory of mind** – suggests that in order to understand ourselves we need to peer into

---

*   The full story is beautifully articulated by Stephen Pinker in *The Language Instinct*.

**   This is not at all the same as the widely discredited 'computer metaphor' which depicts the brain as hardware and the mind as software. Instead, the computational theory sees the mind as a symbol manipulator that follows step-by-step functions and that neural computations explain cognition. See Pinker's *How the Mind Works* for a detailed but readable explanation.

the black box of the human mind wherein mental processes (thinking, memory and knowing) can be explored. In this view, knowledge, memory and thought are interchangeable, and learning is defined as a change in a schema. I'm not subscribing wholesale to this paradigm, but that's certainly where my sympathies lie. Everything we are – our personality, experiences, preferences, thoughts and feelings – are all stored in memory. There is nothing outside of these biological processes; mind and body are not distinct and there is no 'little man' or spooky stuff required to explain how and why we do what we do.[*]

When we think about who we are and what makes us unique, it's remarkably tempting to consider ourselves as made of something special, something beyond the merely biological. We want to believe we have some kind of immortal, intangible essence, but such beliefs are wishful thinking. Even if we don't want to believe something so numinous, we're still tempted to suppose that there must be more to who we are than merely what we know.[3] We work hard to come up with different labels for this stuff (skills, understanding, etc.) but these can just as easily be seen as synonyms for knowledge.

But what of the common-sense observation that knowledge and understanding are different? That wisdom is distinct from skill? Surely, it makes sense to create separate categories for each of these things that I'm grouping together as knowledge? Well, yes, of course it does. I can group Cheddar, Roquefort and mozzarella together as cheese but they each look and taste distinctively different. There are times when it makes sense to specify them and times when it makes sense to group them together. So, we can accept that factual knowledge, skill, wisdom and anything else you might care to speculate about are – *at the same time* – all knowledge and all different. Giving something a different name doesn't alter its reality. Knowledge is all there is.

---

[*] This is not an uncontentious view and there will be plenty of people ready to disagree with this attack on dualism. The debate is beyond the narrow scope of this book, but if you're intrigued you should have a look at Daniel Dennett's *Consciousness Explained* or Matt Ridley's *The Evolution of Everything*.

Thinking about

My position can be summarised in these three propositions:

1. Knowledge is what we think both with and about.

2. We cannot think with or about something we don't know.

3. The more we know about something, the more sophisticated our thinking.

Intelligence depends on knowledge, and making children cleverer depends on making them more knowledgeable.

Nobody can think about something they don't know. Try it for a moment. The best you can do is ask, "What don't I know?" but even then, you're limited to what you *know* you don't know. What we think about are concepts, ideas, experiences and facts – "nothing but facts". We can think about the capital of China (and know that it's Beijing, despite it being called Peking in earlier times). We can think about the length of the Nile (but this is subject to change with the seasons and frequently altering water courses). We can think about our favourite colour (no longer the pink we liked as a child) or what we'd like for our birthday (as long as it's not the same as what we received last year). Some of what seem to us to be immutable facts are temporary ways of holding the world in mind. As our thinking changes, so does what we hold to be true. Knowledge changes us.

We can think about anything we know at least something about, but this can be a shallow, unfulfilling experience. The more things we know, the more detail we possess, the more links and connections we can make. Seeing these links is insight; making these connections is creative. Knowledge attracts knowledge; new stuff sticks to what we already know and our sphere of knowledge expands until, at a certain point, its growth is exponential. Charlie Gordon, who we've met a couple of times previously, was told something similar by his teacher, Miss Kinnian, after the effects of the experimental neurosurgery he underwent began to kick in. She describes him as a "giant sponge", able to soak in knowledge and "see how the different branches of learning are related".[4]

Is this what intelligence really is? The ability to soak things in? The facts, figures and general knowledge that Charlie Gordon soaked in transformed how he saw the world. Facts or propositions are what we think about. Propositional knowledge exists in the realm of conscious thought; when we are aware of a thing, we are thinking about it. Propositional knowledge, declarative memory and crystallised intelligence are, if not the same thing, then broadly synonymous. As with most good ideas, I'm certainly not the first to have thought this. The psychologist John Anderson developed a theory of cognition that he called Adaptive Control of Thought (ACT) in which he stated, "All that there is to intelligence is the simple accrual and tuning of many small units of knowledge that in total produce complex cognition. The whole is no more than the sum of its parts, but it has a lot of parts."[5]

This is something of an understatement. There are many more parts than we will ever be aware of, and the factual, propositional knowledge we possess is just the small part we are able to bring deliberately to mind.

Some examples of propositional knowledge:

- A horse is a quadruped.

- 85% of the people in the world live in 'developed' countries.

- The language Ewoks speak in *Return of the Jedi* is based on ancient Tibetan.

- Brain scans clearly show that we use most of our brain most of the time, even when we're sleeping.

- Cleopatra was born 2,500 years after the Great Pyramid of Giza was built, yet only 2,000 years before the first lunar landing was achieved.

- Ostriches do not bury their heads in the sand to avoid danger.

Are they reasonable? Are they verifiably true? Do you believe them?

Think for a moment about how you felt on reading the list. The first item probably reminded you of the quote from *Hard Times* that opened this chapter. Did that alter the way you thought about it? Maybe some of the propositions surprised you. Maybe you did believe ostriches really do stick their heads in the sand at the sign of danger.* Maybe you still

---

*   In fact, ostriches tend to lie down flat on the ground when they feel threatened.

do and you think I must be wrong, but how would they avoid suffocation? And, for that matter, how would they avoid predators? Moving on, can it really be true that 85% of the world's population live in developed countries? Everyone knows that most of the world's population live in poverty, right?*

Perhaps you have no strong feelings about ostriches or where people live and are inclined to believe these new facts. Perhaps you will verify them later. We change our beliefs all the time and as they change, so do we. It's only rarely that such changes are noticeable, but many small changes have an incremental effect. Slowly, or quickly, knowledge alters who we are.

All of these propositions are formed from a variety of different facts. Think about the one about Cleopatra. You not only have to know who she was, you also have to know what the Great Pyramid is, where Giza is, how these relate to Cleopatra, and something about the moon landings and the scientific progress that led to that moment in human history. You probably also have to know something about time; the fact that 2,000 years is a huge chunk of human history and that the civilisation of ancient Egypt is almost unimaginably old.

While they rely on lots of unstated knowledge, all these propositions are expressed in language. Thinking about these propositions can have the quality of an internal conversation between different perspectives. And while we catch glimpses of thought untethered to language, we can only really think about what we can put into words. That said, the idea that we think in English (or any other language) may be an illusion. The language of thought – call it 'mentalese' – is far more efficient and direct than spoken language, with all its trappings of grammar needed to communicate an idea from one mind to another, but this is something of which we are unaware. Of course, we can have thoughts we're unable to express, but we struggle to think *about* anything without being able to say it. This is something we can test: try thinking about something you cannot say. Hard, isn't it?

Words, and their meanings, are all facts. But, although it can be difficult to discuss concepts for which you have no words, propositional knowledge is much more than a mere list of unconnected facts. Speaking about

---

* You *really* need to read Hans Rosling's remarkable book, *Factfulness*.

his knowledge of birds, everyone's favourite physicist, Richard Feynman, put it like this:

> You can know the name of a bird in all the languages of the world, but when you're finished, you'll know absolutely nothing whatever about the bird ... So let's look at the bird and see what it's doing – that's what counts. I learned very early the difference between knowing the name of something and knowing something.[6]

It's easy to belittle the idea that knowing what things are called is useful. Of course, simply knowing the name of something is quite different from apprehending the thing itself. Knowing that Einstein came up with the special theory of relativity tells you absolutely nothing whatsoever about what the theory means. That second kind of knowing – understanding, if you prefer – requires more facts. The more you know about a thing, the better your understanding. The more you understand it, the better you'll know it.

This is the distinction between *inflexible* and *flexible* knowledge. Knowledge is flexible when it is not tied to superficial features and can be applied to a wide range of contexts. For instance, knowing that Henry II was a medieval king is *in*flexible. It tells you absolutely nothing whatsoever about who Henry was or what it meant to be a medieval monarch. Knowing what medieval kingship entails is flexible and can be deployed to think more widely about a period of history. What we ultimately want is for children to have a flexible understanding that can be applied to a wide variety of new situations, but this is unlikely to occur spontaneously.

Cognitive scientist Daniel Willingham puts it like this:

> Inflexible knowledge is meaningful, but narrow; it's narrow in that it is tied to the concept's surface structure, and the deep structure of the concept is not easily accessed. 'Deep structure' refers to a principle that transcends specific examples; 'surface structure' refers to the particulars of an example meant to illustrate deep structure.[7]

The obvious solution would be to encourage children to think about what we want them to know in deeper, more abstract terms, so they will be better able to generalise what they learn to new contexts. As we'll see in Chapter 9, this doesn't work. In practice, children need to fix their knowledge, however inflexible, in order to incrementally arrive at greater understanding. Knowing inflexibly is a necessary stepping stone to more flexible knowledge.

Even though knowing the name of something may be an inflexible form of knowledge, does that mean learning names isn't worth the effort? Not at all, says Feynman, "knowing the names of things is useful if you want to talk to somebody else – so you can tell them what you're talking about".[8] And this is the point: we use names and labels for reasons of expediency. While I can say, "The theory which determined that the laws of physics are the same for all non-accelerating observers, which shows that the speed of light within a vacuum is the same no matter the speed at which an observer travels," it's quicker and easier to chunk this information as "Einstein's special theory of relativity". Likewise, I can say, "You can use a piece of punctuation that looks like a dot floating above a comma to connect two bits of a sentence if both bits make sense on their own and are also closely related," but this is confusing and time consuming. How much more efficient it would be if I had the schematic knowledge to be able to say, "A semicolon connects two closely related independent clauses." Not only is this more straightforward, it's less ambiguous and consumes less working memory. The act of chunking facts together helps to make them more flexible, and when knowledge becomes flexible we can think with it as well as about it.

Inflexible ideas can be learned by rote. I can memorise a fact such as "commas are used to separate clauses in a sentence", but just knowing this won't necessarily help me to write a better punctuated sentence. On its own it's too abstract to be useful. For this reason, children learn proxies like "put a comma where you take a breath". This sounds plausible and contains knowledge that can be applied, but what if you've just been for a run? What if you have asthma? The limits of inflexible knowledge rapidly become clear. The antidote is more knowledge. I have to show you how to use a comma in a wide variety of contexts and then get you to practise writing correctly punctuated sentences.

Similarly, I can learn the names of all the European capital cities or memorise the times tables, but that doesn't suggest that I will be able to apply this information in any situation other than being directly asked, "What is the capital of Latvia?" or "What is 9×7?" This has resulted in inflexible knowledge being dismissed as only good for pub quizzes. The truth is that inflexibility is a necessary foundation upon which more flexible structures can be built. Let's imagine you have learned about square numbers and know how to apply Pythagoras' theorem to find the lengths of the sides of a right-angled triangle: $a^2 + b^2 = c^2$. Now, if you encounter a problem like the one in Figure 7.1, you should, with minimal prompting, be able to produce the correct answer.

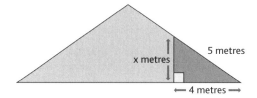

A support beam under a roof space must be at least 2 metres high. Would a beam positioned as shown in the diagram be acceptable? Give a reason for your answer.

Figure 7.1. Example of a maths question which can be solved using Pythagoras' theorem

When we apply inflexible knowledge, we make new schematic connections. We don't just remember facts, we remember all the ways we've thought about and used those facts before.

The more we apply propositional knowledge, the 'chunkier' and increasingly flexible it becomes. Instead of looking at a problem and trying to hold all the steps in mind, we are able to think with the whole schema. Eventually, these schemas can be applied to examples which are less obviously similar because we are able to ignore the superficial differences and concentrate on the similarities. The journey from inflexibility to flexibility produces a positive feedback loop – changes are amplified and enhanced and the new, more expert, way of thinking becomes permanent. In a very real sense, this is what it means to be clever. Eventually, knowledge can be mastered to the point where we no longer have to think about it; our working memory is free to handle chunks of propositional knowledge and arrive at solutions and insights far faster than someone who merely has high fluid intelligence ever could. The general rule is that expert knowledge always trumps raw ability.

We will return to facts and whether some are more worth knowing than others in the next chapter, but for now, so much for Gradgrind and his thirst for facts. All this propositional knowledge is just the tip of an unimaginably enormous iceberg. What of skills?

Thinking with

Although you probably can't explain it, you know how to balance. You know how to recognise thousands of different human faces. And if you're reading this book, you know the relationships between the 44 phonemes and over 170 graphemes that make up the English alphabetic code. These aren't things most people think about, yet we use them to think *with* all the time. At one point you couldn't do these things. You had to learn how. Most of us have forgotten both not knowing and learning because the knowledge of how to do these things transformed us.

All skills are derived from knowledge. In Chapter 5 we dismissed the idea that 'the brain is like a muscle'. We can't expect to get cleverer by exercising our 'mental muscles' because we only get better at what we practice. The benefits of practice don't generalise to things we haven't practised. In the same way, we can't improve our ability to solve problems in organic chemistry by practising solving problems in trigonometry. There's no such thing as a generic ability to be analytical or creative; you can only analyse a given thing or be creative in a particular field. To understand this, we need to deconstruct the idea of skills.

Instead of seeing skills as somehow separate from knowledge, it's more useful to view knowledge and its application as inseparably intertwined and mutually interdependent. When we see people employing what we think of as transferable skills, what we're probably seeing is someone with a wide-ranging body of knowledge in a number of different domains. This is definitely a more helpful way to think about what constitutes skill, but because of the confusion caused it might be preferable to abandon using the term 'skill' altogether in this context.

Is riding a bike a skill? Well, if we mean is it a set of procedures which we can master to the point that we're able to cycle without having to think about it then, yes, it is. Is essay writing a skill? Well, it's not the same sort of thing as riding a bike but, yes, it's another set of procedures which can be learned and practised. What about creativity? Is that a skill? Are there a series of steps which, if you learn, will make you creative? This, as we'll see, is less clear.

In general, skills are more usefully thought of as procedural knowledge. The type of knowledge that makes up how to ride a bike is usually tacit.

If you had to explain to someone else how to ride a bike you might strug-gle to articulate exactly what you meant. You might say something like, "You sit on the saddle, hold the handlebars, balance and then pedal." But would this be useful? We usually learn to ride a bike by having a go. No one can really tell us how to balance; it just 'feels right'. Because we're not sure exactly how we go about riding a bike, swimming or tying our shoelaces, we tend not to think of these things as knowledge, but they are. All these procedures are made up of individual items of hard won knowledge that we've experienced, practised and mastered. Once we've mastered them, they operate in the background beneath our awareness.

Learning to read is a bit like this. Most people have little idea how they're able to read, they just do it. Psycholinguists have become pretty good at understanding how the procedures for learning to read work, but explaining them to children doesn't tend to help much. Acquiring vocabulary knowledge and the process of automatising letter to sound relationships and other word recognition skills is a set of procedures that we commit to memory. With practice they become so well embedded that we can't switch them off; when we see text in a language we can decode, we do so automatically, whether we want to or not.

As such, we're largely unaware of what we do when we read, and we're completely unaware of the cognitive processes involved. The two strands of skilled reading – language comprehension and word recognition – are made up of many other components (vocabulary, verbal reasoning, pho-nological awareness, etc.) but, in fact, all these depend on background knowledge.

Even though you probably don't have any clear memories of what it was like not to be able to read, at some point in your life you didn't know that the squiggles (graphemes) represented sounds (phonemes). You had nei-ther the ability to code your speech into written squiggles, nor the ability to decode those squiggly shapes into sounds. You acquired this knowl-edge slowly and painstakingly. But having learned it, and with sufficient practice, it becomes invisible.

To be able to read at an average reading speed (about 300 words per minute[9]) you must have made all of this automatic. If some of your attention is taken up with trying to work out the sounds produced by the letter combinations or having to rack your brain to think what the words mean, there will be little room left to think about meaning. So-called 'higher level skills', like inference, prediction and analysis, take up a lot of processing space, and if your reading speed falls much below 150 words per minute, your ability to comprehend what you're reading starts to suffer.[*]

These automatised procedures are often so well embedded that we're not even aware of them. Many fluent readers have no conscious grasp of the propositional knowledge on which their ability to read depends. Although they may be unable to think about the process of reading, they think with it instinctively. Knowledge is most truly flexible when it is automatised.

Essay writing is different, but it's still procedural knowledge made up of a body of propositional knowledge that we can apply whenever we have to write an essay. The problem is that the generic knowledge of how to write an essay doesn't necessarily mean we'll be able to write a good essay; we also have to know something about whatever it is we want to write about. Many children have learned how to write an essay, but still manage to produce things like this:

> Miss Brodie looked hard at the door for a long time – this sentence is a simple sentence however they've added the word hard this makes the sentence better they've added an adverb to make it stand out.[**]

This is someone who has learned the form and structure of essay writing, but is still only capable of producing something empty and worthless. I think of this as cargo cult knowledge.

Cargo cults grew up on some of the Melanesian islands during the first half of the 20th century. Amazed islanders watched as Westerners arrived on their islands, built landing strips and then unloaded precious cargo from the aeroplanes which duly landed. That looks easy enough, some canny shaman must have reasoned, if we knock up a bamboo airport then the metal birds will come and lay their cargo eggs for us too. This follows the same logic as the Kevin Costner film *Field of Dreams*: build it and they will come. In Hollywood, magic often happens, but in

....

[*]   If you want to find out more about the science of reading I'd recommend Stanislas Dehaene's *Reading in the Brain* and Maryanne Wolf's *Proust and the Squid*.

[**]   You can see the original version of this here: https://i2.wp.com/www.learningspy. co.uk/wp-content/uploads/2016/11/Screen-Shot-2016-11-09-at-15.12.38.png.

the real world, despite the islanders' best efforts, no cargo arrived. Not only had they no understanding of global geopolitics and Western science, but they'd fundamentally misunderstood the causal relationship between cargo and airports.

Richard Feynman famously appropriated the cargo cult metaphor to describe bad science. He referred to the social sciences as Cargo Cult Science, because "they follow all the apparent precepts and forms of scientific investigation, but they're missing something essential, because the planes don't land".[10] Feynman said that the first principle of science is not to fool yourself and warned, "you are the easiest person to fool".[11] Not fooling ourselves is much easier said than done. Melanesian islanders had lots of theories about how to attract cargo but made very little progress. As a result, most cargo cults died out fairly quickly because it was really hard to continue fooling themselves: the planes didn't land. We don't always have this advantage because, depending on the kind of cargo we desire, it can be much easier to convince ourselves that it has arrived. After all, an essay gets written – no matter how poor – so what we're doing must be working, right? Knowledge of how to write an essay is not enough. In order for the planes to land, you also need knowledge of what you're writing about.

Thankfully, all of this knowledge can be taught and children can, with practice, become better at writing essays. The problem with viewing essay writing as a skill is that it encourages us to think that it is merely a generic set of procedures that can be transferred to each new context. Just because children have mastered writing literature essays does not mean that they'll be equally good at writing about history or economics. Not only does essay writing in these subjects require different content knowledge, it also requires knowledge of the different forms essays are required to take.

The same is true of a 'skill' like inference. In a skills-based approach to education it makes sense to practise inference because by practising it you'll become better at it. But what if there is no such thing as a skill of inference? What if practice doesn't lead to improvement? To be clear, I'm not saying that inference doesn't exist – obviously, you can tell children what an inference is and show them lots of examples – just that it's not a skill that can be practised.

An inference is defined as a conclusion reached on the basis of evidence and reasoning. So, to think about whether it's possible to practise making inferences we need to consider whether by drawing conclusions based on evidence and reason we'll become better at drawing conclusions based on evidence and reason. This sounds logical, but we need to consider *what* we are actually practising. How do you actually draw a conclusion from evidence and reason? Well, first you need to weigh the specific evidence. How do you know what the evidence is telling you? How do you know the importance of the evidence? Then, how do you apply reason to this evidence? Are these generalities that can be learned, or do they depend on specific instances?

Education researcher Robert Marzano says that we can teach inference. All we have to do is pose four simple questions:

1. What is my inference?

2. What information did I use to make this inference?

3. How good was my thinking?

4. Do I need to change my thinking?[12]

Sometimes children will make inferences without realising they've done so. Making them aware of this is the first step. Then they need to consider whether they relied on a clue in the text or on background knowledge. According to Marzano, once we have identified the premises on which they've based their inferences, we can engage in the most powerful part of the process – examining the validity of their thinking. The final step in the process is for children to consider possible changes in their thinking, not to invalidate children's original inferences, but rather to help them develop the habit of continually updating their conclusions as they gather new information.

Pick a passage from *Finnegans Wake* at random and ask Marzano's four questions of it. Too hard? What about this from Kant's *Critique of Pure Reason*:

> A manifold, contained in an intuition, which I call mine, is represented, by means of the synthesis of the understanding, as belonging to the *necessary* unity of self-consciousness; and this is effected by means of the category.

What inferences can you make? What, for instance, is the main idea expressed in this paragraph? Even though you know all the words you may still struggle to work out what the sentence means. Unless, that is, you know something about the categorical imperative; then the passage will be easy to interpret.

It should be clear that what you know is the whole of the game. Once you know that inferences can be made about a text, then you can start trying to make them, but unless you know something about the text you won't be able to make a worthwhile inference. So what does it mean to be skilled at making inferences? Nothing: it is indistinguishable from being knowledgeable.

And what about creativity? Can we provide a set of technical procedures which, if followed, will reliably result in creativity? Probably not. "There is no 'creative thinking' just as there is not 'creative walking'. *Creation* is a result, a place thinking may lead us."[13] So says Kevin Ashton, inventor of the 'internet of things'. We can certainly support the creative impulse and we can provide constraints that force people to be creative in order to overcome the constraint, but most of us want creativity to mean something more than this. Maybe it's something we need to give children experience of, like riding a bike. Well, we can certainly do that, but that still won't make them creative. In order to create new ways of thinking or doing, we need to be very knowledgeable about the old ways of thinking or doing.

A lot of creativity is fairly banal. In essence, it's imagining something we've seen before and altering it to fit a new circumstance. It takes creativity to look through the kitchen cupboards and rustle up a delicious meal. It takes creativity to plant a garden beautifully with limited resources, or to decide to wear those shoes with that dress. All these examples require a solid foundation of knowledge. But, again, most people aren't content with such everyday creativity, preferring instead to obsess about making dents in the universe.

All the great minds throughout history that we celebrate as creative were already experts before they saw a new way of thinking or doing. Consider Newton sitting under the apocryphal apple tree waiting for inspiration to fall. He wasn't just 'being creative' when he formulated his theory of gravity, he was seeing links and connections between the vast store of things he knew about. Indeed, as mentioned in Chapter 1, Newton had probably read everything there was to read about science up to that point. It's much easier to arrive at a new way of thinking or seeing when you already know a tremendous amount.

Wonderful scientist as he was, Newton is not noted for his creativity as a dramatist. He's rarely discussed as a creative politician, military commander or composer. This is because creativity, like the ability to solve problems or think critically, does not transfer between domains. Like every other skill, creativity depends on and is activated by knowledge. In order to be skilled in more than one field you need to be knowledgeable in more than one field.

But maybe you're still dubious. Think of a skill – anything you like. What knowledge do you need to perform this skill? Is there any aspect of this skill that is not knowledge? One possible answer is that some skills require physical capability in addition to knowledge: you might know, in principle, how to deadlift 300 pounds but not be physically strong enough to do so. Or you may know how to knit but have severe arthritis. But apart from physical capacity, what else is there? Do skills *require* knowledge or are they *composed* of knowledge?

What all this comes down to is that becoming skilled is really about becoming knowledgeable. The skill of driving a car depends on acquiring lots of propositional knowledge and then learning how to apply it procedurally. When drivers are insufficiently skilled it will largely be because they lack some aspect of a more skilled driver's knowledge. The same is true of reading, writing, performing calculations, painting, dancing, analysing historical sources and so on. In order to teach a skill, we have to know what it is we want a student to learn and work out how to communicate this knowledge. Once a student has understood, they can act on and practise what has been communicated. Michael Fordham puts it like this: "To be taught, skill must be converted into knowledge, which is the currency of teaching, and then it must be converted back at the other end via practice."[14]

By integrating factual knowledge with procedural knowledge, we encourage children to think with increasing sophistication about the subjects they study. All skills depend on knowledge and all are improved through acquiring more knowledge. This is not always obvious because, as we shall now see, much of the knowledge on which skilled performances depend is tacit.

Unknown knowns

When asked about the lack of evidence of the Iraqi government possessing weapons of mass destruction, the then US Secretary of Defense, Donald Rumsfeld, offered an interesting philosophical discussion on the categories of knowledge:

> … there are known knowns; there are things we know we know. We also know there are known unknowns; that is to say we know there are some things we do not know. But there are also unknown unknowns – the ones we don't know we don't know.[15]

This omits an important category: unknown knowns. While we can explain some of what we're able to do, there are very many things which we're unable to put into words. This sort of knowledge is tacit. As the Hungarian-British polymath Michael Polanyi succinctly said, "We know more than we can tell."[16] Everything we know explicitly depends on a more tacit understanding. He suggested that the closest we could get to articulating our tacit understanding is to come up with proxies or maxims:

> Maxims are rules, the correct application of which is part of the art which they govern. The true maxims of golfing or of poetry increase our insight into golfing or poetry and may even give valuable guidance to golfers and poets; but these maxims would instantly condemn themselves to absurdity if they tried to replace the golfer's skill or the poet's art. Maxims cannot be understood, still less applied by anyone not already possessing a good practical knowledge of the art. They derive their interest from our appreciation of the art and cannot themselves either replace or establish that appreciation.[17]

If you possess the right tacit knowledge then the maxim makes sense. If you can waterski, you'll grasp an explanation of how one waterskis. But if you've never waterskied, then the maxim will miss out too much and be too vague for you to do anything other than copy other waterskiers and work out, through trial and error, what you need to know in order to waterski. This is equally the case for riding bikes, making inferences, writing essays and creativity. Anything that we have automatised – like reading – becomes tacit and therefore very hard to describe to someone who hasn't also automatised it.

Why does this matter? Well, the 'curse of knowledge' is a predictable blind spot in our ability to think. When we come to explain something to others we tend to assume that they have the same background knowledge and share the same points of reference we do. When they don't know what we know they cannot understand what we say. Our explanation seems perfectly perspicacious to us, so we assume it's simple and obvious to other people.

The doctoral research of Elizabeth Newton captures this asymmetry beautifully.[18] She focused on the ability of a pair of subjects: the tapper (to tap out the rhythm to well-known songs) and the listener (to guess the tune). Listeners only managed to correctly guess three out of 120 songs but, astonishingly, tappers estimated that listeners guessed correctly 50% of the time. What would cause such a mismatch? The explanation is that the tappers are 'cursed with knowledge'. They hear the song in their heads and so overestimate how easy it is for others to work out what *they* already know. But if you've ever tried to work out a tune just from hearing a bunch of taps, you'll know that Tchaikovsky's *1812 Overture* sounds pretty similar to the Rolling Stone's 'Satisfaction'. Tappers possess 'expert' knowledge of which listeners are ignorant.

If we possess the right kind of tacit knowledge to be successful, we tend to assume that everyone can 'just do' what we can do. We fail to see how dependent we are on what we have mastered. This results in absurdities, such as saying, "Knowledge isn't all that important because you can always look up whatever you need to know on the internet." Persuasive as this argument can seem, it ignores the fact that a lot of tacit, procedural knowledge – stuff we're not consciously aware of thinking *about* – is what we think *with*. That much – indeed most – of our knowledge is tacit means we're routinely unaware of many things that are of crucial importance to our ability to think.

Those with inflexible knowledge tend only to know what they can say, and this may not be much. Let's imagine you decide to have a go at making a soufflé for the first time. Not having made one before, you follow a recipe. All you know is what is in the recipe book. Since this is necessarily limited, you could state everything you knew about soufflé making.

An experienced chef would possess lots of tacit knowledge and may not be able to articulate all that they know. Because knowledge can be automatised, we no longer have to think about what we're doing in order to do it, and so it's perfectly possible that an expert can produce a masterful performance without consciously being able to explain it. When a pastry chef makes a soufflé, they would almost certainly be able to list the recipe and would probably be able to talk you through the process, but they would leave lots unsaid. They would know things that weren't in the book. They would know things you couldn't put in the book, like what if feels like when the soufflé mixture reaches just the right consistency. They might be able to articulate these things, but even if they could they would be using maxims or proxies, and you wouldn't really understand what they meant.

This is a familiar problem for anyone who has been either a student or a teacher. Teachers are tappers – we confidently communicate what is abundantly clear to us, but it may as well be in ancient Etruscan for all the sense it makes to our perpetually confused students. Not only do they not know what we know, they may not even understand the words on which our explanations depend.

The bottom line here is that we cannot directly teach flexible knowledge because it is tacit. All we can do is teach as broad a range of inflexible knowledge as possible and help children to practise applying it in as broad a range of contexts as possible. Tacit knowledge accumulates by adding to schemas and with practice.

One of the most egregious errors made in discussing the role of knowledge in education is to overlook or belittle the existence of tacit knowledge. Everything – even those precious few things we can articulate – floats in a vast ocean of tacit understanding. Although we can't think *about* it, it is the very stuff we think *with*.*

----

* This is a necessarily brief and incomplete overview. See Harry Collins' book, *Tacit and Explicit Knowledge*, for a much more thorough discussion.

Knowledge is power

The oft wheeled-out aphorism 'knowledge is power'* has become something of a cliché these days, but maybe the reason things become clichéd is because they are true. If we know something we possess it and can leverage it to assist us in our endeavours. Not knowing something – ignorance – is the root of most mistakes.

Our minds are full of different kinds of knowledge and it's what we know that makes us who we are. Our ability to think, reason, problem solve, create and collaborate are all entirely dependent on what we know. In order to think we have to have something to think both with and about. If we don't know lots of useful, powerful and interesting stuff, we'll struggle to be useful, powerful or interesting.

We are unable to think with anything that we are dependent on looking up. 'Thinking with' and 'thinking about' are different ways of handling knowledge but both depend on having the stuff in our heads. If we only know where to look something up, that's the extent of our thinking. Having looked something up, we hold it in our head for just long enough to complete a task and then let it go. In terms of the theory of disuse, such knowledge will have very poor storage strength. If we don't value the knowledge of, say, how to email photos to friends sufficiently to want to memorise it, that's fair enough, but, more importantly, what we look up only makes sense when it's integrated with all that we already know. Only being able to look things up is an impoverishing experience. Knowledge is only knowledge if it lives inside us. In order to understand what we look up we often need to know an awful lot.

E. D. Hirsch, Jr explains further:

> There is a consensus in cognitive psychology that it takes knowledge to gain knowledge. Those who repudiate a fact-filled curriculum on the grounds that kids can always look things up miss the paradox that de-emphasizing factual knowledge actually disables children from looking things up effectively. To stress process at the expense of factual knowledge actually hinders children from learning to learn. Yes, the Internet has placed a wealth of information at our fingertips. But to be able to use that information – to absorb it, to add to our knowledge – we

---

*   Translated from the Latin, *scientia potentia est*, and attributed to either Sir Francis Bacon or Thomas Hobbes, who worked as Bacon's secretary.

> must already possess a storehouse of knowledge. That is the paradox
> disclosed by cognitive research.[19]

The most important individual difference between children is the quality and quantity of what they know. Although differences in fluid intelligence and working memory matter, they are trumped by the advantages of being knowledgeable. Remember Katie and Liam from Chapter 5? Let's imagine that Liam has higher fluid intelligence, but Katie, because of her more advantaged background, has encountered more of the world and knows more facts. Liam and Katie are taught the fact that Thomas Jefferson died on 4 July 1826. Katie remembers that Jefferson was one of America's founding fathers and she's also aware that 4 July was the date that America declared its independence from Britain. Liam has never encountered these facts before and so learning the new information is much harder.

Liam has to rely on his working memory to hold the new information in mind while simultaneously trying to think about it. If they were both equally ignorant of the subject then he would process new information more quickly than Katie. But because Katie already knows more, she can access long-term memories to overcome the limits of her working memory. This means she will have a greater capacity to think analytically and creatively. We would expect that if both Liam and Katie were asked to explain something about the life of Jefferson or the American Declaration of Independence, Katie's performance would be superior.

Some children – often those from more advantaged backgrounds, like Katie – seem to possess a sort of intellectual Velcro which means school stuff sticks more easily. Other children – like Liam – seem perpetually baffled by academic abstractions. What they know isn't as useful and seems to act more like intellectual Teflon.

Facts are never isolated. As we saw in Chapter 6, as soon as we notice connections, new links form between our schemas in long-term memory. What we know is a rich and vibrant web of knowledge. It's not just that some children know more than others, they also know things that are more useful in school. This is yet another instance of the Matthew effect: the knowledge rich get richer while the knowledge poor get (comparatively) poorer.

In *Why Don't Students Like School?* Daniel Willingham conducts a thought experiment on how a small initial difference in knowledge might become incrementally larger over time. Let's reuse our two hypothetical students, Katie and Liam. Let's say Katie knows 10,000 facts whereas Liam only knows 9,000. When introduced to 500 facts, they both try equally hard to learn the material and both succeed in adding to their respective stores of knowledge, but Katie learns 10% of the new information and Liam, because he knows less to begin with, only learns 9%. This is repeated over 10 months, after which Katie now knows 10,500 facts while Liam knows 9,450. The gap has widened from 1,000 to 1,050 facts and will, in all probability, continue to widen.[20] Liam knows less after 10 months than Katie did at the start of the process. Even though he has greater working memory capacity and higher fluid intelligence, to stop the gap from widening further, Liam would have to work considerably harder than Katie. Even if Katie makes less effort than Liam, the gap is unlikely to close. Even if the poor aren't any worse off, the rich are getting ever richer. This is the stark probability of the Matthew effect.

Despite this, many people still seem to feel an instinctive revulsion for the idea that children should be taught to remember facts. There's a deep-rooted suspicion that factual knowledge is in some way detrimental to children's natural ability to learn and understand. In *Seven Myths About Education*, Daisy Christodoulou explores the myth that facts prevent understanding. She reviews the way various thinkers – from Jean-Jacques Rousseau to John Dewey, Paulo Freire and Charles Dickens –write about education and finds that they "all set up polar opposites between facts, which are generally seen as bad, and something else, which is generally seen as good. Facts are opposed with meaning, understanding, reasoning, significance and … imagination or creativity."[21] But as we've seen, our long-term memory is central to who we are and how we think. When we learn new things, they become part of us; they change the way we think and how we see the world. How could knowledge inhibit rather than enhance any of our mental processes?

One possible answer to this question is that the more we know, the less curious we become about the world. Does learning facts crush our ability to wonder about the world? Our response will depend on what we think curiosity is. Psychologist George Loewenstein defines it as the gap "between what we know and what we want to know".[22] In order to feel curiosity we have to know something. We have to be surprised by something not conforming to our expectations or be aware that what we currently know is not enough to fully explain our observations.

Consider this question: Have you ever wondered what the rings of Saturn are made of? If you don't already know, it prompts you to notice that there is something of which you're unaware. As soon as you know that you don't know, you become curious. Disappointingly, it turns out that the rings of Saturn are made of dust. Ice covered dust. There are many occasions when we fail to absorb new information, but when our curiosity is aroused we want to know.

In his aptly named book, *Curious*, the journalist Ian Leslie discusses a concept which he refers to as 'epistemic curiosity'. He suggests that such curiosity about knowledge – or intellectual curiosity – is relatively new and is the result of mass literacy and access to information.[23] Children might well be naturally curious, but as we saw in Chapter 2, they have a motivational bias towards folk knowledge rather than the hard won fruits of human culture. Without direction, children's curiosity is superficial and arrives at dead ends. Without access to biologically secondary knowledge we are dependent on guesswork, superstition and myth. Although culturally accumulated knowledge can be more difficult to make sense of, it opens up new possibilities and ways of seeing. Epistemic curiosity – as opposed to the idle kind – is fed by knowledge: the more we know, the more we realise we don't know. Our knowledge is like an island in a vast sea of ignorance. Our curiosity marks the shoreline where knowledge and ignorance meet. As we act on that curiosity, the shorelines expands and the ocean of ignorance recedes a little more. Far from facts preventing understanding, knowledge feeds curiosity. The more we know, the more capable of curiosity we become.

And it's not just curiosity. What are often conceived of as transferable skills are better thought of as examples of biologically primary adaptions. We learn to collaborate with others, solve problems, think critically and combine ideas creatively long before we get to school. But without the sorts of facts children encounter in school, these adaptive modules are very limited. You have to think critically *about* the facts you have learned. Think of factual knowledge as a pile of bricks. Without interaction and structure, you won't be able to build a house. Similarly, without interaction and structure you don't really know much of any real value. When we know about science, geography, music or history, we can apply our ability to think critically and solve problems to more new and exciting possibilities.

Contrary to the idea that knowledge somehow prevents understanding, Darwin noted that, "ignorance more frequently begets confidence than does knowledge".[24] The Dunning–Kruger effect is the name given to the finding that the poorest performers are the least aware of their own incompetence. Or, put more crudely, ignorant people are too ignorant to recognise their own ignorance. In line with this, 65% of people see themselves as more intelligent than the average.[25]

After comparing participants' tests results with their self-assessment of their performance in such diverse fields as sense of humour, grammar and logic, psychologists David Dunning and Justin Kruger proposed that, for any given area, the incompetent not only fail to recognise their own lack of skill but are also unable to recognise genuine skill in others. Dunning observes, "If you're incompetent, you can't know you're incompetent … the skills you need to produce a right answer are exactly the skills you need to recognize what a right answer is."[26] A little knowledge can be a dangerous thing. When we know part of a problem we can be misled into believing we're an expert. We rarely admit our ignorance; we just rely on heuristics and go with the easiest possible answer. It ought to be obvious that the best antidote to ignorance is knowledge, but then you need knowledge to know that too.

The power of knowledge is such that it also determines what we see. Take a look at Figure 7.2.

Figure 7.2. The offside trap

If you know nothing relevant, all you will be able to see are circles, arrows and lines. Some readers will have enough knowledge to recognise this as a representation of a football pitch with the circles representing players and the arrows representing movement, but those with more specific knowledge of football will see that the darker grey circle labelled 10 is a striker who is offside. They might also infer that the circles labelled 2, 5, 6 and 3 are defenders in the process of executing the 'offside trap'. A real expert will be able to make even more astute observations about the tactics being employed. The point is, to be able to extract any of this information requires quite a lot of knowledge.

What about Figure 7.3?

To the uninitiated this is just sciency stuff. But the more you know about chemistry, the more likely you are to know that you're looking at a distillation experiment. More specific knowledge might tip you off that this is a diagram of the Coffey still and is an example of the continuous distillation of ethyl alcohol. The more you know about a subject, the more you recognise, take in and think about. All this makes learning easier because you have a greater number of potential linkages in your schemas.

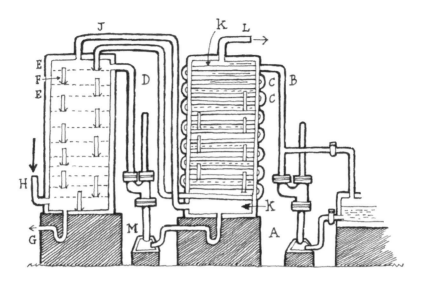

Figure 7.3. The Coffey still

The illusion of knowledge

Perhaps one of the most intractable obstacles in the way of becoming cleverer is the false belief that we know things we don't actually know. The illusion of knowledge – sometimes referred to as the illusion of explanatory depth – affects us all far more than we would like to believe. When we read a book, we think we know it. But after a couple of months, all we'll remember is that we read it and whether or not we liked it. Some time ago, I went to see the physicist Brian Cox give a lecture on the quantum nature of the universe. It was fascinating and I was held spellbound for the couple of hours in which he regaled his audience with tales of the invisible world and its implications for our lives. I left fizzing with ideas, and when I got home, I proceeded to tell my wife how revelatory I found it. After a while she asked, "So what did he say?" I paused for some time before admitting, "I don't know, but it was really good." It's only when people ask us to explain what we think we know that we find out whether we know it.

Rebecca Lawson carried out research into this phenomenon by asking subjects to draw a bicycle. Everyone knows what a bike looks like, right?

Apparently not. Although 96% of the subjects could actually cycle, few were able to draw a working bike. They were given a sketch to which they had to attach pedals and a chain. Over a third of subjects who were not regular cyclists thought that the bicycle chain ran around the front as well as the back wheel of the bicycle. Regular cyclists did a lot better, but still made mistakes. Afterwards they said things like, "Thinking about it in more detail, I realised I had no idea about its structure" and, "I can't believe I found it so difficult to remember what a bike frame looks like!!!"[27]

Although we have a passing familiarity with what a bike looks like, our actual knowledge is pretty shaky. Similarly, although most of us know roughly what a penny looks like, we might have a hard job actually describing its appearance in detail. When we look at a penny – or anything else – our mind focuses on the most salient features and assigns it to a category. We're excellent at seeing similarities and differences between categories, but bad at absorbing detail. Seeing too much would overload working memory. We only notice the key features and fill in the rest.

This is something that has particular significance for anyone studying for an exam. When you reread your notes or highlight text it produces a feeling of familiarity and recognition. "Oh yes," you think, "I know that." Familiarity results in certainty, and when you're certain you stop thinking. A better idea is to test yourself by taking a blank sheet of paper and reconstructing the idea or argument that you need to explain – without referring to your notes. That will be a good indicator of how much you actually know. In Chapter 10, we'll look at some other mechanisms for combatting the illusion of knowledge by helping us to become more aware of our ignorance.

....

In summary, what we've learned in this chapter is that our minds are composed of knowledge. What we know dictates how we think. The good news is that knowledge, unlike generic competencies, is relatively easy to teach. Claiming that a knowledge-rich curriculum is an attempt to just teach factual knowledge is absurd. I'm not even sure how that would be possible. Even if teaching different categories of knowledge separately is possible, it is not desirable.

Once children know something, they're able to use that knowledge to gain more knowledge, think in new ways about what they previously knew and arrive at new understandings of the world. They may find out that some of the things they believed to be true are in need of updating. This happens to us all. Whether we are able to update our world view and keep our knowledge fresh is another product of knowledge. Stubbornly refusing to change our beliefs is the consequence of ignorance. Humility and curiosity are both the result of knowledge.

Chapter 7: key points

- Knowledge is more than just facts – it includes procedural knowledge (skills) as well as tacit knowledge (things we either can't put into words or don't know we know).

- Knowledge is both what we think about and what we think with.

- The more we know, the better we can think; knowing more changes us.

- Learning propositional knowledge (facts) is vital for academic success.

- Knowledge can be inflexible or flexible. The more flexible it is, the more useful it becomes.

- Knowing the names of things allows us to think about and discuss them.

- Thinking about procedural knowledge as 'skills' makes it harder for us to understand how to help students become more skilled. Thinking in terms of procedural knowledge makes it easier.

- All procedures can be practised; some can be practised to the point where they become effortless and automatic.

- Tacit knowledge cannot be taught, it is acquired through experience.

- Because much of our knowledge is tacit, we're often unaware of what we know; we fail to understand how our knowledge developed and what our skill depends on.

- We need knowledge to gain knowledge; the more we know, the easier it is to learn.

- What we know determines how we perceive and think about the world.

- Beware the illusion of knowledge: students often think they know things that they are merely familiar with.

Next, we need to consider what knowledge children need if they are to be cleverer. This is the subject of the next chapter.

Chapter 8
What knowledge?

All knowledge is precious whether or not it serves the slightest human use.

A. E. Housman

- Should school be about all kinds of knowledge, or are some types of knowledge more important than others?

- Are all ways of knowing equally valid?

- Should we care what's considered culturally rich, or is it just the preserve of dead white men?

- What is meant by a broad and balanced curriculum?

While we can make a case that all knowledge is potentially useful and interesting (at least to someone), some things are more useful and interesting than others. In *Bringing Knowledge Back in*, education professor Michael Young came up with the idea of 'powerful knowledge', which he argues provides reliable explanations and a sound basis for making judgements about the world beyond the narrow limits of experience. He distinguishes powerful knowledge from 'common sense'; powerful knowledge is developed systematically by specialists within subject disciplines. It is that which, in the words of Basil Bernstein, allows us to "think the unthinkable and the not yet thought".[1]

As we saw in Chapter 5, there's good reason to believe that children are required to know far less factual knowledge now than they were 100 years ago. In England, the idea that 16-year-olds should have to memorise poetry by heart and learn quotations from a range of literary texts is viewed by many as unfair and the cause of undue stress. In fact, over

100,000 people signed a petition asking the government of the day to reintroduce 'open book' examinations which would not require students to memorise anything because "exams shouldn't be a test on the student's memory, but how we interpret texts".[2] The idea that children might have to learn lists of capital cities or a basic chronology of British history fills many with horror and revulsion. Some even object to the idea that children should be asked to learn times tables, preferring instead that they learn "number sense".[3]

Ideas such as number sense, the ability to interpret texts and various other transferable skills have, at least to some extent, replaced facts in the curriculum. As we saw, the kind of abstract, hypothetical thinking that schools focus on has had some positive effects on society, but without something to think about, children are hampered both in their ability to make sense of the world and in their ability to understand how numbers interact and how texts can be interpreted. Speaking of the ignorance of too many young people, James Flynn says their lack of knowledge of literature, history and geography means that too many people "live in the bubble of the present". What would the world be like, Flynn wonders, if people knew more?

> Imagine how different things would be if most Americans knew that we had been lied into four of our last six wars. You know, the Spanish didn't sink the battleship Maine, the Lusitania was not an innocent vessel but was loaded with munitions, the North Vietnamese did not attack the Seventh Fleet, and, of course, Saddam Hussein hated al Qaeda and had nothing to do with it, and yet the administration convinced 45 per cent of the people that they were brothers in arms, when he would hang one from the nearest lamppost.[4]

The ability to empathise and generalise is all very well, but without facts we are at the mercy of those who want to impose their views of reality. We can't think about things we don't know, and we can't think critically about things we don't know well. The only way to counter this is to prioritise knowledge, but what kind of knowledge?

Powerful knowledge

Young argues that that "education should be an entitlement to knowledge",[5] but suggests that the role of knowledge in the curriculum has been in decline for some years. On the face of it, this seems odd. Why would anyone allow the role of knowledge to decline? How could anyone be against children knowing as much as possible about the world in which they live? Well, as we saw in the previous chapter, there's an increasingly widespread belief that because we can look up whatever we need on the internet, knowing things no longer matters. This lazy, uncritical thinking has been trotted out by a parade of commentators,[6] but the most egregious examples of this logical fallacy tend to come from physicist turned edupreneur Sugata Mitra, who is on record as having said, "knowing is obsolete. People often think I'm saying that knowledge is obsolete, which I'm not. I'm saying putting knowledge in your head – that's obsolete, because you can know anything when you need to know it via the internet."[7] I've already discussed why this is nonsense in the previous chapter and am not about to repeat the argument again. Instead, we'll briefly consider why this reaction to knowledge is so endemic. Is it just because of the rise of the internet?

In *Fear of Knowledge*, the American philosopher Paul Boghossian discusses the belief that science is just one among many ways of understanding the world.[8] This relativist approach to knowledge means that it's easy to argue that there's no such thing as objective truth and that all views and opinions are equally valid. In this world view, what constitutes knowledge is 'socially dependent' rather than objectively true. If everything we know is socially constructed, it can make sense to suggest that some ways of knowing the world are more valid than others because the holders of some forms of knowledge have been oppressed by holders of other forms of knowledge. So, we can have, say, feminist epistemology as distinct from other types of epistemology, which then results in fields like feminist glaciology.* From there it's just a hop, skip and jump to arguing that science is oppressive, that logic is racist and that rationalism is male. Although Boghossian loses little time in pointing out that the world continues to exist regardless of whatever we may believe, and there are ways to arrive at beliefs about the world that are objectively reasonable to anyone capable of appreciating the relevant evidence, regardless of their social or cultural perspective, the suspicions persist.

If all opinions and perspectives are equally valid, what makes a teacher's understanding of their subject more important than whatever the students currently reckon? This has eroded the very idea that teachers ought to be authority figures. After all, why should a teacher be in charge just because they know more than their students? And why should we prioritise what a teacher thinks should be studied over a child's opinions?

We need to distinguish between the knowledge of the powerful and powerful knowledge. The first positions knowledge in terms of its power relations, while the second invites us to consider what sort of knowledge has the greatest potential to explain the world and provide new ways of thinking about it. In Young's view, powerful knowledge is that which "can provide learners with a language for engaging in political, moral, and other kinds of debates".[9]

Young's concept of powerful knowledge assumes that there are indeed many different types of knowledge but that they are not equally valid. For every field of human endeavour there are more useful things to know that improve our ability to think about these subjects. The main distinction Young draws is between 'school knowledge' and 'everyday knowledge'. Everyday knowledge is very useful in navigating the familiar landscape of our day-to-day experiences, but it's less useful at school. Likewise, school knowledge will be really useful in maths or science lessons but of little use in working out what to do when confronted by a tearful friend or

---

* This is not a joke. Carey et al.'s paper 'Glaciers, Gender, and Science: A Feminist Glaciology Framework for Global Environmental Change Research' received quite a bit of media attention when it was published in 2016. It begins, "Glaciers are key icons of climate change and global environmental change. However, the relationships among gender, science, and glaciers – particularly related to epistemological questions about the production of glaciological knowledge – remain understudied." If this seems reminiscent of the physicist Alan Sokal's famous spoof, 'Transgressing the Boundaries: Towards a Transformative Hermeneutics of Quantum Gravity', I couldn't possibly comment.

an irate bus driver. Everyday knowledge is dependent on the context in which it was learned, whereas school knowledge can help children to move beyond the confines of their personal experiences and open up new ways of thinking about aspects of the world which would otherwise be unknown.

It may be true that all knowledge is precious, but not all knowledge is equally precious. The time schools have to teach a curriculum is strictly finite; there isn't time to teach everything. We have to make choices, and so Young suggests that it is the responsibility of schools to "transmit shared and powerful knowledge on behalf of society".[10]

In trying to determine whether knowledge is powerful, Young offers these suggestions:

- Shared and powerful knowledge is verified through learned communities. We need to keep in touch with universities and research and subject associations.

- Children need powerful knowledge to understand and interpret the world. Without it they remain dependent upon those who have it.

- Powerful knowledge is cognitively superior to that needed for daily life. It transcends and liberates children from their daily experience.

- Shared and powerful knowledge enables children to grow into useful citizens. As adults they can use their understanding to cooperate and shape the world together.

- Shared knowledge is a foundation for a just and sustainable democracy. Citizens educated together share an understanding of the common good.

- It is fair and just that all children should have access to this knowledge. Powerful knowledge opens doors: it must be available to all children.

Knowledge can be said to be powerful if it changes children's perceptions, values or understandings. If knowing something causes you to ask new questions and explore different explanations, then that knowledge is powerful. So, finding out that geopolitical realities are the opposite of what most people instinctively assume is powerful. Facts – for example, that income levels have been rising steadily in every country in the world, that many more children than is commonly assumed receive some education, that infant mortality is plummeting and that global population is not out of control – are eye openers.[11] Finding out that your world view is based on systematic bias can be profoundly disorientating.

Not all knowledge is as powerful as that, but finding out that stories are artificial ways of holding on to the world can be a shock for many children, as can the discovery that people lived and thought in profoundly different ways at different times and in different places. Concepts like evolution and gravity – things most people take on faith and wave their hands at – can have a startling impact on how we see the world once we understand them. This sort of powerful knowledge has sometimes been described as being made up of threshold concepts. In the words of Jan Meyer and Ray Land, "A threshold concept can be considered as akin to a portal, opening up a new and previously inaccessible way of thinking about something. It represents a transformed way of understanding, or interpreting, or viewing something without which the learner cannot progress."[12]

The areas of a subject with which children often get stuck seem to be the most important bits. Furthermore, advanced ideas depend on the understanding of certain important fundamentals. In all subject domains and disciplines there are points which lead us into "previously inaccessible ways of thinking". If a concept is a way of organising and making sense of what is known in a particular field, then a threshold concept organises the knowledge and experience which makes an epiphany or 'eureka' moment possible.

Meyer and Land suggest that a threshold concept will most likely possess certain important qualities. These concepts can be described as:

- *Integrative* – once learned, they are likely to bring together different parts of the subject which you hadn't previously seen as connected.

- *Transformative* – once understood, they change the way you see the subject and yourself.

- *Irreversible* – they are difficult to unlearn – once you've passed through it's difficult to see how it was possible not to have understood before.

- *Reconstitutive* – they may shift your sense of self over time. This is initially more likely to be noticed by others, usually teachers.

- *Troublesome* – they are likely to present you with a degree of difficulty and may sometimes seem incoherent or counter-intuitive.

- *Discursive* – the student's ability to use the language associated with that subject changes as they change. It's the change from using scientific key words to talking like a scientist.[13]

Think about learning to read. At some point you started to notice that written letters represent sounds. Over time this liminal state solidified into an ability to decode writing and turn it back into sounds. For most of us, this dramatic shift goes unnoticed and unremarked; it just happens. But it transforms us. From that point on, we are incapable of experiencing writing or texts without this knowledge. We may struggle with new words or unfamiliar structures but we know that the meaning is there, waiting to be unlocked. This change is irreversible; there is no going back to how we were.

Establishing what these concepts are within each domain and mapping them onto the curriculum is the very opposite of misguided generic attempts to describe linear and universal stages of learning. It might not feel comfortable, but it's essential that we acknowledge that there is no straightforward, linear route from 'easy' to 'difficult'.

Some knowledge provides useful tools for thinking about the world. Statistical thinking is a good example. We instinctively focus on how we feel about something without considering what numbers can tell us. Of course, we can also become too reliant on data and fail to stop and think about what we want to use it for. Despite arguing against a 'skill' of inference in the previous chapter, concepts like inference and analysis can be powerful; they provide us with a new framework for thinking about our experiences. It's only when they become misconceived as skills which improve through practice that they lose their power. The scientific method is one of the most powerful of these tools. It involves rigorous scepticism about observations, forming hypotheses and then designing experiments to test a hypothesis. Karl Popper's addition that theories should be falsifiable rather provable is even more powerful and helps scientists to arrive at knowledge that is more likely to be true.

Children will also benefit from knowing things that help them to make generalisations. Remember James Flynn's example of asking his parents how they would feel if they woke up as African-Americans? The ability to make generalisations takes us out of our comfortable bubble and forces us to apply our ideas to people we have never met and to places we will never see. This is easy to say, but the ability to generalise depends on knowledge. Knowledge is powerful in this respect if it enables children to synthesise lots of different information, is widely applicable, possesses analytical power, enables children to explain things which would otherwise be confusing and can be used to make predictions about the future. After all, if you can't imagine a future, you can't think about it.

Children also need knowledge in order that they have power over what they know. Caution is required here as this type of knowledge could easily be misconstrued as 'learning to learn'. Having been dismissive of the idea that children can just look up whatever they need to know as and when they need the information, I need to make clear that children do need to know how to find, select and evaluate information. As Young says, "Knowledge … allows those with access to it to question it and the authority on which it is based and gain the sense of freedom and excitement that it can offer."[14]

Once you've learned something of the world, you also need to know how to question and critique what you've been taught. You need knowledge in order to be independent of the thoughts and beliefs of others. This requires that students know something about how knowledge is developed within, and admitted to, a domain – something of its epistemology. This doesn't have to be technical or abstruse; it can start simply from questions that ask, "How do you know …?" We'll come back to this idea at the end of the chapter.

Cultural literacy and the problem
with dead white men

Knowledge is also powerful if it enables children to follow and participate in debates on significant local, national and global issues. There are sound sociocultural reasons why children should experience the most prevalent and important ideas to have emerged through the iterative processes of accumulating human culture. Young argues that access to powerful knowledge is an entitlement, but if we leave things to chance we'll ensure that those children who are born to literate and wealthy parents will have an additional advantage, as they are more likely to encounter powerful conceptual knowledge than their less advantaged peers.

This idea was taken up by the French sociologist Pierre Bourdieu. He argued that, like material wealth, culturally valuable knowledge is a kind of capital. While we all occupy a position within society, we are defined not only by membership of a social class, but also by the 'capital' we can amass through social relations. Needless to say, as with any other kind of capital, this can, and often does, result in inequality.[15] This suggests that, in choosing what knowledge to teach, we should focus on that which allows children to best compete in the world.

Now, one can argue, as does the economist Bryan Caplan in *The Case Against Education*, that what schools teach is, by and large, useless in terms of what students need to know in the jobs they end up doing. As an English teacher, I have a fair bit of fairly arcane knowledge that few others outside my profession and subject specialism would see as useful. Doctors know all kinds of stuff and are able to save lives, so surely everything they know is vitally important? Well, if it is then I've muddled along without needing to know the vast majority of it. The same goes for everyone else, from greengrocers and figure skaters to lion tamers: the knowledge we have is, largely, only important to us.

But the idea of cultural capital – or cultural literacy, to use E. D. Hirsch, Jr's term – is that it consists of knowledge that it is useful for everyone to know. Being able to quote Shakespeare or knowing Pythagoras' theorem may seem like trivia, but it enables us to access society in a way which would be impossible if we didn't know any of this. It's only important *because* other people know it. This is another example of the Lindy effect – an idea increases in importance the more widely it is shared. If some people know something and others don't, those who don't will find themselves excluded or marginalised from the group which does. If, as is the case in every society human beings have ever developed, those in the more knowledgeable group have more power and influence, those excluded from this group will find themselves on the fringes of society. Whether we like it or not, the powerful routinely decide that what they value is a marker of the elite. If the children of the elite are then given access to this deep pool of accumulated culture, they will perpetuate the divisions and inequalities between the haves and the have-nots. But if the children of those on the margins are taught the same stuff as the wealthy and powerful, they can gain access to opportunities and possibilities denied to their parents. As we saw in the previous chapter, we need knowledge to gain knowledge.

One much chewed bone of contention is who gets to decide what knowledge children should learn. The assumption seems to be that there's some shadowy elite inflicting their preferences on the rest of us. This is nonsense. No one chooses; we all choose. No one person knows enough to make this choice but collectively we have access to the vast accumulation of human culture. The most important things to know are those things that last and which most influence other cultural developments; those things that inspire the most 'conversations' backwards and forwards through time and across space; those things that allow us to trace our cultural inheritance through threads of thought from the discoveries of modern science and the synthesis of modern art back to their ancient origins.

In Chapter 1 we considered Matthew Arnold's oft quoted assertion that children should be taught 'the best'. Clearly, what we consider 'best' is subjective, but, that said, it's rarely arbitrary. It tends to be the product of generations of people agreeing that certain things are inherently good. It is the distilled essence of the Lindy effect. Collectively we decide what is valuable and important.

That is not to claim that this process is not enormously culturally biased, but neither is it entirely subjective. Even if you're utterly unmoved by Darwin's contribution to science or Smith's to economics, you still probably recognise that phrases like 'survival of the fittest' and 'the invisible hand' have permeated social discourse, and that even if you don't really understand them, the theories of evolution and market forces have changed the way we think about ourselves and our place in the universe. The more children know about their cultural inheritance, the more they can question, critique and respond to what has gone before.

Canonical knowledge is regularly condemned as 'stale, male and pale'. Instead of teaching the thoughts and works of the elite, shouldn't we instead prioritise the voices of the more marginalised? Should we de-emphasise what is traditional in favour of what is politically progressive?

These are tough questions. The challenges of a curriculum rooted in powerful knowledge and cultural capital are described by Hirsch in relation to the Core Knowledge programme:

> Because of an inherent and inescapable inertia in the knowledge that is shared among hundreds of millions of people, the Core Knowledge plan was necessarily traditional, and was criticised in the 1990s for being so. It appeared to perpetuate the dominance of the already dominant elements of American life, while the aim of many intellectuals in the 1990s was to reduce that dominance and privilege, and valorize neglected cultures and women. So there was quite a lot of controversy attached to the Core Knowledge plan, which, though egalitarian in purpose and result, looked elitist on the surface. The aim of giving everybody entrée to the knowledge of power ran smack up against the aim of depriveleging those who are currently privileged.[16]

This is a genuine problem. On the face of it, building a curriculum around the thoughts and deeds of historically marginalised groups looks like a really good idea. Who wouldn't want children to know about the achievements of women and people of colour? The trouble is, this isn't shared knowledge. It doesn't allow access to the 'knowledge of power', and, crucially, it doesn't provide much cultural capital. Our dilemma is to navigate the tight confines of the school curriculum to find a way to teach the knowledge "shared among hundreds of millions of people", as well as knowledge that "deprivileges those who are currently privileged". In this endeavour, we must maintain focus on the egalitarian purpose of teaching powerful, culturally rich knowledge so that it can be critiqued.

The canon is not the preserve of any one class, ethnic group or gender. It is a shared cultural heritage that has something to say to us all. Indeed, on reading Sonnet 29, Maya Angelou decided that Shakespeare must have been a black girl. Knowledge is knowledge; it's provenance is interesting but it does not determine its value. Lindsay Johns argues, "There is no apartheid in the philosophical musings of Cicero, no racial segregation in the cosmic grandeur of Dante and no ethnic oppression in the amorous sonnets of Shakespeare." Johns sees attempts by "trendy educationalists" to insist on diversity in the curriculum as signalling their anti-racist credentials and post-colonial guilt. This, he argues, is ultimately unhelpful and leaves those it seeks to help cut off and adrift from the culture that shapes the world in which they live:

> We should accept the truth of history, which is that white men have dominated intellectual life in the west. Let's not resist this; let's run with it. It is western history that has indelibly shaped our consciousness. ... We might hail from Africa or the Caribbean, but our lives, for better or for worse, are lived in the modern western world, and shaped by the traditions that have moulded it. If we acquaint ourselves with the grammars of the west, it will indubitably help us to understand it and then duly succeed here.[17]

Not teaching the thoughts and words of dead white men won't help anyone to understand why people of colour and women have been historically marginalised. When we express our righteous indignation that some knowledge is valued over other knowledge, and decide to teach this other knowledge in the name of liberty and social justice, what we're actually doing is denying children choice. As Hirsch puts it, "If we tried to teach children a fully non-traditional knowledge set, they could not master the existing language of power and success."[18] Deciding that children do not need to know things that some consider elitist or offensive condemns them to ignorance.

There are only two ways out of this bind: firstly, we should be alert to supplementing a core of traditional knowledge with whatever non-traditional knowledge we can find the time and space to add in, and, secondly, we should aim to teach the knowledge with the most cultural capital *and then learn to critique it*. After all, we can't really criticise something we don't understand. No one should be taught to unthinkingly agree that the British Empire was a glorious thing or that Shakespeare is the best writer ever, but if we don't learn about these culturally important aspects of history and literature, we won't know enough to understand the effects of colonialism and that the legacy of the bard is as much to do with cultural imperialism as it is to do with literary merit. Ignorance benefits no one.

But we shouldn't just select what goes into a curriculum based on some arbitrary calculation of cultural worth. We should also be concerned with the cognitive benefit of knowledge. In order to be academically successful children need to read. A lot. In order to understand what they read they need to know whatever writers leave out because they assume their readers will already know it. This presents us with some difficulties, because if we agree that all children, no matter their background, need access to culturally rich, powerful knowledge, how on earth can we know what this background knowledge will be?

What are the most powerful and culturally rich concepts and references? One starting place is the list of facts and concepts that Hirsch included in *Cultural Literacy*. His list of 5,000 names, places, dates and concepts represents the assumed knowledge necessary to read and understand articles in the *New York Times*. Because this knowledge is assumed, it's not discussed or explained but merely referenced, indicating a lattice-work of those things which could empower us to think better about the world. It includes items as varied as the Augean stables, Bering Sea, *caveat emptor*, 'Do Not Go Gentle Into That Good Night', embargo, folklore, Great Depression, David Hume, infinitive, Judas Iscariot, "Lay on, Macduff", metabolism, Nicaragua, orbit, Pharisees, Ramadan, share-cropping, Thomas Malthus, Ursa Major, Victorian, Whistler's Mother, xylem, "You can't serve both God and Mammon" and zeitgeist.[19]

I couldn't claim to know a lot about most of these items, but they are all familiar and connect to existing schemas. If I hear or read any of them, I share something that doesn't then require further explanation. So, knowing these things – that cleaning the Augean stables was one of Hercules' heroic labours; that the Bering Sea separates Russia from Alaska; that *caveat emptor* is the Latin for buyer beware; that Dylan Thomas wrote the poem 'Do Not Go Gentle Into That Good Night' – a perfect example of a villanelle – about death; that an embargo prevents one from acting or trading while it is in place; that folklore is the stuff of old wives' tales; that the Great Depression took place mainly in 1930s America and resulted in Wall Street bankers chucking themselves out of windows; that David Hume was a Scottish philosopher specialising in empiricism and scepticism; that the infinitive is the basic form of a verb which sends traditionally minded grammarians into a coughing fit if split (boldly or otherwise); that Judas Iscariot was a Zealot who betrayed Jesus for 30 pieces of silver; that "Lay on Macduff" comes from Shakespeare's play *Macbeth* and is popularly misquoted as "Lead on";

that metabolism concerns the chemical processes of life; that Nicaragua is a Central American nation made infamous by the US funding of the Contras; that an orbit is the path taken by a planetary body around its sun; that the Pharisees were the priest class who so hated Jesus; that Ramadan is the Islamic month of fasting; that sharecropping is a form of agriculture where a tenant pays rent for the right to farm; that Thomas Malthus observed that population doubles every 25 years unless checked by one or other of the four horsemen (and was wholly incorrect); that Ursa Major is the constellation commonly known as the Great Bear; that Victorian refers to the period in which Queen Victoria ruled the British Empire; that Whistler's Mother is the colloquial name given to a painting of the American artist James McNeill Whistler's maternal parent; that xylem has got something to do with how a plant gets water from its roots to its leaves; that "You can't serve both God and Mammon" is an injunction against the possibility of living a religious life and making money; and that zeitgeist is a German word translating to spirit of the age – does, in a very literal sense, make me cleverer than if I didn't.

Because I know these things, I can think about them. And because I can think about them, I can draw links between them and combine them in interesting ways. Without this knowledge, if I were to see or hear them referred to, I would most probably draw a blank and be unable to continue without recourse to the internet. And, as we saw in the last chapter, knowing how to look something up is pale and desiccated next to having the information live and breathe inside of us.

Another rich seam to mine might be such tomes as Charles Van Doren's marvellous *A History of Knowledge*,[20] which traces the progress of ideas from the ancients through the Middle Ages and the Renaissance, the invention of the scientific method and the start of modernity to the developments of the 20th century, and then speculate about the likely developments of the future.* It covers philosophy, morality, art, theology, economics, politics, science and technology, and traces the influence of great minds from Buddha and Confucius to Christ and Muhammad; from Thales, Democritus and Aristotle to Edison and Einstein; from Sophocles and Euripides to Shakespeare and thence to Samuel Beckett;

---

*   Sadly, Van Doren was disgraced when caught cheating on the 1950s TV quiz show, *Twenty One*. Despite this inexcusably foolish behaviour, *A History of Knowledge* is a terrific read.

from Plato to Kant to Nietzsche and Freud; from Cervantes to Goethe, Yeats, Kafka and Mann. While no one can ever know anything more than a tiny drop of what has been thought and said, it's possible to know enough to equip us to avoid making the most obvious of blunders and to have a rough idea of the extent of our ignorance.

If some people know something and others don't, those who don't will find themselves excluded from and marginalised by the group which does. Of course, simply possessing knowledge is not enough. As we saw in Chapter 4, socio-economic status matters. The children of the wealthy and privileged will continue to have opportunities and access the rest of us can only dream of. Although access to culturally rich knowledge may be insufficient it's still necessary.

I'm not claiming that Hirsch's or Van Doren's lists are either definitive or right; that would be the wrong way to think. Every country would need its own list, but still, the list is not the point. It's just a mechanism for organising information which may – or may not – be worth teaching; it can used badly or well. Our focus should be on schema acquisition and considering the connections between all that a child knows. Just as a map is not the territory, the list (or the curriculum) is merely a way of representing items that should be taught.

It may not be right or fair, but much of this assumed background knowledge consists, inevitably, of the accumulated cultural contributions of dead white men. We don't have to like it, but we do need to teach it. This isn't a scam designed to protect the interests of the rich and powerful, and the argument is bigger than socio-economics. Knowing what is considered culturally important and powerful allows children to have a richer, fuller life; to take part in a community of ideas. As the philosopher Michael Oakeshott famously said:

> ... we are the inheritors, neither of an inquiry about ourselves and the world, nor of an accumulating body of information, but of a conversation, begun in the primeval forests and extended and made more articulate in the course of centuries.[21]

This being the case, schools can induct children into this conversation – between public and private, between the living and the dead – to discover for themselves what they consider to be 'the best'. The curriculum we teach should serve "to remind us that it is access to a 'relation to knowledge' not facts or even scientific laws that is the purpose of education".[22] And, lest we forget, the reason for giving children this access is to make them cleverer, thereby improving their odds of living a happy and fulfilled life.

The hidden cost of bad ideas

When we think in terms of subject domains, powerful knowledge and cultural literacy, it allows us to consider the opportunity cost of pursuing one course over another. Opportunity cost is the value of the next best alternative foregone, where a choice needs to be made between several mutually exclusive alternatives, given limited resources. What this means is that if you've got two choices – go out for a drink (A) or stay home and mark students' books (B) – the opportunity cost of going for a drink is the time and money you spend on going out plus the value of having stayed at home and marked. A traditional cost–benefit analysis doesn't give you the true picture. The true cost (C) of a decision is:

$$A - B = C$$

When calculating the desirability of a course of action, how often do we take into account the value of the best alternative? For every decision, there is an explicit and an implicit cost. The explicit costs are obvious: the resources expended in making the project a success. The implicit costs are the hidden costs represented by the failure to allocate precious resources elsewhere. So our simple equation, $A - B = C$ can be better expressed as:

Explicit value – Cost of chosen option – Implicit value of foregone alternative = True cost

To return to our example, going out for a drink on a Tuesday night might result in accruing units of enjoyment. From this, we have to subtract the cash we've spent on drinks and the enjoyment of ploughing through a pile of marking. Some people might enjoy a few hours of marking but, for most, the night out is a winner in terms of raw enjoyment. But, hang on, what happens on Wednesday? You're hung-over and you've not even looked at those increasingly dog-eared exercise books! Tuesday evening might have been fun, but Wednesday is a living nightmare. In schools, the most precious of our resources is time. Time is always finite. You can only spend it once, and once it's gone, it's gone. The cost of every decision we make in school is explicit value minus implicit value.

When we make a choice about what to teach, our natural tendency is to evaluate that choice on its own merits. We might ask questions like: did students enjoy learning it? Did it enable them to make progress within the subject? Does it connect to other aspects of what they have studied? Did they find it easy or hard? What we very rarely ask is: would it have been better to have taught them something else? It's much harder to evaluate the potential impact of the choice not taken, but unless we try, we will have far less understanding about the power of the choices we make.

Consider an example. A maths teacher decides to spend a few lessons on Roman numerals. She figures that children will encounter them in real life, that they demonstrate how mathematics has developed through history as well as providing another way to represent numbers, and that they might help to reinforce other concepts such as place value or addition and subtraction. She might also conclude that it will be fun. All of these ways of evaluating the teaching of Roman numerals are perfectly valid; they might well achieve all these aims, but would they achieve them as well as doing something else? The justification that learning about Roman numerals might reinforce other mathematical concepts is the least persuasive reason; maybe it would but, arguably, the best way to understand place value is by being taught about and practising using place value. I'm not saying that Roman numerals shouldn't be taught – maybe they should – but if so, they should be taught because they are worth knowing about in their own right. The point of this example is to help us recognise that while children are being taught X they cannot also be taught Y.

Because time is finite children can't study everything. This means teachers have to make a choice. You might have a stock cupboard full of copies of Robert Swindells' novel *Stone Cold*, but the opportunity cost here is the value of studying *Stone Cold* minus the value of studying all the other novels you could possibly choose. Now, you might really like Swindells, but is he a better writer than Chaucer, Shakespeare, Austen or Orwell? Whatever the value in terms of enjoyment of reading *Stone Cold*, what is the cultural capital of Swindells' teen page-turner? To what extent is it going to help build children's vocabulary? What will it teach them about history, society and human nature? Is it really the best choice, or just the easiest?

One of the biggest sticks we've made to beat ourselves with as teachers is the narrowing concept of utility. The regular refrains of "When will I ever need to use this?" or "Why do I need to know this?" are often only ever answered by "Because it's in the exam." This is a terribly limiting way to think about education. If our aim is to make children cleverer, then we can say, "The reason you should know this is because it will make you cleverer." As we saw in the previous chapter, what we know is far more than those things we think *about*. It might be true that the only time many children will actively think *about* trigonometry or plate tectonics is in an exam, but, in reality, we forget a lot of what we've learned and struggle to actively recall most of what we learned at school. Often, we cannot think *about* school subjects directly, but just because we can't recognise how this knowledge has changed us, it doesn't mean that it hasn't. The real power of knowledge is that it is what we think *with*. And the more powerful and culturally rich that knowledge is, the better the quality of our thought.

Here, then, is a list of questions to consider whenever faced with a decision about what to teach:

- Does it add to children's knowledge of what others in society consider to be valuable?

- Does it enable children to take part in discussion or debate that they would otherwise be excluded from?

- Does it enable children to critique what others have decided is important or true?

- Does it allow children to think beyond the confines of their experiences outside of school?

- Does it open up new ways of considering the world?

- Does it allow children to better critically evaluate what they have already been taught?

- Does it make it easier for children to speak to others about abstract concepts?

- Is it rooted in how to perform a task, or in why the task should be performed?

- Would this be good enough for my own children?

- How do I know this choice is better than an alternative?

Answering – or at least thinking about – these questions will go some way to ensuring that what you do in your school or classroom is in the children's best interests and not merely what is most expedient.

A broad and balanced curriculum

The curriculum is much more than the timetable. Clearly, what subjects a school offers and how much time is allocated to each will have a bearing on children's studies, but it does not determine what teachers will teach. We should also be clear that an exam board specification is not a curriculum. Figure 8.1 demonstrates the difference.

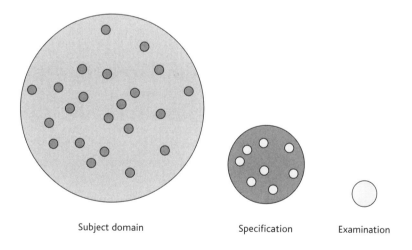

Subject domain   Specification   Examination

Figure 8.1. The domain, the specification and the test

The domain is everything it's possible to know about a subject. For obvious reasons, exam boards select aspects of this domain on which to focus in their courses. This necessarily narrows the curriculum, and, to some extent, exam specifications will exert an inevitable influence on curriculum decisions. The examination narrows the focus further to what it is possible for a pupil to demonstrate in about two hours. A good examination will carefully sample as widely as possible from what is covered by the specification, but exam boards (in an effort to paint exams as being as easy for pupils to do as well in as they possibly can) have gone to enormous efforts to give schools as narrow a range of possibilities on which to focus in classrooms. This is a rational approach to what are perceived to be the levers of accountability, but it creates a perverse incentive for schools to reduce the curriculum to five years' worth of exam practice. No one could reasonably argue that this could ever represent a broad and balanced curriculum.

Subject domains are one of the most useful mechanisms at our disposal for making decisions about what to teach. We have arrived at a reasonably broad consensus of what we mean by mathematics, modern foreign languages and geography (although there's no doubt that the content of some domains is a lot more settled than others). There are some domains, such as history or English literature, where the breadth of content is so impossibly wide that we are forced to make very brutal choices, and others, like maths and science, where the content of what ought to be taught in schools tends to be more broadly accepted.

The aim of making children cleverer is not in conflict with exam success, but a curriculum focused on teaching to the test is most certainly in opposition to the end of making children cleverer.

Here are a few things which do not represent a broad and balanced curriculum:

- Spending class time on SATs practice papers before Christmas in Year 6.

- Neglecting those areas of the Key Stage 2 curriculum that are not examined to concentrate solely on those areas that are.

- Starting GCSEs in Year 9 (or earlier).

- Squeezing out arts subjects in Key Stage 4 to allow for ever greater English and maths allocations.

- Using GCSE exam board specifications as a model for designing the Key Stage 3 curriculum.

If a school does any of these things, it is putting its own interests ahead of those of its students.

While it might feel scary to widen the curriculum and spend less time on exam preparation, this is, counter-intuitively, probably the best way to ensure that children do well in exams. We are all unable to think about anything which we do not know. If knowledge is emphasised, then future possibilities are opened up. Just as aiming a dart at the bullseye increases our chance of hitting the board, so teaching pupils more than they will ever need to know for an examination expands the probability that they will know enough to do well. Conversely, teaching them just enough to do well reduces the likelihood that they will know enough. Instead, it leads to the sort of cargo cult understanding we saw in Chapter 7.

We should also consider what children need to know of science, history, mathematics and geography. In order to follow the arguments in a book or article, we don't need much more than a passing familiarity with assumed background knowledge, but if children are studying trigonometry, plate tectonics, cell division or early modern European history, they will need to possess some foundational knowledge in much greater depth. The unifying concepts that come up repeatedly within a domain will vary enormously from subject to subject, so it makes sense to identify and teach this foundational knowledge early on and to continually return to it.

The educational psychologist Jerome Bruner's notion of the 'spiral curriculum' was predicated on this idea. Bruner dismissed the idea that some kinds of knowledge could be developmentally inappropriate. He said, "any subject can be taught effectively in some intellectually honest form to any child at any stage of development".[23] Hirsch refers to this as the 'Bruner principle': any topic can be taught appropriately to any age of child. Bruner saw the learning of structure, rather than the mastery of facts and techniques, as the central concern of education. He believed that if children were able to understand the structures of different subjects at an early age, then they would find it easier to incorporate new ideas within these domains.

The spiral curriculum sought to introduce the structure of disciplines in a carefully sequenced and logically coherent way. Children should first encounter a simple iteration of an idea and then, on re-encountering it, the complexity should be incrementally increased. This makes intuitive sense and would seem to be supported by what we know about learning and forgetting.

This serves to remind us that simply putting culturally rich, powerful knowledge in front of children is not enough. It must be carefully sequenced and introduced and reintroduced, piece by careful piece.

Domain knowledge

Let's imagine that the circle in Figure 8.2 encapsulates all the knowledge contained within a given domain. Within are all the procedures and propositions which constitute the knowledge of that domain. If the domain in question is chemistry, the circle would contain knowledge of atoms and elements, a homologous series, how to balance an equation and many more items. If the domain is English literature, it would include knowledge of different literary forms and genres, specific knowledge of writers and works of literature, the contexts in which these writers wrote, the various forms of metaphor and rhetorical techniques, traditions of literary criticism and the knowledge of how to construct critical arguments about literature.

Using what we've learned about the formation of schemas, we can think of domains as containing networks of interconnected nodes – chunks of knowledge which all relate to each other and build up to a cohesive whole. This is obviously an oversimplification. Instead of a circle, try thinking of the domain as a sphere, with items connecting hierarchically or laterally and sometimes relating to whole other domains. Either way, children blunder into the middle of the domain with partial and fragmented knowledge.

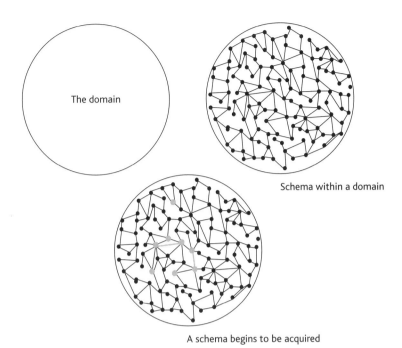

Schema within a domain

A schema begins to be acquired

Figure 8.2. The domain; schema within a domain; a schema begins to be acquired

Source: Adam Boxer, Novices, Experts and Everything In-between:
Epistemology and Pedagogy, *A Chemical Orthodoxy* (10 May 2018).
Available at: https://achemicalorthodoxy.wordpress.com/2018/05/10/
novices-experts-and-everything-in-between-epistemology-and-pedagogy/.

To help children link these fragmentary chunks we need to understand how biologically secondary knowledge is best communicated within a domain. Some pedagogical approaches may be shared by many domains, while some will be peculiar to just one or two. The crucial point is not to confuse learning and doing, pedagogy and epistemology. The production of knowledge is not the same – or even particularly similar – to the transmission of knowledge. In the context of science education, Paul Kirschner offers this distinction:

> The epistemology of most sciences, for example, is often based upon experimentation and discovery and, since this is so, experimentation and discovery should be a part of any curriculum aimed at 'producing' future scientists. But this does not mean that experimentation and discovery should also be the basis for curriculum organization and learning-environment designing.[24]

We've already seen that the best way to learn the solutions to problems is not by solving problems. Problem solving is the means by which new knowledge might be added to the domain; it is not an effective means of learning the knowledge already within the domain. Just as we wouldn't think that the best way to teach children about the Trojan War is to send them off to Turkey on an archaeological dig, we shouldn't conclude that teaching science, maths, English or any other subject bears much resemblance to the way experts in these fields go about practising their professions.

The people who produce new knowledge are often not the people best qualified to teach it. Subject domains in schools – syllabuses as they're usually called – have to select and sequence what is to be taught, but the people who are required to do this work – school teachers – often don't possess the highly specialised knowledge to do so effectively. We rely on someone to provide us with a curriculum and trust that it is fit for purpose. As we've seen, if we turn to examination specifications and work backwards, we arrive at something that is neither broad nor balanced.

....

Building on the ideas that we've covered in this chapter, a curriculum should be:

- Broad. (How much of the domain will pupils experience?)

- Culturally rich. (Does the selected content conform to shared cultural agreements of what is considered valuable to know?)

- Powerful. (Does the selected content allow pupils to think in new and unexpected ways?)

- Coherent. (Does the content link together in a way which builds schemas and allows children to think increasingly effortlessly?)

There's still a vast range of substance to select from in trying to meet these criteria. The point is not to cram in as much as possible, but to select only what can be carefully organised, sequenced and internalised. Remember, planning documents are all very well, but anything that doesn't end up residing in children's minds may as well not have been written down.

Chapter 8: key points

- Not all knowledge is equal – some kinds of knowledge should be privileged in schools.

- Powerful knowledge is distinct from everyday knowledge and allows children to think about concepts outside their narrow experience.

- It's not true that all ways of knowing are equally valid – schools should embrace the idea of teachers as an authority.

- Some knowledge is more culturally rich than other knowledge – that is, it is more valued within society.

- Those who possess powerful, culturally rich knowledge are more likely to be successful – academically and otherwise.

- If only children from privileged backgrounds are given access to powerful, culturally rich knowledge, then injustice and iniquity is perpetuated.

- Children should not be taught to uncritically accept knowledge; instead they should be encouraged to critique what they've learned.

- Because curriculum time is finite, there is always an opportunity cost in what we choose to teach. Schools should endeavour to teach what is most powerful and culturally rich.

- Exam specifications narrow the domain to a test.

- Teaching to the test may feel like a risk-free strategy, but the more of the domain students know, the better they are likely to perform in an exam.

- The domains in which we are experts are vastly larger than the curriculum we teach.

- Expert performance within a domain is necessarily different to teaching knowledge of that domain to novices.

- A curriculum needs careful organisation and sequencing if children are to master powerful knowledge.

It's now time to move to the question of how, in a practical sense, we can ensure that children acquire these powerful, culturally rich ideas. The next chapter focuses on the role of practice in helping children to develop expertise.

Chapter 9
Practice makes permanent

If at first you don't succeed then skydiving definitely isn't for you!

Stephen Wright

- Does practice always lead to improvement?

- Does it matter how we practice, or are some ways of practising more effective than others?

- How does practice change the way we think?

- How are beginners different from those with years of experience?

I was a giver-upper as a child. I gave up on pretty much everything I found tricky and didn't get immediate gratification from – or at least that's what I thought. A few years ago, my mother reminded me of my early struggles with reading. Apparently, my teacher had written home with the bad news that I was mentally subnormal and would probably never learn to read. My mum wasn't having any of that. She took me out of school and spent all day, every day forcing me to read the entire *Janet and John* reading scheme.* My memories of this are pretty murky but the image of those grinning, flaxen haired goody-goodies burns brightly. I hated their parents, their friends and even their dog with a pure and abiding passion. One snapshot of memory that is still crystal clear is the revelation of realising that the word *friend*, which had seemed to make no logical sense at all, could be read as *fry + end*. To this day, this is what

---

* These books were based on the *Alice and Jerry* books written by Mabel O'Donnell. In 1949, UK publishers James Nisbet and Company licensed them and had them rewritten as Janet and John by Mabel O'Donnell and Rona Munro.

I bring to mind whenever I have to spell it. A few weeks later my mum sent me back to school and said to my teacher, "Here you are, he can read now."

Whenever the going got tough and I felt like screaming with exasperation, my well-meaning mother would remind me that 'practice makes perfect'. It turns out – as I've taken great delight in telling her – this is not true. Practice makes permanent. What we repeatedly do we get better at, and if we practise doing the wrong things in the wrong ways, we'll get better at doing things badly. Given that practice is certainly necessary for us to acquire the knowledge we need to get cleverer, it is essential for us to untangle exactly what sort of practice we should be encouraging in children to make sure they're acquiring expertise and not just consolidating mistakes and misconceptions.

Purposeful practice

Most people have heard of the '10,000 hour rule' – the idea that if you put in the hours then anyone can master anything. This appears to be an almost wilful misreading of Anders Ericsson's research into expertise. The journalist Malcolm Gladwell came up with the catchy phrase in his book *Outliers*, and although Ericsson and his colleagues had mentioned the figure in a 1993 report on violin students, there isn't anything special about the number 10,000. Practising for this length of time certainly doesn't confer mastery of anything, not even playing the violin.[1] Of course, practice only takes us so far: genes and motivation will also affect how well we perform.* But in every domain of learning it takes a major investment of time and effort to become an expert. The amount of time required to learn material is roughly proportional to the amount of material there is to learn. As with everything else, the domain matters. It might take far less time to master one domain and far more to master another, depending on their size. Daunting as it might seem, chess is a relatively small domain when compared to, say, biology. And the domain

---

* It's important to note that Ericsson disputes this and has said, "Differences between expert and less accomplished performers reflect acquired knowledge and skills or physiological adaptations effected by training, with the only confirmed exception being height." See Ericsson and Charness (1994), 744.

of times tables is tiny. The more there is to learn, the more you need to practice.

More importantly, the 10,000 hour rule is wrong because *how* you practise matters far more than *how much* you practise. Not all forms of practice are equal. Rote learning – repeating a task over and over – is often dismissed as a laborious, brute force method of ingraining routines in long-term memory, but it can certainly be effective, as anyone who has learned multiplication tables by chanting them aloud can testify. But it is perhaps only *deliberate practice* – which involves attention, rehearsal, repetition over time, precise feedback and getting out of your comfort zone – which enables us to truly develop expertise. Ericsson says, "When most people practice, they focus on the things they already know how to do. Deliberate practice is different. It entails considerable, specific, and sustained efforts to do something you can't do well – or even at all."[2]

Deliberate practice, powerful as it is, has a number of drawbacks for anyone wanting to improve in fields like, say, teaching, writing or gardening. Firstly, Ericsson suggests that domains failing to make the cut include, "Pretty much anything in which there is little or no direct competition … These are not areas where you are likely to find accumulated knowledge about deliberate practice, simply because there are no criteria for superior performance."[3] Secondly, to practise deliberately you need the right kind of teacher. The reason sports, music and chess provide rich opportunities for deliberate practice is because others have gone before, reached elite levels of performance, accrued the knowledge required and then taken on students to pass on their wealth of experience.

Because of these limitations, Ericsson offers us a more achievable version which he has termed *purposeful practice*. Purposeful practice requires the following four ingredients:

1. *Well-defined, specific goals* – the clearer we are about what we want to achieve, the more likely we are to achieve it. If our goal isn't well-defined, how will we know if we've improved? It's useful to have more general goals like, "I want to get better at maths," but in order to improve, these need to be broken down into clear, specific steps.

2. *Focus* – in order to improve, practice requires our full and undivided attention.

3. *Feedback* – we have to know if we've got something right, and if
    we've fallen short, where and why. Feedback doesn't have to come
    from someone else (I have videoed myself performing katas in my
    efforts to get better at karate, for instance), but the assistance of a
    knowledgeable expert is a huge boon.

4. *Being outside your comfort zone* – as soon as we get comfortable we
    stop improving. Flawless performance might be our goal, but in
    order to get better we need to keep paying attention to the details.[4]

This last point requires some additional explanation. In *Human Performance*, Paul Fitts and Michael Posner identify three distinct phases
of practice.[5] When we first begin to practise a new skill, we are acutely
aware of the process. This is the *cognitive stage*. Think of learning to drive
a car: we can feel overwhelmed by having to use three different pedals, the steering wheel, change gear *and* keep an eye on what's going on
outside. As we keep practising, we move into the *associative stage* where
we are less aware of all the different aspects and start to associate them
together. We begin to make fewer mistakes and have greater capacity
to pay attention to our surroundings. Now changing gear and pressing
down the clutch are chunked together as part of a driving schema – they
occur together, without us having to consciously think about it. Further
practice takes us to the *autonomous stage*. At this point we can drive a car
and have a conversation with a passenger at the same time. Driving can
become so automatic that miles can pass by with no conscious awareness
of what we're doing. We quite literally go on autopilot. At this point we
stop improving. This explains why some people (ahem) have been driving for many years and still make the same sloppy mistakes. Joshua Foer
calls this "the OK plateau".[6] To improve further we need to force ourselves back into the cognitive stage, maybe by taking an advanced driving
course.

Think also about the process of learning to teach: at the cognitive stage
we struggle to focus on delivering a lesson and managing children's
behaviour; at the associative stage we become more able to consider what
children are likely to be learning rather than just what they are doing;
and at the autonomous stage we can start to treat children as individuals
without worrying about whether the lesson will work.

Most of us only improve a skill to the point of competency. At the autonomous stage we tend to stop improving because we no longer have to stay conscious of what we're doing. The procedures are stored in long-term memory and our working memory is free to pay attention to new information. Practising to the point of automaticity is a good place to stop for many of the things we want children to learn. But to improve beyond competency we need to continue paying attention, and this is what differentiates purposeful practice from just repeating procedures we have already mastered. This also explains why teachers don't just continue to get better and better with years served.[7] Continued improvement requires purposeful practice.

Progress is easy for beginners. In fact, it's almost guaranteed as long as there is some motivation to improve. It helps if we get some feedback and have opportunities to go over procedures a few times, but beyond that, no problem. Learning only continues if we vary the conditions of practice as we gain mastery, so that a degree of effortful thinking is still required. In this way, novices slowly become increasingly expert.

Not seeing the wood for the trees

We all start life as novices. As such, we think in qualitatively different ways to experts. A novice will know very little about a subject and will have correspondingly little to draw on in long-term memory to help them think and make new connections, whereas an expert has a rich fund of experiences to exploit.

Imagine exploring a wood as either an expert in woodcraft or a novice. The novice immediately plunges into the wood and begins looking carefully and intently at the trees. Not many trees can be seen at any one time and it's impossible to see anything in the distance. There is a bewildering amount of detail but few clues as to the relevance of any of it. The light is poor in the novice's wood and none of the potential paths offer any indication of the way through or out. Some tracks turn out not even to be real paths and a sense of direction is soon lost. Under such circumstances novices can only plan small stratagems which will take them a short way, and hope for the best. It's seldom absolutely clear whether any path is really relevant to the ultimate goal and it's often necessary to retrace their steps. Sometimes it's difficult to tell whether a path has been tried before or not. Inevitably, exploring the wood is largely a matter of trial and error. Novices quickly forget most of the relevant details of a problem and lose their sense of the route taken to reach a solution. Working in the wood as a novice can be oppressive and scary.

While the novice is blundering about speculatively in this dark wood, the expert has remained outside, thinking about how to find a way through, perhaps even walking away from the wood to some higher ground for a better view. The expert will deliberately consider other woods and the general and specific structures of terrain they have experienced. An expert will review their knowledge of woods in general and specifically and think about their structure, but they will also think about solutions – what do I really want from exploring this particular wood, and is it even worth exploring? They may take time for a cup of tea and some peace of mind. They may look up information which they foresee might be useful. The expert enters the wood later, but is then able to recognise which trees, or patterns of trees, are meaningful. They might also consider other topographical features – the alignment to the sun, wind direction or the tracks of particular animals. The expert will have twigged whether it is worth working in this wood at all and, if so, what to look for, why and where. Experts look for, and at, particular features and know what they all mean. There will be few surprises in there.[8]

An expert understands the particular problem but also the generalities of this kind of problem. An expert will recognise the probability that the problem they are faced with is similar to other problems they've solved in important respects. Experts are much more likely to learn something that will be of value next time a similar problem is encountered, particularly if any part of it has been tricky. Novices will have only rather general impressions and will notice and recall very few important details. Worse, little of what they recall will make much sense and almost none of it will be memorable or remembered. At some point when students are 'lost in the woods', teachers will be forced to intervene to minimise the sunk cost of wandering about and not getting anywhere. Ideally, this guidance will come before students begin to practise a new skill, rather than as a result of misconceptions having been embedded.

Because children have yet to pass through the thresholds that lead to expertise, any attempt to short cut the process is only likely to lead to mimicry and inflexibility. We can't expect them to see the deeper structures of the subjects we teach until they've amassed sufficient expertise in the shallows. They need to learn the concrete before they can generalise to the abstract. The way to become an expert is by learning to make ever finer discriminations and to develop new categories and distinctions within the subject. Novices need to learn to recognise metaphorical ways of thinking and to explore what things mean (and don't mean). In this way they come to understand the underlying patterns, the deep structure of the subject, and part of this is the ability to notice analogies: *this is like that in some aspect*. Gradually, novices develop a more flexible understanding that can be applied to a variety of new but fundamentally similar situations, but even so, this will not happen by magic. Novices need guidance – on what to notice, what's important, which distinctions to make and what kind of deep structure they are looking for.

It's tempting to think that students can be become experts if we give them the real-world problems experts engage in and teach them to 'think like experts'. This is unlikely to work. Daniel Willingham explains: "Whenever you see an expert doing something differently from the way a non-expert does it, it may well be that the expert used to do it the way the novice does it, and that doing so was a necessary step on the way to expertise."[9] It is a mistake to think that simply copying what the expert does will lead to success. We need to acquire the accumulated experience to know what to do when things deviate from expectations.

To reiterate, in order to become an expert, we first have to be a novice.

From novice to expert

Although some of these ideas have been alluded to in previous chapters, it will be helpful to reconsider the implications of the various ways in which the thinking of novices and experts deviate from each other. By combining what we have learned about thinking, memory and knowledge, we can get a clearer picture about what it means to make children cleverer.

Broadly speaking, there are two main hallmarks of expertise: (1) automaticity of foundational procedures and (2) the ability to see the 'deep' structure of problems within domains of expertise. We readily accept that an expert knows more than a novice. Experts have mastered a variety of procedural knowledge to the point where they no longer have to think *about* it – instead, they start to think *with* it. They will also have had significant experience of thinking about domain-specific propositional knowledge which helps them to quickly and easily acquire new knowledge within their domain. Much of this becomes tacit background knowledge which, as the name implies, operates in the background. Although we rarely think about it directly, this allows us to make connections beneath the level of consciousness – we grasp subtleties and make inferences without realising anything special is going on. When we have a wide knowledge of a domain, we will also have lots of relevant tacit and procedural knowledge of which we are largely unaware.

As experts, we often assume that others share the same background knowledge as us and so it often goes unsaid. And where expert knowledge is stated, all too often it isn't understood. Experts are unaware of the extent of their knowledge and end up speaking in maxims. As we saw in Chapter 7, such maxims are easily understood by other experts but are meaningless to novices. Where a novice will be confused and frustrated by gaps in explanation, an expert fills them without even realising they're doing it. Such is the curse of knowledge. This lack of insight into the source of expertise can lead us into neglecting the teaching of the vital nuts and bolts on which our expert performances depend.

The more you know about a subject, the more you will learn from reading about, or listening to a lecture on, that subject. This is counter-intuitive because the less you know about a subject, the more there is to learn. This is true, of course, but even though there is a lot more you could learn if you're a novice, you probably won't learn much of it. This is because most of your cognitive reserves are being expended on trying to make sense of the new subject and holding all the fresh information in mind without the necessary prior knowledge to anchor it. Even the information you do attend to will be hard to retrieve because, knowing less, the schemas in your long-term memory will have far fewer connections. This means that there is less for you to 'attach' new knowledge to and far fewer cues to help you retrieve it.

If you're an expert, you'll recognise much of what a fellow expert has to say and be able to turn their taps into a tune. When they move on to novel aspects of the subject, you'll understand how the new information connects with what you already know. The new information will be stored as part of dense schemas with huge numbers of cues, thereby making it easier to retrieve. And the easier it is to retrieve, the easier it becomes to apply. In this way, inflexible knowledge becomes increasingly flexible.

We discussed the distinction between flexible and inflexible knowledge back in Chapter 7. To recap, while a novice may share some of what an expert knows, they are unlikely to know it with the same degree of flexibility. Novices and experts utilise their limited reserves of working memory differently. A novice doesn't possess the schematic structures in long-term memory that an expert does, and so they will need to think about every step of a process and all the components of a proposition individually. This is onerous. As we saw in Chapter 6, most people are only able to handle about four chunks of information at once, and for a novice a chunk might be a single fact. But as we become increasingly familiar with the material we're learning, the cognitive characteristics associated with the material are altered so that it can be handled more efficiently by our working memory. Experts acquire huge, interconnected schemas which they can draw into working memory as single chunks, thus leaving capacity to think about the novel aspects of a problem.

Inflexible knowledge cannot be bypassed; it is a necessary stepping stone to expertise. All experts began with a foundation of inflexible knowledge on which they built increasingly flexible knowledge. It is the flexibility with which we can think about and apply items of knowledge that enables experts to perform effortlessly and solve far more complex problems than novices can.

When trying to solve problems, our minds employ a process called *problem-solving search*. This is the name cognitive scientists have given to our biologically primary ability to solve problems. Problem-solving search depends on both schema acquisition (remembering successful solutions, then recognising similarities between novel and previously solved problems) and *means-end analysis* (working backwards from the goal until a workable solution is found). The ability to use means-end analysis to solve problems is an evolutionary adaption – very young children rapidly learn how to solve the various problems they encounter. They look about themselves to establish what means they have available and then apply these means to achieving their end, whatever that may be. In this way, they learn to roll over, fit blocks together and get adults to do stuff for them. Most of the problems we solve are ones we need to solve again and again. As such, the most efficient way to solve problems is to remember the solution and apply what we did before. With sufficient repetition, we store the solutions to solved problems in long-term memory, which means that when we face the same problem again, we don't even have to think about the solution.[10] How efficient is that?

If most challenges in life are ones we have already overcome, or are close enough that we can generalise solutions from closely related scenarios, then schema acquisition is the key to expert performance within a domain, allowing experts to think about other, possibly more interesting, things as they go about their business. But when novices face a problem for which they don't have a conveniently stored solution, they have to rely on the costlier means-end analysis. This is likely to lead to cognitive overload because it involves trying to work through and hold in mind multiple possible solutions. It's a bit like trying to juggle five objects at once without previous practice. Solving problems is an inefficient way to get better at problem solving. The attention and processing required to engage in means-end analysis results in less capacity to store solutions in long-term memory in a way that can be easily accessed in the future. In order to build up useful schemas, "a problem solver must learn to recognize a problem state as belonging to a particular category of problem states that require particular moves".[11] This takes attention which, if it is being used to search for solutions, will not be available to recognise patterns.

For instance, I know a heck of a lot about *Macbeth*. I've seen four different theatre productions and at least five different film adaptations. On top of that, I must have taught it to perhaps 20 different classes, several times as an A level text (although I never actually studied it as a student). I've also read several books of literary criticism. As a consequence, I'm steeped in the bloody thing! Not only do I know the characters and plot inside out, I can also quote sizeable chunks of it. I know a fair bit about the context in which it was first written and performed and also about how its critical reception has varied over the centuries. While I'd never have the hubris to describe myself as an expert – there's always someone who knows a lot more – I'm not too shabby. In comparison, despite my grounding in literature as an academic study, I know practically nothing about French dramatist Nicolas de Montreux's 1601 tragedy *Sophonisbe*, beyond the fact that it's about a Carthaginian woman who lived during the Second Punic War with Rome.

Now, imagine I had to write an essay about each of these plays. If you gave me any essay question on *Macbeth* I'd feel confident that I'd have something interesting – although perhaps not original – to say because I know its deep structure inside out. But writing about *Sophonisbe*, even if I had a translated copy in front of me, would be tough. Why might this be? Although I'm pretty good at essay writing and know the form a literature essay is supposed to take, I'd struggle to write much worth reading about *Sophonisbe* because I don't know anything about it. I'd have to rely on guesswork, half-formed thoughts and cursory analysis of its superficial features. No doubt I'd do better than many other people who have never studied or taught literature, but I'm pretty sure that any literature undergraduate who had actually read and seen the play would be able to outclass me.

The ability to 'see' structures comes with the experience of thinking about domain-specific knowledge. The more we know and the more practice we have at identifying and solving problems within a domain, the more likely we are to see through the superficial trappings of a problem to the underlying structures beneath. When we become aware of these structures, we become increasingly able to transfer our ideas between contexts. The more I know about the domain of literature, the easier I find it to see connections between different texts. For instance, when I first watched Quentin Tarantino's film *Reservoir Dogs*, with its long monologues and blood-thirsty revenge, especially the set-piece stand-off in the final scene where everyone shoots everyone else, my immediate thought was, *Oh, it's a Senecan tragedy!* How was I able to see past all the silly names and ear slicing to detect this underlying structure? Well, I took classical studies at A level and had read a couple of the Roman dramatist Seneca's plays; then, as part of my English literature degree, I'd been shown Seneca's influence on *Hamlet*, as well as writing an essay comparing Thomas Kyd's *The Spanish Tragedy* and *Titus Andronicus*. It's tempting to say I understood some essential dramatic principle, but that would add an unnecessary layer of obfuscation – I simply *knew* more than lots of other people, who saw the film and arrived at very different conclusions.

In Chapter 7, we considered Daniel Willingham's proposition that inflexible knowledge ties meaning to a concept's superficial features, whereas flexible knowledge "transcends specific examples". Then, in Chapter 8, we looked at Michael Young's definition of powerful knowledge as generalisable concepts rather than narrow, procedural knowledge. Could it be that if knowledge is powerful it is also flexible? If these two really are the same, this provides us with some clues about how to provide children with the flexible, powerful concepts they require; if flexible knowledge comes from inflexible roots, then maybe powerful knowledge must be first encountered in less abstract forms. Probably the best way to 'practise' this kind of propositional knowledge is trying to recall it in different contexts to increase its storage strength. We will discuss retrieval practice in the next chapter.

Procedural knowledge needs to be practised differently. To return to the example of driving a car, at first there is so much on which you must concentrate: your feet, hands, mirrors and the environment outside the car. This all requires enormous cognitive resources: you have to pay attention to *everything*. When you've been driving for a few years, the basic operations for changing gear and taking a right-hand turn have been automatised. Your working memory is free to attend to road conditions and make predictions about what is likely to happen in the next few seconds. Likewise, when writing an essay, a novice will have to pay attention to such minutiae as punctuation, capital letters, sentence structure and academic tone. With practice, these things can be automatised, allowing much greater availability of working memory to think about the content of the essay. This is equally true of any domain of expertise: the less attention we need to give to the basics, the more we can think about what matters. This is how automaticity occurs.

Remember the example of learning to read? This automatisation of the basics is what makes experts so, well, expert. It might help if, instead of talking about 'skills', we talked about expertise; that way we might find it easier to see that all skill comes from learning information and practising how to use it. Hirsch asks us to imagine "how significantly our view of schooling might change if suddenly policy makers, instead of using the term *skill*, had to use the more accurate, knowledge-drenched term *expertise*".[12] Instead of believing that children are simply naturally skilled at music, sport or artistic endeavours, we would see their accomplishments as they rightly are: the result of hard work, purposeful practice and the mastery of specialised knowledge.

One of the hallmarks of the kind of purposeful practice that leads to expertise is the use of 'mental representations'. An expert knows what good looks like; a novice does not. Knowing what expert performance looks and feels like allows us to improve because we know what we're aiming for. Ericsson says that this ability to create rich mental representations is one of the distinguishing features of the kind of practice which is most likely to lead to improvements:

> The relationship between skill and mental representation is a virtuous circle: the more skilled you become, the better your mental representations are, and the better your mental representations are, the more effectively you can practise to hone your skill.[13]

In 2001, Gary McPherson and James Renwick published 'A Longitudinal Study of Self-regulation in Children's Musical Practice', which did exactly what the title suggests.[14] They took 27 children who were learning to play a variety of musical instruments and tried to unpick how and why some children improved more than others over a period of years. All of the children practised, they all put in effort, they were all motivated and had good attitudes, but not all of them got better at the same rate. It's tempting to think that the difference must have been innate ability, but actually the researchers concluded that it was the type of practice in which the children engaged that made the most difference.

McPherson and Renwick counted the number of mistakes children made on first playing a piece and then compared this to the number of mistakes made on a second performance. The lowest performing student made an average of 11 mistakes a minute on her first play-through and was still making 70% of the same mistakes the second time through. The best performing student made an average of 1.4 mistakes the first time round and was able to correct 8 in 10 of these mistakes in his second rendition. The researchers decided that some students had better mental representations of what a good performance would sound like and were able to self-check and provide their own feedback to eliminate as many mistakes as possible.

Of course, a sample of 27 students is unlikely to be representative of the general population, so we should be cautious of making any generalisable claims from this research. Luckily, these findings are supported by a large-scale study on the development of practising strategies, also published in 2001. Instead of the time-consuming approach of videoing and analysing practice sessions undertaken by McPherson and Renwick, Susan Hallam and her colleagues relied on self-report questionnaires to make studying a much larger sample feasible.[15] As with earlier studies, the researchers found that while the quantity of practice and attitudes to learning matter, they don't make nearly as much difference as we might hope. It was the ability to recognise their mistakes and then improve independently that differentiated the most accomplished students. This depended on them being able to visualise what a good performance would feel like as well as sound like.

Mental representations are a particular kind of background knowledge that allow us to visualise and think about a process. An expert musician might be able to hear the notes in her head; an expert firefighter might be able to visualise the steps required to put out a factory fire. Because it helps us to predict potential problems and plan responses, a mental representation allows us to perform better. These representations come from memory. The more practised we are at something, the more we will remember about our past performances. While we're performing we can run a background check that allows us to compare (sometimes consciously, sometimes not) how we're doing against how we want to be doing.

It's worth noting that we can't create mental representations just through study – we have to get our hands dirty by trying to do the thing we want to improve at. Every time we try something, receive feedback on our progress and try again, we're constructing more complete, more idealised mental representations of expert performance and creating a more flexible base of knowledge.

Table 9.1. The difference between novice and expert

Novice	Expert
Little relevant background knowledge	Lots of relevant background knowledge
Relies on working memory	Relies on long-term memory

Novice	Expert
Lacks effective mental representations of successful performance	Has a clear mental representation of successful performance within a domain
Elements of procedures must be remembered and processed individually	Necessary procedural knowledge has been automatised
Only has explicit knowledge	Possesses huge reserves of tacit knowledge
Possesses inflexible knowledge	Knowledge is flexible
Uses means-end analysis to solve problems	Problem solving relies on ability to draw many schemas into working memory as 'chunks'
Sees superficial details	Sees underlying structures
Learns little when exposed to new information	Learns a lot when exposed to information about which they are already knowledgeable
Learns best through explicit instruction and worked examples	Learns best through discovery approaches
Is more likely to experience cognitive overload as attention is swamped by new information	Is less likely to experience cognitive overload as attention is buttressed by memorised 'chunks' of knowledge
Struggles to transfer principles to new contexts	Is able to transfer principles between related domains
Frustrated by challenge	Motivated by challenge
Struggles to perform	Performs confidently and effortlessly
Works backward	Works forward

The single most important thing
for teachers to know

As we saw in Chapter 6, everything we keep in working memory produces a cognitive load. The theoretical underpinnings for this idea have their roots in Miller's work on memory and Chase and Simon's research into chunking. The reason for leaving a discussion of cognitive load theory until now is because it has important implications for teaching both novices and experts. It is so important that Dylan Wiliam has described it as "the single most important thing for teachers to know".[16]

In the early 1980s, Australian psychologist John Sweller was trying to find ways to help students solve mathematical problems. He saw that although students could solve the problems he set, they did not remember how to solve them later. In other words, they focused on the surface features and never saw the deep structure. His theory was born from wondering how someone could successfully solve a problem and yet learn nothing from the experience.[17]

The big idea behind cognitive load theory is that whatever the mechanism or process that transfers information from working to long-term memory is, it actually takes up space in working memory. If our attention is taken up with thinking about solving a problem, there will be insufficient working memory capacity to learn the solution. Working memory has to carry too great a cognitive load. This load can either be *extraneous* or *intrinsic*. Anything distracting or unnecessary produces extraneous load, whereas intrinsic load is the in-built complexity of the task we're trying to think about.* As its name suggests, you can't get rid of intrinsic load, but you can design tasks carefully to make them as simple as possible. Extraneous load, on the other hand, can and should be ruthlessly reduced.

If our working memory capacity is exhausted and we have too many pieces of information to keep in mind, we experience cognitive overload

---

* Researchers have also speculated about a third kind of load called *germane* load – this is an additional burden that has the effect of reducing current performance but increasing schema acquisition over time. This sounds like a neat idea, but researchers quickly realised that germane load made the theory unfalsifiable so have abandoned it. It does, however, overlap nicely with the idea of 'desirable difficulties', explored in the next chapter.

and become increasingly forgetful, confused and frustrated. The working memory of a novice fills up rapidly as they're forced to keep everything they need to know in mind as they attempt to complete a task. Experts rarely succumb to cognitive overload as they rely on being able to draw schemas from long-term memory into working memory as complete chunks.

A simple exercise will demonstrate how this works. Look at the numbers below for five seconds, then look away and see if you can write them down:

601681129166

How did you get on? Some people manage to do quite well at this by chunking the information. Instead of trying to remember 12 different digits, they remember 601, 681, 129 and 166. This is still challenging, but 601 takes up less space in working memory than 6, 0 and 1 do individually.

Now let's try the same exercise but this time as an expert. The numbers have been arranged differently, but otherwise go through the exact same process you did before:

1066 1812 1966

Easy, isn't it? Not only do you only have three chunks to remember, but each of those chunks is already a richly constructed schema. 1066 immediately taps into your Battle of Hastings schema and you might have found yourself thinking about William the Conqueror, Harold with an arrow in his eye and the Bayeux Tapestry. 1812 might have had you thinking of Napoleon's invasion of Russia or of Tchaikovsky's overture. Perhaps you even heard the music and the canon fire. And who can see 1966 without picturing Geoff Hurst, the Charlton brothers and the immortal line, "They think it's all over … It is now"?

The difference between the two exercises is knowledge. The first set of numbers meant nothing, so you had to approach them as a novice. The second set were rich in meaning and so you became an expert.

Here's another example. Try to make sense of this sentence:

The NNB should move jobs outside of the T98, employ more executives of a LRT background, and stop trying to copy HGT's output.

Trying to work out what it means is cognitively demanding because the four acronyms won't relate to anything in your long-term memory. Now try the exercise again:

> The BBC should move jobs outside of the M25, employ more executives of a BME background, and stop trying to copy ITV's output.

This is so much easier because, if you recognised all the initials, meaning is effortlessly supplied by your long-term memory so that you can read the whole thing without having to keep any extraneous information in working memory. This is what it feels like to be an expert.

What cognitive load theory tells us is that, for novices, the best practice approach is to provide explicit instructions and a detailed explanation of worked examples. The finding is that when novices are given a worked example, they're more likely to form the kind of mental representation they need for practice to be more productive. This holds true for novices no matter the subject, but not for experts.

It's sensible to think that the more expert you are, the less guidance you need; in fact, too much direction is likely to prove a distraction. One of the effects noticed by Sweller and his research team has been dubbed the reversal effect. The name refers to the finding that as we become more knowledgeable within a domain, we need less guidance and structure, so much so that instructional techniques that are most effective in helping novices to create long-term memory schemas become increasingly ineffective as novices become experts. Kalyuga and colleagues suggest that "instructional techniques that are highly effective with inexperienced learners can lose their effectiveness and even have negative consequences when used with more experienced learners."[18]

As we become increasingly expert within a domain we begin to benefit from different kinds of instruction to novices. When children don't know much about a topic in which they are expected to solve problems they are forced to rely on their fragile working memory, which is susceptible to cognitive overload, and to a reliance on naive analogies. In contrast, experts already possess mental representations of the topic – sophisticated analogies and models – which provide internal guidance. If additional instructional guidance is supplied, it can result in the processing of redundant information and increased cognitive load as the new guidance has to be reconciled with existing internal strategies. Experts may be prevented from taking advantage of their memorised schemas and their working memory might even become overloaded by the additional (pointless) input: "From this perspective, the expertise reversal effect can be understood as a form of the redundancy effect. It occurs by co-referencing the learners' internal available knowledge structures with redundant, external forms of support."[19]

The two main instances of the reversal effect are:

1. *The worked-example effect* – worked examples (a problem statement followed by a step-by-step demonstration of how to solve it) are often contrasted with open-ended problem solving in which the learner is responsible for providing the step-by-step solution. Although novices benefit more from studying structured worked examples than from solving problems on their own, as knowledge increases, open-ended problem solving becomes more effective.

2. *The imagination effect* – imagining a solution can be more effective than being told how to approach a task. When experts generate and construct their own mental representations of a task, they are likely to store the information in long-term memory more efficiently. However, for novices, structured support is more useful to help alleviate cognitive load.

While the performance of a novice is clumsy, forgetful, halting, vague and unsatisfying, an expert performs smoothly and effortlessly. They carry their expertise lightly and make it look easy. And it often is easy. Experts are so practised that they don't have to concentrate when performing basic or familiar routines. Instead, they are able to use their working memory to monitor their performance, predict possible problems and ensure they are dealt with before they occur. Novices work backward from a solution or a performance, trying to remember how they got there; experts use their expertise to project into the future and then seem to bound forward with intuitive leaps.

All these differences can be further summarised as being differences in domain knowledge. André Tricot and John Sweller argue that "expertise based on biologically secondary, domain-specific knowledge held in long-term memory is by far the best explanation of performance in any cognitive area".[20]

But always remember: we are all novices at something. While the curse of knowledge may blind us to aspects of our expertise in certain areas, the experience of struggle is available anytime we want to try something new. Perhaps one of the tragedies of acquiring expertise in one domain means we are less likely to make ourselves vulnerable by trying to learn another. As adults, we tend only to voluntarily engage in activities at which we are at least competent. We should always remember that novices are not less intelligent, they are less knowledgeable. Everyone gets cleverer the more they know and the more they practise.

Chapter 9: key points

- It is only through practice that we are likely to learn, but not all practice is equal. Only perfect practice makes perfect.

- Purposeful practice is required for students to make progress from competence to mastery.

- Practice of procedural knowledge can lead to automatisation, which frees up space in working memory.

- Novices and experts think differently. Students are novices and teachers are experts. Novices often struggle to understand what experts are trying to communicate.

- All experts used to be novices. There is no shortcut to expertise.

- Experts are prone to suffering from 'the curse of knowledge', which means they are likely to forget what it was like to be a novice.

- Novices and experts benefit from different types of instruction; what feels appropriate to a teacher is a poor guide as to what will work best with students.

- We are all prone to experiencing cognitive overload. Teachers should take care to remove extraneous load from lessons.

The distinctions between novices and experts, and their relationships to domains of knowledge, offer signposts as to how we can help children acquire the knowledge they need to become cleverer. Understanding that practice is what makes the difference between novices and experts is the first step. The next is to acknowledge that what happens in classrooms must be aligned to our aim of helping children to acquire robust schemas full of powerful, culturally rich knowledge. The final chapter will address some practical suggestions for how to go about this process.

Chapter 10
Struggle and success

Knowledge exists to be imparted.

Ralph Waldo Emerson

- Does it matter how we teach if we've got the curriculum right?

- How can we motivate children to want to learn biologically secondary knowledge?

- How do we make sure children are really learning and not just looking competent in lessons?

As we've seen, research into individual differences suggests that intelligence is fairly stable and that environmental factors – parenting and teaching – seem to wear off over time. At the same time, the huge rise in IQ scores over the last century clearly demonstrate that something really is changing and that these changes have real-world significance. This presents us with a paradox, which perhaps can be explained by saying that *g* (the tendency of cognitive abilities to correlate with each other in individuals) is real but that individual cognitive factors can be disproportionately affected by social attitudes and so increase with corresponding rises in other cognitive abilities. We should also remember that no matter how stable a construct is, if it changes, it changes. Remember the example of the phone number: under most conditions we expect our phone number to stay the same, but if we change it we expect it to stay changed. The same may well be true for intelligence.

In Chapter 3, we considered James Flynn's suggestion of what the different components of intelligence might be. Here they are again:

- *Mental acuity* – the ability to come up with solutions to problems about which we have no prior knowledge.

- *Habits of mind* – the ways in which we are accustomed to using our minds.

- *Attitudes* – how the society in which we live tends to view and think about the world.

- *Knowledge and information* – vocabulary, arithmetic, general knowledge, etc.

- *Speed of information processing* – how quickly we assimilate new data.

- *Memory* – our ability to retrieve information when it will be useful.

Of these, the final two – speed of information processing and memory – are fluid components and, as such, are probably beyond the ability of teachers to affect.

While the other four may all be malleable to different extents, the conclusion we've been building to over the course of this book is that our best bet for making kids cleverer is to increase the quantity and quality of what they know. If we can only think about things we know, then in the real world, creativity, problem solving and critical thinking are sharply increased by knowing more. As teachers, this should give us some confidence that increasing intelligence is both likely to work (it's easy to see that if you teach something to a child you can then check whether they know it) and likely to be effective (once they know something you can assess the effects of applying this knowledge).

The next question to consider is, if we've decided to teach children mastery of the various domains of knowledge they will encounter by providing them with culturally rich, powerful knowledge, does it matter how they are taught?

The case for explicit instruction

Broadly speaking, instruction tends to follow two distinct approaches: either focusing on getting children to remember information or on getting them to solve problems. Although a teacher might prioritise one or the other of these approaches, most teachers will, in all likelihood, do a bit of both. There's nothing wrong with this per se, but the order in which we engage in these approaches is important.

As we've seen, all human beings have a limited capacity for paying attention to information, and we can only hold about four chunks of information in mind at any given time. These chunks can be well-developed schemas or single, unrelated items of information. Although it might seem reasonable to suggest that either of our two approaches could result in learning (schematic changes to long-term memory) this seems not to be the case.

While no one would deny that the ability to solve problems is an important end, it's not necessarily an effective means. As we saw in the previous chapter, working memory limitations restrict how much of an experience reaches our long-term memory, and the capacity we need to handle information may leave little space for schema acquisition, even if a problem is solved. The issue is that the mechanism for solving problems, the 'problem-solving search', depletes our working memory reserves: "As a consequence, learners can engage in problem-solving activities for extended periods and learn almost nothing."[1]

What this tells us is that children can concentrate on solving problems and they can concentrate on tasks which contribute to developing their schemas, but if the task is challenging they are unlikely to manage both. Even though problem-solving activities certainly have their place in strengthening schematic connections once a schema has been acquired, they are a poor way of helping children to remember what they need to know in order to solve problems.

When teaching new material, especially when it is abstract or counter-intuitive, we need to ensure that children's working memories are not overloaded. The problem with more inductive 'discovery' methods of teaching is that they require children to juggle too much novel information in mind at the same time, with the result that they are so busy attempting to solve problems that they are less able to perceive the relationships and patterns we want them to understand. As such, explicit instruction is almost certainly a better bet than providing relatively little guidance using problem-solving or open-enquiry methods.

It's worth pointing out at this point that the term 'explicit instruction' does not mean simply giving a lecture. Instead, it involves using carefully considered explanations, worked examples and accurate analogies alongside questioning, modelling and scaffolding, structured discussion and lots of opportunities for purposeful practice. Then, once children have learned the propositional and procedural knowledge they need, they can switch their attention to solving increasingly complex problems.

This is not a matter of preference or opinion; it is the clear consensus of a considerable body of research.[2] Of course, you can ignore this weight of evidence, but doing so is likely to favour those children from more privileged backgrounds at the cost of those from poorer homes. Those children who come to school with greater mental acuity and faster speed of processing, or those who come from a background where they have been exposed to more useful knowledge of the world, already have a serious advantage over their less fortunate peers. If, for instance, we give children problems to solve without having first spent time on activities designed to help everyone remember the information needed to solve the problems, we will unwittingly be further privileging the already privileged.

By this point, I hope I have convinced you that teaching powerful, culturally rich knowledge with the aim of making children cleverer should be our aim. This being the case, it makes sense to follow an approach that balances the need to build up schemas of powerful knowledge with the need to keep children motivated; success followed by struggle.

Struggle before success

By all accounts, Sisyphus, the king of Ephyra, was a fairly unpleasant character. He killed travellers and stole their stuff in violation of the laws of hospitality. Mightily offended, the Greek god, Zeus, punished Sisyphus by condemning him to an eternity of pushing a huge rock up a hill only to have it roll down again as soon as he got it to the top. One can imagine that Sisyphus was not a happy chap.

Pushing a boulder up a hill with no prospect of ever reaching the top has become the very image of futility. Most people only persist with something difficult when they believe success is possible. Children are no different. It's pointless having the expectation that children will work hard to get good grades if they're unable to see how this might be achieved. Success and struggle must be balanced.

Since first encountering Robert and Elizabeth Bjork's concept of 'desirable difficulties', I've thought a lot about what the phrase means and how best to explain it. The sorts of difficulties the Bjorks have studied are designed to reduce performance during instruction in order to increase retention and transfer over the longer term. These desirable difficulties include:

- *Retrieval practice* – asking questions about material which has already been covered rather than restudying it in order to prevent children developing a false sense of familiarity and fluency.

- *Spacing* – allowing children to forget some of the material covered before it's reintroduced.

- *Interleaving* – mixing up different content in order to prevent children developing the illusion of knowledge.

- *Variation* – changing the conditions in which instruction takes place in order to prevent contextual cues from building up and making it harder for children to transfer what they've learned to new contexts.

- *Reducing and delaying feedback* – progressively reducing the frequency and quantity of feedback given in order to prevent children from becoming dependent on external sources of expertise.

There's something of a vogue for failure at the moment. I've noticed that when talking to teachers about these things, the message sometimes gets misinterpreted as just making work more difficult or as a justification for not helping children when they struggle. Some people seem to believe that children should be encouraged – even forced – to get things wrong and to cope with unachievable tasks. There are important benefits to making mistakes (as we'll see shortly) but, on the whole, this approach is a bad idea. The point of these desirable difficulties is to confront us with the illusion of knowledge and reveal the true extent of our ignorance.

Struggle is worthwhile because it's the only way in which we continue to improve. When we stop struggling we reach a plateau beyond which we stop making progress. We may think we're getting better, but we're probably just becomingly increasingly confident and may even fall victim to the Dunning–Kruger effect (see page 195). As we saw in the previous chapter, developing mastery or expertise requires concentration; we must think about what we're doing. As soon as we're able to perform a task on autopilot, we're no longer learning.

The problem is that struggling isn't much fun. Most people prefer the feeling of being able to fluently perform a task at a lower level of expertise than pushing themselves to be better. If students simply struggle they will learn to hate school. If they struggle too much, or too soon, this will also be undesirable. Struggle is only desirable after success has been encoded. What I mean by this is that most children will find it demotivating to struggle with something if they see little hope of success. But if they have a clear mental representation of what success looks and feels like, they're more likely to persevere in the face of setbacks.

Instruction should begin with the express purpose of encoding success: clear explanations, careful modelling of high expectations, well-structured scaffolding and guided practice with lots of feedback. Only then, when some measure of success has been experienced, should we introduce struggle.

At this point, the aim of instruction should shift to promoting internalisation. Children will only be independent when they have the means to accomplish a task within themselves. If they're relying on something outside themselves, they will never master challenging content. Once success is encoded, therefore, children should be ready to have some of the scaffolding we've used to artificially boost their performance removed. They're ready for less detailed, less frequent feedback on their progress and increasingly independent practice. This inevitably means that it's more difficult for children to perform well in class, but because they have a clear mental representation of success, they're better able to contend with difficulties. That said, if at any point they look to be struggling too much, the best thing to do is to restore some of the support and offer clearer feedback. *The point is not that children should sink or swim, it's that they should all swim.*

Introducing struggle should always be balanced against children's sense of self-efficacy. Too much struggle is likely to backfire; what they're most likely to learn is that they've reached a limit beyond which they're not capable of improving. They will either decide to settle for a more seemingly achievable target or give up entirely because they don't want to feel stupid. Only when we believe improvement is possible do we put up with having to struggle.

Introducing struggle is important and valuable, but it is also risky. If we get it wrong, children won't enjoy school and will probably give up. But if they never have to struggle at all, they may well develop an unrealistic view of their own ability and believe they know more than they actually do. In our efforts to make children cleverer we should follow these steps:

1. Encode success.

2. Promote internalisation.

3. Increase challenge.

4. Repeat.

Encoding success

If children are to access the knowledge they need to become cleverer, they need a firm foundation in the systems we use to encode and decode biologically secondary knowledge – that is, written grammar and mathematics. Effortless access to times tables, for example, allows children to tackle more demanding problems such as long division and algebra. Having to mentally calculate each component of a maths problem makes the cognitive load imposed by a task much higher. Novices quickly lose track of where they are in a procedure or make simple errors which prevent them from solving the problem. Likewise, effortless grapheme to phoneme conversion allows children to cope with more complex, low-frequency and technical vocabulary. If basic reading is effortful, the process imposes such a large cognitive load that children are unlikely to pick out relevant information in a maths or science word-based problem, and are unlikely to read a book for pleasure.

Beyond unlocking the ability to encode and decode cultural knowledge, we should also consider the sequence of learning within subjects. Every domain has some basic facts and concepts which are used repeatedly over the course of study and are fundamental to understanding more complex ideas. Presenting these basics early in the curriculum, and affording children the opportunities to commit these to long-term memory through the cycle of forgetting and relearning, liberates precious working memory resources.

Some of what students learn in school can be at odds with the biologically primary knowledge they have built up through observation and interaction with the world. What children already know can help them to learn more easily, but where it involves misconceptions the process can backfire. For example, most students believe plants get their mass from the soil rather than primarily from carbon dioxide in the atmosphere, because when you see them growing it's a lot easier to believe that they somehow come out of the soil rather than the scientific reality that they come out of the air. When presented with problems involving the conservation of mass, this folk knowledge explanation leads children to make mistakes. Even though teachers work hard to correct misconceptions, memory tends to drift back towards familiar schemas. Thus, it's important to assess these misconceptions and provide carefully paced, explicit explanations which draw attention to the differences between everyday observations and counter-intuitive reality.

Some of what children need to learn is quite distant from biologically primary knowledge and is consequently hard to integrate into schemas. Children find it easier to incorporate troubling new knowledge into existing schemas if we connect abstractions to concrete representations of the same concept. One way to do this is by using analogies: *this is like that*. However, care must be taken to explicitly direct children's attention to the key similarities between the familiar concrete model and the unfamiliar abstract knowledge so they don't end up fixating on irrelevancies. For instance, if children are told that white blood cells are like soldiers, that would be memorable: the new concept (blood cells) is related to prior knowledge (soldiers). However, they might end up believing that cells wear uniforms, take orders or march in step. For the analogy to work, we would need to explain *how* white blood cells are like soldiers.

Sometimes misconceptions stem from having been taught an overly simplified analogy. As noted on page 179, children have learned that when writing a sentence, they should put a comma where they take a breath. The correct way to use a comma depends on understanding the relationship between an independent and a dependent clause. This is a much more abstract explanation and so is harder for kids to grasp. They readily revert to the common-sense heuristic that you put a comma where you take a breath because it's concrete. In this case, they need to be retaught the correct explanation multiple times alongside regular reminders that their old understanding doesn't work. Developing good explanations and accurate analogies is probably the key area of subject specialist knowledge teachers most need to develop.

So, novices learn best when teachers give concrete examples to exemplify abstract concepts and explain how the examples and big ideas connect. Making content explicit through carefully paced explanation, modelling and examples can help prevent children from becoming overloaded. It should be noted that explanation does not mean that the teacher does all the talking while the kids just listen – effective instruction requires interaction, questioning and dialogue.

We all receive information through two primary pathways – auditory (for the spoken word) and visual (for the written word and graphic or pictorial representations). It stands to reason that children will find learning easier if teachers use both mechanisms to present new information. As we saw in Chapter 6, our working memory is made up of several interacting modules, two of which, the phonological loop and the visuo-spatial sketchpad, process information differently. Although performing two tasks which require the same component of working memory can quickly overload our capacity, we're able to use different components of working memory at the same time without difficulty. This is referred to as *dual coding*. The phonological loop and the visuo-spatial sketchpad can be utilised at the same time by, for instance, providing anchor images to support a complex verbal explanation. Everybody benefits from experiencing information through more than one modality. Multiple modalities usually just means a mix of words and images. A modality engages children's senses; the more senses we engage, the more likely we are to encode information in long-term memory.

In practice, speaking at the same time as showing a graphic enhances learning if the two types of information complement one another (e.g. showing an animation while describing it out loud). But if the two sources of information are not complementary, children's attention will be divided, forcing them to task switch. Contrary to popular belief, humans can't multitask. Not even women. What we can do is switch our attention between different tasks. We pause one task in order to undertake another and then switch back. This switch requires attention and forces us to shift our mental processes from accessing one schema to accessing another. Every time we make this kind of switch we pay a price as our brain engages in a 'reinstatement search'. As Figure 10.1 shows, this price – the task-switching penalty – is both a loss of time and an increase in errors.[3]

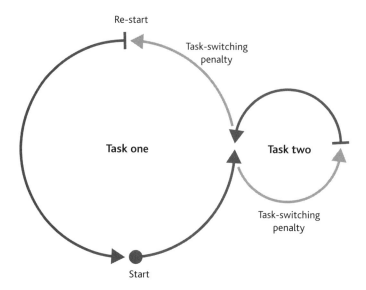

Figure 10.1. The task-switching penalty

Richard Mayer suggests five principles for reducing extraneous cognitive load when designing learning materials: coherence, signalling, redundancy, spatial contiguity and temporal contiguity. Essentially, we should delete extraneous material, highlight relevant material, avoid unnecessary text, place text near visuals and make sure spoken words and images correspond. Mayer also found that students learn more from multi-modal instruction when the words are spoken aloud rather than printed.[4]

Ruth Colvin Clark has investigated the most effective ways to combine words and images and has come up with a number of useful recommendations to help teachers design better resources and presentations. She suggests that there are four different types of visuals we should be aware of:

- Organisational images (flow charts, concept maps, etc.) help children to see qualitative relationships in the content they are learning.

- Relational images (pie charts, bar charts, use of colour to show variation) help to summarise quantitative data.

- Transformational images (animations or overlaying arrows on line drawings to show direction or movement) can help to demonstrate changes in time and space.

- Interpretive images (some simulations and animations) can help children to make connections between abstract concepts and concrete examples.[5]

Certain types of visuals are more suitable for specific purposes. Whenever teachers design resources, the type of visual selected should be carefully aligned to the intended purpose.

Whenever we use images or other visuals to present information we should also consider the following:

- Combining words and images can help children to build coherent mental models of unfamiliar material and concepts.

- A poorly selected visual might actually interfere with learning. Teachers should avoid images which place extraneous demands on children's limited working memory capacity or are distracting, because children may focus on unintended or irrelevant features of the image rather than the parts which relate to our explanation.

- Ideally any text should be incorporated into the image to minimise the effort of switching attention back and forth and so connections are clear.

- Simple visuals communicate ideas more clearly and concisely. Where possible, use flat two-dimensional images rather than elaborate three-dimensional options.

- When images are self-explanatory it's better to avoid unnecessary words. Conversely, if a diagram is complex, accompanying text may help children to process the information.

Children can also benefit from creating their own visuals. When they are asked to produce drawings while they are reading, students are likely to learn more than they would by writing a summary or from other techniques commonly used to help make things stick.[6] We can ease cognitive load by providing partially completed drawings, such as the opening stages of a timeline or some of the connections in a causal relationship diagram. This can be particularly effective when tasks rely on complex problem solving.

Using a narrative structure within a teaching sequence can help children to tap into our evolved propensity for remembering stories. Stories are one of the most important ways we have of trying to make sense of the world. We look at all the coincidences, connections, curiosities and contradictions that surround us and weave them into a plausible narrative in which everything makes sense and inconsistencies are explained away. This incredibly useful skill enables us to interpret an otherwise incomprehensible world – without narrative there would be little way for us to make meaning of our experiences. Almost everything we encounter we repackage as a story – scientific discoveries, news events, love affairs, the broad sweep of history. It's all grist to our mental story mills.

The fact that visual and verbal information can be processed simultaneously without putting additional load on working memory is something teachers should regularly exploit. When explaining new material, it's helpful to find a visual presentation relevant to the learning. Examples include a Venn diagram showing how categories of information can be organised, an animation or representation of a process, a graph showing key information or simply a picture of what you're explaining.

It's worth being aware that if we try to draw on the same component of working memory more than once, we're likely to overload it. Thus, we should avoid giving a verbal explanation while presenting different text on the board. Attempting to follow along in their own copy of a text while simultaneously having to listen as the text is read aloud is impossible. Children are forced to task switch between the printed material and the sound of the teacher's voice, meaning they lose track of what it is they're supposed to be reading and remember far less than if they had either read or listened without trying to do both at once.

It's also worth considering how we can minimise the amount of task switching children need to do. Having to shift attention from one part of a page (e.g. a diagram) to another (e.g. some labels) imposes additional load on working memory, which probably isn't helpful. When children need to do this (e.g. an exam question involving a graph on one page and a description on another), encourage them to break the task into component steps and tackle each one separately before attempting to combine the components together.

And, of course, effective instruction must include effective feedback. Surprisingly, there is empirical evidence that "delaying, reducing, and summarizing feedback can be better for long-term learning than providing immediate, trial-by-trial feedback". Nicholas Soderstom and Robert Bjork also point out that "Numerous studies – some of them dating back decades – have shown that frequent and immediate feedback can, contrary to intuition, degrade learning."[7]

The analogy of navigation provides a useful analogy. If you're making a journey, using a map requires effort, and so if you intend to make the journey more than once it makes sense to memorise the route rather than to have to map-read your way every time. A satnav, on the other hand, is the perfect machine for giving feedback: its GPS knows exactly where you are, you tell it exactly where you want to go and it provides immediate, trial-by-trial feedback on your progress. If you make a mistake it adapts and provides new instructions to compensate for the error. Navigation becomes effortless and memorising routes is hardly worth the trouble. If students are at the beginning of a course they will lack the knowledge to successfully perform a task without carefully scaffolded feedback. Being shown how to perform well and being given 'satnav feedback' will help motivate them to see that they can be successful. Once they have encoded the belief that they can be successful, it's time to move to promoting internalisation.

Promoting internalisation

As time goes by and students become increasingly confident, teachers ought to reduce the amount of feedback they give and raise their expectations of how much struggle children can reasonably cope with. At this stage, the most effective kind of feedback is of the 'map-reading' variety – having to struggle helps children recognise that it's worth the effort to memorise how to solve specific types of problems and to internalise certain procedures. Once these things have been internalised, students are no longer dependent on teachers' feedback and performance becomes increasingly effortless. By the time the end of a course is approaching, there should be little need for teachers to give feedback at all, as children should have learned everything they need to be successful. There's little point investing effort in providing feedback that children do not internalise.

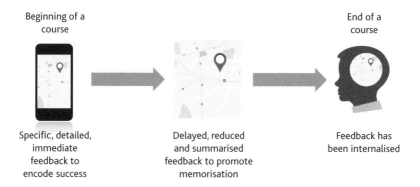

Figure 10.2. The feedback continuum

Clearly, it takes more than reduced and summarised feedback for children to internalise what they need to learn. Often, the biggest barrier to learning biologically secondary knowledge is that it seems too abstract, too counter-intuitive, too difficult and, frankly, too boring. Once students accept that success is possible, that their efforts will be rewarded with improved outcomes, then it's time to switch our focus away from external props and scaffolds and towards getting them to internalise the knowledge they need to be successful.

We all want learning to be quick and easy, but this might be an inherently short-term approach. The long-term goals of learning are long term. In order to meet these fundamental goals, it is crucial that we understand the distinction between performance and learning. Performance is measurable, but learning can only be inferred from performance – it cannot be observed directly. That is to say, performance is easy to observe whereas learning is not. You can tick a box to show that a student's performance has moved from X to Y, but you can't necessarily tell whether learning has taken place.

Not only is our current performance a poor indicator of future learning, but the better our performance is at the point we encounter new information, the less likely we are to retain and be able to transfer this information to different fields. Remember the Bjorks' theory of disuse? What increases retrieval strength in the short term does not lead to increased storage strength in the longer term. The idea that you can judge progress in learning within a lesson is misleading and unhelpful. No matter how well planned a teaching sequence is, we have to accommodate the uncomfortable truth that much of what children learn will be quickly forgotten. If we want to improve learning, we might have to strategically reduce children's performance by introducing desirable difficulties.

As we have seen, one of the most robust findings from research into memory is that trying to retrieve something from memory helps us to form stronger schematic connections for that material. Teachers can exploit this aspect of memory in a variety of ways. One technique is to use questions to introduce a new topic. These help to activate the schemas relevant to the new learning, reintroduce children to ideas they will need in the lesson and allow the teacher to assess their background knowledge, as well as any misconceptions they might have. Questions also provoke children's curiosity by making them aware of gaps in their knowledge. The more curious they are, the more invested they will be in learning the answers.

Regular low-stakes quizzes and reviews also tap into this testing effect. These can take the form of quick questions on the board at the start of a lesson, multiple-choice quizzes online or self-tests that children design themselves. The format of the practice of retrieving information probably doesn't matter that much. So, if you've taught children to create mind maps, simply encourage them to practise recreating them from memory. If your students are in the habit of creating flash cards, ensure they are not passively rereading them but actively testing their ability to remember (e.g. by jotting down what's on the card from memory). We should also be aware of the hypercorrection effect – the finding that the more confident someone is that an incorrect answer they have given is correct, the more likely they are to learn from their mistake and not make it again. As long as we're corrected, making mistakes seems to produce stronger schemas than when we don't make mistakes.[8]

Herman Ebbinghaus, who first discovered the forgetting curve, also conducted experiments into how information could be retained for as long as possible. He found that if we allow some forgetting to take place before reviewing the material to be learned, the curve of forgetting starts to flatten off.

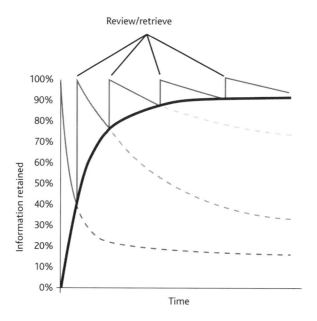

Figure 10.3. The spacing effect

If we revisit information at regular intervals we are much more likely to remember it, but the real reason this is so effective is that, as we forget, we are more receptive to learning new information. And what's more, because new learning (or relearning) depends on what has gone before, the optimal spacing of content provides a foundation for subsequent learning.

There are also optimum spacing intervals depending on how long we want to retain information:

Table 10.1. Optimal intervals for retaining information

Time to test	Optimum interval between study sessions
1 week	1–2 days
1 month	1 week
2 months	2 weeks
6 months	3 weeks
1 year	4 weeks

Source: Adapted from Nicholas J. Cepeda, Edward Vul, Doug Rohrer, John T. Wixted and Harold Pashler, Spacing Effects in Learning: A Temporal Ridgeline of Optimal Retention, *Psychological Science* 19 (2008): 1095–1102.

If you've got a test next week, wait a day or so before restudying the material you've covered. If the test is in a month, give yourself a week to forget. And if your test is a year hence, you're best off waiting at least a month. The further away the test date, the longer the interval between study sessions.

Teachers can harness the spacing effect by structuring sequences of learning so that children gain practice over time – for example, reviewing previously taught content across weeks or months. An easy way to do this is to move from modular to cumulative assessment over the course of the year. Rather than teaching a topic and testing that topic, make sure the test includes other topics covered previously in the year. Cumulative tests ensure that children are exposed to key content on a regular basis and that repeated practice at recalling that knowledge is spaced over time.

As well as distributing practice over time, there may be some benefit to mixing up the types of practice. This strategy, known as interleaving, offers an alternative to what is usually called 'massed practice'. Massed practice allows us to focus on learning one topic or skill area at a time. The topic or skill is repeatedly practised for a period of time and then we move on to another skill and repeat the process. Interleaving practice, on the other hand, involves working on multiple skills in parallel.

Interleaving the practice of different types of content when setting problem-solving tasks in lessons appears to be particularly effective in mathematics teaching. For example, if children are adding, subtracting, multiplying and dividing fractions, typically it's more effective to mix up, or interleave, the practice of different problem types rather than practise just one type of problem and then move on to the next.

As well as introducing desirable difficulties, we can also teach children to be metacognitive. Metacognition – or thinking about thinking – can be a useful process to help us internalise what we're learning about. One way to become more metacognitive is to consider the accuracy of our judgements of learning. Metacognitive judgements are the assessments children make about how well they have learned particular information – that is, how likely it is they will remember the material when given an exam question. These assessments influence how much revision students tend to do and which topics they decide require further study.

It seems likely that there are several processes taking place when we form judgements about what we are learning. We tend to make fairly quick evaluations based on our familiarity with the material before investing any mental effort in retrieving information from long-term memory. We may also form a slower, more considered judgement of how readily we can retrieve that information based on actually trying to recall it.

When students revise key material in preparation for tests or exams they often overestimate how much they can securely recall. This is the illusion of knowledge (see page 197). The poor accuracy of these judgements relates back to the rather lazy (or, more charitably, effort-efficient) way human beings have evolved to process information. We tend to stop processing information once the analysis relevant to the task has been carried out. For example, it's fairly easy to mistake recognition for recall, so if a page in a textbook looks very familiar, the student may incorrectly judge that they have good recall of the material it contains and stop revising.

Teachers can help students in a few different ways. Firstly, we can help them to identify what they know well and what needs further study by providing feedback on what they have learned. This feedback will be more effective if we are fairly specific about where and how students can improve. Secondly, we can teach students about the importance of making delayed judgements of learning when studying independently so they are less likely to fall victim to the illusion of knowledge. In general, we are more accurate at predicting later performance when there is a delay between studying material and making a judgement about how much we can securely recall. Finally, encourage students to test that judgement by attempting tasks or questions from memory. The process of self-testing not only taps into the testing effect, but it also helps to improve students' judgement about where they need to focus their efforts.

Increasing challenge

Once children have experienced a measure of success and internalised the processes required to repeat their successes, they're ready for additional challenge. If we meet too much challenge we may well decide that it's not worth pushing for greater fluency and expertise and will settle for the level of competence we have achieved. It's tempting to commit time to interventions designed to increase children's self-efficacy or resilience, but such efforts are rarely worth it. Resilience and self-efficacy are, like all other mental attributes, context specific. As we've seen, motivation is a product of being successful.[9] Once we've experienced some success we're ready for greater challenge. The level of challenge needs to be ramped up slowly and carefully.

One of the potential problems with teachers pushing for 'higher order skills', as depicted in Bloom's taxonomy, is that it's easy to overlook the importance of that foundation of knowledge which supports everything else. Bloom himself saw knowledge as the basis for all thinking; not as a category of thinking skill but as the necessary precondition for putting these skills and abilities into practice.[10] The starting point for the transfer of learning is ensuring that children have the background knowledge to understand the context of novel problems. However, as we discussed in the previous chapter, in order to successfully transfer that knowledge to a novel problem, children need to ignore superficial differences and understand the deep underlying structure.

The more abstract the problem, the harder it is to work out the underlying structure. Abstractions are difficult to internalise, as are problems with multiple steps. When there are lots of steps, there is a risk that working memory will quickly become overloaded. We can use worked examples to reduce the cognitive load involved in learning complex processes and procedures. It may be helpful to start with highly scaffolded examples – for example, step-by-step presentations of how to solve a problem. We can help independence by gradually removing this guidance as children tackle more examples so they are encouraged to internalise more of the steps.

Varying the conditions of practice is a desirable difficulty that increases the load on working memory, but it is also an effective tool for ensuring that children are applying mental effort when engaging with material. Try asking them to compare different types of problems to highlight the same underlying structure – for example, mixing word problems with more abstract problems may help them to recognise the unifying concepts involved in both. Word problems tend to have a more concrete basis, such as working out the volume of a water tank, whereas an abstract problem might simply require the application of a mathematical formula.

We should also be mindful that increased challenge is not just for those children we consider to be the most able. The general principle is that everyone should experience struggle when they are ready for it, but what is challenging will be different for different people. Because of this, it's impossible to offer specific advice on what challenge should look like.

The idea that instruction benefits from being differentiated – that within the same lesson different children will be working on different tasks and using different resources – most likely arose as a way to overcome this difficulty. This approach is probably unhelpful. It's better to think instead of teaching being adaptive – responding to children's needs as they become clear by checking for understanding, giving additional explanations and providing additional support where necessary.

As children start to believe they can be successful at a more challenging level, then we can start to move our focus back to helping them internalise coping with increased complexity and difficulty. And so the cycle continues. In this way, no one is left behind and all children become cleverer.

Chapter 10: key points

- Not all instructional approaches are equal. Focusing on the efficient formation of schemas before moving to problem-solving activities is crucial if we want to make children cleverer.

- Instruction should focus on encoding success, promoting internalisation and then increasing challenge.

- When teaching new material, especially when it is abstract or counter-intuitive, we need to ensure that students are not overloaded.

- Careful use of worked examples and problem-solving tasks is one way to help manage cognitive load and improve the transfer of learning.

- By mixing in problem-solving exercises, so that students alternate between exploring worked solutions and trying to solve problems more independently, we can help students to transfer knowledge to novel contexts in the future.

- The effort of trying to remember something aids future recall more than other studying techniques do.

The project of making children cleverer requires that we focus on the minutiae as well as trying to maintain a sense of the bigger picture. How we teach is only meaningful if we have made good decisions about what we teach. And thinking about what we teach is enhanced by remembering that our aim is to help children become more creative, be better problem solvers, think more critically and be more collaborative.

We now move to the concluding arguments of the book and assess whether it's possible to close the achievement gap between the most and least advantaged children.

Conclusion:
Shifting the bell curve

It is so easy to be wrong – and to persist in being wrong – when the costs of being wrong are paid by others.

Thomas Sowell

As teachers, we like to believe we can see the good in all children. Schools are intended to be nurturing environments which shape and socialise young minds. We're deeply aware of the need to close the attainment gap between the haves and the have-nots, and social disadvantage is seen as the single biggest problem for us to overcome. But there might be some difficulties with this idea that no one really wants to talk about. Maybe there is no way to close the attainment gap in schools.

How do you solve a problem like the bell curve?

Writing a book about intelligence and education is scarcely possible without making some mention of Richard Herrnstein and Charles Murray's hugely controversial book, *The Bell Curve*.[1] In essence, Herrnstein and Murray's thesis can be boiled down to three main claims:

1. The importance of intelligence, as measured by IQ tests, increased exponentially over the 20th century as society became increasingly technical and complex.

2. Changes in society saw an 'invisible migration' in which a cognitive elite – those at the upper end of the IQ distribution – found their way to the top of business, government and the professions and are

set to become ever more dominant and prosperous. At the same time, those on the lower end of the IQ distribution are falling ever further behind.

3. Because IQ is substantially inherited, there's nothing anyone can really do about this. Poverty is more to do with low intelligence than circumstance, and the reason so many African-Americans are poor is not due to slavery, Jim Crow laws and structural racism, but because of bad genes. Probably the best we can do is offer a universal basic income and make these people feel productive and useful.

This presents a stark view of the world, and one in which education offers scant hope:

> Formal schooling offers little hope of narrowing cognitive inequality on a large scale in developed countries, because so much of its contribution has already been realized with the advent of universal twelve-year systems. Special programs to improve intelligence within the school have had minor and probably temporary effects on intelligence. ...
>
> Taken together, the story of attempts to raise intelligence is one of high hopes, flamboyant claims, and disappointing results. For the foreseeable future, the problems of low cognitive ability are not going to be solved by outside interventions to make children smarter.[2]

So, is the message I've tried to argue in this book a self-indulgent waste of time? Am I simply engaging in "high hopes" and "flamboyant claims" which will inevitably lead to "disappointing results"?

As to their first claim, I think they're right. Intelligence is probably more important now than ever before. Their second claim about the 'cognitive elite' might be true, but it might also be the sort of instinctive gap thinking that Hans Rosling warns us against. The cognitive elite represents, at most, 10–15% of people; almost 70% of us have an IQ score between 85 and 115. No one in their right mind would advocate an approach to education that wrote off 85–90% of the population. Even if their claim that the gap between the lives of the elite and the rest of us is getting ever wider were true (and there's good reason to doubt it), it is a counsel of despair. Our concern should be for the lives of everyone else. Happily, their third claim is dead wrong: genes obviously make some difference but it is our environment that determines whether we have the chance to get cleverer.

It's true that (depending on how we measure it) attainment, like IQ, is distributed normally and there is always going to be a spread of ability and attainment across any population. There will always be successes and failures, winners and losers, haves and have-nots. With intelligence, it's all relative. The IQ bell curve has been specifically designed so that for someone who is on the right of centre, there will be someone else on the left. As you raise the overall level of intelligence, the whole curve shifts to the right, but the average is then reset at 100. It's an abstract concept which means that an IQ score is not absolute but relative to the population in general. It is therefore meaningless to talk of raising everybody's IQ. This is also Herrnstein and Murray's objection. While accepting that attempts to raise intelligence might have some benefit for those at the bottom of the distribution, they warn that "one must be careful to understand what is and is not being improved: The performance of those at the bottom might improve, but they could end up being even further behind their brighter classmates."[3]

This is true, but trivially so. We need to pry the mathematical construct of IQ apart from the real-world concept of intelligence. The argument I've made in this book is that it is what children know that makes them clever. Thinking in terms of IQ points doesn't really mean anything, but thinking in terms of powerful concepts and culturally rich information allows us to pinpoint the effects of an intervention. If a child learns something new they can start thinking about it. Language and concepts are often indistinguishable – you can't learn about osmosis without also learning the word. This makes a tangible difference to what happens inside children's brains. Every new item of knowledge is one more thing that can be prodded, fitted together, twisted into shape, questioned, rejected or used. Worrying about whether you can measure the change misses the point – the change is real.

Herrnstein and Murray also suggest that although interventions deigned to raise intelligence might make some difference, "the size of the effect is small".[4] Again, thinking in terms of knowledge rather than IQ points allows us to see what really matters. Maybe increasing intelligence in the population would be like raising everyone's living standards by increasing their income by a fixed amount. Everybody would see a personal improvement in their circumstances, but as everyone got richer, there would still be a gap between the highest and the lowest. However, the improvement would be experienced asymmetrically. In very crude terms, if everyone got an extra £100, everyone would be richer, but for those who started from a high base rate an extra £100 won't mean much. For those starting from a low base rate, £100 is a windfall. According to economic historian Deirdre McCloskey, although the rich have certainly got richer, the poor have benefitted disproportionately from the average rise in incomes. In her words, "millions more have gas central heating, cars, smallpox vaccinations, indoor plumbing, cheap travel, rights for women, lower child mortality, adequate nutrition, taller bodies, doubled life expectancy, schooling for their kids, newspapers, a vote, a shot at university and respect".[5] It's ridiculous to claim that small effects don't matter. A greater emphasis on teaching powerful, culturally rich knowledge might have parallel benefits on the intellect. Either way, we must try to control the instinct to obsess over the extremes and acknowledge that the majority of people occupy the gap in-between.

Although everyone is getting richer and poverty is becoming less severe for billions of people, income does not distribute normally.[6] Most of the wealth in the world is owned by a relatively small percentage of its population. Where IQ is symmetrical, wealth is not. And neither is knowledge. Ironically, only the knowledgeable have the luxury of dismissing the importance of knowledge. Learning a powerful new concept might mean little to those who already know much, but it could have a disproportionately beneficial effect on those who know least.

What we should do differently

First and foremost, if we want to make children cleverer, it is schools that will make the most difference. Politicians and education reformers may be guilty of labouring under the misapprehension that better home environments lead to success, and that if we could replicate those environments then achievement gaps would disappear. But, as we saw in Chapter 4, individual differences in intelligence and academic outcomes are largely a result of the interplay between genes and the school environment, not family background. Our efforts will be best spent trying to close the advantage gap afforded by different schools.

One obvious mistake to avoid is academic selection. This might well work for those students who attend selective schools, but such children do well whatever school they attend. Where you have selective schools, you must necessarily also have schools where those who fail the selection test end up. It's not impossible for a non-selective school within a selective system to offer the kind of academic environment that leads to making children cleverer, but neither is it easy. If we accept that children's ability is, at least in part, the consequence rather than the cause of what they experience at school, then putting the children who most need powerful, culturally rich knowledge in an environment where they're least likely to get these things is unforgiveable.

Having avoided a selection system, we next need to ensure that all children have access to a broad and balanced curriculum, taught using explicit instruction. Currently, what happens in many schools favours those children from more advantaged backgrounds over those from less advantaged backgrounds, and those with higher fluid intelligence over those with less. Why should those who are already benefiting from winning the social and genetic lotteries be further advantaged by an education system determined to focus on biologically primary adaptions? Of course, few people working in education would intentionally skew the system in favour of the most fortunate. No one deliberately sets out to create schools where it's harder for children to get cleverer, but that's what happens.

The aim of the ideas presented in this book is not just to provide a level playing field, but to slant it so that it asymmetrically benefits those who start with least. The main arguments I've put forward are:

- An increase in intelligence is likely to lead to increases in health and happiness, among other things.

- We have a motivational bias towards the biologically primary and against what's biologically secondary.

- The aspect of intelligence we're most able to affect is crystallised intelligence – knowledge stored in long-term memory.

- The factor most likely to determine whether schools make children cleverer is the peer culture. Peer culture can be shaped by schools for better or worse.

- A barrier to improving intelligence is the bottleneck of working memory – a tiny advantage in working memory is likely to lead to huge academic advantages.

- The best way to overcome this limit is to acquire robust schemas which can be drawn into working memory as chunks.

- Some knowledge can be so well acquired that it takes up no space in working memory and becomes automatised.

- Knowledge is both what we think about (propositions) and what we think with (automatised procedures and tacit knowledge).

- Some knowledge is both more powerful (allows for thinking more thoughts) and more culturally rich (has a higher cultural value) than other kinds of knowledge; as such, it results in more useful schemas.

- Explicit instruction and purposeful practice are our best bets to support children to build biologically secondary schemas.

- A knowledge-rich curriculum and explicit instruction will make children cleverer and increase the likelihood that they live happier, healthier and more secure lives.

- The children who are likely to benefit most from this approach to education are those on the left hand side of the bell curve.

Any approach to education that does not prioritise powerful, culturally rich knowledge and explicit instruction is – wittingly or not – both adding to social injustice and discriminating against those children on the lower end of the normal distribution.

While intelligence cannot grow in a vacuum, schools can provide more of the sort of nurturing environment that allows intelligence to flourish. We know that the peer effects within schools have a strong influence on learning. Where there is a culture of failure or of opting out, this needs to be turned around so that becoming more intelligent is seen as desirable by all children. And once there is a peer culture where it's socially desirable to work hard and be successful, then it doesn't matter that much what schools do. If you're already advantaged, being given the further advantage of an academically orientated peer group is likely to benefit you more than whatever dubious policies are enacted by schools. Unless schools emphasise a curriculum focused on powerful, culturally rich knowledge and explicit instruction, the peer culture that is likely to develop will not be one in which hard work and academic excellence are valued. Inevitably, children's disadvantages are compounded.

We know what to do; now we need to do it. There is no excuse. We know about the limitations of working memory, the transformational power of rich background knowledge and the tendency of children to be more motivated to engage in biologically primary evolutionary adaptions rather than focus on the hard task of mastering new biologically secondary modules. Ignoring this information wilfully and deliberately increases societal inequities. The assertion that there is 'no best way' to teach, that child-centred approaches are as valid as explicit instruction, is responsible for poorer children from less advantaged backgrounds being further squeezed out of the best universities and the best-paid jobs. In maintaining this belief, we pursue a policy where no one gets a hand up or a hand out; survival of the fittest and to hell with everyone else.

All this goes to show the huge importance of education. If we want to make all children cleverer, the fairest scenario is one where the differences between children's academic outcomes are due to their genes and not their backgrounds. Although schools cannot – and should not – seek to eliminate these genetic differences, they can attempt to move the entire bell curve further to the right.

If our approach to education is primarily 'child-centred', we're conceding to children's motivational bias towards the biologically primary and away from the biologically secondary. If we focus on developing generic skills, rather than building the knowledge base which makes such skills possible, then we confer a further advantage on those children who already have the advantages of higher fluid intelligence and greater access to cultural capital. And, if we ignore the evidence on prioritising powerful, culturally rich knowledge and explicit instruction, then we ensure that the gap between the haves and the have-nots grows ever greater.

If all children knew more, they would all be able to think about more things. They would be able to use this knowledge to solve problems, be creative, think critically and collaborate on meaningful projects. This knowledge would help them to make better, wiser decisions, which would lead to them being safer and healthier, and living longer, more fulfilled lives. Of course, all these things must be caveated with the phrase 'on average'. No one can predict the life course of an individual, but we can reasonably assume that all children will, in the most tangible sense of the word, become cleverer.

We can still imagine a society in which the advantages of a high IQ today could be enjoyed by those with an average IQ tomorrow. Therefore, in aiming to make kids cleverer, we shouldn't be interested in making them cleverer than someone else – this is the futile game of winners and losers. Instead, we should aim to help everyone get cleverer than they currently are.

At the end of *Flowers for Algernon*, the attempt to raise Charlie Gordon's intelligence through surgery ends in tragedy. He forgets all he has learned and, after suffering the agonies of experiencing his abilities slough away, he returns to the state of happy ignorance in which he began the story. In his final journal entry, he expresses the wish that he could be as smart as he had been, because if he could he'd read all the time.

What happened to Charlie is fiction. Our efforts to make children cleverer will not end in this way. Here in the real world there is cause for real optimism. There are schools, organisations and individual teachers who are realising the potential of the approaches outlined in this book. They have understood that if children from disadvantaged backgrounds are given the same access to powerful knowledge as their more privileged peers, they can start to close the advantage gap. There are always barriers and excuses. But while some prevaricate, others are proving that all children can become cleverer.[7]

We are all born different, each endowed with our own gifts, talents and potential; no two of us are exactly alike. But the sad truth is that not only do we inherit our genes, we also inherit our environments. Some children have far more advantages than others. This is something we can at least try to alleviate. Schools can mitigate against asymmetric environmental influences by teaching children powerful, culturally rich knowledge in a way that they are most likely to remember and be able to apply to the circumstances of their lives.

If we expend our efforts on trying to make everyone the same we shall surely fail. There will always be a difference between the most and least intelligent, and the most intelligent are always likely to be the most advantaged, but this advantage should not be based on the good fortune of being born into wealth. Instead, if our energies are directed towards trying to improve everyone's average, all children will improve.

We cannot all be geniuses, but we can all get cleverer.

Notes

Introduction

1   Paul Dolan, *Happiness by Design: Finding Pleasure in Everyday Life* (London: Penguin, 2014).

2   Linda S. Gottfredson, Mainstream Science on Intelligence: An Editorial with 52 Signatories, History, and Bibliography, *Intelligence* 24 (1997): 13–23 at 13.

3   Jon Andrews, David Robinson and Jo Hutchinson, *Closing the Gap? Trends in Educational Attainment and Disadvantage* (London: Education Policy Institute, 2017), p. 6. Available at: https://epi.org.uk/wp-content/uploads/2017/08/Closing-the-Gap_EPI-.pdf.

4   John Jerrim, *Global Gaps: Comparing Socio-economic Gaps in the Performance of Highly Able UK Pupils Internationally* (London: Sutton Trust, 2017), p. 4. Available at: https://www.suttontrust.com/wp-content/uploads/2017/02/Global-Gaps_FINAL_V2_WEB.pdf. These figures are specifically for achievement in science. The differences in reading and mathematics are nearer the OECD average.

5   Hans Rosling with Ola Rosling and Anna Rosling Rönnlund, *Factfulness: Ten Reasons We're Wrong About the World – And Why Things Are Better Than You Think* (London: Sceptre, 2018), pp. 19–46.

6   Arthur Scargill, *The Sunday Times* (10 January 1982).

7   Dylan Wiliam, *Leadership for Teacher Learning: Creating a Culture Where All Teachers Improve So That All Students Succeed* (West Palm Beach, FL: Learning Sciences International, 2016), p. 6.

Chapter 1: The purpose of education

1   Matt Ridley, *The Evolution of Everything: How Ideas Emerge* (London: Fourth Estate, 2015), pp. 188–189.

2   Eric Kalenze, *Education is Upside-Down: Reframing Reform to Focus on the Right Problems* (Lanham, MD: Rowman & Littlefield, 2014).

3   Robert de Vries and Jason Rentfrow, *A Winning Personality: The Effects of Background on Personality and Earnings* (London: Sutton Trust, 2016), p. 4. Available at: https://www.suttontrust.com/wp-content/uploads/2016/01/Winning-Personality-FINAL.pdf.

4   Kristján Kristjánsson, *The Sutton Trust Report and Its Fallout: Some Curious Ideas about the Shaping of Personality as 'Character Education'* (Birmingham: Jubilee Centre for Character and Virtues, 2016), p. 2 [original emphasis]. Available at: https://www.jubileecentre.ac.uk/userfiles/jubileecentre/pdf/insight-series/

Kristjansson%20K%20-%20The%20Sutton%20Trust%20Report%20and%20
Its%20Fallout.pdf.

5   Annie Murphy Paul, *The Cult of Personality: How Personality Tests Are Leading Us to
Miseducate Our Children, Mismanage Our Companies, and Misunderstand Ourselves*
(New York: Free Press, 2004).

6   Jubilee Centre for Character and Virtues, *A Framework for Character Education
in Schools* (Birmingham: Jubilee Centre for Character and Virtues, 2017), p. 2.
Available at: https://www.jubileecentre.ac.uk/userfiles/jubileecentre/pdf/character-
education/Framework%20for%20Character%20Education.pdf.

7   Jonathan Haidt, *The Righteous Mind: Why Good People Are Divided by Politics and
Religion* (London: Penguin, 2012).

8   Philip E. Tetlock, Social Functionalist Frameworks for Judgment and Choice:
Intuitive Politicians, Theologians, and Prosecutors, *Psychological Review* 109(3)
(2002): 451–471.

9   Haidt, *The Righteous Mind*, p. 91.

10   Adam Smith, *The Theory of Moral Sentiments* (London: Andrew Millar; Edinburgh:
Alexander Kincaid and J. Bell, 1759).

11   Richard Buckminster Fuller, *Critical Path,* 2nd rev. edn (New York: St Martin's Press,
1981).

12   IBM Global Technology Services, The Toxic Terabyte: How Data-Dumping Threatens
Business Efficiency (July 2006). Available at: http://www.ibm.com/services/no/cio/
leverage/levinfo_wp_gts_thetoxic.pdf.

13   See https://www.youtube.com/watch?v=emx92kBKads.

14   Leonard Mlodinow, *Elastic: Flexible Thinking in a Time of Change* (New York:
Pantheon, 2018).

15   Daniel J. Boorstin, A Case of Hypochondria, *Newsweek* (6 July 1970).

16   Alison Wolf, *Does Education Matter? Myths About Education and Economic Growth*
(London: Penguin, 2002), p. 16.

17   Allan Bloom, *The Closing of the American Mind: How Higher Education Has Failed
Democracy and Impoverished the Souls of Today's Students* (New York: Simon &
Schuster, 1987), p. 239.

18   Matthew Arnold, *Culture and Anarchy* (Oxford: Oxford University Press, 2006
[1869]), p. 5.

19   Letter from Rt Hon Michael Gove MP to Tim Oates, Chair of the Expert Panel on
Curriculum (11 June 2012). Available at: http://media.education.gov.uk/assets/
files/pdf/l/secretary%20of%20state%20letter%20to%20tim%20oates%20
regarding%20the%20national%20curriculum%20review%202011%20june%20
2012.pdf.

20   Arnold, *Culture and Anarchy*, p. 9.

21   Martin Luther King, Jr, The Purpose of Education, *The Maroon Tiger* [Morehouse
College Student Paper] (1947). Available at: https://www.drmartinlutherkingjr.com/
thepurposeofeducation.htm.

22   Nassim Nicholas Taleb, *Antifragile: Things That Gain from Disorder* (London: Penguin,
2013), p. 318.

23   Andrew Marr, *A History of the World* (London: Pan Macmillan, 2013), pp. 310–311.

24   Marr, *A History of the World*, p. 311.

Chapter 2: Built by culture

1   Kevin N. Laland, *Darwin's Unfinished Symphony: How Culture Made the Human Mind*
(Princeton, NJ: Princeton University Press, 2017), p. 7.

2   Albano Beja-Pereira, Gordon Luikart, Philip R. England, Daniel G. Bradley, Oliver
     C. Jann, Giorgio Bertorelle et al., Gene-Culture Coevolution Between Cattle Milk
     Protein Genes and Human Lactase Genes, *Nature Genetics* 35 (2003): 311–313.

3   Roger Lewin and Robert A. Foley, *Principles of Human Evolution*, 2nd edn
     (Cambridge: Wiley-Blackwell, 2004).

4   Mario Cáceres, Joel Lachuer, Matthew A. Zapala, John C. Redmond, Lili Kudo, Daniel
     H. Geschwind et al., Elevated Gene Expression Levels Distinguish Human from
     Non-Human Primate Brains, *Proceedings of the National Academy of Sciences of
     the United States of America* 100(22) (2003): 13030–13035.

5   Magnus Enquist, Stefano Ghirlanda, Arne Jarrick and Carl Adam Wachtmeister, Why
     Does Human Culture Increase Exponentially?, *Theoretical Population Biology* 74(1)
     (2008): 46–55.

6   Laland, *Darwin's Unfinished Symphony*, p. 30.

7   Laland, *Darwin's Unfinished Symphony*.

8   See Richard Dawkins, *The Selfish Gene: 40th Anniversary Edition* (Oxford: Oxford
     University Press, 2016), ch. 25.

9   Ecclesiastes 1:9, KJV.

10   Jerome S. Bruner, *Toward a Theory of Instruction* (Cambridge, MA: Belknap Press,
     1966), p. 101.

11   Michael Young, What Are Schools For?, *Educação, Sociedade & Culturas* 32 (2011):
     145–155 at 150.

12   James Mark Baldwin, Consciousness and Evolution, *Psychological Review* 3
     (1896): 300–309 at 301. Available at: https://brocku.ca/MeadProject/Baldwin/
     Baldwin_1896_b.html.

13   David C. Geary, Educating the Evolved Mind: Conceptual Foundations for an
     Evolutionary Educational Psychology. In Jerry S. Carlson and Joel R. Levin (eds),
     *Educating the Evolved Mind: Conceptual Foundations for an Evolutionary Educational
     Psychology* (Charlotte, NC: Information Age Publishing, 2007), pp. 1–99.

14   Laland, *Darwin's Unfinished Symphony*, p. 134.

15   Karl Popper, *All Life is Problem Solving* (Abingdon: Routledge, 2001), p. 100.

16   This is not an established fact and there are many criticisms of 'just so stories'
     resulting from evolutionary psychology. For an overview see Paul Howard-Jones,
     Evolution of the Learning Brain: Or How You Got to Be So Smart (Abingdon:
     Routledge, 2018), pp. 158–160.

17   See, for example, Amina Youssef, Paul Ayres and John Sweller, Using General
     Problem-Solving Strategies to Generate Ideas in Order to Solve Geography
     Problems, *Applied Cognitive Psychology* 26(6) (2012): 872–877.

18   Dylan Wiliam, *Creating the Schools Our Children Need: What We're Doing Now
     Won't Help Much (And What We Can Do Instead)* (West Palm Beach, FL: Learning
     Sciences International, 2018), p. 125.

19   David C. Geary and Daniel B. Berch, Evolution and Children's Cognitive and
     Academic Development. In David C. Geary and Daniel B. Berch (eds), *Evolutionary
     Perspectives on Child Development and Education* (Basel: Springer International
     Publishing, 2016), pp. 217–250 at p. 234.

20   Steven Pinker, *The Language Instinct: How the Mind Creates Language* (London:
     Penguin, 2015).

21   Andrew R. George, In Search of the é.dub.ba.a: The Ancient Mesopotamian School
     in Literature and Reality. In Yitzhak Sefati, Pinhas Artzi, Chaim Cohen, Barry L.
     Eichler and Victor A. Hurowitz (eds), *An Experienced Scribe Who Neglects Nothing:
     Ancient Near Eastern Studies in Honor of Jacob Klein* (Potomac, MD: CDL Press,
     2005), pp. 127–137 at p. 127.

22   George, In Search of the é.dub.ba.a, p. 130.

23   Alexandra Kleinerman, *Education in Early 2nd Millennium BC Babylonia: The Sumerian Epistolary Miscellany* (Leiden: Brill, 2011).

24   Egbert of Liège, *The Well-Laden Ship*, tr. Robert G. Babcock (Cambridge, MA: Harvard University Press, 2013), p. 68.

25   Alvarus Pelagius, *The Plaint of the Church*. In Brian Tierney (ed.), *The Middle Ages*, Vol. 1: *Sources of Medieval History*, 5th edn (New York: McGraw-Hill Education, 1992), pp. 296–297 at p. 296.

26   Catherine Moriarty (ed.), *The Voice of the Middle Ages: In Personal Letters 1100–1500* (New York: Peter Bedrick Books, 1989), p. 105.

27   Douglas K. Detterman, Education and Intelligence: Pity the Poor Teacher Because Student Characteristics are More Significant Than Teachers or Schools, *Spanish Journal of Psychology* 19(93) (2016): 1–11 at 2.

28   James Tooley, *The Beautiful Tree: A Personal Journey into How the World's Poorest People Are Educating Themselves* (New Delhi: Penguin; Washington, DC: Cato Institute, 2009).

29   Daniel C. Dennett, *The Intentional Stance* (Cambridge, MA: MIT Press, 1987).

30   Andrew N. Meltzoff, Born to Learn: What Infants Learn from Watching Us. In Nathan A. Fox, Lewis A. Leavitt and John G. Worhol (eds), *The Role of Early Experience in Infant Development* (Skillman, NJ: Johnson & Johnson, 1999), pp. 145–160.

31   Sidney Strauss, Margalit Ziv and Adi Stein, Teaching as a Natural Cognition and Its Relations to Preschoolers' Developing Theory of Mind, *Cognitive Development* 17 (2002): 1473–1487 at 1482.

32   Edgar C. Reinke, Quintilian Lighted the Way, *Classical Bulletin* 51 (1975): 65–71.

Chapter 3: Is intelligence the answer?

1   Peter Lattman, The Origins of Justice Stewart's 'I Know It When I See It', *Wall Street Journal Law Blog* (27 September 2007). Available at: https://blogs.wsj.com/law/2007/09/27/the-origins-of-justice-stewarts-i-know-it-when-i-see-it/.

2   These responses come from Edward Thorndike, Lewis Terman, Stephen Colvin, Vivian Allen, Charles Henmon and Herbert Woodrow. See Intelligence and Its Measurement: A Symposium, *Journal of Educational Psychology* 12(3) (1921): 123–147.

3   Edwin Boring, Intelligence as the Tests Test It, *New Republic* 36 (1923): 35–37 at 35.

4   Robert J. Sternberg and Douglas K. Detterman (eds), *What is Intelligence? Contemporary Viewpoints on Its Nature and Definition* (Norwood, NJ: Ablex, 1986).

5   Shane Legg and Marcus Hutter, A Collection of Definitions of Intelligence, *Frontiers in Artificial Intelligence and Applications* 157 (2007): 17–24 at 19.

6   David Adam, *The Genius Within: Smart Pills, Brain Hacks and Adventures in Intelligence* (London: Picador, 2018), p. 46.

7   James R. Flynn, *What is Intelligence? Beyond the Flynn Effect* (Cambridge: Cambridge University Press, 2007), pp. 53–54.

8   For reviews showing that IQ is the most reliable indicator of job performance see Nathan R. Kuncel and Sarah A. Hezlett, Fact and Fiction in Cognitive Ability Testing for Admissions and Hiring Decisions, *Current Directions in Psychological Science* 19(6) (2010): 339–345; Frank L. Schmidt, In-Sue Oh and Jonathan A. Shaffer, The Validity and Utility of Selection Methods in Personnel Psychology: Practical and Theoretical Implications of 100 Years of Research Findings. Fox School of Business

Research Paper (17 October 2016). Available at: https://papers.ssrn.com/sol3/papers.cfm?abstract_id=2853669.

9   For the positive correlation between IQ and physical and mental health see Catherine R. Gale, G. David Batty, Per Tynelius, Ian J. Deary and Finn Rasmussen, Intelligence in Early Adulthood and Subsequent Hospitalization and Admission Rates for the Whole Range of Mental Disorders: Longitudinal Study of 1,049,663 Men, *Epidemiology* 21(1) (2010): 70–77; Marius Wrulich, Martin Brunner, Gertraud Stadler, Daniela Schalke, Ulrich Keller and Romain Martin, Forty Years On: Childhood Intelligence Predicts Health in Middle Adulthood, *Health Psychology* 33(2) (2014): 292–296.

10 Catherine M. Calvin, G. David Batty, Geoff Der, Caroline E. Brett, Adele Taylor, Alison Pattie et al., Childhood Intelligence in Relation to Major Causes of Death in 68 Year Follow-up: Prospective Population Study, *BMJ* 357 (2017): j2708.

11 Arvind Suresh, Autism Increase Mystery Solved? No, It's Not Vaccines, GMOs, Glyphosate – Or Organic Foods, *Genetic Literacy Project* (22 September 2016). Available at: https://geneticliteracyproject.org/2016/09/22/autism-increase-mystery-solved-no-its-not-vaccines-gmos-glyphosate-or-organic-foods/.

12 The correlations between cognitive ability and measures of work performance are taken from Kuncel and Hezlett, Fact and Fiction in Cognitive Ability Testing, 341.

13 Kuncel and Hezlett, Fact and Fiction in Cognitive Ability Testing.

14 Emily C. Nusbaum and Paul J. Silvia, Are Intelligence and Creativity Really So Different? Fluid Intelligence, Executive Processes, and Strategy Use in Divergent Thinking, *Intelligence* 39(1) (2011): 36–45.

15 Miriam A. Mosing, Nancy L. Pedersen, Guy Madison and Fredrik Ullén, Genetic Pleiotropy Explains Associations between Musical Auditory Discrimination and Intelligence, *PLOS ONE* 9(11) (2014): e113874.

16 Jonathan Wai, David Lubinski and Camilla P. Benbow, Creativity and Occupational Accomplishments Among Intellectually Precocious Youths: An Age 13 to Age 33 Longitudinal Study, *Journal of Educational Psychology* 97(3) (2005): 484–492.

17 Gale et al., Intelligence in Early Adulthood.

18 Daniel Nettle, Intelligence and Class Mobility in the British Population, *British Journal of Psychology* 94 (2003): 551–561.

19 Afia Ali, Gareth Ambler, Andre Strydom, Dheeraj Rai, Claudia Cooper, Sally McManus et al., The Relationship Between Happiness and Intelligence Quotient: The Contribution of Socio-economic and Clinical Factors, *Psychological Medicine* 43(6) (2013): 1303–1312.

20 Ian J. Deary, Steve Strand, Pauline Smith and Cres Fernandes, Intelligence and Educational Achievement, *Intelligence* 35(1) (2007): 13–21.

21 Timothy C. Bates, Fluctuating Asymmetry and Intelligence, *Intelligence* 35(1) (2007): 41–46.

22 Steven Pinker, *The Better Angels of Our Nature: A History of Violence and Humanity* (London: Penguin, 2011).

23 Ian J. Deary, Why Do Intelligent People Live Longer?, *Nature* 456 (2008): 175–176.

24 Daniel Keyes, *Flowers for Algernon* (New York: Harcourt, 1966), p. 35.

25 Howard Gardner, *Frames of Mind: The Theory of Multiple Intelligences* (New York: Basic Books, 1983).

26 Howard Gardner, Multiple Intelligences: Prelude, Theory, and Aftermath. In Robert J. Sternberg, Susan T. Fiske and Donald J. Foss (eds), *Scientists Making a Difference: One Hundred Eminent Behavioral and Brain Scientists Talk About Their Most Important Contributions* (New York: Cambridge University Press, 2016), pp. 167–170 at p. 169.

27   Gardner, Multiple Intelligences, p. 169.

28   C. Branton Shearer and Jessica M. Karanian, The Neuroscience of Intelligence: Empirical Support for the Theory of Multiple Intelligences?, *Trends in Neuroscience and Education* 6 (2017): 211–223 at 212.

29   See https://youtu.be/OL6-x0modwY.

30   Michael Beldoch, Sensitivity to Expression of Emotional Meaning in Three Modes of Communication. In Joel R. Davitz and Michael Beldoch (eds), *The Communication of Emotional Meaning* (New York: McGraw-Hill, 1964), pp. 31–42.

31   Daniel Goleman, *Emotional Intelligence: Why It Can Matter More Than IQ* (London: Bloomsbury, 1995).

32   Flavia Cavazotte, Valter Moreno and Mateus Hickmann, Effects of Leader Intelligence, Personality and Emotional Intelligence on Transformational Leadership and Managerial Performance, *Leadership Quarterly* 23(3) (2012): 443–455.

33   Dana Joseph and Daniel A. Newman, Emotional Intelligence: An Integrative Meta-Analysis and Cascading Model, *Journal of Applied Psychology* 95(1) (2010): 54–78.

34   Edward L. Thorndike, Intelligence and Its Uses, *Harper's Magazine* 140 (1920): 227–235 at 228.

35   David Weschler, *The Measurement and Appraisal of Adult Intelligence*, 4th edn (Baltimore, MD: Williams & Wilkins, 1958), p. 75.

36   Martin E. Ford and Marie S. Tisak, A Further Search for Social Intelligence, *Journal of Educational Psychology* 75(2) (1983): 196–206.

37   Robert J. Sternberg and Cynthia A. Berg, Quantitative Integration: Definitions of Intelligence. A Comparison of the 1921 and 1986 Symposia. In Robert J. Sternberg and Douglas K. Detterman (eds), *What is Intelligence? Contemporary Viewpoints on Its Nature and Definition* (Norwood, NJ: Ablex 1986), pp. 155–162.

38   Phillip L. Ackerman and Eric D. Heggestad, Intelligence, Personality, and Interests: Evidence for Overlapping Traits, *Psychological Bulletin* 121(2) (1997): 219–245.

39   Gardner, Multiple Intelligences, p. 169; Sternberg and Berg, Quantitative Integration.

40   Michael J. A. Howe, Can IQ Change? *The Psychologist* 11 (1998): 69–72 at 71.

41   Robert Serpell, How Specific Are Perceptual Skills? A Cross-Cultural Study of Pattern Reproduction, *British Journal of Psychology* 70(3) (1979): 365–380.

42   Jared Diamond, *Guns, Germs and Steel: A Short History of Everybody for the Last 13,000 Years* (London: Vintage, 1998), pp. 20–21.

43   Richard J. Haier, *The Neuroscience of Intelligence* (New York: Cambridge University Press, 2017), p. 71.

Chapter 4: Nature via nurture

1   Stephen Jay Gould, *The Mismeasure of Man* (New York: Norton & Co., 1981), pp. 185–186.

2   Maria Konnikova, Practice Doesn't Make Perfect, *The New Yorker* (28 September 2016). Available at: https://www.newyorker.com/science/maria-konnikova/practice-doesnt-make-perfect.

3   In fact, it's likely that genes account for 30–60% of the variance across psychological traits, which means everything else accounts for the remaining 40–70%. See Robert Plomin, John C. DeFries, Valerie S. Knopik and Jenae M. Neiderhiser, *Behavioral Genetics*, 6th edn (New York: Worth Publishers, 2013).

4   Choe Sang-Hun, South Korea Stretches Standards for Success, *New York Times* (22 December 2009). Available at: https://www.nytimes.com/2009/12/23/world/asia/23seoul.html.

5   Richard E. Nisbett, Schooling Makes You Smarter: What Educators Need to Know About IQ, *American Educator* 37(1) (2013): 10–19 at 13. Available at: https://www.aft.org/sites/default/files/periodicals/Nisbett.pdf.

6   See Eric Turkheimer, Andreana Haley, Mary Waldron, Brian D'Onofrio and Irving I. Gottesman, Socioeconomic Status Modifies Heritability of IQ in Young Children, *Psychological Science* 14(6) (2003): 623–628; Eric Turkheimer, Clancy Blair, Aaron Sojourner, John Protzko and Erin Horn, Gene Environment Interaction for IQ in a Randomized Clinical Trial. Unpublished manuscript. University of Virginia, Charlottesville, VA (2012).

7   Leo Tolstoy, *Anna Karenina*, tr. R. P. L. Volokhonsky (New York: Viking Penguin, 2001 [1875–1877]). The Anna Karenina principle was first identified by Jared Diamond in *Guns, Germs and Steel* to explain the reasons behind animal domestication – see ch. 9.

8   See Roger W. Simmons, Tara Wass, Jennifer D. Thomas and Edward P. Riley, Fractionated Simple and Choice Reaction Time in Children with Prenatal Exposure to Alcohol, *Alcoholism: Clinical and Experimental Research* 26(9) (2002): 1412–1419; Susan Astley, FAS/FAE: Their Impact on Psychosocial Child Development with a View to Diagnosis. In Richard E. Tremblay, Ronald G. Barr and Ray DeV. Peters (eds), *Encyclopedia on Early Childhood Development* (2003). Available at: http://www.child-encyclopedia.com/documents/AstleyANGxp.pdf.

9   See Alan Lucas, Ruth Morley, Tim J. Cole, Gill Lister and Catherine Leeson-Payne, Breast Milk and Subsequent Intelligence Quotient in Children Born Preterm, *The Lancet* 339(8788) (1992): 261–264; James W. Anderson, Bryan M. Johnstone and Daniel T. Remley, Breast-Feeding and Cognitive Development: A Meta-Analysis, *American Journal of Clinical Nutrition* 70(4) (1999): 525–535; Erik L. Mortensen, Kim F. Michaelsen, Stephanie A. Sanders and June A. Reinisch, The Association between Duration of Breastfeeding and Adult Intelligence, *Journal of the American Medical Association* 287(18) (2002): 2365–2371.

10 Betty Hart and Todd R. Risley, *Meaningful Differences in the Everyday Experience of Young American Children* (Baltimore, MD: Brookes Publishing, 1995).

11 Douglas E. Sperry, Linda L. Sperry and Peggy J. Miller, Reexamining the Verbal Environments of Children from Different Socioeconomic Backgrounds, *Child Development* (2018). doi:10.1111/cdev.13072

12 Kathryn Asbury and Robert Plomin, *G is for Genes: The Impact of Genetics on Education and Achievement* (Chichester: Wiley, 2013), p. 27.

13 Stefan Samuelsson, Brian Byrne, Richard K. Olson, Jacqueline Hulslander, Sally Wadsworth, Robin Corley et al., Response to Early Literacy Instruction in the United States, Australia and Scandinavia: A Behavioural-Genetic Analysis, *Learning and Individual Differences* 18(3) (2008): 289–295.

14 Asbury and Plomin, *G is for Genes*, p. 28.

15 Matt Ridley, *The Evolution of Everything: How Ideas Emerge* (London: Fourth Estate, 2015), p. 166.

16 Gene Nakajima, Gertrude Stein's Medical Education and Her Evolving Feminism. Unpublished manuscript. Chesney Archives, Johns Hopkins Medical Institutions, MD (1986).

17 Linda S. Gottfredson, Mainstream Science on Intelligence: An Editorial with 52 Signatories, History, and Bibliography, *Intelligence* 24 (1997): 13–23 at 15.

18 Alan R. Templeton, Human Races: A Genetic and Evolutionary Perspective, *American Anthropologist* 100(3) (1998): 632–650.

19   William T. Dickens and James R. Flynn, Black Americans Reduce the Racial IQ Gap: Evidence from Standardization Samples, *Psychological Science* 17(10) (2006): 913–920.

20   Lawrence Wright, *Twins: And What They Tell Us About Who We Are* (Hoboken, NJ: Wiley, 1997).

21   Thomas J. Bouchard, Jr, Genetic Influence on Human Psychological Traits: A Survey, *Current Directions in Psychological Science* 13(4) (2004): 148–151 at 151.

22   Robert Plomin and Ian J. Deary, Genetics and Intelligence Differences: Five Special Findings, *Molecular Psychiatry* 20(1) (2015): 98–108.

23   Judith Rich Harris, *The Nurture Assumption: Why Children Turn Out the Way They Do* (London: Bloomsbury, 1999), p. 357.

24   Harris, *The Nurture Assumption*, p. 248.

25   Claude M. Steele and Joshua Aronson, Stereotype Threat and the Test Performance of African Americans, *Journal of Personality and Social Psychology* 69(5) (1995): 797–811.

26   Stephen J. Spencer, Claude M. Steele and Diane M. Quinn, Stereotype Threat and Women's Math Performance, *Journal of Experimental Social Psychology* 35(1) (1999): 4–28.

27   Keith E. Stanovich, Matthew Effects in Reading: Some Consequences of Individual Differences in the Acquisition of Literacy, *Reading Research Quarterly* 22 (2017): 360–407. This can be found repeatedly in the Bible. Most sources reference Matthew 25:29, but Matthew 13:12 says something very similar, as does Luke 19:26, Luke 8:18 and Mark 4:25. The first person to coin the phrase 'Matthew effect' was Robert K. Merton, referring to the finding that citations of academic papers are asymmetric: The Matthew Effect in Science, *Science* 159(3810) (1968): 56–63.

28   Harris, *The Nurture Assumption*, p. 245.

29   Asbury and Plomin, *G is for Genes*, p. 89.

Chapter 5: Can we get cleverer?

1   James R. Flynn, *Are We Getting Smarter? Rising IQ in the Twenty-First Century* (Cambridge: Cambridge University Press, 2012), p. 1.

2   Christian Brinch and Ann Galloway, Schooling in Adolescence Raises IQ Scores, *Proceedings of the National Academy of Sciences of the United States of America* 109 (2011): 425–430.

3   Kjell Härnqvist, Relative Changes in Intelligence from 13 to 18. I: Background and Methodology, *Scandinavian Journal of Psychology* 9(1) (1968): 50–64.

4   For an extensive review see Stephen J. Ceci, How Much Does Schooling Influence General Intelligence and Its Cognitive Components? A Reassessment of the Evidence, *Developmental Psychology* 27(5) (1991): 703–722.

5   Philipp A. Freund and Heinz Holling, Who Wants to Take an Intelligence Test? Personality and Achievement Motivation in the Context of Ability Testing, *Personality and Individual Differences* 50(5) (2011): 723–728.

6   Ceci, How Much Does Schooling Influence General Intelligence, 717.

7   Stuart J. Ritchie and Elliot M. Tucker-Drob, How Much Does Education Improve Intelligence? A Meta-Analysis, *Psychological Science* 29(8) (2018). https://doi.org/10.1177/0956797618774253

8   Sorel Cahan and Nora Cohen, Age versus Schooling Effects on Intelligence Development, *Child Development* 60 (1989): 1239–1249.

9   See, for example, Ingeborg Stelzl, Ferdinand Merz, Theodor Ehlers and Herbert Remer, The Effect of Schooling on the Development of Fluid and Cristallized

Intelligence: A Quasi-Experimental Study, *Intelligence* 21(3) (1995): 279–296; Christina Cliffordson and Jan-Eric Gustafsson, Effects of Age and Schooling on Intellectual Performance: Estimates Obtained from Analysis of Continuous Variation in Age and Length of Schooling, *Intelligence* 36(2) (2008): 143–152.

10   Ulric Neisser, Gwyneth Boodoo, Thomas J. Bouchard, Jr, A. Wade Boykin, Nathan Brody, Stephen J. Ceci et al., Intelligence: Knowns and Unknowns, *American Psychologist* 51(2) (1996): 77–101 at 87.

11   Douglas K. Detterman, Education and Intelligence: Pity the Poor Teacher Because Student Characteristics are More Significant Than Teachers or Schools, *Spanish Journal of Psychology* 19(93) (2016): 1–11.

12   Karsten T. Hansen, James J. Heckman and Kathleen J. Mullen, The Effect of Schooling and Ability on Achievement Test Scores, *Journal of Econometrics* 121(1–2) (2004): 39–98.

13   See Ceci, How Much Does Schooling Influence General Intelligence; Keith E. Stanovich, Matthew Effects in Reading: Some Consequences of Individual Differences in the Acquisition of Literacy, *Reading Research Quarterly* 22 (1993): 360–407; and Stuart J. Ritchie, Timothy C. Bates and Robert Plomin, Does Learning to Read Improve Intelligence? A Longitudinal Multivariate Analysis in Identical Twins from Age 7 to 16, *Child Development* 86 (2015): 23–36.

14   Stuart J. Ritchie, Timothy C. Bates and Ian J. Deary, Is Education Associated with Improvements in General Cognitive Ability, or in Specific Skills?, *Developmental Psychology* 51(5) (2015): 573–582.

15   Raymond B. Cattell, *Abilities: Their Structure, Growth, and Action* (Boston, MA: Houghton Mifflin, 1971).

16   Magnus Carlsson, Gordon B. Dahl, Björn Öckert and Dan-Olof Rooth, The Effect of Schooling on Cognitive Skills, *Review of Economics and Statistics* 97(3) (2015): 533–547.

17   Ted Nettlebeck and Carlene Wilson, The Flynn Effect: Smarter Not Faster, *Intelligence* 32(1) (2004): 85–93.

18   Elliot M. Tucker-Drob, Differentiation of Cognitive Abilities Across the Life Span, *Developmental Psychology* 45(4) (2009): 1097–1118. See also Daniel Murman, The Impact of Age on Cognition, *Seminars in Hearing* 36(3) (2015): 111–121.

19   James R. Flynn, Massive IQ Gains in 14 Nations: What IQ Tests Really Measure, *Psychological Bulletin* 101(2) (1987): 171–191.

20   Arthur Conan Doyle, *The Sign of Four* (London: Penguin, 2001 [1890]), p. 92.

21   Ulric Neisser, Rising Scores on Intelligence Tests: Test Scores are Certainly Going Up All Over the World, But Whether Intelligence Itself Has Risen Remains Controversial, *American Scientist* 85(5) (1997): 440–447 at 445.

22   James R. Flynn, *What is Intelligence? Beyond the Flynn Effect* (Cambridge: Cambridge University Press, 2007), p. 11.

23   Flynn, *What is Intelligence?*, p. 25. See also Alexander Romanovich Luria, *Cognitive Development: Its Cultural and Social Foundations*, ed. Michael Cole (Cambridge, MA: Harvard University Press, 1976).

24   Flynn, *Are We Getting Smarter?*

25   Cavan Sieczkowski, 1912 Eighth-Grade Exam Stumps 21st-Century Test-Takers, *Huffington Post* (8 December 2013). Available at: https://www.huffingtonpost.co.uk/entry/1912-eighth-grade-exam_n_3744163?guccounter=1.

26   Jeremy E. Genovese, Cognitive Skills Valued by Educators: Historical Content Analysis of Testing in Ohio, *Journal of Educational Research* 96 (2002): 101–114.

27   Flynn, *Are We Getting Smarter?*, p. 20.

28   Steven Pinker, *The Better Angels of Our Nature: A History of Violence and Humanity* (London: Penguin, 2011), p. 793.

29   Theodore Roosevelt, *The Winning of the West*. Vol. 1: *From the Alleghanies to the Mississippi, 1769–1776* (New York: Cornell University Library, 1889), p. 65.

30   James W. Loewen, *Lies My Teacher Told Me: Everything Your American History Textbook Got Wrong* (New York: New Press, 1995), pp. 22–31.

31   Johann Hari, The Two Churchills, *New York Times* (12 August 2010). Available at: https://www.nytimes.com/2010/08/15/books/review/Hari-t.html.

32   Examples are detailed by Pinker, *The Better Angels of Our Nature*, pp. 796–797.

33   David P. Farrington, Origins of Violent Behavior Over the Life Span. In Daniel J. Flannery, Alexander T. Vazsonyi and Irwin D. Waldman (eds), *The Cambridge Handbook of Violent Behavior and Aggression* (Cambridge: Cambridge University Press, 2007), pp. 19–48 at pp. 22–23, pp. 26–27.

34   Garrett Jones, Are Smarter Groups More Cooperative? Evidence from Prisoner's Dilemma Experiments, 1959–2003, *Journal of Economic Behaviour & Organisation* 68(3–4) (2008): 489–497.

35   Ian J. Deary, G. David Batty and Catherine R. Gale, Bright Children Become Enlightened Adults, *Psychological Science* 19(1) (2008): 1–6.

36   Pinker, *The Better Angels of Our Nature*, pp. 791–810.

37   Peera Wongupparaj, Veena Kumari and Robin G. Morris, A Cross-Temporal Meta-Analysis of Raven's Progressive Matrices: Age Groups and Developing Versus Developed Countries, *Intelligence* 49 (2015): 1–9.

38   Lisa Trahan, Karla K. Stuebing, Merril K. Hiscock and Jack M. Fletcher, The Flynn Effect: A Meta-Analysis, *Psychological Bulletin* 140(5) (2014): 1332–1360.

39   Jennifer Crocker, Marc-Andre Olivier and Noah Nuer, Self-Image Goals and Compassionate Goals: Costs and Benefits, *Self and Identity* 8 (2009): 251–269.

40   Test available at www.mindsetonline.com.

41   See http://www.intropsych.com/ch01_psychology_and_science/self-report_measures.html.

42   Carol S. Dweck, Carol Dweck Revisits the 'Growth Mindset', *Education Week* (23 September 2015). Available at: https://www.stem.org.uk/system/files/community-resources/2016/06/DweckEducationWeek.pdf.

43   Christine Gross-Loh, How Praise Became a Consolation Prize [interview with Carol Dweck], *The Atlantic* (16 December 2016). Available at: https://www.theatlantic.com/education/archive/2016/12/how-praise-became-a-consolation-prize/510845/.

44   See, for example, Dave Paunesku, Mindset Misconceptions: Trying Hard ≠ Growth Mindset, *medium.com* (17 November 2015). Available at: https://medium.com/learning-mindset/mindset-misconceptions-trying-hard-growth-mindset-8ceb12a33636.

45   Bryan Caplan, *The Case Against Education: Why the Education System is a Waste of Time and Money* (Princeton, NJ: Princeton University Press, 2018), p. 59.

46   Jo Boaler, *The Educators*, BBC Radio 4 [audio] (29 September 2014). Available at https://www.bbc.co.uk/programmes/b04gw6rh.

47   Jason S. Mosel, Hans S. Schroder, Carrie Heeter, Tim P. Moran and Yu-Hao Lee, Mind Your Errors: Evidence for a Neural Mechanism Linking Growth Mind-Set to Adaptive Posterror Adjustments, *Psychological Science* 22(12) (2011): 1484–1489.

48   Gross-Loh, How Praise Became a Consolation Prize.

49   Gross-Loh, How Praise Became a Consolation Prize.

50   Philip H. Gosse, *Omphalos: An Attempt to Untie the Geological Knot* (London: John Van Voorst, 1857).

51   Cinzia Rienzo, Heather Rolfe and David Wilkinson, *Changing Mindsets: Evaluation Report and Executive Summary* (London: Education Endowment Foundation, 2015). Available at: https://v1.educationendowmentfoundation.org.uk/uploads/pdf/Changing_Mindsets.pdf.

52   Yue Li and Timothy C. Bates, Does Growth Mindset Improve Children's IQ, Educational Attainment or Response to Setbacks? Active-Control Interventions and Data on Children's Own Mindsets (2017). Available at: https://osf.io/preprints/socarxiv/tsdwy.

53   Carol Dweck quoted in Tom Chivers, A Mindset 'Revolution' Sweeping Britain's Classrooms May Be Based on Shaky Science, *BuzzFeed* (14 January 2017). Available at: https://www.buzzfeed.com/tomchivers/what-is-your-mindset?utm_term=.lv42Bb4l9#.ucWBv7RQG.

54   John A. Bargh, Priming Effects Replicate Just Fine, Thanks, *Psychology Today* (11 May 2012). Available at: https://www.psychologytoday.com/blog/the-natural-unconscious/201205/priming-effects-replicate-just-fine-thanks.

55   Education Week Research Center, *Mindset in the Classroom: A National Study of K-12 Teachers* (2016). Available at: http://www.edweek.org/media/ewrc_mindsetintheclassroom_sept2016.pdf.

56   David S. Yeager, Paul Hanselman, David Paunesku, Christopher Hulleman, Carol Dweck, Chandra Muller et al., Where and For Whom Can a Brief, Scalable Mindset Intervention Improve Adolescents' Educational Trajectories? (2018) (manuscript under revision). Available at: https://doi.org/10.31234/osf.io/md2qa.

57   Victoria F. Sisk, Alexander P. Burgoyne, Jingze Sun, Jennifer L. Butler and Brooke N. Macnamara, To What Extent and Under Which Circumstances Are Growth Mind-Sets Important to Academic Achievement? Two Meta-Analyses, *Psychological Science* 29(4) (2018): 549–571 at 549.

58   Daniel T. Willingham, *Why Don't Students Like School? A Cognitive Scientist Answers Questions About How the Mind Works and What It Means for the Classroom* (San Francisco, CA: Jossey-Bass, 2009), p. 109.

59   Robert J. Sternberg, Increasing Fluid Intelligence Is Possible After All, *Proceedings of the National Academy of Sciences of the United States of America* 105(19) (2008): 6791–6792 at 6791.

60   Susanne M. Jaeggi, Martin Buschkuehl, John Jonides and Walter J. Perrig, Improving Fluid Intelligence with Training on Working Memory, *Proceedings of the National Academy of Sciences of the United States of America* 105(19) (2008): 6829–6833 at 6829.

61   Sternberg, Increasing Fluid Intelligence Is Possible After All, 6791.

62   See David Didau and Nick Rose, *What Every Teacher Needs to Know About Psychology* (Woodbridge: John Catt Educational, 2016), pp. 62–69.

63   David E. Moody, Can Intelligence Be Increased by Training on a Task of Working Memory?, *Intelligence* 37(4) (2009): 327–328 at 327 and 328.

64   Tyler L. Harrison, Zach Shipstead, Kenny L. Hicks, David Z. Hambrick, Thomas S. Redick and Randall W. Engle, Working Memory Training May Increase Working Memory Capacity But Not Fluid Intelligence, *Psychological Science* 24(12) (2013): 2409–2419 at 2409.

65   Jacky Au, Ellen Sheehan, Nancy Tsai, Greg J. Duncan, Martin Buschkuehl and Susanne M. Jaeggi, Improving Fluid Intelligence with Training on Working Memory: A Meta-Analysis, *Psychonomic Bulletin & Review* 22(2) (2014): 366–377 at 366.

66   Daniel J. Simons, Walter R. Boot, Neil Charness, Susan E. Gathercole, Christopher F. Chabris, David Z. Hambrick and Elizabeth A. L. Stine-Morrow, Do 'Brain-Training'

Programs Work?, *Psychological Science in the Public Interest* 17(3) (2016): 103–186 at 103.

67   Although not peer reviewed before this book went to print, see Giovanni N. Sala, Deniz Aksayli, K. Semir Tatlidil, Tomoko Tatsumi, Yasuyuki Gondo and Fernand Gobet, Near and Far Transfer in Cognitive Training: A Second-Order Meta-Analysis (2018). Available at: https://psyarxiv.com/9efqd/.

68   Have a look at http://www.thinkingclassroom.co.uk/ThinkingClassroom/ThinkingSkills.aspx if you require further examples.

69   Caplan, *The Case Against Education*, p. 59.

70   See http://www.cie.org.uk/images/164766-2016-syllabus.pdf.

71   See http://www.cie.org.uk/images/198157-june-2014-question-paper-11.pdf.

72   See, for example, http://www.letsthink.org.uk/wp-content/uploads/2014/06/developing_science_in_KS3.pdf.

73   Philip Adey and Michael Shayer, *Really Raising Standards: Cognitive Intervention and Academic Achievement* (London and New York: Routledge, 1994).

74   See https://educationendowmentfoundation.org.uk/our-work/projects/lets-think-secondary-science/.

75   Carl Sagan, Encyclopaedia Galactica (Episode 12), *Cosmos* [video]. PBS (14 December 1980).

76   Douglas K. Detterman, The Case for the Prosecution: Transfer as an Epiphenomenon. In Douglas K. Detterman and Robert J. Sternberg (eds), *Transfer on Trial: Intelligence, Cognition, and Instruction* (Westport, CT: Ablex Publishing, 1993), pp. 1–23 at p. 17.

77   David P. Ausubel, An Evaluation of the Conceptual Schemes Approach to Science Curriculum Development, *Journal of Research in Science Teaching* 3 (1965): 255–264 at 257.

78   See https://educationendowmentfoundation.org.uk/evidence-summaries/teaching-learning-toolkit/setting-or-streaming/.

79   Robert Rosenthal and Lenore Jacobson, Pygmalion in the Classroom, *Urban Review* 3(1) (1968): 16–20.

80   Lee Jussim and Kent D. Harber, Teacher Expectations and Self-Fulfilling Prophecies: Knowns and Unknowns, Resolved and Unresolved Controversies, *Personality and Social Psychology Review* 9(2) (2005): 131–155 at 131.

81   Graham Nuthall, *The Hidden Lives of Learners* (Wellington: New Zealand Council for Educational Research Press), p. 84.

82   Dylan Wiliam, Reliability, Validity, and All That Jazz, *Education 3–13* 29(3) (2001): 17–21 at 19.

Chapter 6: How memory works

1   Paul A. Kirschner, John Sweller and Richard E. Clark, Why Minimal Guidance During Instruction Does Not Work: An Analysis of the Failure of Constructivist, Discovery, Problem-Based, Experiential, and Inquiry-Based Teaching, *Educational Psychologist* 41(2) (2006): 75–86 at 76.

2   Daniel C. Dennett, *Consciousness Explained* (London: Penguin, 1991), p. 39.

3   Benjamin H. Kennedy, *The Theaetetus of Plato*, with translation and notes (Cambridge: Cambridge University Press, 1881), p. 268.

4   Dennett, *Consciousness Explained*, p. 223.

5   Kirschner et al., Why Minimal Guidance During Instruction Does Not Work, 77.

6   John Sweller, Paul Ayres and Slava Kalyuga, *Cognitive Load Theory: Explorations in the Learning Sciences, Instructional Systems and Performance Technologies* (New York: Springer, 2011), p. 35.

7   George A. Miller, The Magical Number Seven, Plus or Minus Two: Some Limits on Our Capacity for Processing Information, *Psychological Review* 63(2) (1956): 81–97.

8   William G. Chase and Herbert A. Simon, Perception in Chess, *Cognitive Psychology* 4(1) (1973): 55–81.

9   Nelson Cowan, The Magical Number 4 in Short-Term Memory: A Reconsideration of Mental Storage Capacity, *Behavioral and Brain Sciences* 24(1) (2001): 87–114.

10 André Bisseret, Mémoire opérationelle et structure du travail [Working Memory and Work Structure], *Bulletin de Psychologie* 24 (1970): 280–294. English summary published as: Analysis of Mental Processes Involved in Air Traffic Control, *Ergonomics* 14 (1971): 565–570.

11 Miller, The Magical Number Seven, 84.

12 Arthur Conan Doyle, *A Study in Scarlet* (London: Penguin, 2001 [1887]).

13 Thomas M. Bartol, Jr, Cailey Bromer, Justin Kinney, Michael A. Chirillo, Jennifer N. Bourne, Kristen M. Harris and Terrence J. Sejnowski, Nanoconnectomic Upper Bound on the Variability of Synaptic Plasticity, *eLife* 4 (2015): e10778.

14 André Tricot and John Sweller, Domain-Specific Knowledge and Why Teaching Generic Skills Does Not Work, *Educational Psychology Review* 26(2) (2014): 265–283 at 279.

15 Though whether conscious access is the defining characteristic of these types of memory is debatable – see Katharina Henke, A Model for Memory Systems Based on Processing Modes Rather Than Consciousness, *Nature Reviews Neuroscience* 11(7) (2010): 523–532.

16 For a neurobiological account of how all this works see Robert Cabeza and Morris Moscovitch, Memory Systems, Processing Modes, and Components: Functional Neuroimaging Evidence, *Perspectives on Psychological Science* 8(1) (2013): 49–55.

17 Duncan R. Godden and Alan D. Baddeley, Context-Dependent Memory in Two Natural Environments: On Land and Underwater, *British Journal of Psychology* 66(3) (1975): 325–331.

18 Elizabeth F. Loftus and John C. Palmer, Reconstruction of Automobile Destruction: An Example of the Interaction between Language and Memory, *Journal of Verbal Learning and Verbal Behavior* 13(5) (1974): 585–589.

19 Henry L. Roediger and Kathleen McDermott, Creating False Memories: Remembering Words Not Presented in Lists, *Journal of Experimental Psychology: Learning, Memory, and Cognition* 21(4) (1995): 803–814.

20 Frederic C. Bartlett, Experiments on the Reproduction of Folk-Stories, *Folklore* 31(1) (1920): 30–47.

21 Hermann Ebbinghaus, *Memory: A Contribution to Experimental Psychology*, tr. Henry A. Ruger and Clara E. Bussenius (New York: Teachers College, Columbia University, 1913 [1885]). These experiments have recently been replicated by Jaap M. J. Murre and Joeri Dros, Replication and Analysis of Ebbinghaus' Forgetting Curve, *PLOS ONE* 10(7) (2015): e0120644.

22 Elizabeth Bjork and Robert A. Bjork, Intentional Forgetting Can Increase, Not Decrease, Residual Influences of To-Be-Forgotten Information, *Journal of Experimental Psychology: Learning, Memory, and Cognition* 29(4) (2003): 524–531.

23 From a Go Cognitive interview with Robert Bjork on the theory of disuse and the role of forgetting in human memory: http://gocognitive.net/interviews/theory-disuse-and-role-forgetting-human-memory.

24 Joshua Foer, *Moonwalking with Einstein: The Art and Science of Remembering Everything* (New York: Penguin, 2012).

25   Joshua Foer, Feats of Memory Anyone Can Do, *TED.com* [video] (2012). Available at: http://www.ted.com/talks/joshua_foer_feats_of_memory_anyone_can_do?awesm=on.ted.com_Foer&utm_campaign=&utm_medium=on.ted.com-static&utm_source=t.co&utm_content=awesm-publisher.

26   Kathryn McWeeny, Andrew Young, Dennis Hay and Andrew Ellis, Putting Names to Faces, *British Journal of Psychology* 78 (1987): 143–146.

Chapter 7: You are what you know

1   Daniel Keyes, *Flowers for Algernon* (New York: Harcourt, 1966), p. 167.

2   John B. Watson, *Behaviourism*, rev. edn (Chicago, IL: University of Chicago Press, 1930), p. 82.

3   For a thorough explanation of why dualism is such a 'forlorn' concept see Daniel C. Dennett, *Consciousness Explained* (London: Penguin, 1991), pp. 33–42.

4   Keyes, *Flowers for Algernon*, p. 55.

5   John R. Anderson, ACT: A Simple Theory of Complex Cognition, *American Psychologist* 51(4) (1996): 355–365 at 356.

6   See Richard P. Feynman, Names Don't Constitute Knowledge [video of Yorkshire Television interview] (1973). Available at: https://youtu.be/lFlYKmos3-s.

7   Daniel T. Willingham, Inflexible Knowledge: The First Step to Expertise, *American Educator* 26 (2002): 31–33. Available at: http://www.aft.org/periodical/american-educator/winter-2002/ask-cognitive-scientist.

8   Feynman, Names Don't Constitute Knowledge.

9   John Hattie and Gregory Yates, *Visible Learning and the Science of How We Learn* (Abingdon: Routledge, 2014), p. 53.

10   Richard P. Feynman, Cargo Cult Science: Some Remarks on Science, Pseudoscience, and Learning How to Not Fool Yourself (1974). Available at: http://calteches.library.caltech.edu/51/2/CargoCult.htm.

11   Feynman, Cargo Cult Science.

12   Robert J. Marzano, The Art and Science of Teaching/Teaching Inference, *Educational Leadership* 67(7) (2010): 80–81. Available at: http://www.ascd.org/publications/educational-leadership/apr10/vol67/num07/Teaching-Inference.aspx.

13   Kevin Ashton, *How to Fly a Horse: The Secret History of Creation, Invention and Discovery* (London: Windmill Books, 2015), p. 31.

14   Michael Fordham, Knowledge as the Currency of Teaching, *Clio et cetera* (12 October 2017). Available at: https://clioetcetera.com/2017/10/12/knowledge-as-the-currency-of-teaching.

15   United States Department of Defense, News Briefing: Secretary Rumsfeld and Gen. Myers [news transcript] (12 February 2002). Available at: http://archive.defense.gov/Transcripts/Transcript.aspx?TranscriptID=2636.

16   Michael Polyani, *The Tacit Dimension* (Abingdon: Routledge, 1966), p. 4.

17   Michael Polyani, *Personal Knowledge: Towards a Post-Critical Philosophy* (New York: Psychology Press, 1998 [1958]).

18   Elizabeth Newton, Overconfidence in the Communication of Intent: Heard and Unheard Melodies. PhD dissertation. Stanford University, CA (1990).

19   Eric Donald Hirsch, Jr, 'You Can Always Look It Up' … Or Can You?, *American Educator* 24(1) (2000): 4–9. Available at: https://www.aft.org/sites/default/files/periodicals/LookItUpSpring2000.pdf.

20   "I have of course made up all the numbers in [this] example, but we know that the basics are correct – the rich get richer": Daniel T. Willingham, *Why Don't Students Like School? A Cognitive Scientist Answers Questions About How the Mind Works and What It Means for the Classroom* (San Francisco, CA: Jossey-Bass, 2009), p. 45.

21   Daisy Christodoulou, *Seven Myths About Education* (Abingdon: Routledge, 2014), p. 13.

22   Quoted in Jonah Lehrer, The Itch of Curiosity, *Wired* (8 March 2010). Available at https://www.wired.com/2010/08/the-itch-of-curiosity/.

23   Ian Leslie, *Curious: The Desire to Know and Why Your Future Depends on It* (London: Quercus Editions, 2014), p. 17.

24   Charles Darwin, *The Descent of Man, and Selection in Relation to Sex* (London: John Murray, 1871). Available at: http://darwin-online.org.uk/content/frameset?pageseq =1&itemID=F937.1&viewtype=text.

25   Patrick R. Heck, Daniel J. Simons and Christopher F. Chabris, 65% of Americans Believe They Are Above Average in Intelligence: Results of Two Nationally Representative Surveys, *PLOS ONE* 13(7) (2018): e0200103. Available at: https://journals.plos.org/plosone/article?id=10.1371/journal.pone.0200103.

26   Errol Morris, The Anosognosic's Dilemma: Something's Wrong But You'll Never Know What It Is (Part 1) [interview with David Dunning], *New York Times Opinionator Blog* (20 June 2010). Available at: https://opinionator.blogs.nytimes.com/2010/06/20/the-anosognosics-dilemma-1/.

27   Rebecca Lawson, The Science of Cycology: Failures to Understand How Everyday Objects Work, *Memory & Cognition* 34(8) (2006): 1667–1675 at 1669.

Chapter 8: What knowledge?

1   Quoted in Michael Young, The Curriculum and the Entitlement to Knowledge. Edited text of a talk given at Magdalene College, Cambridge, 25 March 2014. Available at: http://www.cambridgeassessment.org.uk/Images/166279-the-curriculum-and-the-entitlement-to-knowledge-prof-michael-young.pdf.

2   See https://petition.parliament.uk/archived/petitions/172405.

3   Jo Boaler, Fluency Without Fear: Research Evidence on the Best Ways to Learn Math Facts, *YouCubed* (28 January 2015). Available at: https://www.youcubed.org/evidence/fluency-without-fear/.

4   James R. Flynn, Why Our IQ Levels are Higher Than Our Grandparents', *TED.com* (2013). Available at: https://www.ted.com/talks/james_flynn_why_our_iq_levels_are_higher_than_our_grandparents/transcript.

5   Young, The Curriculum and the Entitlement to Knowledge.

6   See, for example, George Monbiot, In An Age of Robots, Schools Are Teaching Our Children to Be Redundant, *The Guardian* (15 February 2017). Available at: https://www.theguardian.com/commentisfree/2017/feb/15/robots-schools-teaching-children-redundant-testing-learn-future; Caitlin Moran, Why I Should Run Our Schools, *The Times* (29 April 2017). Available at: https://www.thetimes.co.uk/article/caitlin-moran-why-i-should-be-education-secretary-9llh939r2.

7   Quoted in Carole Cadwalladr, The 'Granny Cloud': The Network of Volunteers Helping Poorer Children Learn, *The Guardian* (2 August 2017). Available at: https://www.theguardian.com/education/2015/aug/02/sugata-mitra-school-in-the-cloud.

8   Paul Boghossian, *Fear of Knowledge: Against Relativism and Constructivism* (New York: Oxford University Press, 2007).

9   Michael Young, Powerful Knowledge: An Analytically Useful Concept or Just a 'Sexy Sounding Term'? A Response to John Beck's 'Powerful Knowledge, Esoteric Knowledge, Curriculum Knowledge', *Cambridge Journal of Education* 43(2) (2013): 195–198 at 196.

10   Young, The Curriculum and the Entitlement to Knowledge, 10.

11   For detailed statistical analysis see Hans Rosling with Ola Rosling and Anna Rosling
      Rönnlund, *Factfulness: Ten Reasons We're Wrong About the World – And Why Things
      Are Better Than You Think* (London: Sceptre, 2018), pp. 19–46.

12   Jan Meyer and Ray Land, Threshold Concepts and Troublesome Knowledge:
      Linkages to Ways of Thinking and Practising. In Chris Rust (ed.), *Improving Student
      Learning: Theory and Practice Ten Years On* (Oxford: Oxford Centre for Staff and
      Learning Development, 2003), pp. 412–424 at p. 414.

13   Adapted from http://www.ee.ucl.ac.uk/~mflanaga/thresholds.html.

14   Michael Young, Knowledge, Curriculum and the Future School. In Michael Young,
      David Lambert, Carolyn Roberts and Martin Roberts, *Knowledge and the Future
      School: Curriculum and Social Justice* (London: Bloomsbury Academic, 2014), pp.
      8–40 at p. 20.

15   Pierre Bourdieu, *Cultural Reproduction and Social Reproduction in Knowledge,
      Education and Cultural Change* (London: Tavistock, 1973).

16   Eric Donald Hirsch, Jr, *Why Knowledge Matters: Rescuing Our Children from Failed
      Educational Theory* (Cambridge, MA: Harvard Education Press, 2016), p. 160.

17   Lindsay Johns, In Praise of Dead White Men, *Prospect* (October 2010). Available at:
      https://www.prospectmagazine.co.uk/magazine/in-defence-of-dead-white-men.

18   Hirsch, *Why Knowledge Matters*, p. 160.

19   Eric Donald Hirsch, Jr, *Cultural Literacy: What Every American Needs to Know*
      (Boston, MA: Houghton Mifflin, 1988).

20   Charles Van Doren, *A History of Knowledge* (New York: Birch Lane Press, 1991).

21   Michael Oakeshott, *Rationalism in Politics and Other Essays* (London: Methuen,
      1962), p. 198.

22   Young, The Curriculum and the Entitlement to Knowledge, 6.

23   Jerome S. Bruner, *The Process of Education* (Cambridge, MA: Harvard University
      Press, 1960), p. 33.

24   Paul A. Kirschner, Epistemology or Pedagogy, That Is the Question. In Sigmund
      Tobias and Thomas M. Duffy (eds), *Constructivist Instruction: Success or Failure?*
      (Abingdon and New York: Routledge, 2009), pp. 144–157 at p. 151. Available
      at: https://dspace.ou.nl/bitstream/1820/2326/1/Epistemology%20or%20
      Pedagogy%20-%20That%20is%20the%20Question.pdf.

Chapter 9: Practice makes permanent

1   K. Anders Ericsson, Ralf Th. Krampe and Clemens Tesch-Römer, The Role of
      Deliberate Practice in the Acquisition of Expert Performance, *Psychological Review*
      100(3) (1993): 361–406.

2   K. Anders Ericsson, Michael J. Prietula and Edward T. Cokely, The Making of an
      Expert, *Harvard Business Review* 85(7–8) (2007): 114–121 at 116.

3   Anders Ericsson and Robert Pool, *Peak: Secrets from the New Science of Expertise*
      (London: Bodley Head, 2016), p. 98.

4   Ericsson and Pool, *Peak*, pp. 15–18.

5   Paul M. Fitts and Michael I. Posner, *Human Performance* (Westwood, CT:
      Greenwood Press, 1979).

6   Joshua Foer, *Moonwalking with Einstein: The Art and Science of Remembering
      Everything* (New York: Penguin, 2012), p. 170.

7   This is the subject of an academic debate. On the one side we have Tara Kini
      and Anne Podolsky, Does Teaching Experience Increase Teacher Effectiveness? A
      Review of the Research, *Learning Policy Institute* (3 June 2016). Available at: https://
      learningpolicyinstitute.org/product/does-teaching-experience-increase-teacher-
      effectiveness-review-research; and on the other Steven G. Rivkin, Eric A. Hanushek

and John F. Kain, Teachers, Schools and Academic Achievement, *Econometrica* 73(2) (2005): 417–458.

8   The metaphor comes from Hugo Kerr's *The Cognitive Psychology of Literacy Teaching: Reading, Writing, Spelling, Dyslexia (& A Bit Besides)*. Available at: http://www.hugokerr.info/book.pdf.

9   Daniel T. Willingham, *Why Don't Students Like School? A Cognitive Scientist Answers Questions About How the Mind Works and What It Means for the Classroom* (San Francisco, CA: Jossey-Bass, 2009), p. 110.

10   John Sweller, Cognitive Load During Problem Solving: Effects on Learning, *Cognitive Science* 12(2) (1988): 257–285.

11   Sweller, Cognitive Load During Problem Solving, 261.

12   Eric Donald Hirsch, Jr., *Why Knowledge Matters: Rescuing Our Children from Failed Educational Theory* (Cambridge, MA: Harvard Education Press, 2016), p. 13.

13   Ericsson and Pool, *Peak*, p. 80.

14   Gary E. McPherson and James M. Renwick, A Longitudinal Study of Self-regulation in Children's Musical Practice, *Music Education Research* 3(2) (2001): 169–186.

15   Susan Hallam, Tiija Rinta, Maria Varvarigou, Andrea Creech, Ioulia Papageorgi, Teresa Gomes and Jennifer Lanipekun, The Development of Practising Strategies in Young People, *Psychology of Music* 40(5) (2012): 652–680.

16   In a tweet on 26 January 2017, Wiliam said, "I've come to the conclusion that Sweller's Cognitive Load Theory is the single most important thing for teachers to know." Available at: goo.gl/gnfRbj.

17   John Sweller, Story of a Research Program. In Sigmund Tobias, J. Dexter Fletcher and David C. Berliner (series eds), Acquired Wisdom Series. *Education Review* 23 (2016). http://dx.doi.org/10.14507/er.v23.2025

18   Slava Kalyuga, Paul Ayres, Paul Chandler and John Sweller, The Expertise Reversal Effect, *Educational Psychologist* 38 (2003): 23–31 at 23.

19   Chee Ha Lee and Slava Kalyuga, Expertise Reversal Effect and its Instructional Implications. In Victor A. Benassi, Catherine E. Overson and Christopher M. Hakala (eds), *Applying Science of Learning in Education: Infusing Psychological Science into the Curriculum* (Washington, DC: American Psychological Association, 2014), pp. 31–44 at p. 35. Available at: http://teachpsych.org/Resources/Documents/ebooks/asle2014.pdf.

20   André Tricot and John Sweller, Domain-Specific Knowledge and Why Teaching Generic Skills Does Not Work, *Educational Psychology Review* 26(2) (2014): 265–283 at 281.

Chapter 10: Struggle and success

1   Paul A. Kirschner, John Sweller and Richard E. Clark, Why Minimal Guidance During Instruction Does Not Work: An Analysis of the Failure of Constructivist, Discovery, Problem-Based, Experiential, and Inquiry-Based Teaching, *Educational Psychologist* 41(2) (2006): 75–86 at 80.

2   See, for example, Richard E. Clark, Paul A. Kirschner and John Sweller, Putting Students on the Path to Learning: The Case for Fully Guided Instruction, *American Educator* 36(1) (2012): 6–11. Available at: https://www.aft.org/sites/default/files/periodicals/Clark.pdf; Barak Rosenshine, Principles of Instruction: Research Based Strategies That All Teachers Should Know, *American Educator* 36(1) (2012): 12–19. Available at: https://www.aft.org/sites/default/files/periodicals/Rosenshine.pdf; John Dunlosky, Strengthening the Student Toolbox: Study Strategies to Boost Learning, *American Educator* 37(3) (2013): 12–21. Available at: https://www.aft.org/sites/default/files/periodicals/dunlosky.pdf; and Deans for Impact, *The*

Science of Learning (Austin, TX: Deans for Impact, 2015). Available at: http://www. deansforimpact.org/pdfs/The_Science_of_Learning.pdf.

3   A recent study has shown that attention split between a lecture and laptops or smartphones not only harms the test scores of the student using the device, but their classmates as well. See Arnold L. Glass and Mengxue Kang, Dividing Attention in the Classroom Reduces Exam Performance, *Educational Psychology* (26 July 2018). Available at: https://www.tandfonline.com/doi/full/10.1080/01443410.201 8.1489046.

4   See Richard E. Mayer and Roxana Moreno, Nine Ways to Reduce Cognitive Load in Multimedia Learning, *Educational Psychologist* 38(1) (2003): 43–52; and Richard E. Mayer, Research-Based Principles for Designing Multimedia Instruction. In Victor A. Benassi, Catherine E. Overson and Christopher M. Hakala (eds), *Applying Science of Learning in Education: Infusing Psychological Science into the Curriculum* (Washington, DC: American Psychological Association, 2009), pp. 59–70. Available at: http://teachpsych.org/Resources/Documents/ebooks/asle2014.pdf.

5   Ruth Colvin Clark, *Evidence-Based Training Methods* (Alexandria, VA: ATD Press, 2015).

6   Ruth Colvin Clark, Frank Nguyen and John Sweller, *Efficiency in Learning: Evidence-Based Guidelines to Manage Cognitive Load* (San Francisco, CA: Pfeiffer, 2006).

7   Nicholas C. Soderstrom and Robert A. Bjork, Learning Versus Performance. In Dana S. Dunn (ed.), *Oxford Bibliographies Online: Psychology* (New York: Oxford University Press, 2013), p. 23. Available at: https://bjorklab.psych.ucla.edu/ wp-content/uploads/sites/13/2016/07/Soderstrom_Bjork_Learning_versus_ Performance.pdf.

8   Janet Metcalfe and Bridgid Finn, People's Hypercorrection of High Confidence Errors: Did They Know It All Along?, *Journal of Experimental Psychology: Learning, Memory, and Cognition* 37(2) (2011): 437–448.

9   Hui-Ju Liu, The Relation of Academic Self-Concept to Motivation among University EFL Students, *Feng Chia Journal of Humanities and Social Sciences* 20 (2010): 207–225.

10   Benjamin S. Bloom, *Taxonomy of Educational Objectives*. Vol. 1: *The Classification of Educational Goals* (London: D. McKay, 1956).

Conclusion: Shifting the bell curve

1   Richard J. Herrnstein and Charles Murray, *The Bell Curve: Intelligence and Class Structure in American Life* (New York: Free Press, 1996).

2   Herrnstein and Murray, *The Bell Curve*, p. 389.

3   Herrnstein and Murray, *The Bell Curve*, p. 394.

4   Herrnstein and Murray, *The Bell Curve*, p. 394.

5   Deirdre McCloskey, Equality Lacks Relevance If the Poor Are Growing Richer, *Financial Times* (11 August 2014). Available at: https://www.ft.com/ content/4c62ddaa-e698-11e3-9a20-00144feabdc0.

6   Hans Rosling with Ola Rosling and Anna Rosling Rönnlund, *Factfulness: Ten Reasons We're Wrong About the World – And Why Things Are Better Than You Think* (London: Sceptre, 2018), pp. 51–53.

7   See, for example, *Battle Hymn of the Tiger Teachers: The Michaela Way,* edited by Katherine Birbalsingh (Woodbridge: John Catt, 2016), which tells the extraordinary story of Michaela Community School in Brent, North West London.

Bibliography

Ackerman, Phillip L. and Eric D. Heggestad (1997). Intelligence, Personality, and Interests: Evidence for Overlapping Traits, *Psychological Bulletin* 121(2): 219–245.

Adam, David (2018). *The Genius Within: Smart Pills, Brain Hacks and Adventures in Intelligence* (London: Picador).

Adey, Philip and Michael Shayer (1994). *Really Raising Standards: Cognitive Intervention and Academic Achievement* (London and New York: Routledge).

Ali, Afia, Gareth Ambler, Andre Strydom, Dheeraj Rai, Claudia Cooper, Sally McManus, Scott Weich, H. Meltzer, Simon Dein and Angela Hassiotis (2013). The Relationship Between Happiness and Intelligence Quotient: The Contribution of Socio-economic and Clinical Factors, *Psychological Medicine* 43(6): 1303–1312.

Alvarus Pelagius (1992). *The Plaint of the Church*. In Brian Tierney (ed.), *The Middle Ages*, Vol. 1: *Sources of Medieval History*, 5th edn (New York: McGraw-Hill Education), pp. 296–297.

Anderson, James W., Bryan M. Johnstone and Daniel T. Remley (1999). Breast-Feeding and Cognitive Development: A Meta-Analysis, *American Journal of Clinical Nutrition* 70(4): 525–535.

Anderson, John R. (1996). ACT: A Simple Theory of Complex Cognition, *American Psychologist* 51(4): 355–365.

Andrews, Jon, David Robinson and Jo Hutchinson (2017). *Closing the Gap? Trends in Educational Attainment and Disadvantage* (London: Education Policy Institute). Available at: https://epi.org.uk/wp-content/uploads/2017/08/Closing-the-Gap_EPI-.pdf.

Arnold, Matthew (2006 [1869]). *Culture and Anarchy* (Oxford: Oxford University Press).

Asbury, Kathryn and Robert Plomin (2013). *G is for Genes: The Impact of Genetics on Education and Achievement* (Chichester: Wiley).

Ashton, Kevin (2015). *How to Fly a Horse: The Secret History of Creation, Invention and Discovery* (London: Windmill Books).

Astley, Susan (2003). FAS/FAE: Their Impact on Psychosocial Child Development with a View to Diagnosis. In Richard E. Tremblay, Ronald G. Barr and Ray DeV. Peters (eds), *Encyclopedia on Early Childhood Development*. Available at: http://www.child-encyclopedia.com/documents/AstleyANGxp.pdf.

Au, Jacky, Ellen Sheehan, Nancy Tsai, Greg J. Duncan, Martin Buschkuehl and Susanne M. Jaeggi (2014). Improving Fluid Intelligence with Training on Working Memory: A Meta-Analysis, *Psychonomic Bulletin & Review* 22(2): 366–377.

Ausubel, David P. (1965). An Evaluation of the Conceptual Schemes Approach to Science Curriculum Development, *Journal of Research in Science Teaching* 3: 255–264.

Baddely, Alan (2012). Working Memory: Theories, Models, and Controversies, *Annual Review of Psychology* 63: 1–29.

Baldwin, James Mark (1896a). A New Factor in Evolution, *American Naturalist* 30: 441–451: 536–553.

Baldwin, James Mark (1896b). Consciousness and Evolution, *Psychological Review* 3: 300–309. Available at: https://brocku.ca/MeadProject/Baldwin/Baldwin_1896_b.html.

Bargh, John A. (2012). Priming Effects Replicate Just Fine, Thanks, *Psychology Today* (11 May). Available at: https://www.psychologytoday.com/blog/the-natural-unconscious/201205/priming-effects-replicate-just-fine-thanks.

Barrett, David B., George T. Kurian and Todd M. Johnston (2001). *World Christian Encyclopedia: A Comparative Survey of Churches and Religions in the Modern World* (New York: Oxford University Press).

Bartlett, Frederic C. (1920). Experiments on the Reproduction of Folk-Stories, *Folklore* 31(1): 30–47.

Bartol, Jr, Thomas M., Cailey Bromer, Justin Kinney, Michael A. Chirillo, Jennifer N. Bourne, Kristen M. Harris and Terrence J. Sejnowski (2015). Nanoconnectomic Upper Bound on the Variability of Synaptic Plasticity, *eLife* 4: e10778.

Bates, Timothy C. (2007). Fluctuating Asymmetry and Intelligence, *Intelligence* 35(1): 41–46.

Beja-Pereira, Albano, Gordon Luikart, Philip R. England, Daniel G. Bradley, Oliver C. Jann, Giorgio Bertorelle et al. (2003). Gene-Culture Coevolution Between Cattle Milk Protein Genes and Human Lactase Genes, *Nature Genetics* 35: 311–313.

Beldoch, Michael (1964). Sensitivity to Expression of Emotional Meaning in Three Modes of Communication. In Joel R. Davitz and Michael Beldoch (eds), *The Communication of Emotional Meaning* (New York: McGraw-Hill), pp. 31–42.

Birbalsingh, Katherine (ed.) (2016). *Battle Hymn of the Tiger Teachers: The Michaela Way* (Woodbridge: John Catt Educational).

Bisseret, André (1970). Mémoire opérationelle et structure du travail [Working Memory and Work Structure], *Bulletin de Psychologie* 24: 280–294. English summary published as: Analysis of Mental Processes Involved in Air Traffic Control, *Ergonomics* 14 (1971): 565–570.

Bjork, Elizabeth and Robert A. Bjork (2003). Intentional Forgetting Can Increase, Not Decrease, Residual Influences of To-Be-Forgotten Information, *Journal of Experimental Psychology: Learning, Memory, and Cognition* 29(4): 524–531.

Bjork, Robert A. (n.d.). The Theory of Disuse and the Role of Forgetting in Human Memory [video]. Available at: http://gocognitive.net/interviews/theory-disuse-and-role-forgetting-human-memory.

Bjork, Robert A. and Marcia C. Linn (2002). Introducing Desirable Difficulties for Educational Applications in Science (IDDEAS). Available at: https://belmontteach.files.wordpress.com/2015/09/bjork-introducing-desirable-difficulties.pdf.

Bloom, Allan (1987). *The Closing of the American Mind: How Higher Education Has Failed Democracy and Impoverished the Souls of Today's Students* (New York: Simon & Schuster).

Bloom, Benjamin S. (1956). *Taxonomy of Educational Objectives*. Vol. 1: *The Classification of Educational Goals* (London: D. McKay).

Boaler, Jo (2014). *The Educators*, BBC Radio 4 [audio] (29 September). Available at https://www.bbc.co.uk/programmes/b04gw6rh.

Boaler, Jo (2015). Fluency Without Fear: Research Evidence on the Best Ways to Learn Math Facts, *YouCubed* (28 January). Available at: https://www.youcubed.org/evidence/fluency-without-fear/.

Boghossian, Paul (2007). *Fear of Knowledge: Against Relativism and Constructivism* (New York: Oxford University Press).

Boorstin, Daniel J. (1970). A Case of Hypochondria, *Newsweek* (6 July).

Boring, Edwin (1923). Intelligence as the Tests Test It, *New Republic* 36: 35–37.

Bouchard, Jr, Thomas J. (2004). Genetic Influence on Human Psychological Traits: A Survey, *Current Directions in Psychological Science* 13(4): 148–151.

Bourdieu, Pierre (1973). *Cultural Reproduction and Social Reproduction in Knowledge, Education and Cultural Change* (London: Tavistock).

Boxer, Adam (2018). Novices, Experts and Everything In-between: Epistemology and Pedagogy, *A Chemical Orthodoxy* (10 May). Available at: https://achemicalorthodoxy.wordpress.com/2018/05/10/novices-experts-and-everything-in-between-epistemology-and-pedagogy/.

Bratsberg, Bernt and Ole Rogeberg (2018). Flynn Effect and its Reversal Are Both Environmentally Caused, *Proceedings of the National Academy of Sciences of the United States of America* 115(26). doi:10.1073/pnas.1718793115

Brinch, Christian and Ann Galloway (2011). Schooling in Adolescence Raises IQ Scores, *Proceedings of the National Academy of Sciences of the United States of America* 109: 425–430.

Bruner, Jerome S. (1960). *The Process of Education* (Cambridge, MA: Harvard University Press).

Bruner, Jerome S. (1966). *Toward a Theory of Instruction* (Cambridge, MA: Belknap Press).

Cabeza, Robert and Morris Moscovitch (2013). Memory Systems, Processing Modes, and Components: Functional Neuroimaging Evidence, *Perspectives on Psychological Science* 8(1): 49–55.

Cáceres, Mario, Joel Lachuer, Matthew A. Zapala, John C. Redmond, Lili Kudo, Daniel H. Geschwind, David J. Lockhart, Todd M. Preuss and Carrolee Barlow (2003). Elevated Gene Expression Levels Distinguish Human from Non-Human Primate Brains, *Proceedings of the National Academy of Sciences of the United States of America* 100(22): 13030–13035.

Cadwalladr, Carole (2015). The 'Granny Cloud': The Network of Volunteers Helping Poorer Children Learn, *The Guardian* (2 August). Available at: https://www.theguardian.com/education/2015/aug/02/sugata-mitra-school-in-the-cloud.

Cahan, Sorel and Nora Cohen (1989). Age versus Schooling Effects on Intelligence Development, *Child Development* 60: 1239–1249.

Calvin, Catherine M., G. David Batty, Geoff Der, Caroline E. Brett, Adele Taylor, Alison Pattie et al. (2017). Childhood Intelligence in Relation to Major Causes of Death in 68 Year Follow-up: Prospective Population Study, *BMJ* 357: j2708.

Caplan, Bryan (2018). *The Case Against Education: Why the Education System is a Waste of Time and Money* (Princeton, NJ: Princeton University Press).

Carey, Benedict (2014). *How We Learn* (London: Macmillan).

Carey, Mark, M. Jackson, Alessandro Antonello and Jaclyn Rushing (2016). Glaciers, Gender, and Science: A Feminist Glaciology Framework for Global Environmental Change Research, *Progress in Human Geography* 40(6): 770–793.

Carlsson, Magnus, Gordon B. Dahl, Björn Öckert and Dan-Olof Rooth (2015). The Effect of Schooling on Cognitive Skills, *Review of Economics and Statistics* 97(3): 533–547.

Carraher, Terezinha N., David W. Carraher and Analúcia D. Schliemann (1985). Mathematics in the Street and in School, *British Journal of Developmental Psychology* 3: 21–29.

Cattell, Raymond B. (1971). *Abilities: Their Structure, Growth, and Action* (Boston, MA: Houghton Mifflin).

Cavazotte, Flavia, Valter Moreno and Mateus Hickmann (2012). Effects of Leader Intelligence, Personality and Emotional Intelligence on Transformational Leadership and Managerial Performance, *Leadership Quarterly* 23(3): 443–455.

Ceci, Stephen J. (1991). How Much Does Schooling Influence General Intelligence and Its Cognitive Components? A Reassessment of the Evidence, *Developmental Psychology* 27(5): 703–722.

Cepeda, Nicholas J., Edward Vul, Doug Rohrer, John T. Wixted and Harold Pashler (2008). Spacing Effects in Learning: A Temporal Ridgeline of Optimal Retention, *Psychological Science* 19: 1095–1102.

Chandler, Paul and John Sweller (1992). The Split-Attention Effect as a Factor in the Design of Instruction, *British Journal of Educational Psychology* 62(2): 233–246.

Chase, William G. and Herbert A. Simon (1973). Perception in Chess, *Cognitive Psychology* 4(1): 55–81.

Chi, Michelene T. H., Paul J. Feltovich and Robert Glaser (1981). Categorization and Representation of Physics Problems by Experts and Novices, *Cognitive Science* 5: 121–152.

Chivers, Tom (2017). A Mindset 'Revolution' Sweeping Britain's Classrooms May Be Based on Shaky Science, *BuzzFeed* (14 January). Available at: https://www.buzzfeed.com/tomchivers/what-is-your-mindset?utm_term=.lv42Bb4l9#.ucWBv7RQG.

Christodoulou, Daisy (2014). *Seven Myths About Education* (Abingdon: Routledge).

Clark, Richard E., Paul A. Kirschner and John Sweller (2012). Putting Students on the Path to Learning: The Case for Fully Guided Instruction, *American Educator* 36(1): 6–11. Available at: https://www.aft.org/sites/default/files/periodicals/Clark.pdf.

Clark, Ruth Colvin (2015). *Evidence-Based Training Methods* (Alexandria, VA: ATD Press).

Clark, Ruth Colvin, Frank Nguyen and John Sweller (2006). *Efficiency in Learning: Evidence-Based Guidelines to Manage Cognitive Load* (San Francisco, CA: Pfeiffer).

Cliffordson, Christina and Jan-Eric Gustafsson (2008). Effects of Age and Schooling on Intellectual Performance: Estimates Obtained from Analysis of Continuous Variation in Age and Length of Schooling, *Intelligence* 36(2): 143–152.

Cohen, Gillian (1990). Why is it Difficult to Put Names to Faces?, *British Journal of Psychology* 81: 287–297.

Collins, Harry (2010). *Tacit and Explicit Knowledge* (Chicago, IL: University of Chicago Press).

Conan Doyle, Arthur (2001 [1887]). *A Study in Scarlet* (London: Penguin).

Conan Doyle, Arthur (2001 [1890]). *The Sign of Four* (London: Penguin).

Connor, Charles E. (2005). Neuroscience: Friends and Grandmothers, *Nature* 435: 1036–1037.

Cowan, Nelson (2001). The Magical Number 4 in Short-Term Memory: A Reconsideration of Mental Storage Capacity, *Behavioral and Brain Sciences* 24(1): 87–114.

Crocker, Jennifer, Marc-Andre Olivier and Noah Nuer (2009). Self-Image Goals and Compassionate Goals: Costs and Benefits, *Self and Identity* 8: 251–269.

Darwin, Charles (1871). *The Descent of Man, and Selection in Relation to Sex* (London: John Murray). Available at: http://darwin-online.org.uk/content/frameset?pageseq=1&itemID=F937.1&viewtype=text.

Dawkins, Richard (2016). *The Selfish Gene: 40th Anniversary Edition* (Oxford: Oxford University Press).

Deans for Impact (2015). *The Science of Learning* (Austin, TX: Deans for Impact). Available at: http://www.deansforimpact.org/pdfs/The_Science_of_Learning.pdf.

Deary, Ian J. (2001). *Intelligence: A Very Short Introduction* (New York: Oxford University Press).

Deary, Ian J. (2008). Why Do Intelligent People Live Longer?, *Nature* 456: 175–176.

Deary, Ian J., G. David Batty and Catherine R. Gale (2008). Bright Children Become Enlightened Adults, *Psychological Science* 19(1): 1–6.

Deary, Ian J., Steve Strand, Pauline Smith and Cres Fernandes (2007). Intelligence and Educational Achievement, *Intelligence* 35(1): 13–21.

Dehaene, Stanislas (2010). *Reading in the Brain: The New Science of How We Read* (London: Penguin).

Dennett, Daniel C. (1987). *The Intentional Stance* (Cambridge, MA: MIT Press).

Dennett, Daniel C. (1991). *Consciousness Explained* (London: Penguin).

Detterman, Douglas K. (1993). The Case for the Prosecution: Transfer as an Epiphenomenon. In Douglas K. Detterman and Robert J. Sternberg (eds), *Transfer on Trial: Intelligence, Cognition, and Instruction* (Westport, CT: Ablex Publishing), pp. 1–23.

Detterman, Douglas K. (2016). Education and Intelligence: Pity the Poor Teacher Because Student Characteristics are More Significant Than Teachers or Schools, *Spanish Journal of Psychology* 19(93): 1–11.

de Vries, Robert and Jason Rentfrow (2016). *A Winning Personality: The Effects of Background on Personality and Earnings* (London: Sutton Trust). Available at: https://www.suttontrust.com/wp-content/uploads/2016/01/Winning-Personality-FINAL.pdf.

Diamond, Jared (1998). *Guns, Germs and Steel: A Short History of Everybody for the Last 13,000 Years* (London: Vintage).

Dickens, William T. and James R. Flynn (2006). Black Americans Reduce the Racial IQ Gap: Evidence from Standardization Samples, *Psychological Science* 17(10): 913–920.

Didau, David (2015). *What If Everything You Knew About Education Was Wrong?* (Carmarthen: Crown House Publishing).

Didau, David and Nick Rose (2016). *What Every Teacher Needs to Know About Psychology* (Woodbridge: John Catt Educational).

Dolan, Paul (2014). *Happiness by Design: Finding Pleasure in Everyday Life* (London: Penguin).

Dunlosky, John (2013). Strengthening the Student Toolbox: Study Strategies to Boost Learning, *American Educator* 37(3): 12–21. Available at: https://www.aft.org/sites/default/files/periodicals/dunlosky.pdf.

Dunlosky, John and Thomas O. Nelson (1994). Does the Sensitivity of Judgements of Learning (JoLs) to the Effects of Various Study Activities Depend Upon When the JoLs Occur?, *Journal of Memory and Language* 33: 545–565.

Dunlosky, John, Katherine A. Rawson, Elizabeth J. Marsh, Mitchell J. Nathan and Daniel T. Willingham (2013). Improving Students' Learning with Effective Learning Techniques: Promising Directions from Cognitive and Educational Psychology, *Psychological Science in the Public Interest* 14(1): 4–58.

Dweck, Carol S. (2015a). Carol Dweck Revisits the 'Growth Mindset', *Education Week* (23 September). Available at: https://www.stem.org.uk/system/files/community-resources/2016/06/DweckEducationWeek.pdf.

Dweck, Carol S. (2015b). *Mindset: How You Can Fulfill Your Potential* (London: Constable & Robinson).

Dweck, Carol S. (2018). Growth Mindset Interventions Yield Impressive Results, *The Conversation* (26 June). Available at: https://theconversation.com/growth-mindset-interventions-yield-impressive-results-97423.

Ebbinghaus, Hermann (1913 [1885]). *Memory: A Contribution to Experimental Psychology*, tr. Henry A. Ruger and Clara E. Bussenius (New York: Teachers College, Columbia University).

Education Week Research Center (2016). *Mindset in the Classroom: A National Study of K-12 Teachers*. Available at: http://www.edweek.org/media/ewrc_mindsetintheclassroom_sept2016.pdf.

Egbert of Liège (2013). *The Well-Laden Ship*, tr. Robert Gary Babcock (Cambridge, MA: Harvard University Press).

Enquist, Magnus, Stefano Ghirlanda and Kimmo Eriksson (2011). Modelling the Evolution and Diversity of Cumulative Culture, *Philosophical Transactions B* 366(1563): 412–423.

Enquist, Magnus, Stefano Ghirlanda, Arne Jarrick and Carl Adam Wachtmeister (2008). Why Does Human Culture Increase Exponentially?, *Theoretical Population Biology* 74(1): 46–55.

Epstein, David (2014). *The Sports Gene: Talent, Practice and the Truth About Success* (London: Yellow Jersey).

Ericsson, K. Anders (2007). Deliberate Practice and the Modifiability of Body and Mind: Toward a Science of the Structure and Acquisition of Expert and Elite Performance, *International Journal of Sport Psychology* 38(1): 4–34.

Ericsson, K. Anders and Neil Charness (1994). Expert Performance: Its Structure and Acquisition, *American Psychologist* 49(8): 725–747.

Ericsson, K. Anders, Ralf Th. Krampe and Clemens Tesch-Römer (1993). The Role of Deliberate Practice in the Acquisition of Expert Performance, *Psychological Review* 100(3): 361–406.

Ericsson, Anders and Robert Pool (2016). *Peak: Secrets from the New Science of Expertise* (London: Bodley Head).

Ericsson, K. Anders, Michael J. Prietula and Edward T. Cokely (2007). The Making of an Expert, *Harvard Business Review* 85(7–8): 114–121.

Farrington, David P. (2007). Origins of Violent Behavior Over the Life Span. In Daniel J. Flannery, Alexander T. Vazsonyi and Irwin D. Waldman (eds), *The Cambridge Handbook of Violent Behavior and Aggression* (Cambridge: Cambridge University Press), pp. 19–48.

Feynman, Richard P. (1973). Names Don't Constitute Knowledge [video of Yorkshire Television interview]. Available at: https://youtu.be/lFIYKmos3-s

Feynman, Richard P. (1974). Cargo Cult Science: Some Remarks on Science, Pseudoscience, and Learning How to Not Fool Yourself. Available at: http://calteches. library.caltech.edu/51/2/CargoCult.htm.

Fisch, Karl (2008). Shift Happens [video]. Available at: https://www.youtube.com/ watch?v=emx92kBKads.

Fitts, Paul M. and Michael I. Posner (1979). *Human Performance* (Westwood, CT: Greenwood Press).

Flynn, James R. (1987). Massive IQ Gains in 14 Nations: What IQ Tests Really Measure, *Psychological Bulletin* 101(2): 171–191.

Flynn, James R. (2007). *What is Intelligence? Beyond the Flynn Effect* (Cambridge: Cambridge University Press).

Flynn, James R. (2012). *Are We Getting Smarter? Rising IQ in the Twenty-First Century* (Cambridge: Cambridge University Press).

Flynn, James R. (2013). Why Our IQ Levels are Higher Than Our Grandparents', *TED.com*. Available at: https://www.ted.com/talks/james_flynn_why_our_iq_levels_ are_higher_than_our_grandparents/transcript.

Foer, Joshua (2012a). Feats of Memory Anyone Can Do [video], *TED.com*. Available at: http://www.ted.com/talks/joshua_foer_feats_of_memory_anyone_can_do?awesm=on. ted.com_Foer&utm_campaign=&utm_medium=on.ted.com-static&utm_source=t. co&utm_content=awesm-publisher.

Foer, Joshua (2012b). *Moonwalking with Einstein: The Art and Science of Remembering Everything* (New York: Penguin).

Ford, Martin E. and Marie S. Tisak (1983). A Further Search for Social Intelligence, *Journal of Educational Psychology* 75(2): 196–206.

Fordham, Michael (2017). Knowledge as the Currency of Teaching, *Clio et cetera* (12 October). Available at: https://clioetcetera.com/2017/10/12/ knowledge-as-the-currency-of-teaching.

Freund, Philipp A. and Heinz Holling (2011). Who Wants to Take an Intelligence Test? Personality and Achievement Motivation in the Context of Ability Testing, *Personality and Individual Differences* 50(5): 723–728.

Fuller, Richard Buckminster (1981). *Critical Path*, 2nd rev. edn (New York: St Martin's Press).

Gale, Catherine R., G. David Batty, Per Tynelius, Ian J. Deary and Finn Rasmussen (2010). Intelligence in Early Adulthood and Subsequent Hospitalization and Admission Rates for the Whole Range of Mental Disorders: Longitudinal Study of 1,049,663 Men, *Epidemiology* 21(1): 70–77.

Gardner, Howard (1983). *Frames of Mind: The Theory of Multiple Intelligences* (New York: Basic Books).

Gardner, Howard (2016). Multiple Intelligences: Prelude, Theory, and Aftermath. In Robert J. Sternberg, Susan T. Fiske and Donald J. Foss (eds), *Scientists Making a Difference: One Hundred Eminent Behavioral and Brain Scientists Talk About Their Most Important Contributions* (New York: Cambridge University Press), pp. 167–170.

Geary, David C. (2007). Educating the Evolved Mind: Conceptual Foundations for an Evolutionary Educational Psychology. In Jerry S. Carlson and Joel R. Levin (eds), *Educating the Evolved Mind: Conceptual Foundations for an Evolutionary Educational Psychology* (Charlotte, NC: Information Age Publishing), pp. 1–99.

Geary, David C. and Daniel B. Berch (2016). Evolution and Children's Cognitive and Academic Development. In David C. Geary and Daniel B. Berch (eds), *Evolutionary Perspectives on Child Development and Education* (Basel: Springer International Publishing), pp. 217–250.

Genovese, Jeremy E. (2002). Cognitive Skills Valued by Educators: Historical Content Analysis of Testing in Ohio, *Journal of Educational Research* 96: 101–114.

George, Andrew R. (2005). In Search of the é.dub.ba.a: The Ancient Mesopotamian School in Literature and Reality. In Yitzhak Sefati, Pinhas Artzi, Chaim Cohen, Barry L. Eichler and Victor A. Hurowitz (eds), *An Experienced Scribe Who Neglects Nothing: Ancient Near Eastern Studies in Honor of Jacob Klein* (Potomac, MD: CDL Press), pp. 127–137.

Gladwell, Malcolm (2009). *Outliers: The Story of Success* (London: Penguin).

Glass, Arnold L. and Mengxue Kang (2018). Dividing Attention in the Classroom Reduces Exam Performance, *Educational Psychology* (26 July). Available at: https://www. tandfonline.com/doi/full/10.1080/01443410.2018.1489046.

Godden, Duncan R. and Alan D. Baddeley (1975). Context-Dependent Memory in Two Natural Environments: On Land and Underwater, *British Journal of Psychology* 66(3): 325–331.

Goleman, Daniel (1995). *Emotional Intelligence: Why It Can Matter More Than IQ* (London: Bloomsbury).

Gosse, Philip H. (1857). *Omphalos: An Attempt to Untie the Geological Knot* (London: John Van Voorst).

Gottfredson, Linda S. (1997). Mainstream Science on Intelligence: An Editorial with 52 Signatories, History, and Bibliography, *Intelligence* 24: 13–23.

Gould, Stephen Jay (1981). *The Mismeasure of Man* (New York: Norton & Co.).

Gross-Loh, Christine (2016). How Praise Became a Consolation Prize [interview with Carol Dweck], *The Atlantic* (16 December). Available at: https://www.theatlantic.com/education/archive/2016/12/how-praise-became-a-consolation-prize/510845/.

Guardian, The (2018a). Atlas Jogged: Humanoid Robot Can Now Run Through a Park All By Itself (11 May). Available at: https://www.theguardian.com/technology/2018/may/11/boston-dynamics-atlas-jog-humanoid-robot-run-through-park.

Guardian, The (2018b). Can These Robots Build An Ikea Chair? (18 April). Available at: https://www.theguardian.com/technology/video/2018/apr/18/can-these-robots-build-an-ikea-chair-video.

Haidt, Jonathan (2012). *The Righteous Mind: Why Good People Are Divided by Politics and Religion* (London: Penguin).

Haier, Richard J. (2017). *The Neuroscience of Intelligence* (New York: Cambridge University Press).

Hallam, Susan, Tiija Rinta, Maria Varvarigou, Andrea Creech, Ioulia Papageorgi, Teresa Gomes and Jennifer Lanipekun (2012). The Development of Practising Strategies in Young People, *Psychology of Music* 40(5): 652–680.

Hansen, Karsten T., James J. Heckman and Kathleen J. Mullen (2004). The Effect of Schooling and Ability on Achievement Test Scores, *Journal of Econometrics* 121(1–2): 39–98.

Harari, Yuval Noah (2016). *Homo Deus: A Brief History of Tomorrow* (London: Penguin).

Hari, Johann (2010). The Two Churchills, *New York Times* (12 August). Available at: https://www.nytimes.com/2010/08/15/books/review/Hari-t.html.

Härnqvist, Kjell (1968). Relative Changes in Intelligence from 13 to 18. I: Background and Methodology, *Scandinavian Journal of Psychology* 9(1): 50–64.

Harris, Judith Rich (1999). *The Nurture Assumption: Why Children Turn Out the Way They Do* (London: Bloomsbury).

Harrison, Tyler L., Zach Shipstead, Kenny L. Hicks, David Z. Hambrick, Thomas S. Redick and Randall W. Engle (2013). Working Memory Training May Increase Working Memory Capacity But Not Fluid Intelligence, *Psychological Science* 24(12): 2409–2419.

Hart, Betty and Todd R. Risley (1995). *Meaningful Differences in the Everyday Experience of Young American Children* (Baltimore, MD: Brookes Publishing).

Hattie, John (2008). *Visible Learning: A Synthesis of Over 800 Meta-Analyses Relating to Achievement* (Abingdon: Routledge).

Hattie, John and Gregory Yates (2014). *Visible Learning and the Science of How We Learn* (Abingdon: Routledge).

Heath, Chip and Dan Heath (2007). *Made to Stick: Why Some Ideas Take Hold and Others Come Unstuck* (London: Arrow Books).

Heck, Patrick R., Daniel J. Simons and Christopher F. Chabris (2018). 65% of Americans Believe They Are Above Average in Intelligence: Results of Two Nationally Representative Surveys, *PLOS ONE* 13(7): e0200103. Available at: https://journals. plos.org/plosone/article?id=10.1371/journal.pone.0200103.

Henke, Katharina (2010). A Model for Memory Systems Based on Processing Modes Rather Than Consciousness, *Nature Reviews Neuroscience* 11(7): 523–532.

Herrnstein, Richard J. and Charles Murray (1996). *The Bell Curve: Intelligence and Class Structure in American Life* (New York: Free Press).

Hirsch, Jr, Eric Donald (1988). *Cultural Literacy: What Every American Needs to Know* (Boston, MA: Houghton Mifflin).

Hirsch, Jr, Eric Donald (2000). 'You Can Always Look It Up' … Or Can You?, *American Educator* 24(1): 4–9. Available at: https://www.aft.org/sites/default/files/periodicals/ LookItUpSpring2000.pdf.

Hirsch, Jr, Eric Donald (2016). *Why Knowledge Matters: Rescuing Our Children from Failed Educational Theory* (Cambridge, MA: Harvard Education Press).

Hofstadter, Douglas and Emmanuel Sander (2013). *Surfaces and Essences* (New York: Basic Books).

Howard-Jones, Paul (2018). *Evolution of the Learning Brain: Or How You Got to Be So Smart* (Abingdon: Routledge).

Howe, Michael J. A. (1998). Can IQ change?, *The Psychologist* 11: 69–72.

Howe, Michael J. A. (1999). *Genius Explained* (Cambridge: Cambridge University Press).

IBM Global Technology Services (2006). The Toxic Terabyte: How Data-Dumping Threatens Business Efficiency (July). Available at: http://www.ibm.com/services/no/ cio/leverage/levinfo_wp_gts_thetoxic.pdf.

Intelligence and Its Measurement: A Symposium (1921). *Journal of Educational Psychology* 12(3): 123–147.

Jaeggi, Susanne M., Martin Buschkuehl, John Jonides and Walter J. Perrig (2008). Improving Fluid Intelligence with Training on Working Memory, *Proceedings of the National Academy of Sciences of the United States of America* 105(19): 6829–6833.

Jerrim, John (2017). *Global Gaps: Comparing Socio-economic Gaps in the Performance of Highly Able UK Pupils Internationally* (London: Sutton Trust). Available at: https:// www.suttontrust.com/wp-content/uploads/2017/02/Global-Gaps_FINAL_V2_ WEB.pdf.

Johns, Lindsay (2010). In Praise of Dead White Men, *Prospect Magazine* (23 September). Available at: https://www.prospectmagazine.co.uk/magazine/ in-defence-of-dead-white-men.

Jones, Garrett (2008). Are Smarter Groups More Cooperative? Evidence from Prisoner's Dilemma Experiments, 1959–2003, *Journal of Economic Behaviour & Organisation* 68(3–4): 489–497.

Joseph, Dana and Daniel A. Newman (2010). Emotional Intelligence: An Integrative Meta-Analysis and Cascading Model, *Journal of Applied Psychology* 95(1): 54–78.

Jubilee Centre for Character and Virtues (2017). *A Framework for Character Education in Schools* (Birmingham: Jubilee Centre for Character and Virtues). Available at: https://www.jubileecentre.ac.uk/userfiles/jubileecentre/pdf/character-education/Framework%20for%20Character%20Education.pdf.

Jussim, Lee and Kent D. Harber (2005). Teacher Expectations and Self-Fulfilling Prophecies: Knowns and Unknowns, Resolved and Unresolved Controversies, *Personality and Social Psychology Review* 9(2): 131–155.

Kalenze, Eric (2014). *Education is Upside-Down: Reframing Reform to Focus on the Right Problems* (Lanham, MD: Rowman & Littlefield).

Kalyuga, Slava, Paul Ayres, Paul Chandler and John Sweller (2003). The Expertise Reversal Effect, *Educational Psychologist* 38(1): 23–31.

Kennedy, Benjamin H. (1881). *The Theaetetus of Plato*, with translation and notes (Cambridge: Cambridge University Press).

Kerr, Hugo (n.d.). *The Cognitive Psychology of Literacy Teaching: Reading, Writing, Spelling, Dyslexia (& A Bit Besides)*. Available at: http://www.hugokerr.info/book.pdf.

Keyes, Daniel (1966). *Flowers for Algernon* (New York: Harcourt).

King, Jr, Martin Luther (1947). The Purpose of Education, *The Maroon Tiger* [Morehouse College Student Paper]. Available at: https://www.drmartinlutherkingjr.com/thepurposeofeducation.htm.

Kini, Tara and Anne Podolsky (2016). Does Teaching Experience Increase Teacher Effectiveness? A Review of the Research, *Learning Policy Institute* (3 June). Available at: https://learningpolicyinstitute.org/product/does-teaching-experience-increase-teacher-effectiveness-review-research.

Kirschner, Paul A. (2009). Epistemology or Pedagogy, That Is the Question. In Sigmund Tobias and Thomas M. Duffy (eds), *Constructivist Instruction: Success or Failure?* (Abingdon and New York: Routledge), pp. 144–157. Available at: https://dspace.ou.nl/bitstream/1820/2326/1/Epistemology%20or%20Pedagogy%20-%20That%20is%20the%20Question.pdf.

Kirschner, Paul A., John Sweller and Richard E. Clark (2006). Why Minimal Guidance During Instruction Does Not Work: An Analysis of the Failure of Constructivist, Discovery, Problem-Based, Experiential, and Inquiry-Based Teaching, *Educational Psychologist* 41(2): 75–86.

Kleinerman, Alexandra (2011). *Education in Early 2nd Millennium BC Babylonia: The Sumerian Epistolary Miscellany* (Leiden: Brill).

Konnikova, Maria (2016). Practice Doesn't Make Perfect, *The New Yorker* (28 September). Available at: https://www.newyorker.com/science/maria-konnikova/practice-doesnt-make-perfect.

Kristjánsson, Kristján (2016). *The Sutton Trust Report and Its Fallout: Some Curious Ideas About the Shaping of Personality as 'Character Education'* (Birmingham: Jubilee Centre for Character and Virtues). Available at: https://www.jubileecentre.ac.uk/userfiles/jubileecentre/pdf/insight-series/Kristjansson%20K%20-%20The%20Sutton%20Trust%20Report%20and%20Its%20Fallout.pdf.

Kuncel, Nathan R. and Sarah A. Hezlett (2010). Fact and Fiction in Cognitive Ability Testing for Admissions and Hiring Decisions, *Current Directions in Psychological Science* 19(6): 339–345.

Laland, Kevin N. (2017). *Darwin's Unfinished Symphony: How Culture Made the Human Mind* (Princeton, NJ: Princeton University Press).

Larkin, Jill, John McDermott, Dorothea P. Simon and Herbert A. Simon (1980). Expert and Novice Performance in Solving Physics Problems, *Science* 208(4450): 1335–1342.

Lattman, Peter (2007). The Origins of Justice Stewart's 'I Know It When I See It', *Wall Street Journal Law Blog* (27 September). Available at: https://blogs.wsj.com/law/2007/09/27/the-origins-of-justice-stewarts-i-know-it-when-i-see-it/.

Lave, Jean (1988). *Cognition in Practice: Mind, Mathematics, and Culture in Everyday Life* (Cambridge, MA: Cambridge University Press).

Lawson, Rebecca (2006). The Science of Cycology: Failures to Understand How Everyday Objects Work, *Memory & Cognition* 34(8): 1667–1675.

Lee, Chee Ha and Slava Kalyuga (2014). Expertise Reversal Effect and its Instructional Implications. In Victor A. Benassi, Catherine E. Overson and Christopher M. Hakala (eds), *Applying Science of Learning in Education: Infusing Psychological Science into the Curriculum* (Washington, DC: American Psychological Association). Available at: http://teachpsych.org/Resources/Documents/ebooks/asle2014.pdf, pp. 31–44.

Legg, Shane and Marcus Hutter (2007). A Collection of Definitions of Intelligence, *Frontiers in Artificial Intelligence and Applications* 157: 17–24.

Lehrer, Jonah (2010). The Itch of Curiosity, *Wired* (8 March). Available at: https://www.wired.com/2010/08/the-itch-of-curiosity/.

Leslie, Ian (2014). *Curious: The Desire to Know and Why Your Future Depends on It* (London: Quercus Editions).

Lewin, Roger and Robert A. Foley (2004). *Principles of Human Evolution*, 2nd edn (Cambridge: Wiley-Blackwell).

Li, Yue and Timothy C. Bates (2017). Does Growth Mindset Improve Children's IQ, Educational Attainment or Response to Setbacks? Active-Control Interventions and Data on Children's Own Mindsets. Available at: https://osf.io/preprints/socarxiv/tsdwy.

Liu, Hui-Ju (2010). The Relation of Academic Self-Concept to Motivation among University EFL Students, *Feng Chia Journal of Humanities and Social Sciences*, 20: 207–225.

Loewen, James W. (1995). *Lies My Teacher Told Me: Everything Your American History Textbook Got Wrong* (New York: New Press).

Loftus, Elizabeth F. and John C. Palmer (1974). Reconstruction of Automobile Destruction: An Example of the Interaction between Language and Memory, *Journal of Verbal Learning and Verbal Behavior* 13(5): 585–589.

Lorentz, Hendrik Antoon (1909). The Theory of Electrons and its Applications to the Phenomena of Light and Radiant Heat; A Course of Lectures Delivered in Columbia University, New York, in March and April, 1906 (Leipzig: B. G. Teubner; New York: G. E. Stechert & Co.).

Lucas, Alan, Ruth Morley, Tim J. Cole, Gill Lister and Catherine Leeson-Payne (1992). Breast Milk and Subsequent Intelligence Quotient in Children Born Preterm, *The Lancet* 339(8788): 261–264.

Luria, Alexander Romanovich (1976). *Cognitive Development: Its Cultural and Social Foundations*, ed. Michael Cole (Cambridge, MA: Harvard University Press).

McCloskey, Deirdre (2014). Equality Lacks Relevance If the Poor Are Growing Richer, *Financial Times* (11 August). Available at: https://www.ft.com/content/4c62ddaa-e698-11e3-9a20-00144feabdc0.

McInerney, Laura (2016). Profiles: Andrew Sabisky, Political Forecaster, *Schools Week* (5 July). Available at: https://schoolsweek.co.uk/andrew-sabisky-political-forecaster/.

McPherson, Gary E. and James M. Renwick (2001). A Longitudinal Study of Self-regulation in Children's Musical Practice, *Music Education Research* 3(2): 169–186.

McWeeny, Kathryn, Andrew Young, Dennis Hay and Andrew Ellis (1987). Putting Names to Faces, *British Journal of Psychology* 78: 143–146.

Marr, Andrew (2013). *A History of the World* (London: Pan Macmillan).

Marzano, Robert J. (2010). The Art and Science of Teaching/Teaching Inference, *Educational Leadership* 67(7): 80–81. Available at: http://www.ascd.org/publications/educational-leadership/apr10/vol67/num07/Teaching-Inference.aspx.

Mayer, Richard E. (2009). Research-Based Principles for Designing Multimedia Instruction. In Victor A. Benassi, Catherine E. Overson and Christopher M. Hakala (eds), *Applying Science of Learning in Education: Infusing Psychological Science into the Curriculum* (Washington, DC: American Psychological Association). Available at: http://teachpsych.org/Resources/Documents/ebooks/asle2014.pdf, pp. 59–70.

Mayer, Richard E. and Roxana Moreno (2003). Nine Ways to Reduce Cognitive Load in Multimedia Learning, *Educational Psychologist* 38(1): 43–52.

Meltzoff, Andrew N. (1999). Born to Learn: What Infants Learn from Watching Us. In Nathan A. Fox, Lewis A. Leavitt and John G. Worhol (eds), *The Role of Early Experience in Infant Development* (Skillman, NJ: Johnson & Johnson), pp. 145–160.

Merton, Robert K. (1968). The Matthew Effect in Science, *Science* 159 (3810): 56–63.

Metcalfe, Janet and Bridgid Finn (2011). People's Hypercorrection of High Confidence Errors: Did They Know It All Along?, *Journal of Experimental Psychology: Learning, Memory, and Cognition* 37(2): 437–448.

Meyer, Jan and Ray Land (2003). Threshold Concepts and Troublesome Knowledge: Linkages to Ways of Thinking and Practising. In Chris Rust (ed.), *Improving Student Learning: Theory and Practice Ten Years On* (Oxford: Oxford Centre for Staff and Learning Development), pp. 412–424.

Miller, George A. (1956). The Magical Number Seven, Plus or Minus Two: Some Limits on Our Capacity for Processing Information, *Psychological Review* 63(2): 81–97.

Millon, Theodore, Erik Simonsen, Morten Birket-Smith and Roger D. Davis (eds) (1998). *Psychopathy: Antisocial, Criminal, and Violent Behavior* (New York: Guilford Press).

Mlodinow, Leonard (2018). *Elastic: Flexible Thinking in a Constantly Changing World* (London: Allen Lane).

Monbiot, George (2017). In An Age of Robots, Schools Are Teaching Our Children to Be Redundant, *The Guardian* (15 February). Available at: https://www.theguardian.com/commentisfree/2017/feb/15/robots-schools-teaching-children-redundant-testing-learn-future.

Moody, David E. (2009). Can Intelligence Be Increased by Training on a Task of Working Memory?, *Intelligence* 37(4): 327–328.

Moran, Caitlin (2017). Why I Should Run Our Schools, *The Times* (29 April). Available at: https://www.thetimes.co.uk/article/caitlin-moran-why-i-should-be-education-secretary-9llh939r2.

Moriarty, Catherine (ed.) (1989). *The Voice of the Middle Ages: In Personal Letters 1100–1500* (New York: Peter Bedrick Books).

Morris, Errol (2010). The Anosognosic's Dilemma: Something's Wrong But You'll Never Know What It Is (Part 1) [interview with David Dunning], *New York Times Opinionator Blog* (20 June). Available at: https://opinionator.blogs.nytimes.com/2010/06/20/the-anosognosics-dilemma-1/.

Mortensen, Erik L., Kim F. Michaelsen, Stephanie A. Sanders and June A. Reinisch (2002). The Association between Duration of Breastfeeding and Adult Intelligence, *Journal of the American Medical Association* 287(18): 2365–2371.

Mosel, Jason S., Hans S. Schroder, Carrie Heeter, Tim P. Moran and Yu-Hao Lee (2011). Mind Your Errors: Evidence for a Neural Mechanism Linking Growth Mind-Set to Adaptive Posterror Adjustments, *Psychological Science* 22(12): 1484–1489.

Mosing, Miriam A., Nancy L. Pedersen, Guy Madison and Fredrik Ullén (2014). Genetic Pleiotropy Explains Associations between Musical Auditory Discrimination and Intelligence, *PLOS ONE* 9(11): e113874.

Murman, Daniel (2015). The Impact of Age on Cognition, *Seminars in Hearing* 36(3): 111–121.

Murphy, James and Dianne Murphy (2018). *Thinking Reading: What Every Secondary Teacher Needs to Know About Reading* (Woodbridge: John Catt Educational).

Murphy Paul, Annie (2004). *The Cult of Personality: How Personality Tests Are Leading Us to Miseducate Our Children, Mismanage Our Companies, and Misunderstand Ourselves* (New York: Free Press).

Murre, Jaap M. J. and Joeri Dros (2015). Replication and Analysis of Ebbinghaus' Forgetting Curve, *PLOS ONE* 10(7): e0120644.

Nakajima, Gene (1986). Gertrude Stein's Medical Education and Her Evolving Feminism. Unpublished manuscript. Chesney Archives, Johns Hopkins Medical Institutions, MD.

Neisser, Ulric (1997). Rising Scores on Intelligence Tests: Test Scores are Certainly Going Up All Over the World, But Whether Intelligence Itself Has Risen Remains Controversial, *American Scientist* 85(5): 440–447.

Neisser, Ulric, Gwyneth Boodoo, Thomas J. Bouchard, Jr, A. Wade Boykin, Nathan Brody, Stephen J. Ceci et al. (1996). Intelligence: Knowns and Unknowns, *American Psychologist* 51(2): 77–101.

Nettle, Daniel (2003). Intelligence and Class Mobility in the British Population, *British Journal of Psychology* 94: 551–561.

Nettlebeck, Ted and Carlene Wilson (2004). The Flynn Effect: Smarter Not Faster, *Intelligence* 32(1): 85–93.

Newton, Elizabeth (1990). *Overconfidence in the Communication of Intent*: Heard *and* Unheard Melodies. PhD dissertation. Stanford University, CA.

Nisbett, Richard E. (2010). *Intelligence and How to Get it: Why Schools and Cultures Count* (New York: W. W. Norton & Co).

Nisbett, Richard E. (2013). Schooling Makes You Smarter: What Educators Need to Know About IQ, *American Educator* 37(1): 10–19. Available at: https://www.aft.org/sites/default/files/periodicals/Nisbett.pdf.

Nusbaum, Emily C. and Paul J. Silvia (2011). Are Intelligence and Creativity Really So Different? Fluid Intelligence, Executive Processes, and Strategy Use in Divergent Thinking, *Intelligence* 39(1): 36–45.

Nuthall, Graham (2007). *The Hidden Lives of Learners* (Wellington: New Zealand Council for Educational Research Press).

Oakeshott, Michael (1962). *Rationalism in Politics and Other Essays* (London: Methuen).

Original Positions (2013). Finnegans Wake – Book I Chapter 1 (22 December). Available at: http://www.originalpositions.com/2013/12/finnegans-wake-book-i-chapter-1/.

Pashler, Harold, Patrice M. Bain, Brian A. Bottge, Arthur Graesser, Kenenth Koedinger, Mark McDaniel and Janet Metcalfe (2007). *Organizing Instruction and Study to Improve Student Learning* (NCER 2007–2004) (Washington, DC: National Center for Education Research, Institute of Education Sciences, US Department of Education). Available at: https://files.eric.ed.gov/fulltext/ED498555.pdf.

Paunesku, Dave (2015). Mindset Misconceptions: Trying Hard ≠ Growth Mindset, *medium.com* (17 November). Available at: https://medium.com/learning-mindset/mindset-misconceptions-trying-hard-growth-mindset-8ceb12a33636.

Pinker, Steven (1999). *How the Mind Works* (London: Penguin).

Pinker, Steven (2002). *The Blank Slate: The Modern Denial of Human Nature* (London: Penguin).

Pinker, Steven (2011). *The Better Angels of Our Nature: A History of Violence and Humanity* (London: Penguin).

Pinker, Steven (2015). *The Language Instinct: How the Mind Creates Language* (London: Penguin).

Plomin, Robert and Ian J. Deary (2015). Genetics and Intelligence Differences: Five Special Findings, *Molecular Psychiatry* 20(1): 98–108.

Plomin, Robert, John C. DeFries, Valerie S. Knopik and Jenae M. Neiderhiser (2013). *Behavioral Genetics*, 6th edn (New York: Worth Publishers).

Polanyi, Michael (1966). *The Tacit Dimension* (Abingdon: Routledge).

Polanyi, Michael (1998 [1958]). *Personal Knowledge: Towards a Post-Critical Philosophy* (New York: Psychology Press).

Pomerance, Laura, Julie Greenberg and Kate Walsh (2016). *Learning About Learning: What Every New Teacher Needs to Know* (Washington, DC: National Council on Teacher Quality). Available at: http:// www.nctq.org/dmsView/Learning_About_Learning_Report.

Popper, Karl (2001). *All Life is Problem Solving* (Abingdon: Routledge).

Quigley, Alex (2018). *Closing the Vocabulary Gap* (Abingdon: Routledge).

Ragan, C. Ian, Imre Bard and Ilina Singh (2013). What Should We Do About Student Use of Cognitive Enhancers? An Analysis of Current Evidence, *Neuropharmacology* 64: 588–595.

Reinke, Edgar C. (1975). Quintilian Lighted the Way, *Classical Bulletin* 51: 65–71.

Richardson, Ken (2017). *Genes, Brains and Human Potential: The Science and Ideology of Intelligence* (New York and Chichester: Columbia University Press).

Ridley, Matt (1999). *Genome: The Autobiography of a Species in 23 Chapters* (London: Harper Perennial).

Ridley, Matt (2015). *The Evolution of Everything: How Ideas Emerge* (London: Fourth Estate).

Rienzo, Cinzia, Heather Rolfe and David Wilkinson (2015). *Changing Mindsets: Evaluation Report and Executive Summary* (London: Education Endowment Foundation). Available at: https://v1.educationendowmentfoundation.org.uk/uploads/pdf/Changing_Mindsets.pdf.

Ritchie, Stuart J. (2015). *Intelligence: All That Matters* (London: Hodder & Stoughton).

Ritchie, Stuart J. and Elliot M. Tucker-Drob (2018). How Much Does Education Improve Intelligence? A Meta-Analysis, *Psychological Science* 29(8). https://doi.org/10.1177/0956797618774253

Ritchie, Stuart J., Timothy C. Bates and Ian J. Deary (2015). Is Education Associated with Improvements in General Cognitive Ability, or in Specific Skills?, *Developmental Psychology* 51(5): 573–582.

Ritchie, Stuart J., Timothy C. Bates and Robert Plomin (2015). Does Learning to Read Improve Intelligence? A Longitudinal Multivariate Analysis in Identical Twins from Age 7 to 16, *Child Development* 86: 23–36.

Rivkin, Steven G., Eric A. Hanushek and John F. Kain (2005). Teachers, Schools and Academic Achievement, *Econometrica* 73(2): 417–458.

Roediger, Henry L. and Kathleen McDermott (1995). Creating False Memories: Remembering Words Not Presented in Lists, *Journal of Experimental Psychology: Learning, Memory, and Cognition* 21(4): 803–814.

Roosevelt, Theodore (1889). *The Winning of the West*. Vol. 1: *From the Alleghanies to the Mississippi, 1769–1776* (New York: Cornell University Library).

Rosenberg, Marc (2017). Marc My Words: The Coming Knowledge Tsunami, *Learning Solutions* (10 October). Available at: https://www.learningsolutionsmag.com/articles/2468/marc-my-words-the-coming-knowledge-tsunami.

Rosenshine, Barak (2012). Principles of Instruction: Research Based Strategies That All Teachers Should Know, *American Educator* 36(1): 12–19. Available at: https://www.aft.org/sites/default/files/periodicals/Rosenshine.pdf.

Rosenthal, Robert and Lenore Jacobson (1968). Pygmalion in the Classroom, *Urban Review* 3(1): 16–20.

Rosling, Hans, with Ola Rosling and Anna Rosling Rönnlund (2018). *Factfulness: Ten Reasons We're Wrong About the World – And Why Things Are Better Than You Think* (London: Sceptre).

Rosner, Mordechai and Michael Belkin (1987). Intelligence, Education, and Myopia in Males, *Archives of Ophthalmology* 105(11): 1508–1511.

Sabisky, Andrew (2015). Five Myths About Intelligence. In David Didau, *What If Everything You Knew About Education Was Wrong?* (Carmarthen: Crown House Publishing), pp. 395–412.

Sagan, Carl (1980). Encyclopaedia Galactica (Episode 12), *Cosmos* [video]. PBS (14 December).

Sala, Giovanni N., Deniz Aksayli, K. Semir Tatlidil, Tomoko Tatsumi, Yasuyuki Gondo and Fernand Gobet (2018). Near and Far Transfer in Cognitive Training: A Second-Order Meta-Analysis. Available at: https://psyarxiv.com/9efqd/.

Samuelsson, Stefan, Brian Byrne, Richard K. Olson, Jacqueline Hulslander, Sally Wadsworth, Robin Corley, Erik G. Willcutt and John C. DeFries (2008). Response to Early Literacy Instruction in the United States, Australia and Scandinavia: A Behavioural-Genetic Analysis, *Learning and Individual Differences* 18(3): 289–295.

Sang-Hun, Choe (2009). South Korea Stretches Standards for Success, *New York Times* (22 December). Available at: https://www.nytimes.com/2009/12/23/world/asia/23seoul.html.

Scarborough, Hollis S. (2001). Connecting Early Language and Literacy to Later Reading (Dis)Abilities: Evidence, Theory, and Practice. In Susan B. Neuman and David K. Dickinson (eds), *Handbook of Early Literacy* (New York: Guilford Press), pp. 97–110.

Scargill, Arthur (1982). *The Sunday Times* (10 January).

Schmidt, Frank L., In-Sue Oh and Jonathan A. Shaffer (2016). The Validity and Utility of Selection Methods in Personnel Psychology: Practical and Theoretical Implications of 100 Years of Research Findings. Fox School of Business Research Paper (17 October). Available at: https://papers.ssrn.com/sol3/papers.cfm?abstract_id=2853669.

Serpell, Robert (1979). How Specific Are Perceptual Skills? A Cross-Cultural Study of Pattern Reproduction, *British Journal of Psychology* 70(3): 365–380.

Shearer, C. Branton and Jessica M. Karanian (2017). The Neuroscience of Intelligence: Empirical Support for the Theory of Multiple Intelligences?, *Trends in Neuroscience and Education* 6: 211–223.

Shenk, D. (2010). *The Genius in All of Us: Why Everything You've Been Told About Genes, Talent and Intelligence Is Wrong* (London: Icon Books).

Sieczkowski, Cavan (2013). 1912 Eighth-Grade Exam Stumps 21st-Century Test-Takers, *Huffington Post* (8 December). Available at: https://www.huffingtonpost.co.uk/entry/1912-eighth-grade-exam_n_3744163?guccounter=1.

Simmons, Roger W., Tara Wass, Jennifer D. Thomas and Edward P. Riley (2002). Fractionated Simple and Choice Reaction Time in Children With Prenatal Exposure to Alcohol, *Alcoholism: Clinical and Experimental Research* 26(9): 1412–1419.

Simons, Daniel J., Walter R. Boot, Neil Charness, Susan E. Gathercole, Christopher F. Chabris, David Z. Hambrick and Elizabeth A. L. Stine-Morrow (2016). Do 'Brain-Training' Programs Work?, *Psychological Science in the Public Interest* 17(3): 103–186.

Sisk, Victoria F., Alexander P. Burgoyne, Jingze Sun, Jennifer L. Butler and Brooke N. Macnamara (2018). To What Extent and Under Which Circumstances Are Growth Mind-Sets Important to Academic Achievement? Two Meta-Analyses, *Psychological Science* 29(4): 549–571.

Smith, Adam (1759). *The Theory of Moral Sentiments* (London: Andrew Millar; Edinburgh: Alexander Kincaid and J. Bell).

Smith, Steven M. (1985). Background Music and Context-Dependent Memory, *American Journal of Psychology* 98(4): 591–603.

Soderstrom, Nicholas C. and Robert A. Bjork (2013). Learning Versus Performance. In Dana S. Dunn (ed.), *Oxford Bibliographies Online: Psychology* (New York: Oxford University Press). Available at: https://bjorklab.psych.ucla.edu/wp-content/uploads/sites/13/2016/07/Soderstrom_Bjork_Learning_versus_Performance.pdf.

Sokal, Alan G. (1996). Transgressing the Boundaries: Towards a Transformative Hermeneutics of Quantum Gravity, *Social Text* 46/47: 217–252.

Son, Lisa K. and Janet Metcalfe (2005). Judgements of Learning: Evidence for a Two-Stage Process, *Memory & Cognition* 33(6): 1116–1129.

Sowell, Thomas (1995). *The Vision of the Anointed: Self-Congratulation as a Basis for Social Policy* (New York: Basic Books).

Spearman, Charles (1904). 'General Intelligence,' Objectively Determined and Measured, *The American Journal of Psychology* 15(2): 201–292.

Spencer, Stephen J., Claude M. Steele and Diane M. Quinn (1999). Stereotype Threat and Women's Math Performance, *Journal of Experimental Social Psychology* 35(1): 4–28.

Sperry, Douglas E., Linda L. Sperry and Peggy J. Miller (2018). Reexamining the Verbal Environments of Children from Different Socioeconomic Backgrounds, *Child Development*. doi:10.1111/cdev.13072

Stanovich, Keith E. (2017). Matthew Effects in Reading: Some Consequences of Individual Differences in the Acquisition of Literacy, *Reading Research Quarterly* 22: 360–407.

Steele, Claude M. and Joshua Aronson (1995). Stereotype Threat and the Test Performance of African Americans, *Journal of Personality and Social Psychology* 69(5): 797–811.

Stelzl, Ingeborg, Ferdinand Merz, Theodor Ehlers and Herbert Remer (1995). The Effect of Schooling on the Development of Fluid and Cristallized Intelligence: A Quasi-Experimental Study, *Intelligence* 21(3): 279–296.

Sternberg, Robert J. (2008). Increasing Fluid Intelligence Is Possible After All, *Proceedings of the National Academy of Sciences of the United States of America* 105(19): 6791–6792.

Sternberg, Robert J. and Cynthia A. Berg (1986). Quantitative Integration: Definitions of Intelligence: A Comparison of the 1921 and 1986 Symposia. In Robert J. Sternberg and Douglas K. Detterman (eds), *What is Intelligence? Contemporary Viewpoints on Its Nature and Definition* (Norwood, NJ: Ablex), pp. 155–162.

Sternberg, Robert J. and Douglas K. Detterman (eds) (1986). *What is Intelligence? Contemporary Viewpoints on Its Nature and Definition* (Norwood, NJ: Ablex).

Strauss, Sidney, Margalit Ziv and Adi Stein (2002). Teaching as a Natural Cognition and Its Relations to Preschoolers' Developing Theory of Mind, *Cognitive Development* 17: 1473–1487.

Suresh, Arvind (2016). Autism Increase Mystery Solved? No, It's Not Vaccines, GMOs, Glyphosate – Or Organic Foods, *Genetic Literacy Project* (22 September). Available at: https://geneticliteracyproject.org/2016/09/22/autism-increase-mystery-solved-no-its-not-vaccines-gmos-glyphosate-or-organic-foods/.

Sweller, John (1988). Cognitive Load During Problem Solving: Effects on Learning, *Cognitive Science* 12(2): 257–285.

Sweller, John (2016). Story of a Research Program. In Sigmund Tobias, J. Dexter Fletcher and David C. Berliner (series eds), Acquired Wisdom Series. *Education Review* 23. http://dx.doi.org/10.14507/er.v23.2025

Sweller, John, Paul Ayres and Slava Kalyuga (2011). *Cognitive Load Theory: Explorations in the Learning Sciences, Instructional Systems and Performance Technologies* (New York: Springer).

Taleb, Nassim Nicholas (2013). *Antifragile: Things That Gain from Disorder* (London: Penguin).

Templeton, Alan R. (1998). Human Races: A Genetic and Evolutionary Perspective, *American Anthropologist* 100(3): 632–650.

Tetlock, Philip E. (2002). Social Functionalist Frameworks for Judgment and Choice: Intuitive Politicians, Theologians, and Prosecutors, *Psychological Review* 109(3): 451–471.

Thorndike, Edward L. (1920). Intelligence and Its Uses, *Harper's Magazine* 140: 227–235.

Tolstoy, Leo (2001 [1875–1877]). *Anna Karenina*, tr. R. P. L. Volokhonsky (New York: Viking Penguin).

Tooley, James (2009). *The Beautiful Tree: A Personal Journey into How the World's Poorest People Are Educating Themselves* (New Delhi: Penguin; Washington, DC: Cato Institute).

Trahan, Lisa, Karla K. Stuebing, Merril K. Hiscock and Jack M. Fletcher (2014). The Flynn Effect: A Meta-Analysis, *Psychological Bulletin* 140(5): 1332–1360.

Tricot, André and John Sweller (2014). Domain-Specific Knowledge and Why Teaching Generic Skills Does Not Work, *Educational Psychology Review* 26(2): 265–283.

Trzaskowski, Maceij, Nicole Harlaar, Rosalind Arden, Eva Krapohl, Kaili Rimfeld, Andrew McMillan et al. (2014). Genetic Influence on Family Socioeconomic Status and Children's Intelligence, *Intelligence* 42(100): 83–88.

Tucker-Drob, Elliot M. (2009). Differentiation of Cognitive Abilities Across the Life Span, *Developmental Psychology* 45(4): 1097–1118.

Turkheimer, Eric, Clancy Blair, Aaron Sojourner, John Protzko and Erin Horn (2012). Gene Environment Interaction for IQ in a Randomized Clinical Trial. Unpublished manuscript. University of Virginia, Charlottesville, VA.

Turkheimer, Eric, Andreana Haley, Mary Waldron, Brian D'Onofrio and Irving I. Gottesman (2003). Socioeconomic Status Modifies Heritability of IQ in Young Children, *Psychological Science* 14(6): 623–628.

Tzanakis, Michael (2011). Bourdieu's Social Reproduction Thesis and the Role of Cultural Capital in Educational Attainment: A Critical Review of Key Empirical Studies, *Educate* 11(1): 76–90.

United States Department of Defense (2002). News Briefing: Secretary Rumsfeld and Gen. Myers [news transcript] (12 February). Available at: http://archive.defense.gov/Transcripts/Transcript.aspx?TranscriptID=2636.

Van Doren, Charles (1991). *A History of Knowledge* (New York: Birch Lane Press).

Wai, Jonathan, David Lubinski and Camilla P. Benbow (2005). Creativity and Occupational Accomplishments Among Intellectually Precocious Youths: An Age 13 to Age 33 Longitudinal Study, *Journal of Educational Psychology* 97(3): 484–492.

Watson, John B. (1930). *Behaviourism*, rev. edn (Chicago, IL: University of Chicago Press).

Weingartner, Herbert, Halbert Miller and Dennis L. Murphy (1977). Mood-State-Dependent Retrieval of Verbal Associations, *Journal of Abnormal Psychology* 86(3): 276–284.

Weschler, David (1958). *The Measurement and Appraisal of Adult Intelligence*, 4th edn (Baltimore, MD: Williams & Wilkins).

Wiliam, Dylan (2001). Reliability, Validity, and All That Jazz, *Education 3–13* 29(3): 17–21.

Wiliam, Dylan (2016). *Leadership for Teacher Learning: Creating a Culture Where All Teachers Improve So That All Students Succeed* (West Palm Beach, FL: Learning Sciences International).

Wiliam, Dylan (2018). *Creating the Schools Our Children Need: What We're Doing Now Won't Help Much (And What We Can Do Instead)* (West Palm Beach, FL: Learning Sciences International).

Willingham, Daniel T. (2002). Inflexible Knowledge: The First Step to Expertise, *American Educator* 26: 31–33. Available at: http://www.aft.org/periodical/american-educator/winter-2002/ask-cognitive-scientist.

Willingham, Daniel T. (2007). Critical Thinking: Why Is It So Hard To Teach?, *American Educator* 31: 8–19. Available at: https://www.aft.org/sites/default/files/periodicals/Crit_Thinking.pdf.

Willingham, Daniel T. (2009). *Why Don't Students Like School? A Cognitive Scientist Answers Questions About How the Mind Works and What It Means for the Classroom* (San Francisco, CA: Jossey-Bass).

Wolf, Alison (2002). *Does Education Matter? Myths about Education and Economic Growth* (London: Penguin).

Wolf, Maryanne (2008). *Proust and the Squid: The Story and Science of the Reading Brain* (London: Icon Books).

Wongupparaj, Peera, Veena Kumari and Robin G. Morris (2015). A Cross-Temporal Meta-Analysis of Raven's Progressive Matrices: Age Groups and Developing Versus Developed Countries, *Intelligence* 49: 1–9.

Wright, Lawrence (1997). *Twins: And What They Tell Us About Who We Are* (Hoboken, NJ: Wiley).

Wrulich, Marius, Martin Brunner, Gertraud Stadler, Daniela Schalke, Ulrich Keller and Romain Martin (2014). Forty Years On: Childhood Intelligence Predicts Health in Middle Adulthood, *Health Psychology* 33(2): 292–296.

Yeager, David S., Paul Hanselman, David Paunesku, Christopher Hulleman, Carol Dweck, Chandra Muller et al. (2018). Where and For Whom Can a Brief, Scalable Mindset Intervention Improve Adolescents' Educational Trajectories? (manuscript under revision). Available at: https://doi.org/10.31234/osf.io/md2qa.

Young, Michael (2007). *Bringing Knowledge Back in: From Social Constructivism to Social Realism in the Sociology of Education* (Abingdon: Routledge).

Young, Michael (2011). What Are Schools For?, *Educação, Sociedade & Culturas* 32: 145–155.

Young, Michael (2013). Powerful Knowledge: An Analytically Useful Concept or Just a 'Sexy Sounding Term'? A Response to John Beck's 'Powerful Knowledge, Esoteric Knowledge, Curriculum Knowledge', *Cambridge Journal of Education* 43(2): 195–198.

Young, Michael (2014a) The Curriculum and the Entitlement to Knowledge. Edited text of a talk given at Magdalene College, Cambridge, 25 March. Available at: http://www.cambridgeassessment.org.uk/Images/166279-the-curriculum-and-the-entitlement-to-knowledge-prof-michael-young.pdf.

Young, Michael (2014b). Knowledge, Curriculum and the Future School. In Michael Young, David Lambert, Carolyn Roberts and Martin Roberts, *Knowledge and the Future School: Curriculum and Social Justice* (London: Bloomsbury Academic), pp. 8–40.

Young, Michael (2014c). Powerful Knowledge as a Curriculum Principle. In Michael Young, David Lambert, Carolyn Roberts and Martin Roberts, *Knowledge and the Future School: Curriculum and Social Justice* (London: Bloomsbury Academic), pp. 65–88.

Youssef, Amina, Paul Ayres and John Sweller (2012). Using General Problem-Solving Strategies to Generate Ideas in Order to Solve Geography Problems, *Applied Cognitive Psychology* 26(6): 872–877.

Index

10,000 hour rule 13, 228–229

A

ability grouping 142–146
accent 98–99, 100
accountability
 of children 25
 of schools 33, 220
Ackerman, Phillip 286
Adam, David 57, 284
Adey, Philip 140, 292
advantage gap 8, 116, 274, 278
Ali, Afia 285
Alvarus Pelagius 284
Anderson, James 287
Anderson, John 176, 294
Andrews, Jon 281
Angelou, Maya 211
Anna Karenina principle 89, 287
Aristotle 49, 50, 172
Arnold, Matthew 30, 210, 282
Asbury, Kathryn 91, 92, 109, 287, 288
Ashton, Kevin 186, 294
Astley, Susan 287
Au, Jacky 291
Ausubel, David 142, 292
automatisation 238, 246

B

Baddeley, Alan 153, 154, 293
Baker/baker paradox 168–169
Baldwin, James Mark 41, 43, 283

Bargh, John 134
Bargh fallacy 134
Bartol, Jr, Thomas M. 293
Bartlett, Frederic 163, 293
Bates, Timothy 116, 133, 285, 289, 291
behaviourism 173
Beja-Pereira, Albano 283
Beldoch, Michael 74, 286
Belkin, Michael 2
bell curve 71, 93, 123, 271–279
Bernstein, Basil 201
Birbalsingh, Katherine 298
Bisseret, André 293
Bjork, Elizabeth 165, 253, 293
Bjork, Robert 165, 167, 253, 261, 293, 298
Blair, Tony 17
blob, the 33
Bloom, Allan 30, 282
Bloom, Benjamin 267, 298
Bloom's taxonomy 267
Boaler, Jo 131, 290, 295
Boghossian, Paul 203, 204, 295
Boorstin, Daniel 29, 282
Boring, Edwin 57, 284
Bouchard, Jr, Thomas J. 101, 103, 288
Bourdieu, Pierre 209, 296
Boxer, Adam 223
brain training 12, 113, 120, 136–137, 146, 147
Bratsberg, Bernt 129

breastfeeding 90
Brinch, Christian 288
Bruner, Jerome 40, 221, 283, 296

C

Cabeza, Robert 293
Cáceres, Mario 283
Cahan, Sorel 115, 288
Calvin, Catherine 285
Caplan, Bryan 131, 139–140, 209, 290, 292
Carey, Mark 204
Carlsson, Magnus 289
Carlyle, Thomas 17
cargo cults 183–184
Cattell, Raymond 117, 289
Cavazotte, Flavia 74, 286
Ceci, Stephen 115, 288, 289
central executive 153–154
Cepeda, Nicholas J. 265
character 17, 21–25, 31, 35, 99
Charlie Gordon 1, 70, 114, 171, 175, 278;
    see also Flowers for Algernon
chess 122, 142, 146, 229
Chesterton, G. K. 34
Chomsky, Noam 173
Christodoulou, Daisy 193, 294
chunking 155, 159, 170, 179, 180, 222,
    223, 230, 235, 241, 242–243, 251, 276
Churchill, Winston 96, 128
Clark, Richard E. 297
Clark, Ruth Colvin 259, 298
classical conditioning 160
Cliffordson, Christina 289
cognitivism 173
Cognitive Acceleration through Science
    Education (CASE) 140–141
cognitive load theory 242, 244
cognitive overload 236, 241, 242–243,
    244, 246
Cohen, Nora 115, 288
Collins, Harry 190
Conan Doyle, Arthur 289, 293
Core Knowledge 211

correlation 61–69, 74, 100–101, 133, 135,
    136, 144
Cowan, Nelson 293
creativity 7, 10, 25, 28, 59, 60, 61, 65, 67,
    181–182, 186, 188, 250
Crick, Francis 37
Crocker, Jennifer 290
culture, peer 104, 107, 111, 275, 276–277
culture, transmission of 10, 20, 30, 37–41
cultural
    capital 209, 211, 212, 218, 277
    literacy 209, 216
curiosity, epistemic 194
curriculum:
    knowledge-rich 15, 198, 276
    spiral 221–222

D

Darwin, Charles 195, 295
Dawkins, Richard 39, 283
dead white men 32, 201, 209, 212, 215
Deans for Impact 297
Deary, Ian 116, 285, 288, 289, 290
Dehaene, Stanislas 183
Dennett, Daniel 51, 150, 151, 174, 284,
    292, 294
desirable difficulties 253–254, 263
Detterman, Douglas 49, 57, 116,
    141–142, 284, 289, 292
de Vries, Robert 281
Dewey, John 193
Diamond, Jared 79, 286, 287
Dickens, Charles 171, 193
Didau, David 291
disuse, theory of 165–166, 191, 263
domain:
    folk 42, 43, 44
    primary and secondary 43, 44, 45, 137
    subject 156, 158, 181, 187, 206, 207,
        219–221, 222–224, 225, 228–229,
        234, 237, 244, 245, 256
Dolan, Paul 281
dual coding 257
Dunlosky, John 297

Dunning, David 195
Dunning–Kruger effect 195, 254
Dweck, Carol 129, 130–134, 135, 290, 291

E

Ebbinghaus, Herman 164, 165, 264, 293
eduba(s) 48, 49, 50
Education Endowment Foundation 133, 140, 141, 142, 291
Education Policy Institute 8
Education Week Research Center 291
Egbert of Liège 48, 284
Einstein, Albert 151, 178, 179, 214
Emerson, Ralph Waldo 249
enculturation 20
Enquist, Magnus 283
environment
    and learning 38, 39, 43
    and genes 86–94
    school 53, 106, 111, 135, 142, 271, 274, 275, 276
    shared and non-shared 98, 99, 100–101, 103–104, 108
    social 79
    unfamiliar 71
environmental
    influences 11, 58, 59–60, 65, 76–78, 98, 109–110, 114, 121, 124–125
    stimuli 44–46, 139, 152–153
episodic buffer 153
episteme 172
epistemology 172, 203–204, 208, 223
Epstein, David 87
Ericsson, K. Anders 86, 87, 228, 229, 239, 296, 297
eugenics 96
evolutionary:
    adaption 10, 43, 52, 235, 277
    advantage 24
    biology 37–38, 53, 124, 167
    psychology 10, 43, 46

expertise:
    experts 13, 180, 187, 223, 228, 231–233, 233–241, 242–246
    reversal effect 244–245

F

facts 25, 26, 121, 126, 149, 171–173, 175–176, 177–181, 192–193
falsifiability 73, 132–133, 207, 242
Farrington, David P. 290
feedback 180, 229, 230, 239, 240, 253, 254, 255, 261–262, 267
Feynman, Richard 73, 178, 179, 184, 294
Fitts, Paul 230, 296
Flowers for Algernon 1, 70, 114, 278, 285, 294
Flynn effect 123–125, 128–129
Flynn, James 57, 113, 123, 124–126, 127, 202, 208, 250, 284, 288, 289, 295
Foer, Joshua 168, 169, 230, 293, 294, 296
Foley, Robert A. 283
folk disciplines:
    biology xiii, 41, 42
    physics 41, 42, 163
    psychology 41, 42, 75
Ford, Martin E. 286
Fordham, Michael 187, 294
forgetting 121, 149, 164–167, 256
forgetting curve 164, 264
Freire, Paulo 193
Freund, Philipp A. 288
Fuller, Richard Buckminster 26, 282

G

g 66, 67, 116–117, 121, 125, 249
Gale, Catherine R. 285
Gardner, Howard 72–73, 76, 285, 286
Geary, David 42, 43, 44, 47, 52, 283
gene expression 38
Genovese, Jeremy E. 289
George, Andrew R. 283, 284
George Washington Social Intelligence Test 75
Gilbert, Christine 33

Gladwell, Malcolm 228
Glass, Arnold L. 297
Godden, Duncan R. 293
Golem effect 144
Goleman, Daniel 74, 286
Gosse, Philip Henry 133, 290
Gottfredson, Linda S. 7, 57, 75, 281, 287
Gould, Steven Jay 86, 286
Gove, Michael 30, 33, 282
Gradgrind 171, 180
group differences:
    race 95–96, 105
    sex 105–106
group socialisation theory 99, 104
groupness 106

H

habits of mind 57, 58, 114, 250
Haidt, Jonathan 24, 282
Haier, Richard J. 286
Hallam, Susan 240, 297
Hamlet 237
Hansen, Karsten T. 289
Harber, Kent D. 144, 292
Härnqvist, Kjell 288
Harris, Judith Rich 99, 104, 105, 107, 288
Harrison, Tyler L. 291
Hart, Betty 287
Hattie, John 294
health quotient (HQ) 108, 109
Heck, Patrick R. 295
Heggestad, Eric D. 286
Henke, Katharina 293
heritability 65, 88, 89, 91, 93, 99,
    101–103, 104, 105, 111
Herrnstein, Richard 271, 273, 298
Hirsch, Jr, E. D. 191, 209, 211, 212, 213,
    221, 238, 294, 296, 297
Hitch, Graham 154
Hofstadter, Douglas 119
Howard-Jones, Paul 283
Howe, Michael 77, 286
Hutter, Marcus 57, 284

hypercorrection effect 264
hyperthymesia 156

I

IBM Global Technology Services 282
imagination effect 245
inference 183, 184–185, 186, 207
intelligence:
    abstract 74
    crystallised 11, 77, 117–118, 119–122,
        123, 124, 136, 140, 147, 153–154
    emotional (EQ) 74
    fluid 11, 12, 14, 77, 117–118, 119–
        122, 124, 136, 137, 147, 153–154,
        180, 192–193, 275, 277
    general 72, 75, 80, 121, 125; *see also g*
    practical 74, 75
    social 74–75
interleaving 253, 266
internalisation 254, 262–263, 266, 268,
    269
IQ:
    scores 60, 65, 66, 67, 71, 75, 76, 77, 78,
        81, 83, 87, 89, 96, 97, 104, 114, 115,
        122, 123, 124, 125, 127, 272–273
    tests 55, 60, 65, 66–67, 68, 71–72,
        75, 76, 77, 78–81, 82–83, 87, 111,
        114–115, 119, 121, 123, 125, 127

J

Jacobson, Lenore 144, 292
Jaeggi, Susanne 136–137, 291
Jefferson, Thomas 128, 192
Jerrim, John 281
Johns, Lindsay 211–212, 296
Jones, Garrett 290
Joseph, Dana 286
Jubilee Centre 22, 23, 281, 282
Jussim, Lee 144, 292

K

Kalenze, Eric 21, 25, 281
Kalyuga, Slava 154, 244, 292, 297
Kerr, Hugo 297
Keyes, Daniel 1, 285, 294

King, Jr, Martin Luther 31, 282
Kini, Tara 296
Kirschner, Paul A. iii–v, 152, 223, 292, 296, 297
Kleinerman, Alexandra 284
knowledge:
  background 28, 158, 182, 185, 189, 213, 215, 221, 234, 240, 263, 268, 277
  biologically primary and secondary 43, 44, 45, 52, 53–54, 256
  curse of 189, 234, 246
  doubling curve 26
  explicit 241
  flexible and inflexible 178–179, 180, 189, 235, 238, 241
  illusion of 167, 197–199, 200, 253, 254, 266, 267
  powerful 201, 203–206, 209, 211, 213, 216, 222, 225–226, 238, 278
  procedural 172, 181–182, 183, 187–188, 189, 199, 234, 238, 241, 246
  propositional 139, 172, 176, 177–178, 180, 183, 187, 199, 234, 238
  tacit 160, 172, 188–189, 190, 199, 241, 276
Konnikova, Maria 286
Kristjánsson, Kristján 281
Kuncel, Nathan R. 284, 285
Ku Klux Klan 128

L

Laland, Kevin 38, 43, 282, 283
Land, Ray 206, 296
Larkin, Philip 97
Lattman, Peter 284
Lawson, Rebecca 197, 295
learning, social and asocial 38–41, 44
Lee, Chee Ha 297
Legg, Shane 57, 284
Leslie, Ian 194, 295
Let's Think Secondary Science 140–141; see also Cognitive Acceleration through Science Education (CASE)
Lewin, Roger 283

Li, Yue 133, 291
library 17, 18–19
Lindy effect 31, 39, 52, 209, 210
Liu, Hui-Ju 298
Loftus, Elizabeth 162, 293
Loewen, James W. 290
Loewenstein, George 193
Lucas, Alan 287
Luria, Alexander Romanovich 125–126, 289

M

Macbeth 214, 236, 237
McCloskey, Deirdre 274, 298
McPherson, Gary 239–240, 297
McWeeny, Kathryn 294
Mandarin 159
Marr, Andrew 32, 282
Marzano, Robert 185, 294
massed practice 266
Matthew effect 106, 146, 192, 193, 288
Matrix, The 168
matrix reasoning tests 119, 124
maxim 188–189, 190, 234
Mayer, Richard 259, 298
Medawar, Peter 55
means-end analysis 235, 236, 241
Meltzoff, Andrew 51, 284
Mencken, H. L. 20
Mendel, Gregor 96
memory:
  associative 160
  declarative and non-declarative 160–161, 163, 172, 176
  episodic and semantic 161–163
  long-term 12, 15, 117, 120, 121, 136, 149, 152–158, 160, 165, 170, 172, 192, 193, 229, 231, 234, 235–236, 240, 243–244, 245, 251, 256, 258, 266, 275
  working 12, 117, 118, 120–121, 136–137, 145, 152–158, 159, 170, 179, 180, 192, 193, 198, 231, 235, 238, 240, 241, 242–245, 246, 251,

256, 257, 259, 260–261, 268, 276, 277
working memory model 13, 154
mental representations 239, 240, 241, 244, 245, 254, 255
Merton, Robert K. 288
meta-beliefs 58–59
metacognition 266
Metcalfe, Janet 298
Meyer, Jan 206, 296
Miller, George 154, 155–156, 242, 293
Millon, Theodore 23
Minnesota Twin Family Study 100
mindset:
fixed 129, 130, 132–133, 136
growth 129–135, 147
Mitra, Sugata 203
Mlodinow, Leonard 29, 282
modalities 258
modelling 25, 252, 254, 257
Molière 113
Monbiot, George 295
Montreux, Nicolas de 237
Moody, David 137, 291
Moran, Caitlin 295
Moravec's paradox 46
Moriarty, Catherine 284
Morris, Errol 295
Mortensen, Erik L. 287
Mosel, Jason 132, 290
Mosing, Miriam A. 285
motivational bias 43, 54, 194, 275, 277
multiple intelligences, theory of 56, 72–73, 133
Murman, Daniel 289
Murphy, Dianne 146
Murphy, James 146
Murray, Charles 271, 273, 298
Murre, Jaap M. J. 293

N

Nakajima, Gene 287
Neisser, Ulric 116, 125, 289
Nettle, Daniel 285

Nettlebeck, Ted 289
Newton, Elizabeth 189, 294
Newton, Isaac 28, 44, 187
Nisbett, Richard E. 287
novices 13, 223, 225, 231–241, 242–247, 256, 257
Nusbaum, Emily C. 285
Nuthall, Graham 144, 292

O

Oakeshott, Michael 215, 296
opportunity cost 216, 217, 225
Organisation for Economic Co-operation and Development (OECD) 8, 281

P

Palmer, John 162, 293
parenting 61, 85, 92, 97–98, 100, 103–104, 107, 111, 249
Paul, Annie Murphy 23, 282
Paunesku, Dave 290
Pavlov, Ivan 160
pedagogy 223
peer groups 98, 99, 106, 107, 111
personal development 20
personality:
'Big Five' 22
MBTI (Myers–Briggs Type Indicator) 55
MMPI (Minnesota Multiphasic Personality Indicator) 55
OCEAN 23
phonological loop 153, 154, 155, 257
phronesis 172
Pinker, Steven 46, 47, 68, 128, 173, 283, 285, 289, 290
Plato 49, 50, 151, 166, 292
Plomin, Robert 91, 92, 109, 286, 287, 288, 289
Polanyi, Michael 188, 294
Popper, Karl 44–45, 207, 283
Posner, Michael 230, 296

practice:
deliberate 229
purposeful 228–229, 231, 238–239, 246, 252, 276
priming 105, 106, 160
problem solving 7, 10, 25, 45, 129, 140, 181, 224, 235, 236, 237, 241, 245, 250, 251–252, 260, 269
Proust, Marcel 157
proxy measure 60, 70–71, 82, 83
pseudoscience 73, 133
Pygmalion effect 144
Pythagoras' theorem 152, 180, 209

Q

Quigley, Alex 91
Quintilian 52

R

Raiders of the Lost Ark 157
Reinke, Edgar C. 284
Renwick, James 239–240, 297
Reservoir Dogs 237
retrieval:
practice 59, 161, 238, 253
strength 165–167, 170, 263
Ridley, Matt 20, 93–94, 174, 281, 287
Rienzo, Cinzia 291
Ritchie, Stuart 116–117, 118, 288, 289
Rivkin, Steven G. 296
Roediger, Henry L. 293
Rogeberg, Ole 129
Rogers, Samuel 149
Roosevelt, Theodore 128, 290
Rose, Nick 291
Rosenshine, Barak 297
Rosenthal, Robert 144, 292
Rosling, Hans 8–9, 171, 177, 272, 281, 295, 298
Rosner, Mordechai 2
Rousseau, Jean-Jacques 193
Rumsfeld, Donald 188, 294
Rutherford, Adam 85

S

Sagan, Carl 141, 292
Sala, Giovanni N. 292
Samuelsson, Stefan 287
Sander, Emmanuel 119
Sang-Hun, Choe 286
scaffolding 252, 254–255, 263, 268
Scargill, Arthur 9, 281
schema 12, 139, 155, 158–159, 163, 167–168, 170, 174, 179, 180, 190, 193, 196, 213, 215, 222–224, 230, 234–236, 241, 243, 244–245, 251, 252, 256, 258, 263, 264, 269, 276
Schmidt, Frank L. 284
selection
academic 83, 106, 142, 275
natural 24, 37, 47, 53, 80
Seneca 237
Serpell, Robert 78–79, 286
skills:
21st century 12, 26, 35, 44, 45, 46
thinking 138–142, 146, 147, 267
transferable 27, 127, 181, 194, 202
Shakespeare, William 169, 209, 211, 212, 213, 217
Shayer, Michael 140, 292
Shearer, C. Branton 286
Sherlock Holmes 124, 156
Sieczkowski, Cavan 289
Simmons, Roger W. 287
Simons, Daniel 138, 291, 295
Sisk, Victoria F. 291
Sisyphus 253
Smith, Adam 24, 85, 210, 282
Soderstrom, Nicholas C. 298
socialisation 20, 29, 99, 104
socio-economic status 81, 82, 89, 106, 114, 135, 215
Socrates 25, 27
Sokal, Alan G. 204
Sophonisbe 236, 237
Sowell, Thomas 271
spacing effect 264, 265
Spanish Tragedy, The 237

Spencer, Stephen J. 288
Sperry, Douglas E. 287
Stanovich, Keith E. 106, 288, 289
Strauss, Sidney 51, 284
Steele, Claude 105, 288
Stein, Gertrude 94
Stelzl, Ingeborg 288
stereotype threat 105, 134
Sternberg, Robert 57, 136–137, 284, 286, 291
Stewart, Justice Potter 56
Stone Cold 217
Sumeria 48, 49, 50
Suresh, Arvind 64, 285
survivorship bias 6, 19
Sutton Trust 6, 21, 22, 281
Sweller, John 154, 156, 242, 244, 245, 292, 297
Swindells, Robert 217–218

T

Taleb, Nassim Nicholas 31, 282
task switching 258, 261
techne 172
Templeton, Alan R. 287
Tetlock, Philip 24, 282
Thatcher, Margaret 8
theory of mind 42, 51, 173
Thorndike, Edward 74, 75, 284, 286
Titus Andronicus 237
Tolstoy, Leo 89, 287
Tooley, James 50, 284
Trahan, Lisa 290
transfer 127, 136–137, 139–142, 155, 169, 187, 237, 241, 253, 263, 267–268, 269
Tricot, André 156, 245, 293, 297
Tucker-Drob, Elliot M. 289
Turkheimer, Eric 287

U

United States Department of Defense 294

V

Van Doren, Charles 214, 215, 296
visuo-spatial sketchpad 153, 154, 257
vocabulary 47, 60, 90–91, 117, 118, 119–120, 123–125, 157, 159, 182, 250, 256

W

Wai, Jonathan 285
Ward Beecher, Henry 31
Watson, John B. 173, 294
Weschler, David 286
Wiliam, Dylan 46, 145, 242, 281, 283, 292, 297
Willingham, Daniel 136, 178, 193, 233, 238, 291, 294, 297
Wilson, Woodrow 128
Wolf, Alison 29, 282
Wolf, Maryanne 183
Wongupparaj, Peera 290
worked example effect 245
Wright, Lawrence 288
Wright, Stephen 227
Wrulich, Marius 285

Y

Yeager, David S. 291
Young, Michael 40, 201, 203, 204, 205, 208, 209, 238, 283, 295
Youssef, Amina 283

The Perfect (Ofsted) English Lesson

David Didau

ISBN: 978-178135052-2

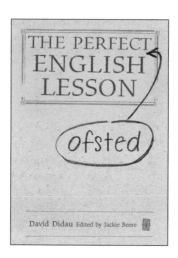

Another from Jackie Beere's 'Perfect' stable, David Didau's simple but effective little book is designed to help bring the best out of all English departments during that all-important Ofsted visit.

Packed full of ideas, strategies and simple yet effective innovations, *The Perfect (Ofsted) English Lesson* is an essential tool in the toolkit of every English department – and not just for the inspection either! With topics including assessment for learning, progress, the learning environment and planning outstanding lessons, this is the book for every English teacher's desk drawer.

The Secret of Literacy

Making the implicit explicit

David Didau

ISBN: 978-178135127-7

Literacy? That's someone else's job, isn't it? This is a book for all teachers on how to make explicit to students those things we do implicitly.

In the Teachers' Standards it is stated that all teachers must demonstrate an understanding of, and take responsibility for promoting, high standards of literacy, articulacy and the correct use of Standard English, whatever the teacher's specialist subject.

In *The Secret of Literacy* David Didau inspires teachers to embrace the challenge of improving students' life chances through improving their literacy.

Topics include:

- Why literacy is important
- Oracy – improving classroom talk
- How we should teach reading
- How to get students to value writing
- How written feedback and marking can support literacy

What If Everything You Knew About Education Was Wrong?

David Didau

ISBN: 978-178583157-7

If you feel a bit cross at the presumption of some oik daring to suggest everything you know about education might be wrong, please take it with a pinch of salt. It's just a title. Of course, you probably think a great many things that aren't wrong.

The aim of this book is to help you 'murder your darlings'. David will question your most deeply held assumptions about teaching and learning, expose them to the fiery eye of reason and see if they can still walk in a straight line after the experience. It seems reasonable to suggest that only if a theory or approach can withstand the fiercest scrutiny should it be encouraged in classrooms. David makes no apologies for this; why wouldn't you be sceptical of what you're told and what you think you know? As educated professionals, we ought to strive to assemble a more accurate, informed or at least considered understanding of the world around us.